St. Francis of America

St. Francis of America

How a Thirteenth-Century Friar
Became America's Most Popular Saint

Patricia Appelbaum

The University of North Carolina Press CHAPEL HILL

Publication of this book was supported in part by a generous gift from Cyndy and John O'Hara.

Chapter 1 is adapted from the following publication: "St. Francis in the Nineteenth Century," by Patricia Appelbaum. *Church History*, Volume 78, Issue 04 (December 2009), pp. 792–813. Copyright © 2009 American Society of Church History. Reprinted with the permission of Cambridge University Press.

Jacket illustration: *Brother Francis: A Canticle to Creation*, by Nancy Earle, SMIC (Courtesy of the artist)

Library of Congress Cataloging-in-Publication Data
Appelbaum, Patricia Faith.
    St. Francis of America: how a thirteenth-century friar became America's most popular saint / Patricia Appelbaum.
        pages cm
    Includes bibliographical references and index.
    ISBN 978-1-4696-2374-0 (cloth : alk. paper) — ISBN 978-1-4696-2375-7 (ebook)
1. Francis, of Assisi, Saint, 1182–1226.   2. Popular culture—United States.   3. Popular culture—Religious aspects—Christianity.   4. United States—Religious life and customs.
I. Title.
    BX4700.F6A766 2015
    271'.302—dc23   2014048331

For Meg

Let all things their Creator bless

Contents

Figures

Acknowledgments

We are told that St. Francis was deeply skeptical toward books and learning, and that he lived joyfully without a home or an office. I have never claimed to follow his example in these respects. But Francis did not reject companionship or community, and it is clear that he thought very highly of gratitude—so I take this opportunity to express mine.

Thanks first of all to the libraries of Amherst College, Mount Holyoke College, and Smith College for access and study space. A large bouquet to the W. E. B. Du Bois Library at the University of Massachusetts at Amherst, especially to its tireless interlibrary loan staff. During the early part of my research, I did not have access to your services, and I can scarcely tell you how much I appreciate them now. An even bigger bouquet to Brian Shelburne, Annie Sollinger, and Mike Foldy at the UMass Image Collection Library for the beautiful digital reproductions of many of the images that illustrate this book.

For their generous help with illustrations, I thank Kia Campbell of the Library of Congress, Barbara Polowy of the Hillyer Art Library at Smith College, and Adam Lerner and Jo-Anne Chapin of the Amherst College Library, all of whom went beyond the call of duty. Thanks also to Caleb Wetmore of Collective Copies. Especially, I thank all the copyright holders who granted permission to reproduce images.

I am very grateful to Joye Bowman and the History Department at UMass for access and support. Many thanks also to Rob Eveleigh of the UMass Information Technology service for invaluable help with assistive technology.

One of the unexpected delights of this project was meeting and corresponding with so many researchers, both professional and avocational. I owe a particular debt of gratitude to scholars (in alphabetical order) Michael Clawson, Larry Eskridge, Laura Hobgood-Oster, Sharon McLean, David Morgan, Victoria Morse, William North, and J. R. Watson; to archivists Diane Ney of Washington National Cathedral and Ann Upton of Haverford College; and to Maria Lynch Dumoulin of Kenneth Lynch and Sons, Eva Schwarz of Barbara Israel Garden Antiques, and Hutton Wilkinson, business partner of the late Tony Duquette. All of them generously shared time, resources, and deep background knowledge with me. Many dedicated local historians and historical societies have been equally kind and generous: Ann Lightman and Val Crompton of the Church of St. John the Baptist in Adel, Leeds, Yorkshire; Ann Lowell and the Society of the Companions of the Holy Cross; and Christina Abbott, researcher on Frederick Warren Allen; as well as the staff and volunteers at the historical societies of Dublin, New Hampshire; New Canaan, Connecticut; and Pomfret, Connecticut. You are the custodians of great treasures.

I met Linda Ferranti when I inadvertently wandered onto her private property looking for the Kershaw house. She and her family, the current owners, have been extremely generous in sharing archival photographs, oral history, and historical documents. I wish I could have published more of the pictures. The Rev. Richard Cassius Lee Webb and the Rev. Ann Webb, summer clergy at the Chapel of St. Francis in Marlborough, New Hampshire, took time to open the chapel to me and shared historical background and photographs. I am deeply grateful.

Many friends and colleagues read one or more chapters and offered invaluable suggestions. Special thanks to Jon Roberts and the Boston American Religious History Group and to the Five College History Seminar, generous colleagues all. Margaret Bendroth of the Congregational Library has been a steady supporter and conversation partner. She and Christopher Beneke, Brian Bixby, Healan Gaston, Stephen Prothero, and Roberta Wollons offered valuable comments on various chapter drafts. Many thanks also to Dan McKanan and David Morgan for their thoughtful and illuminating commentary on the manuscript. And I am particularly grateful to Lisa Kleinholz and Marla Solomon for their astute observations as fellow writers and nonspecialist readers. Any errors or infelicities that remain are, of course, mine alone.

My profound gratitude goes out to all who answered my survey with such openness and generosity. Many thanks also to all the friends and relatives who kept an eye out for interesting information and passed it along to me. I don't think I can name you all, but I want at least to mention Betsy Mathews for suggesting *Rabbit Hill*; Anna, Bill F., and Bill R. for help with Alcoholics Anonymous literature; and Barbara, Gail, Lorraine, Mary, and Sally. I ask the indulgence of anyone I've neglected to mention.

As always, I thank my editor Elaine Maisner for her wise advice and cheerful encouragement.

Last but not least, I want to express my appreciation to my family, both immediate and extended, for their steady presence, interest, and support.

My sister Lorraine Appelbaum has been a patient listener and insightful conversation partner. My husband, William L. Holladay, has read most of this book in manuscript (parts of it several times!) and has shared many conversations and perplexities about it. He also organized and proofread the bibliography, assisted with the index, and provided much household support. My daughter Margaret Holladay has served as an able research assistant on several occasions, sought out and photographed St. Francis images at home and overseas, and in general, has made my life easier and happier in so many ways.

St. Francis of America

Introduction

I don't know when I first heard of St. Francis. Maybe I had seen a garden statue somewhere; I have dim recollections of some children's books; there was a St. Francis Hospital in the city near our small town. Wherever it came from, I absorbed an idea of a gentle, kindly figure in a brown robe who loved birds, animals, and children. He was certainly no threat to our Quaker household, even though we didn't "believe in" saints or statues.

It was not until I was an adult, far along in my education, that I read any of Francis's own writings.[1] And what a shock that was! I was astonished to find that Francis promised reverence to the pope, honored priests, loved churches, emphasized obedience, and insisted that his followers should be orthodox Catholics. This was not the St. Francis I knew—or thought I knew. Later, when I was working on my doctoral thesis, I was struck by the frequency with which liberal Protestants—who also didn't "believe in" saints—referred to St. Francis as an ideal or a standard. Among the mid-twentieth-century pacifists I studied, he was considered a model of nonviolence and peacemaking.

In these experiences is the genesis of this book. Of course I am not the only person ever to have noticed that popular images of Francis sometimes differ from historical accounts. What I want to do here, though, is to trace the history and variety of those popular interpretations.

For contemporary Americans, St. Francis of Assisi is one of the most widely recognized saints and one of the best loved. Not only Catholics and Protestants, but other believers and "spiritual but not religious" people know who he is and name him among their favorite religious figures. And his reach extends far beyond formal religious life. You can buy a statue of him at a garden center, see a movie about him, or download songs about him from iTunes. How did this happen? How did a thirteenth-century Roman Catholic saint become a familiar figure in American religion and popular culture? And what does it mean that he did?

This book sets out to answer those questions. In it I describe the ways American non-Catholics have encountered, interpreted, and constructed the figure of St. Francis of Assisi and reflect on the meanings of those interpretations in American religion and culture. I begin with the rediscovery of Francis in the mid-nineteenth century and end with the recent past, the early twenty-first century.

Many people assume that St. Francis has always been as popular and beloved as he is today, and that everyone agrees about who he was and what he means for the contemporary world. This book will question those assumptions. We shall see how depictions of Francis have changed over time—in print; in illustrations and visual art; in music, drama, and film. We shall also consider how Protestant images have differed from Catholic ones, and how non-Christian and secular sources have constructed Francis.

The non-Catholic appropriation of Francis was and is an international phenomenon. I am focusing on the United States in order to understand the phenomenon within the context of American religion and culture. But it is impossible to treat it in complete isolation. Overseas events and experiences shaped Americans' perceptions. Seminal studies about Francis came from continental Europe, as did works of art. English-language texts tended to cross national boundaries very quickly. Consequently I will at times refer to European and other sources for context. It will also be important to look occasionally at Roman Catholic events and interpretations—as background, as points of comparison to Protestant ideas, and as context for the non-Catholic conversation.[2]

Why Francis?

Why St. Francis? Most people, when asked to describe St. Francis, would mention the same things I knew about in childhood: his closeness to nature and his love of animals. The best-known legends about him say that he spoke to birds, who stopped singing to gather around and listen to him; that he tamed a wolf who was terrorizing a local town, using nothing more than his words and his gentle spirit; that he called lambs and crickets his brothers and sisters. One of the few authentic writings we have from Francis himself is the "Canticle of the Sun" (see chapter 1), in which he refers to "Brother Sun" and "Sister Moon," "Sister Water" and "Brother Fire." Today, a popular church service is the "blessing of the animals," to which members and visitors bring their pets, on the October feast day of St. Francis.

Other people might quote the "prayer of St. Francis": "Lord, make me an instrument of thy peace. Where there is hatred, let me sow love; where there is injury, pardon; where there is doubt, faith . . . ." (See chapter 4.)

Like the garden statues, this prayer is everywhere: on greeting cards, plaques, and coffee mugs, in song lyrics, and at Alcoholics Anonymous meetings. It is not in fact authentic to Francis—it dates from the early twentieth century, as we shall see. But those who use it believe that it expresses his true spirit, a spirit of love, selflessness, and peacemaking. Perhaps they also notice that it does not mention either Jesus or any kind of institution. Christians and non-Christians, individualists and joiners can all find this Francis equally accessible.

The novelist Donna Tartt wrote in 2005 that "Francis's popularity . . . has continued undiminished from his death in 1226 to the present day." As I have noted, this is not quite accurate. Francis's popularity among non-Catholics is in fact a relatively new phenomenon, dating from a revival of interest in the mid-nineteenth century. The Protestant reformers of the sixteenth century had largely rejected Catholic notions of sainthood, and Protestants' sense of history tended to skip over the Middle Ages as a time of superstition and corruption. This was especially true in the Reformed and evangelical traditions that dominated the early United States, but even the more moderate Anglican church kept more distance from its Catholic roots then than it does today. Only in the nineteenth century did Protestants begin to come to terms with Catholicism, in an ambivalent, approach-avoidance kind of way.[3]

Nor did those who loved Francis in the nineteenth century always see him the way twenty-first-century devotees do. Although nineteenth-century devotees knew about the sermon to the birds, it did not become a primary focus until later. Instead, the earliest writers had to begin by making the case to their readers for studying saints at all. Many emphasized Francis's reforming capacities and his preaching—presenting him as, in effect, a proto-Protestant. Another early argument in his favor was his importance to the world of art and literature; scholars argued that he inspired the groundbreaking work of the Renaissance painter Giotto and that his poetry in the Italian language—instead of Latin—paved the way for Dante. Later, a multitude of other interpretations arose: Francis as mirror of the life of Jesus, as mystic, as man of the people, as revolutionary. Many of these ideas overlapped; they were not mutually exclusive, but were part of an extended common discussion. This discussion took place in the popular press as much as in the scholarly world.

Tartt was right in one respect, though. St. Francis's popularity continues undiminished today. When the newest pope chose his name in 2013, the world was newly reminded of Francis's life, and he continues to be a standard of comparison for the pope's decisions and actions. But even before 2013, there was a steady stream of commentary about Francis. A complete set of new translations began publication in 1999. A classic biography was reissued in 2003, and two new biographies came out in 2012. Recent works have considered Francis's relationship with Islam, his representations in literature and art, and his "afterlife" through history. He has been presented as a model for evangelicals, a true Catholic, and a near-Buddhist. Children's books about him appear regularly. A recent work describes Francis's popularity among rock and punk musicians. Digital media have multiplied the images of Francis and generated new kinds of folklore.[4]

Culture and Alternatives

My book makes two interlocking—and somewhat paradoxical—arguments. The first is that the various images of St. Francis are historically conditioned: they reflect the cultural preoccupations of their time. They arise in response to the needs, desires, interests, and tensions of particular times and people. This does not, of course, mean that any one image is correct or incorrect. It does mean that these images are often limited or partial.

My second point, though, is that these images very often represent alternatives to historical conditions—alternatives to the cultural preoccupations of their times. In the nineteenth century, for example, middle- and upper-class people valued the cultivation of taste in fine or high art. Such people often encountered Francis precisely through the study of art and assessed his importance in artistic terms. This seldom happens today; it reflects nineteenth-century preoccupations. Yet the Francis they found through art was not a person of taste, elegance, or cultivation, but a rebel against convention—both artistic and social. Or, for a more contemporary example, we may consider garden statuary. In one way it is an expression of consumer culture. A way to feel close to St. Francis is to buy a statue of him; a way to express one's religious and spiritual choices is through consumption. Yet that St. Francis statue serves as a continual reminder of what one lacks and perhaps longs for—a life free of possessions; a life that is not dominated by money or property or, in fact, consumerism.

Although this book is not primarily about spirituality, thoughtful readers will find much here to nurture their spiritual lives. Let me say at the outset that I am not going to uncover a "real" St. Francis or promote any particular interpretation of him. Nor do I plan to tell readers how to engage spiritually with St. Francis, how to follow him, or how to interpret him for today. There is other literature that addresses all of those questions admirably. What I would like to do is to encourage readers to broaden their views. Most of us tend to read Francis selectively—to choose the parts of his story or character that speak to our own conditions and to ignore or explain away the rest. In showing some of the ways this has been done in the past, I hope to offer my readers a way to query their own interpretations of Francis—to think about what they include, what they leave out, how they use the things they know, and how other people and other times have understood Francis. In so doing, I hope, they will be encouraged to reflect more deeply on his life and meaning.

Finally, the book will keep three themes in view: sainthood, place, and history. First, sainthood: what is the meaning of someone like Francis for communities that have no formal category of sainthood? Second is the sense of place. Early Protestants rejected pilgrimage as well as sainthood, and with it, rejected the idea that any particular place was more sacred than any other. Yet modern Protestants have persistently found special meaning in Assisi. Why, and what has changed? And finally, history: in what ways have religious Americans adopted, appreciated, related to, or avoided the past? With St. Francis, historicity seems to be a key factor in non-Catholics' acceptance of him—he is historical and therefore "real," not mythical or supernatural. And his devotees have often looked to professional historical writing to learn about his life and work. Yet they have also felt free to interpret, imagine, and engage spiritually with St. Francis, without conforming to the limits of historicity. What does this tell us about religion, history, and spirituality?

A word about terminology: I have sometimes referred to an image or idea of Francis as a "construction." This is a term coined by philosophers of postmodernism who have argued that there is no objective truth. Rather, what we call "truth" is socially constructed: it depends on unspoken agreements throughout society to recognize some things as true and to refuse to see others, often in response to the needs of power structures. Critics can expose these alleged truths by "deconstructing" them, but whatever is built in their place will also be socially constructed and therefore not absolute. From this point of view, it is arguable, I think, that images of Francis are constructed: that various social groups have unconsciously collaborated to create images of Francis in response to societal desires and anxieties. My purpose is not to claim that they are false images but to remind readers of the energies behind the many visions of Francis. What is more, social construction need not always serve the powerful. It can also be a way in which ordinary or marginalized people create meaning. In any case, this book is not primarily focused on deconstructing these images or the discourses of power that may underlie them. I use the term "construction" lightly, as a useful concept, while leaving a full-scale theoretical treatment to others.

Where We Begin

In order to study popular public appropriation of St. Francis, I wanted to begin with sources that were available to a wide public. My starting point, as a rough measure of popular interest, is the *Readers' Guide to Periodical Literature*. This index gives an overview of a broad range of general-interest magazines that appeal to a wide readership. Of course, the editors of these periodicals had some power to shape public tastes and interests. But they also had to respond to public demand, so their choices of what to publish suggest that they expected a reasonable level of public interest. In addition, I trace rising and falling interest through records of book publication. Biographies, document collections, novels, and imaginative treatments of Francis are markers of cultural interest and frequently reflect or generate new interpretations. I have pointed to major works in Franciscan scholarship as benchmarks, but a complete history of scholarly discussion—which is very extensive—is beyond the scope of this book.

Beyond these starting points, I have drawn on other resources as appropriate. For the early twentieth century, the American Periodicals Series database of full-text articles was a valuable archive. For the years since 1990 or so, there is, of course, the Internet. The major books and periodical articles have referred me onward to less obvious sources. I have drawn on manuscript and archival sources, events and performances, visual imagery, and occasionally music—although there is more to be said about music than I have had space for here. What I explore in depth are the cultural "products"—texts, visual images, trends, rituals—that have had wide popularity or lasting importance; those that have been important to the history of the interpretation of St. Francis; those that provide significant or illuminating responses to cultural conditions; or all of these features together. This book places all these sources in the context of American religious history—especially Protestant institutions and movements, popular religion, and history of practice. It attends to large-scale historical events, ideas, and cultural shifts.

The Life of Francis

The historical Francis, like the historical Jesus, can be drawn in outline but remains elusive in detail. There are a number of biographical sources on Francis, but none conforms to modern ideas of scientific history. None was written during his lifetime, and all had agendas of various kinds, and they drew on diverse strands of oral tradition.

Francis's own writings offer only scattered biographical details: the most significant is the Testament dictated near the end of his life. He begins, "The Lord granted me, Brother Francis, to begin to do penance in this way: While I was in sin it seemed very bitter to me to see lepers. And the Lord himself led me among them and I had mercy upon them. . . . and afterward I lingered a little and left the world." Later he says, "And after the Lord gave me brothers, no one showed me what I should do, but the Most High Himself revealed to me that I should live according to the form of the Holy Gospel. And I had this written down simply and in a few words and the Lord Pope confirmed it for me." The remainder of the document reminds the brothers how they are to live.

There are three early biographical accounts of Francis: two by Thomas of Celano, informally known as the First and Second Life (*Life of St. Francis,* or *Vita Prima,* about 1228–29, and *Remembrance of the Desire of a Soul,* or *Vita Secunda,* about 1245–47); and one by St. Bonaventure, general minister of the Order of Friars Minor (the oldest order of Franciscan men), completed about 1263. Thomas's First Life remembers Francis's saintliness. The Second Life is more concerned with the life of the order. Bonaventure's Life was something of an official treatment, and after its completion, friaries were ordered to destroy earlier documents. Only a very few of these documents survive today. Among them are several collections of stories about Francis. Some of these writings, like the "Legend of the Three Companions" (1241–47), claimed to have been composed by brothers who knew Francis, while other writings are more distant or derivative. Of later sources, the *Fioretti,* or *Little Flowers of St. Francis* (c. 1375) was a major collection of oral tradition and folklore about Francis and a popular devotional text. Many readers have taken it as an evocation of his personality if not as historical fact. Other important sources were the Bollandist *Acta Sanctorum* (1643–1940), a Jesuit collection of lives of the saints; and a history of the Franciscan Order compiled by the friar Luke Wadding, beginning in 1625.[5] The following is a summary of Francis's life as outlined in most of the sources.[6]

Francesco Bernardone was born in Assisi in 1181 or 1182. Christened Giovanni (John), he was renamed Francesco (Francis) at an early age. His father was a wealthy cloth merchant and his mother came from a prominent family. As a young man Francis was lighthearted, outgoing, and extravagant. In his early twenties he moved gradually toward religious commitment, following experiences of battle, imprisonment, and illness. He also tried to identify with the poor and sick: he was said to have exchanged clothes with a beggar in Rome for a day, and his first embrace of a leper was a turning point in his life.

Soon afterward, Francis heard a divine call to "rebuild my church," which he took to mean physical reconstruction of a crumbling chapel known as the Portiuncula, or "Little Portion." To fund this enterprise, he sold a quantity of his father's cloth and his own horse. Confronted by his angry father, Francis gave back all his father's property—not only the price of the cloth, but, in a dramatic gesture, all the clothes he was wearing. Henceforth, declared Francis, his only father would be God.

Francis soon gathered a group of close companions whose intention was to be poor and to serve the poor. They supported themselves by manual work and begging, accepting only in-kind gifts, never money. In 1208 Francis sought approval from Pope Innocent III for a simple rule of life. The pope at first refused, then approved the rule and the fellowship, including their itinerant preaching. Four years later a young noblewoman, Clara Scifi, known to us as Clare, left her father's house to adopt a life of poverty similar to the brothers'; however, she and the women's order she founded were cloistered. Later Francis created a "third order" for people living in the world. As the orders grew and became more regularized, Francis gradually lost or relinquished supervision of them.

The stories I mentioned earlier are among those that we will encounter often in the course of this book. The Canticle of the Sun is generally accepted as authentic to Francis. Of the legends, a favorite was, and is, the story of Francis preaching to the birds, who grew silent to listen to him. This tale survived in several different versions. It has often been retold and is frequently depicted in art. Another favorite is the story of the wolf of Gubbio, in which Francis persuaded the wolf to stop harassing the townspeople, and in turn persuaded the people to feed him.

Beyond these, many commentators have recounted the narrative of "true and perfect joy." Talking with a brother, Francis names many desirable things that are nevertheless not "perfect joy"—bringing new brothers into the order, converting nonbelievers, and healing the sick, for example.

Finally he tells the brother what joy really is—to arrive late at the brothers' dwelling, in mud and icy cold, to be refused admission, to be thrown out and beaten, and yet to remain patient: this is true and perfect joy. As vivid as the story is, its meaning remains somewhat mysterious. A surprising number of modern commentators quote it without explaining it, as we shall see.

Another important narrative concerns Francis's visit to the sultan of Egypt. If it is historical, as many authorities think it is, it took place in 1219, during the Fifth Crusade. Francis traveled to the besieged city of Damietta (Dumyat) and went on foot to visit the Egyptian commander, hoping to convert him to Christianity and thereby bring about peace between the two sides. The sultan declined to convert, but treated Francis with respect and allowed him to leave unharmed.

Toward the end of his life Francis was said to have received the stigmata—wounds in his hands, feet, and sides resembling the wounds of Christ. Signs of his identification with Christ, they were said to have been given by an angel as Francis prayed on a mountaintop. No Christian figure had received this bodily manifestation before Francis.

Francis died in October 1226. His death was immediately followed by controversy among Franciscans between the early vision and a more systematized order. The spontaneity and extreme poverty of the early years were difficult to sustain.

Over the next seven hundred years there were periods of conflict, decline, reform, and reorganizing. As a result, there are several different Franciscan orders. Originally, the First Order was for men, the Second for women, and the Third Order for laypeople of both sexes living in the world. Today, the First Order has evolved into three principal branches: the Order of Friars Minor (OFM) or Regular Franciscans, the Conventuals, and the Capuchins. The Second Order, known as Poor Clares or Poor Ladies, is cloistered. The Third Order continues to attract lay members. It has also generated newer communities, many of them for women, whose members live under vows but are active in the world rather than being cloistered. Episcopalians and other Protestants have also adopted versions of the Third Order.

Where We Are Going

Chapter 1 traces the ways St. Francis first became known to Protestants and to the wider Anglo-American culture—through travel, art, literature, and Protestant historicism, as well as an uneasy attraction to Catholic aesthetics and spirituality. It then outlines the innovative biography of Francis by the French Protestant Paul Sabatier and its impact on twentieth-century perceptions. By the early twentieth century Francis had been thoroughly embraced by American Protestant culture. Chapter 2 begins by surveying this widespread appropriation. Its second section turns to the place of Francis and Sabatier in Progressive-era Christian social reform. Third, this chapter considers the emerging importance of the sense of place. Finally, it outlines Catholic responses to Protestant appropriation of Francis.

Chapter 3 considers the period between the world wars. Literary treatments of Francis were increasingly personal and imaginative, and he was "acted out" in drama and social action. This chapter looks at the pacifist construction of Francis and at efforts toward voluntary poverty during the Great Depression. Chapter 4 traces the origins of three important and lasting cultural artifacts: the "peace prayer," the hymn "All Creatures of Our God and King," and garden statuary. Chapter 5 looks at the post–World War II "consensus culture" and at the spiritual ferment on its margins. Fictional treatments of Francis by Robert Lawson for children, and Bernard Malamud for adults, are especially important in this era.

In the watershed era of the 1960s, Francis is known as a hippie and begins to be known as an environmentalist. Chapter 6 traces his connections with San Francisco hippies and alternative Christian churches, his place in the nascent "ecology" movement, and the culturally resonant movie by Franco Zeffirelli. Chapter 7 begins by surveying significant events of the 1980s, including evangelicals' embrace of Francis, changes in environmentalist movements, and several manifestations of Francis in popular art forms. It then focuses on a history and description of "blessing of the animals" rituals, which have become embedded in popular culture since about 1985.

Chapter 8 pauses to listen to some living voices as the narrative approaches the contemporary period. Here I analyze responses to a survey I conducted in 2013. Chapter 9 looks at three recent trends—the postmodern Francis, Francis and Islam, and contemporary folklore. An epilogue outlines developments since 2000 and offers concluding reflections on the meaning of St. Francis in American culture and religious history. It also returns to the themes of sainthood, place, and history.

CHAPTER ONE

The Nineteenth Century

A Protestant Catholic and Catholic Protestants

An English-speaking Protestant of the mid-nineteenth century, preparing to explore continental Europe for the first time, might have picked
up Octavian Blewitt's 1850 guidebook to central Italy. Along with its descriptions of Rome, Florence, and Ravenna, the book noted that "Assisi
is the sanctuary of early Italian art." A similar book in 1905, however,
declared, "Assisi is the city of St. Francis." In the space of some fifty years,
St. Francis of Assisi went from an insignificant, almost unknown figure
to a universally familiar one. How did this transformation take place?
Why was St. Francis the center of a description of Assisi in 1905, but
not in 1850?[1]

This chapter shows how American non-Catholics gradually grew acquainted with the figure of St. Francis during the second half of the
nineteenth century. As we shall see, many events and cultural forces contributed to the process. First of all, Protestants were beginning to realize
that the history of Christianity before the Reformation was also their own
history. At the same time, travel to Europe was becoming more accessible,
which meant more exposure to European art and architecture, including
many images of saints. American Protestants were also encountering
Catholics more often at home. All of this, along with broader cultural
currents, led to a reassessment of their relationship with Catholic traditions in general and saints in particular.

Other saints also caught Protestants' interest, but none became as
popular as Francis. He was attractive for many reasons—not least the fact
that there was a reasonable amount of historical evidence for his life. It
was clear that he had actually lived, and in a particular place, at a particular
time. But not all readers interpreted the evidence the same way, and it
is incomplete in any case. Thus a number of different images of Francis
emerged during the nineteenth century, emphasizing different features
of Francis and meeting different needs. Francis was a subject for imaginative elaboration, personal relationship, and collective appropriation. All
of these images, however, grew out of the culture and concerns of the

nineteenth century. And instead of affirming cultural standards, most of them proposed alternatives.

A chronological outline gives us a good overview of the way Francis became familiar to non-Catholics. A body of literature about Francis written by non-Catholics built up slowly from the 1840s until about 1870. Around that year the pace of publication increased. Events in 1870—the first Vatican Council and the final unification of Italy—drew international attention to Italy. More broadly, the last quarter of the nineteenth century was a time of growing prosperity and also of an emerging cultural critique. Both of these forces contributed, in different ways, to the increasing interest in Francis. The seven-hundredth anniversary of Francis's birth, in 1881–82, prompted a new outpouring of scholarly literature and popular works. Thus by 1888 it was possible for a book reviewer to say, "The story of St. Francis has been fully and frequently related." And in 1893, a new biography shaped perceptions of Francis for the twentieth century. The process was not uniform—some writers in the 1880s and 1890s still had to explain who Francis was and why Protestants should be interested in him—but this was the general trajectory.

Cultural Currents

The Protestant rediscovery of Francis began in the context of an ambivalent Protestant encounter with Catholicism. In the United States, this encounter began in the late eighteenth century, but gained force after 1830, with increased immigration from Catholic countries, the annexation of the Southwest, and the gradual growth of overseas travel. The literary historian Jenny Franchot argued in a classic work that Protestants reacted with both approach and avoidance, attraction and repulsion. Since the Reformation of the sixteenth century, Protestantism had generally regarded Roman Catholicism as a threatening "other." In nineteenth-century America, anti-Catholicism was common and sometimes violent.[2]

But many non-Catholics responded to the encounter with curiosity, appreciation, and selective appropriation. Travel and genteel education exposed them to the surprising attractions of pre-Reformation art and architecture. Midcentury travel literature dwelt on Catholic peasant and urban life as well. Some writers of fiction—notably Nathaniel Hawthorne and Harriet Beecher Stowe, descendants of New England Puritans—explored such Catholic themes as confession and intercession. There were a few prominent public conversions to Catholicism and a small but steady stream of less visible ones.

There were many dimensions to Protestants' ambivalence. First, Catholic power attracted and puzzled them. They could not quite account for the Roman church's survival "after [its] having been directed offstage nearly four centuries earlier." Saints also proved puzzling. Franchot argues that Protestant writers came to terms with them by framing them as heroic individuals acting in spite of, or even against, the church—not as holy or divinely gifted persons. As we shall see, this tendency continued well into the twentieth century and was surely a way of thinking about Francis. Catholic worship posed yet another problem. The Anglican churches struggled for years over the Oxford Movement, which among other things encouraged the revival of pre-Reformation practices. At the same time, many American Protestants developed a "deeply mixed fascination for Roman Catholic worship." As historian Ryan Smith has observed, Gothic buildings, visual symbolism such as crosses, and liturgical practices such as processions were derided as "popery" in the 1830s, but were common in mainstream Protestantism—including its Anglican branch—by the 1890s.[3]

A related phenomenon was the medievalist movement, which was well established in Britain by 1850, reached its height in the United States after the Civil War, and remained influential long after that time. Medievalism was not only an artistic movement but a far-reaching cultural one. Against the dominant ideology of progress and the growing industrial economy, medievalism appealed to a desire for simplicity, self-reliance, and closeness to nature. These qualities were thought to foster a more deeply grounded local and national identity. Proponents regarded the Middle Ages as a time of almost childlike innocence, fresher and purer than the jaded nineteenth century. Gothic architecture shared in the ideal of purity because it followed forms found in nature. More significantly, it relied on human craft, in contrast to the anonymous production of the industrial model.

Both medievalism and the encounter with Catholicism contributed to a late-century cultural phenomenon known as antimodernism. Historian T. J. Jackson Lears has described the complex mental world of educated Victorians who reacted against the alienation and impersonality of modernity, especially in the years between 1880 and 1920. For these antimodernists, the Middle Ages represented authentic experience and cultural unity. Peasants, saints, and mystics embodied innocence, simplicity (both material and spiritual), faith, imagination, vitality, nature, access to sacred mystery, and "primal irrationality," together with, paradoxically, moral strength and self-control. In this reading Francis epitomized the medieval ideal for late-century antimodernists.[4]

Protestantism struggled with modernity in another dimension as well. The nineteenth century brought stunning challenges to traditional belief—most significantly the rising authority of science, the theory of evolution, and the historical criticism of the Bible. At the same time, a popular theology of consistent, all-forgiving love began to displace the long tradition of self-scrutiny and conviction of sin that was rooted in American Calvinism. One consequence of these shifts was a reconsideration of the idea of Jesus. Historical criticism generated interest in the historical Jesus—questions about what was really "true" about him. At the same time, it intensified questions about the truth of miraculous and supernatural claims. On the other hand, many liberals, "seekers," and dissenters distinguished between Jesus himself and church teachings about him, retaining a sense of personal relationship to Jesus even when they drifted away from formal ecclesial structures. The result was a widespread emphasis on the human Jesus, his teachings, and his love.[5]

A final factor was the ideology of nature. Idealization of the natural world was a long and complex cultural tradition, but in the later nineteenth century it functioned especially as an outlet for disaffection with urban and industrial growth and as a way of resisting religious authority. It drew not only on the long Romantic tradition but on the particular expression of that tradition in New England transcendentalism and, later in the century, on nostalgia for the vanishing wilderness.[6] Francis's close association with nature was a far less prominent theme in the nineteenth century than it is in the twenty-first, but it was a persistent undercurrent. Distinctive among saints, this connection with nature undoubtedly resonated with nineteenth-century sensibilities, even among those who resisted formal religious ties.

Within these contexts I want to look more closely at the process by which American non-Catholics came to know about Francis and affirmed his legitimacy, and at the images of Francis they constructed. Much of this process drew on European sources, as we shall see.

Protestants, Francis, and History

From Martin Luther onward, most Protestants thought that religious orders were unnecessary at best and ungodly at worst. Franciscan friars were widely regarded as lazy, greedy, and corrupt. But Protestant thinking about Francis and his followers began to change in the mid-nineteenth century.[7]

One of the earliest sources of this altered thinking was Protestant historicism. "Church history" as a modern academic discipline began to emerge during the first half of the nineteenth century. As it developed, Protestants gradually, and not without controversy, came to realize that the history of the pre-Reformation church pertained also to them. Thus the earliest non-Catholic works on Francis—and many later ones as well—present themselves in the first instance as historical projects.[8]

Perhaps the most important of these works, especially for the general public, was an essay by Sir James Stephen. Stephen was a British government official, an evangelical Anglican, and, at that time, an avocational historian. His essay, published in 1847, was itself a review of two French biographies and made reference to an unfinished "History of the Monastic Orders" by the poet Robert Southey. The essay appeared in periodicals on both sides of the Atlantic and was reprinted in an 1849 collection.[9]

Stephen first had to argue that it was all right to study monastic orders—that they were "legitimate object[s] of ecclesiastical history." By "monastic," he meant all religious orders, although Franciscans were technically not monastics but mendicants. Like any good historian, Stephen discussed the sources on Francis, noting that they were "more than usually copious and authentic." And he looked for the causes of historical events in human sources rather than in supernatural ones. In this context he recounted and reflected on the story of the saint's life.[10]

Stephen was not alone in his work. At least three general histories of the church or of monasticism were published between 1855 and 1861. Charles Forbes de Montalembert's *Monks of the West, from St. Benedict to St. Bernard* began publication in Paris in 1860 and appeared in English translation in both Boston and Edinburgh within a year. General ecclesiastical histories, such as Henry Hart Milman's, also included biographies of saints. And in 1856, the German historian Karl von Hase published a life of St. Francis frequently cited by Anglophone writers. Thus scholars and educated readers encountered Francis through the study of history.[11]

Protestants found much with which to identify. Stephen, for example, argued that the Franciscan order survived its founder's death because it was a forerunner of the Reformation. Unlike the Benedictines and other settled monastic orders, he said, the mendicant Franciscans restored religious purity, engaged with the world, and sided with the weak and humble. Above all, they fostered "the Mission and the Pulpit"—a Protestant trope that was still being repeated as late as 1886. The historian C. K. Adams wrote in 1870 that Francis's purpose was "the work of a Reformation in the church" in the period when "the human intellect [sought] to rise up against the Roman yoke and throw it off." His Baptist colleague Samuel L. Caldwell added, "There is a lesson, too, of the power there is in preaching." Later authors suggested that Franciscans were the Puritans or Methodists of their day; one source in 1884 went so far as to compare Francis with the popular evangelist Dwight Moody. This proto-Protestant image of Francis, then, provided both a point of connection and a sense of reassurance for Protestants ambivalent about Catholicism.[12]

The image did not go unchallenged, however. The *Cyclopædia of Biblical, Theological, and Ecclesiastical Literature* (1870), whose editorial committee was a veritable *Who's Who* of evangelical American Protestant scholars, was sharply critical of most claims about Francis. The *Cyclopædia* cited the documentary sources on the saint, but found in them evidence of an unstable and immoral figure. Francis "imagin[ed]" he heard a call from heaven and "pretended" to perform miracles. The pope's approval of the order, said the writer, was the cynical use of a madman for the pope's own purposes and also served Francis's "ambition." As for Francis's moral character, the author comments, "Romish casuists say that [Francis's sale of his father's goods] was justified by the simplicity of his heart. It is clear that his religious training had not instructed him in the ten commandments." Nevertheless, the *Cyclopædia* mentioned the stories about birds with a touch of sentimentality, even while condemning the potential for pantheism. And it made an entirely favorable judgment of Francis's emphasis on love.[13]

Even among more sympathetic readers, the contested areas of Francis's story were those that were most distant from Protestantism. These readers struggled with his relationship to Catholic institutions, his obedience to the pope, the power structures of the Franciscan order, corruption within the order, and the meaning of the divine command to "rebuild my church." They were concerned about Francis's apparent disregard for ordinary morality. They were also uneasy about his treatment of his body, starved and deprived in ascetic discipline and finally mutilated by the stigmata. Difficult as these issues were, however, non-Catholic thinkers did not ignore them, but thought and argued about them. In the end most followed Stephen, consciously or not, by attempting to distinguish usable parts of the Franciscan tradition from "the sophistries or the superstitions of the ages in which they flourished." Or, as a popular article forty years later put it, they admired Francis despite the fact that his teaching was "marred by certain errors of Popery."[14]

Travel and Art

English-speaking Protestants also encountered Francis through travel. Travel on the European continent, formerly the province of the wealthy or of artistic expatriates, became increasingly accessible to the middle classes during the nineteenth century, with particularly large numbers participating after 1870. As Malcolm Bradbury has argued, tourists before about 1840 had gone abroad to explore, to discover what was to them the unknown. For mid- and late-century travelers, however, the way had already been charted. "Culture" displaced discovery as the object of the search. In this context "culture" meant two things: a personal grasp of important intellectual and aesthetic objects and, more broadly, the experience of a whole way of life. Travel was a ritual, a visit to cultural "shrines," the encounter with which was expected to have a transforming effect. Italy had special importance to Americans, for whom Rome was the cradle of democracy and Italian art the epitome of beauty.[15]

Assisi was not among these shrines at first. In the midcentury period, most tourists passed it by in order to explore the larger cities. Assisi became more accessible, however, at the same time that public interest in St. Francis was increasing, with a new railway line built in 1866. Thus John Murray's 1857 travel guide said, "There are no inns, properly speaking, at Assisi." By 1874, though, things had changed enough for Henry James to comment wryly, "[Baedeker] was at Assisi in force."[16]

Appropriating culture meant, in large measure, looking at art. Developing artistic taste and judgment was an essential part of nineteenth-century cultural education; art was understood to be a manifestation of the highest and best human sensibilities. Thus it is not surprising that travel guidebooks concentrated overwhelmingly on the works of art to be found in any given place. Indeed, these books could be myopic about other meanings of the sites in question. Murray, for example, advised tourists to stop for a rest at an active Franciscan monastery, but remarked that it "has little to interest the traveller" beyond a handful of paintings.[17]

One of the earliest essays on Francis in English addressed cultural interests, even while drawing on Stephen as a source. This essay appeared in the British writer Anna Jameson's 1850 collection *Legends of the Monastic Orders*. Originally a guide for the growing masses of Anglophone tourists, this book was a standard work in art history through the end of the century. Jameson wanted to explain "those works of Art which the churches and galleries of the Continent . . . have rendered familiar to us as objects of taste while they have remained unappreciated as objects of thought." She went so far as to say that saints and other sacred figures "have, for us, a deep, a lasting, interest." Thus she offered sacred art to the (generally Protestant) traveler as a vehicle not only of culture and beauty, but of religious meaning.[18]

Jameson's treatment of St. Francis was balanced and extensive. Monastic subjects in general were problematic for Jameson, since she accepted the prevalent Protestant view of monasticism as unnatural, ugly, and painfully ascetic. But, like Stephen, she argued that monasticism was historically important. As for Franciscans, she thought their religious sensibility was overly focused on retribution instead of love, and, unlike many later writers, she acknowledged some of the more bizarre qualities of Franciscan legend. Yet she saw in Francis early signs of the "tender spirit of Christianity." She admired his inclusion of animals in the divine life and the "mission of Christ." One of the many images she chose as illustrations was a version of Francis preaching to the birds (see figure 1).[19]

Jameson and many others linked Francis to the artist Giotto di Bondone (1276–1337), a transitional figure between the Middle Ages and the Renaissance. Giotto's painting appealed to nineteenth-century medievalists, who thought it modeled simplicity, innocence, and unselfconscious passion. At the same time, Giotto was recognized as an innovator and a humanist, one who departed from the conventions of medieval drawing to depict individual faces and spontaneous gestures. Some of his most important work, as it was then understood, depicted St. Francis—notably scenes from the saint's life and death, found in the church of Santa Croce in Florence, and a cycle of twenty-eight frescoes depicting his life, in the basilica of San Francesco at Assisi. (In recent years critics have questioned his responsibility for the latter, but in the nineteenth century it was rarely challenged.) Thus anyone looking at Giotto's work for aesthetic or historical purposes was exposed to narratives about St. Francis (see figure 2).[20]

More than that, though, many commentators attributed Giotto's innovations precisely to his effort to portray St. Francis, assuming that the saint's

FIGURE 1 St. Francis preaching to the birds. Engraving, after Giotto, in Mrs. Jameson's *Legends of the Monastic Orders*, 1852.

humanness and naturalness required a new mode of expression. This idea was circulating as early as the 1850s. It was most fully articulated, however, in a later work—Henry Thode's widely cited *Franz von Assisi und die Anfänge der Kunst der Renaissance in Italien* (Francis of Assisi and the beginnings of Renaissance art in Italy), published in 1885. "The men whose hearts glowed with new and burning love for Christ could not rest satisfied with the stiff and hard types of the old Greek art," said one reviewer. And, "it is not till we come to Giotto that we realize all that art owes to Francis."[21]

Art, then, offered a legitimate approach to sainthood for ambivalent Protestants, and Giotto's work offered a legitimate channel to Catholic art. For artistic commentators Francis was a realistic, human figure, a simple and passionate soul, a model of premodern authenticity. They saw in him the unity of culture and spirit that they attributed to the Middle Ages. Yet he also represented a break with the past, recalling the Francis of reform. And he signified for them a true, "tender" Christianity that implicitly transcended institutions.

FIGURE 2 Giotto di Bondone (attributed). St. Francis preaching to the birds. Ca. 1300. Fresco, Basilica di San Francesco, Assisi. This famous image is only one of twenty-eight pictures in a cycle depicting the life of St. Francis.

Literature and Spirituality

Thoughtful Victorians also encountered Francis in literature. Their first and most important source was Dante, who was highly regarded in the nineteenth century and offered another reason for Protestants to explore Catholicism. The influential American writers Henry Wadsworth Longfellow and Charles Eliot Norton undertook translations of his works beginning in 1859, supplementing the standard 1814 version by Henry Francis Cary. Together with James Russell Lowell, they formed the Dante Society in 1881.[22]

Readers of the *Divine Comedy* encountered Francis in the *Paradiso*, primarily in canto 11, which reflects on his marriage to Lady Poverty. But Francis was also understood as a forerunner to Dante, particularly through the well-known work of Frédéric Ozanam. A Catholic social critic and historian, Ozanam argued in 1852 that Francis was the first Italian vernacular poet, and as such was both the precursor of Dante and a voice of the people. (Jameson made a similar point, although Ozanam was more frequently cited.) This argument was not universally accepted; one American magazine commented in 1865 that Francis's writing was full of "life and fervor, but little more," and described one fragment as "but a pensive, monotonous wail." On the other hand, an influential essay by the poet and critic Matthew Arnold followed Ozanam in describing Francis's poetry as the "humble upper waters of a mighty stream."[23]

Arnold's essay "Pagan and Mediæval Religious Sentiment" summarized Francis for a generation of literary readers. First published in 1864, it remained in print until at least 1932. The essay reflected on the breadth and richness of historical Catholicism compared to dry Protestant rationality and went on to compare a late Roman "pagan" text with St. Francis's Canticle of the Sun. Arnold thought pagan religion was reasoned, cheerful, and anchored in present reality. But St. Francis, he wrote, understood suffering, particularly as experienced by common people. Francis responded to suffering not with his senses but with his "heart and imagination," and the Canticle offered not superficial cheerfulness but joy. This, by implication, was true Christianity, transcending suffering rather than denying it.[24]

Here is Arnold's translation of the Canticle:

O most high, almighty, good Lord God, to thee belong praise,
   glory, honour, and all blessing!

Praised be my Lord God with all his creatures; and specially our
brother the sun, who brings us the day, and who brings us
the light; fair is he, and shining with a very great splendor:
O Lord, he signifies to us thee!

Praised be my Lord for our sister the moon, and for the stars,
the which he has set clear and lovely in heaven.

Praised be my Lord for our brother the wind, and for air and cloud,
calms and all weather, by the which thou upholdest in life all
creatures.

Praised be my Lord for our sister water, who is very serviceable
unto us, and humble, and precious, and clean.

Praised be my Lord for our brother fire, through whom thou givest
us light in the darkness; and he is bright, and pleasant, and very
mighty, and strong.

Praised be my Lord for our mother the earth, the which doth
sustain us and keep us, and bringeth forth divers fruits, and
flowers of many colours, and grass.

Praised be my Lord for all those who pardon one another for his
love's sake, and who endure weakness and tribulation; blessed
are they who peaceably shall endure, for thou, O most Highest,
shalt give them a crown!

Praised be my Lord for our sister, the death of the body, from
whom no man escapeth. Woe to him who dieth in mortal sin!
Blessed are they who are found walking by thy most holy will,
for the second death shall have no power to do them harm.

Praise ye, and bless ye the Lord, and give thanks unto him, and
serve him with great humility.[25]

Arnold's argument recalled once again the simplicity and emotional
fervor that outsiders attributed to medieval Catholicism. The Francis who
is the source of vernacular poetry is expressive, often spontaneous, and
full of imagination and feeling. But he is also poor, humble, and acquainted with suffering. He is implicitly Christlike, without the strictures
of organized Christianity. And as a man of the people, speaking the language of the people, he is associated with the emergence of Italian national

identity, particularly as expressed in language, folklife, and artistic traditions.

Arnold was one of many religious liberals, seekers, discontents, and utopians who contributed—alongside more conventional Protestants—to the appropriation and interpretation of Francis. We have already encountered some of these dissenters in other roles. For example, Hase, the biographer, was an anti-Catholic polemicist of liberal orientation as well as a historian. Montalembert, the son of a Scottish convert to Catholicism, was a liberal Catholic and an advocate for medieval French art and architecture. Ozanam was a friend of Montalembert and was also the founder of the Society of St. Vincent de Paul, a religious order devoted to serving the poor. New England Unitarians were early participants in the conversation. Arnold resisted the rationalist Anglicanism of his upbringing, but read widely in religious texts, including the Bible, the *Imitatio Christi* of Thomas à Kempis, the Bhagavad Gita, and American transcendentalist writings.[26]

These seekers were instrumental in establishing another image of Francis: as imitation of Christ. In him they saw a historical figure, an ordinary human being, who had conformed almost perfectly to Jesus' example. "[Francis's] life was beatitude, an embodiment of the Sermon on the Mount," said a writer in a Unitarian periodical. To be sure, Protestants of a more orthodox stripe cautioned against identifying Francis fully with Christ. For seekers, though, Francis's human imitation of Jesus meant that other ordinary people might in turn emulate him—even, or especially, if they were alienated from the wider church. And, in the face of contemporary anxieties about biblical criticism, Francis's life reinforced arguments for Jesus' historicity.[27]

The French philosopher and historian Ernest Renan (1823–92) developed this idea most fully. In 1866, when he published his essay "Saint François d'Assise" ("Saint Francis of Assisi"), he was already well known as a religious liberal and author of the *Vie de Jésus* (*Life of Jesus*, 1863)— which had been roundly criticized by the important historian Philip Schaff. The essay on Francis was widely cited from the French, reissued in 1884, and published in English translation in 1891.[28]

Renan's essay was a meditation on Hase's biography. He began with the question of historical authenticity, which he thought was well established by both Hase and Hase's French translator, Charles Berthoud. Yet, said Renan, the historical record presented a figure of legendary proportions. He argued against too narrow an interpretation of the record, maintaining instead that the legends pointed to genuine qualities of Francis's character.

Renan presented Francis as a perfect image of Jesus—the Jesus of the synoptic Gospels and the Sermon on the Mount. The life of Francis, he said, was indirect evidence of the truth of the Gospels, because it showed that Jesus' way of living was possible. Francis sought only "primitive Christian perfection," and his followers were simple people "with very little theology." He possessed such purity that he soared above dogma and church. He did not even acknowledge the existence of evil. Yet he was not unearthly: he saw meaning in all of nature, and he was a man of feeling. Here Renan echoed Matthew Arnold, but where Arnold contrasted Francis's compassion with late Roman religion, Renan contrasted it with the cool detachment of Buddhism. At the same time, his language echoed the long-standing Protestant tropes of primitivism and direct response to the Gospel.[29]

Renan also contrasted Francis with the nineteenth century—its materialism, its cynicism, its mediocrity. He argued that Francis's central idea was that "to possess is wrong." Christian poverty was not deprivation, however, but freedom, immersed in nature and dependent on God. Renan argued that Francis's liberated poverty eventually had a profound effect not only on religious freedom, as might be expected, but on art, which calls for lofty ideals and a communal sensibility. "I cannot conceive what a society founded on the selfishness of individual possession can produce that is great," he wrote. Thus by embracing the gospel of poverty, Francis made a lasting impact "which our great men of action and our capitalists will never be capable of." This anticapitalist version of Francis reappeared with great force in the 1890s and flourished in the twentieth century, as we shall see.[30]

In 1870, literature and spiritual seeking converged in the first book-length treatment of Francis's life written in English. Its author, Margaret Oliphant, combined a historical reading with imaginative and spiritual interpretation. Oliphant had been Montalembert's Edinburgh translator. She was also a novelist who asked searching religious questions in response to her own unconventional life.[31]

Oliphant's *Francis* appeared in a series directed at a pious but serious Protestant readership—the Macmillan Company's "Sunday Library for Household Reading." Published from 1868 through 1873, this series looked at missionaries, English saints, classical wisdom, hermits, mystics, French Jansenists, English poetry, and German hymnody. Thus it drew on the history of Catholic Europe as well as of Protestant Britain—but very carefully, looking more at rebels, humanists, and individualists than at theologians or churchmen.[32]

Oliphant herself was sensitive to historical practice and was careful to distinguish history from legend. Her book, which drew on the Franciscan sources, Hase, and Ozanam, was in many ways a straightforward account of what was then known about Francis. Yet, like Renan, she also drew on the legends, using them to enhance her narrative. She also used the narrative as occasion for spiritual reflections. For instance, as she describes Francis's loss of interest in lighthearted pursuits, she argues that his distraction was not caused by the prospect of embracing poverty. Rather, it was "that startled sense of incongruity which strikes the finer-toned and more sensitive mind" when faced with contrast of "heaven above so calm and distant, and the aching, moaning earth below."[33]

Like her contemporaries, Oliphant simultaneously affirmed Protestant values and showed sympathy for Catholic faith and practice. She argued, for instance, that the extension of papal power was founded in a liberating idea of universal priesthood, however corrupted, and she alluded to Catholic texts such as the *Imitatio Christi* of Thomas à Kempis. Yet, for her Protestant audience, she stated unequivocally that Francis's life was "wholly evangelical." Both he and St. Dominic, she wrote, "literally [made], as near as they could in the simplicity of their age, a material copy of [Jesus'] life and work."[34]

A few years later John Ruskin—the medievalist, art critic, prophet of the Arts and Crafts movement, professor, prolific writer, and social reformer—entered into a kind of personal communion with Francis. Ruskin had long since rejected the evangelical Protestantism of his youth, but he was then returning to Christian language, though not to Christian institutions, and he was trying to integrate that language with his aesthetic, moral, and political principles. Among his many projects was the Guild of St. George, a proposed spiritual community that would incorporate art, study, and labor on communally owned land. In 1874—the year that Henry James complained about tourism—Ruskin went to Assisi to study and write about Giotto's paintings. He lived in the sacristan's cell in the old Franciscan monastery and kept a piece of St. Francis's cloak. He wrote that Francis had appeared to him in a dream and made him a member of the Third Order, a membership he considered valid. And his copy of an early portrait of Francis by Cimabue, a forerunner of Giotto, came out looking like a self-portrait.[35]

FIGURE 3 St. Francis blessing Assisi. Engraving after François-Léon Benouville (1821–59), frontispiece to Mrs. Oliphant's *Francis of Assisi*, 1874. Nineteenth-century publishers used a variety of images and subjects: the iconography of Francis had not yet settled on birds.

So Renan, Oliphant, and Ruskin, in different ways, reached beyond the proto-Protestant Francis of mission and pulpit to claim that Francis represented a true Christianity in a broader way—a way that was less doctrinal, more personal, more expressive, but at the same time more sensitive to the needs of the poor and outcast. To be sure, it was a severe and difficult way, but it was also childlike in its simplicity, and filled with joy. This Francis offered an alternative to the alienation that sometimes accompanied Victorian wealth and comfort.

And so did the Francis of nature. This image, so widely prevalent in our own time, was often a minor point or an afterthought in nineteenth-century works; it was hardly ever a central theme (see figure 3). However, nearly every source at least mentions the poetic Canticle of the Sun, or the miracle stories about animals, or the story of Francis preaching to the birds—the scene famously portrayed by Giotto and reproduced in Mrs. Jameson's guidebook. Non-Catholic writers recognized these stories as legends, but again, argued that they conveyed a truth about Francis's character. In any case they seemed unable to resist repeating them. In addition, Francis's poverty and mendicancy meant of course that he lived much of his life outdoors. Thus Francis offered a way to affirm the goodness of nature in an industrialized society that was beginning to long for its lost wilderness—and in religious communities that had tended to fear or ignore the natural world.[36]

As noted earlier, the seven-hundredth anniversary of Francis's birth occurred in about 1881, and by the late 1880s he was a widely familiar figure. Accessible to middle-class and educated Protestant audiences, Francis's story also pointed toward social criticism. It spoke to longings for simplicity of soul and undivided spiritual passion. It embraced the paradoxes of premodern economics and aesthetic refinement, humanness and myth, and nature and the supernatural.[37]

Sabatier and Beyond

In 1893 Paul Sabatier's biography of Francis, *Vie de Saint François d'Assise* ("Life of Saint Francis of Assisi"), was a publishing sensation. Sabatier (1858–1928) was a French Protestant and a Socialist. Born in Strasbourg, he served as a pastor until the early 1890s, when he turned his full attention to Franciscan studies. At the same time, he lived on the land as a peasant. His book was published in French in 1893, in English in 1894, went into twenty editions (i.e., printings) by 1898, and continued in print until the 1930s. The Vatican placed it on its "Index" of forbidden books in 1894. Travel guides and reference works added it to their lists of recommended reading about Francis and Assisi. Tolstoy praised it and was said to have had it translated into Russian. It remained a reference point for serious Protestant study until the mid-twentieth century and has recently been issued yet again.[38]

Scholars have been more skeptical about this biography than its popularity might suggest. The 1910 *Encyclopædia Britannica* commented that Sabatier's Francis was an anachronism, "a modern pietistic French Protestant of the most liberal type." John Moorman's classic *History of the Franciscan Order* cited Sabatier's distinguished work on textual sources but rejected his interpretations. Augustine Thompson's recent biography called Sabatier's Francis "a remarkably modern individualist . . . anachronistic to medieval Italy." Most studies agree, though, that Sabatier's work initiated modern scholarship on Francis. Especially significant is the "Franciscan question," the long and complex discussion of the age and authenticity of the early sources.[39]

Still, few scholars have noticed that Sabatier's work represented a culmination as much as a beginning. His thought was very much a product of the later nineteenth century, following trajectories set by earlier thinkers. He began with historical questions and sought to recover the human Francis from the accretions of legend and of ecclesiastical politics. At the same time, he had an undisguised emotional appreciation of Francis. He was in some measure a Christian believer but questioned received interpretations and institutional inertia. He associated Francis with common people, national identity, alternatives to capitalism, and the possibility of radical social reform. Whether or not he consciously drew on existing studies, then, it is certain that the ground was prepared for him.[40]

Sabatier's Francis was in every way an accessible, authentic model of a serious individualistic Christian. For Sabatier, Francis was a flesh-and-blood human being, the "genius" or guiding spirit of the Italian soul, and the embodiment of religious democracy. He offered a religion of action—the imitation of Jesus as the expression of love. Although Sabatier was antiecclesial, antidoctrinal, and almost anti-intellectual, he did tentatively acknowledge the reality of the supernatural, manifested not so much in spectacular miracles as in experiential spirituality. He disposed of Protestant moral concerns with relative ease, arguing for Francis's purity in every respect.[41]

Sabatier argued that Francis became a man of the people by actively rejecting the identity to which he was born—wealthy and perhaps noble—and identifying with the poor and outcast. He claimed for himself and his followers the identity and social rank of *minori*, or lesser citizens. This identification with common people encouraged the development of a national identity, expressed in part in the development of a common Italian language and vernacular poetry. National identity also implied political and religious democracy, the rule of common people, and individual conscience. In Sabatier's view, the Franciscan movement had been coopted and repressed beyond recognition by Rome, with the cooperation of power-hungry Franciscans. Had this not happened, the church would have looked very different.[42]

True Christianity, in Sabatier's view, was a religion of love and action, and it should be engaged with the world. Doctrine, ritual, institutions, and any but the simplest worship were generally corrupt. Faith was something to be lived. While Sabatier described Francis as a mystic, he was careful to distinguish this mysticism from cloistered contemplation. For Francis, he thought, mysticism was a direct experience of Jesus and led directly into action. Sabatier differed from many of his spiritually minded contemporaries by disparaging Thomas à Kempis's *Imitatio*: it was, he thought, too mysterious and too focused on the cloistered life.

Nature signified purity for Sabatier. He argued that Francis saw it for what it was, while other medieval figures tended to overinterpret it. This freshness and simplicity were reflected in artistic representations of Francis, such as Giotto's, and these in turn opened the way to Renaissance realism. Sabatier treated the nature stories as especially clear representations of who St. Francis was. Like Oliphant and others, he distinguished them from historical truth, regarding them instead as iconic images.

The sermon to the birds was the linchpin of his argument. "The sermon to the birds," he wrote, "closed the reign of Byzantine art and of the thought of which it was the image. It is the end of dogmatism and authority; it is the coming in of individualism and inspiration; . . . marking a date in the history of the human conscience." Nature, art, freedom, spirituality, equality: all are here linked to Francis and the birds.[43]

By the end of the nineteenth century, St. Francis was a permanent feature of the Protestant landscape. At that point interpretations burgeoned. An oratorio—written by a Catholic but performed for general audiences in London, New York, and other cities—depicted evening falling over Assisi accompanied by "arpeggios by the strings" and included a "Ballad of Poverty" with "the chorus joining in the refrain." Francis's call came, not in illness or through scripture, but direct from heaven ("women's chorus"). In 1895 Staff-Captain Eileen Douglas of the Salvation Army presented St. Francis as a role model for that organization. A year later Canon Knox Little of Worcester (England) Cathedral offered his flock and his readership a Francis for the Anglican *via media* (middle way). Though this Francis was sensitive and impulsive, he was endowed with a "balanced mind," "frankness," and "common sense." His devotion to the Cross issued in "practical, sustained, self-sacrificing effort," not mere idle contemplation—nor the unfocused melancholy that James Stephen saw in Francis half a century earlier. In the next chapter we will see how the interpretation of Francis unfolds.[44]

Emerging Pictures

American Protestants encountered Francis in the nineteenth century through history, travel, art, and literature, in the context of an ambivalent encounter with Catholicism and a struggle with emergent modernity. Non-Catholics' interest in Francis, and their interpretation of him, arose from cultural concerns such as "scientific" history, artistic self-cultivation, and religious faith. Yet those who admired Francis almost always saw in him an alternative to their society and culture, not an affirmation of it. Historians found in him a usable Catholic past, medievalists a simpler and more unified culture than their own, elite literary critics a friend of common people. For art critics, Francis signaled a break with the past and a source of new inspiration; for dissatisfied Christians and seekers, spiritual integrity; for social critics, a life free of materialism.

Franchot's classic work proposed that Protestants' interest in Catholicism was largely voyeuristic, a kind of religious tourism from which they could return to the safe haven of simple, rational Protestantism. Others have followed this line of thought. But nineteenth-century works about St. Francis suggest a more mixed picture, as Smith and Lears have argued. Protestants were not just spectators; they also borrowed and reshaped Catholic materials, just as tourists might return with new ideas and reshaped perceptions. In the process, Protestants' practice and expression often moved a little closer to the Catholic side of their heritage. Equally often, though, they gave the Catholic sources a more Protestant or universalistic interpretation.

Unlike many saints, Francis was clearly a historical figure and could be studied as such. Protestants could understand his life in the familiar language of missions, morals, and Gospel freedom. This image of Francis never disappeared entirely, but it was gradually supplanted by the late-century piety of individuality, personality, aesthetic feeling, nature worship, and unmediated spiritual experience. Protestants' access to Francis through art began a long process of visualizing Francis, as Protestant culture began to explore the visual and aesthetic dimensions of religion. At the same time, Francis's story came to represent a political and economic critique. Above all, it signified the imitation of Christ— the possibility that any person, not just a specially gifted one, could live as Jesus did.

CHAPTER TWO

The Early 1900s

Everyone's Saint

From the 1890s until the beginning of World War I, new publications about St. Francis came out at a steady pace—sources, translations, biographies, scholarly studies, and popular works. "At no time has his name been more familiar or his legend more often repeated than in our own day," said a prominent clergyman in 1905—adding significantly, "He has been re-canonized."[1]

Sabatier was the reference point for much of this work. The Francis we see in religious and literary works, theology and biography, popular articles and verse, is most often the one that Sabatier presented: anti-institutional, independent, an imitator of Jesus, identified with the common man, a social and political activist, mystical and artistic. In many cases the connections with Sabatier are quite explicit. A 1912 review claims that his book was "known to thousands of modern readers and students, and has been incorporated into text-books and college courses." As we have seen, it was standard reading for travelers as well. One writer referred to churchmen "explaining the 20th century spirit of St. Francis in Sabatier meetings," as if they were a common thing. Above all, he was a guiding light for social Christianity, including Christian socialism and the Social Gospel movement.[2]

But other themes emerged as well. Anti-modernism, with its weary longing and its hopeful experiments, reached its fullest expression in the era between 1880 and 1920. An emerging sense of place and pilgrimage gave shape to emotional connections with Francis. Roman Catholic writers challenged non-Catholics about the "real" St. Francis.

Early-twentieth-century constructions of Francis were embedded in mainstream culture and drew on common cultural sources. Yet they often pointed to a better world or a deeper spiritual life. This chapter begins by surveying the breadth and variety of American appropriations of Francis in the early twentieth century, with special attention to his meaning as a model of true Christianity. Next, it turns to progressive-era Protestant social reformers. The third section considers place and pilgrimage and their meanings, and the final section outlines Roman Catholic critiques of the Protestant appropriation of Francis.

The turn of the twentieth century was known as both the Gilded Age and the Progressive Era, a fact that suggests its inherent tensions. In the broadest sense, this period was part of a long shift from a decentralized society of agriculture and craft to a rationalized, bureaucratic economy and state, on its way to a culture of consumption. As Gilded Age, the period was a high point of American wealth, expansion, and extravagance. Yet the nation struggled with the effects of unregulated capitalism. Crowded cities, poverty, and labor unrest generated growing awareness of social and economic inequities. Similar tensions attended geographic expansion. The United States was proud of having attained its "manifest destiny" by spreading across the continent—yet 1893 marked the "closing of the frontier," the end of limitless expansion and a challenge to European Americans' self-image as pioneers, to say nothing of the final decisive losses for Native Americans. Antimodernism was one response to this series of transitions and changes in American culture. Another response was the loose coalition of journalistic, political, and religious movements that worked for reform and gave the Progressive Era its name. At the same time, other groups responded to Americans' changing relationships with the natural world by promoting conservation, outdoor recreation, and the establishment of national parks. All these movements overlapped at times with antimodern sentiment.

In a slightly different way, it was also a transitional age for American Protestantism. In one sense, the Protestant mainstream, like the American mainstream, reached the height of its power around the turn of the century. The denominations we know as "mainline" enjoyed great cultural authority and supported a vast international movement in the form of missions. Part of their strength came from their relative unity: there was not yet a firmly fixed dividing line between "evangelical" and "liberal." The mainline coalesced from a broad evangelical tradition, and by the turn of the century, most of the mainstream denominations had come to terms with modernity. Formal theologies embraced new knowledge and circumstances, and as we have seen, popular theology was softening the outlines of doctrine and truth claims, while all affirmed their evangelical heritage and their love of Jesus. Moreover, there were some intentional moves toward Christian unity: the Federal Council of Churches, for example, was founded in 1908.[3]

Yet there were challenges. The spiritually restless seekers of the nineteenth century had long since expressed their unease with traditional Christianity. They set in motion a continuing tradition of quiet dissent. From another direction, a movement back to "the fundamentals" was in its early stages, suggesting a different kind of discomfort with mainstream trends. Social Christianity, though more closely tied to the mainstream, still criticized the societal structures in which the churches were embedded.[4]

Another source of unease for hegemonic Protestantism was the fact that Roman Catholic and Jewish populations in America had soared. They posed a complicated challenge to the self-understanding of American Protestants—sometimes a sense of threat, but often an attraction or a search for common ground. Catholic institutions, especially, were developing a more assertive voice. The Roman Catholic Church had its own responses to modernity. The important encyclical *Rerum novarum* (1891), on labor and economics, was a benchmark in Catholic social teaching. *Pascendi* (1907) set severe limits on the modernist theology that had been emerging.

In a classic work, William R. Hutchison and colleagues described the period from 1900 onward as a time of "travail" for the mainline Protestant establishment. These Protestants began the century with a triumphal sense of a unified, hegemonic, modern Christianity. But there was already an undercurrent of dissent and a growing awareness of other Christianities and other religions. And by 1960, according to Hutchison, the dominant "social reality" of America was religious pluralism, not Protestant triumphalism. Protestants of the turn of the century were living through the beginning of this transition.[5]

A Cultural Reference Point

With Francis "re-canonized," non-Catholics no longer needed to justify their attention to historical saints. Francis became familiar across the spectrum of mainline Protestantism. Periodicals such as the *New York Evangelist* (Presbyterian) and the *Christian Advocate* (Methodist) referred to him, as did the psychologist George Coe and the famous Christian writer Charles Sheldon in *Zion's Herald* (Methodist). The *Congregationalist* quoted him in its collections of meditations. Quaker magazines both Orthodox and Hicksite mentioned him. A Baptist community sponsored a lecture series. The *Chautauquan* regularly retold stories about Francis and mentioned reading and study groups—some of them still using Mrs. Oliphant's biography. General-interest periodicals ranging from *Harper's Bazaar* to *Overland Monthly and Out West Magazine* gave attention to Francis as well.[6]

Francis was also featured on the lecture circuit. In 1902, for example, "Boston's latest literary fad" was a lecture series by Professor Edward Howard Griggs. Several sources agreed that his best lecture was on St. Francis. Griggs frequently turned to Francis as an example in his various series on great leaders and teachers.[7]

Francis often served as a sort of cultural reference point, a standard of comparison for a wide range of people and events. When President McKinley was assassinated, an Anglican bishop called his wounds "more truly stigmata" than those of St. Francis. Another clergyman, addressing the Massachusetts Fish and Game Protective Association in 1905, likened their work feeding the hungry birds to that of St. Francis. In another realm, the modern dancer Isadora Duncan was compared to Francis for her originality and simplicity. Many other prominent figures, ranging from Napoleon to Oscar Wilde, were compared with St. Francis in some way.[8]

Francis was also a reference point for new realms of thought—psychology and world religions. The Countess Evelyn Martinengo Cesaresco, an English observer of Italy, compared Francis to figures from other religions who have an affinity for animals—fakirs, dervishes, yogis, and classical divinities like Bacchus and Orpheus. But she hastened to assure her mostly Christian readers that "St. Francis . . . in some respects, stands alone," as a historical and highly individual figure motivated by "tender feeling." The emergent discipline of psychology also took an interest in Francis. William James, in his seminal work *Principles of Psychology*, considered stigmata as an example of the power of hypnotic suggestion. More optimistically, advocates of hypnotism pointed to the stigmata as evidence of its effectiveness. On the other hand, Rufus Jones, a historian of mysticism, was skeptical about traditional mystical experiences like ecstasy, trance, visions, and bodily manifestations. These, he thought, were more likely to be signs of ill health than spiritual gifts; perhaps they arose from "hysteria."[9]

Americans incorporated Francis into their shifting relationship with nature. The conservationist John Muir was compared to Francis, although Muir himself seems not to have been especially attached to him. Samuel

Crothers, a prominent Unitarian clergyman, was more direct: "And there is the increasing number of the nature-lovers who enter into the religious feelings which St. Francis voiced in 'The Song of the Creatures.' They loved one who could worship out of doors.... As they sit around their campfires they join heartily in the praise of Brother Fire."[10]

Finally, Francis was increasingly presented to children and imagined as a children's saint. This trend is especially important in the history of interpretation. While images of Francis for children were not unknown in the nineteenth century, they became commonplace during the twentieth. On one level this sometimes meant that Francis was trivialized, his meanings oversimplified. But on another level, it meant that he was integrated into American culture in an especially profound way, through the memories of children.

Specific interpretations varied. In 1894, the *New York Evangelist* published a short account of the life of St. Francis for children, emphasizing the birds. This account also made reference to "a very interesting book ... by a French pastor, Paul Sabatier." In the same year, a Catholic writer suggested that the tale of Francis might make more attractive reading than stories of martyrdom and self-mortification. She mentioned Oliphant as a source. The *Youth's Companion*, in a different vein, offered Francis as an encouraging example of standing out from the crowd. Wellesley professor Sophie Jewett connected him especially with place and with peace.[11]

True Christianity

Francis had great breadth of meaning in turn-of-the-century America, but one meaning predominated, and it undoubtedly reflected Sabatier's influence. In this material Francis is, above all, a true follower of Jesus, a model of true Christianity. This is not itself surprising, since observers since the thirteenth century have remarked on Francis's likeness to Christ. What is notable is the variety of Francis's company and contexts. Lecturers and essayists often compiled selections of great, exemplary, or truly devoted Christians—not unlike the book series in which Oliphant published her biography of Francis. Most of these series and collections included heroes of Protestantism, chiefly reformers and evangelists. Wycliffe, Luther, and Wesley were popular. The collections also routinely included figures from the pre-Reformation

Catholic Church, and occasionally even post-Reformation figures such as the missionary Francis Xavier. But other choices varied, as we shall see. Some of these lists were later replicated in stained glass and church ornament.[12]

For example, the Reverend Charles Edward Jefferson, of Broadway Tabernacle (Congregationalist) in New York, argued that God periodically renewed the Christian faith by calling "another Twelve" disciples. After the age of the apostles, he said, these were the church fathers Tertullian and Augustine, the medieval figures Anselm, Aquinas, and Thomas à Kempis along with Francis, and the reformers Savonarola, Hus, Luther, Melanchthon, Zwingli, and Calvin. A subsequent group of twelve included Henry Ward Beecher and Dwight L. Moody. The biblical historian Joseph Barber Lightfoot placed Francis among the "great servants of God." The radical activist George Herron, advocating "the recovery of Jesus from Christianity," claimed in 1901 that the "idea of Jesus [broke] forth" in Francis as in Ambrose, Bernard of Clairvaux, and John Wycliffe. The well-known Unitarian minister Edward Everett Hale, addressing a bicentennial celebration of John Wesley in 1903, added Milton, Swedenborg, and Emerson to the list. For mystics, Francis appeared alongside Madame Guyon, Tauler, and Boehme; for missionaries, with Judson and the Jesuits, David Livingstone, or Wilfred Grenfell; for social visionaries, with the Salvation Army or with Tolstoy. In one of the few explicitly masculine-gendered references to St. Francis, the *Congregationalist and Christian World* used him as an example of "the virility of goodness," along with Paul, Luther, Charles Kingsley, Horace Bushnell, and Phillips Brooks.[13]

On one level, these collections simply reflect a literary convention of the time. But in a deeper sense, they suggest an underlying question, even anxiety, about what exactly true Christianity is. If the biblical worldview was now a thing of the past, what would Christianity look like in the future? When Catholics refused to become Protestants, and Protestants embraced Catholic aesthetics, and divided denominations cooperated in mission, who exactly was a true Christian? Was America really a Protestant nation? What "fundamentals" were still true? What was most important—cognition or emotion, spiritual experience or reforming energy? Sabatier's Francis, a true Christian for the modern world, offered a kind of answer—not so much an intellectual solution as a lived and embodied one.[14]

Sabatier and Social Christianity

Sabatier's Francis was also important in the Protestant social criticism that flourished during the Progressive Era. The critical tradition that developed in this period extended far into the twentieth century. We will look at three exemplars of this tradition, but it is important to note that each of them was connected with a wide community. For them, Francis signified social critique and reform, resistance to institutions, and a new way of living out Christian faith.

Social Christianity, or the Social Gospel, is an umbrella term for a diffuse but influential movement. In its narrowest meaning, the Social Gospel is a theological claim that salvation is not only individual but communal. In this view, societies and churches, as well as individuals, can sin and therefore need salvation, and individuals' sins can be shaped by social systems, not only by personal failings. Social Gospellers therefore argued that Christians must go beyond charity and soul saving to look at the systems that cause social ills. The term "Social Gospel" is also used more broadly to refer to various Protestant responses to the problems of industrial capitalism, from settlement houses to Christian socialism. There were parallel responses in Europe and in the Roman Catholic Church.

Walter Rauschenbusch (1861–1918) is remembered today as the principal spokesperson for the Social Gospel idea. A Northern Baptist and the son of immigrants, he developed a strong sense of social concern in the late 1880s while serving as a pastor in New York City. From a small clergy-support group, he and others developed the Brotherhood of the Kingdom in the early 1890s—a loosely organized fellowship of a few dozen pastors, theologians, and laypeople concerned with integrating their Protestant Christianity with their social concerns. Rauschenbusch's best-known works built on the work of the Brotherhood and articulated the arguments for social Christianity for a wider audience. They have continued to influence Christian social thought into the twenty-first century.[15]

Francis was an inspiration to the Brotherhood from early on. One member jokingly described its annual meetings as "Rauschenbusch's Assisi." Louise Seymour Houghton, Sabatier's English-language translator, was a member, and the group studied Sabatier for a year. Their pamphlets and other writings make it clear that Francis was one of their guiding lights.[16]

Rauschenbusch's Social Gospel Francis looks very much like Sabatier's. In a seminal work, *Christianizing the Social Order*, Rauschenbusch wrote of Francis, "This most famous and beloved saint of the Middle Ages was the great friend and ideal of the common people, a very incarnation of Christian democracy. In its infancy, before the church twisted it and wrested it to its own taste and use, the Franciscan movement was charged with an almost revolutionary social sympathy." In a footnote, he added that "Sabatier's 'Life of St. Francis' is still the classical interpretation of that wonderful soul." Rauschenbusch made similar comments in *Christianity and the Social Crisis* and in *A Theology for the Social Gospel.*[17]

Here again, Francis was a model of true Christianity. Rauschenbusch grouped the early Franciscans with Gospel-based lay movements like the Waldensians and the early Methodists, the Salvation Army, and the foreign mission movement. He regarded them all as democratic renewals of the faith, "expressions of lay religion and working-class ethics." But Francis was not just a social activist. For Rauschenbusch, he was an example of the fullest expression of Christian spiritual life, one of those great souls who had "escaped from themselves and learned to depend on God."[18]

Rauschenbusch's contemporary Rufus M. Jones (1863–1948) had a similar take on Francis: a holy figure, an exemplar of true Christianity, and a model for social action. His interpretation was both parallel to and different from Rauschenbusch's. Jones was a key figure in twentieth-century liberal religion. As an academic and a popular speaker and writer, he redefined Quakerism for the modern age in a way that appealed to both insiders and outsiders. He also mediated the idea of mysticism to a broad middle-class audience, paving the way for later developments in twentieth-century spirituality. In addition, his activism reached a wide public, notably through the American Friends Service Committee and through his advocacy for legal conscientious objection. Jones argued that the Quaker faith combined mystical spirituality—by which he meant direct experience of God's presence—and action in the world. Raised in the Orthodox-evangelical stream of Quakerism, he maintained close ties with both evangelicals and liberals.[19]

Like Rauschenbusch, Jones came of age in the era when Francis was becoming widely known. Jones had a direct link to Sabatier, since they had met as graduate students, when Sabatier was studying the history of mysticism. Jones considered Sabatier the greatest interpreter of Francis, and the parallels in their thought are clear. But Jones wrote that his deepest personal connection with Francis began in 1903, after a period of personal tragedy. At that time, he said, Francis "came to me with his rich revealing power," and a colleague's insights on Francis "opened up new understanding of the meaning of love." Although he did not visit Assisi until 1929, the trip was a high point for him and he frequently referred to it afterward.[20]

As a social activist, Jones responded to the same concerns as the Social Gospel movement. In an early work, he emphasized Francis's humanity and his concern for everyday people, and in a later one, he made Francis the model of active peacemaking. At the same time, Jones believed above all that Francis was a model of true "primitive" Christianity, that is to say, the Christianity of the first followers of Jesus.

For example, in his important *Studies in Mystical Religion* (1909), Jones devoted a chapter to St. Francis and some of his successors. He first argued that Francis was interested in ordinary people—the "common man," or "concrete men"—not in theological abstractions. When he kissed the leper, or fed the robbers, or reached out to the poor, he was living his beliefs: "He *practised* the love and tenderness which were the warp and woof of his message." In addition, Francis "made Christianity once again a lay religion," not a churchly one. Not surprisingly, Jones's Francis is distinctly antiecclesial—a fresh breeze in an era of "gloomy superstitions, whose preaching was in sharp contrast to the formal, barren services in the churches."[21]

Twenty years later, in *The New Quest* (1928), Jones set Francis alongside Gandhi in a discussion of "experiments in heroic love." Both served as examples of pacifism and active peacemaking. Here, Jones again dismissed many traditional ideas about the meaning of Francis. Friars, poverty, asceticism: these were not really important. The "real miracle" was overcoming evil with good. Jones then reviewed the familiar stories in those terms. This time, when Francis kissed the leper, or welcomed the robbers, or reached out to rich as well as poor, he was acting out not only his personal love, but the ultimate power of love and goodness. As modern-day examples of such power, Jones evenhandedly mentioned Quaker war relief and famous missionaries.[22]

Jones also liked to connect Francis with Quakerism directly. He did this not only through mysticism and pacifism, but by retelling an often overlooked story from the *Little Flowers*. This is the story of Brother Giles's encounter with King Louis IX of France, later St. Louis. The story says that when they met, they sat together in silence for some hours. They then parted without speaking. When questioned, Giles said, "I read his heart, and he read mine." For Jones, this story implied that silent worship was timeless and truthful. He was less interested, though, in the natural world: he gave very little attention to the Franciscan nature stories, whether the sermon to the birds or the Canticle of the Sun.[23]

Like Rauschenbusch and Jones, Vida Scudder (1861–1954) was engaged with the issues of her time and found inspiration in St. Francis. As a professor of English, a Christian Socialist, and a prolific writer, Scudder integrated religious and social concerns with much of her work and life. She was important in women's activism, women's education, and Christian social thought. She also maintained a deeper personal involvement with St. Francis than either Rauschenbusch or Jones.

Scudder was born to Congregationalist missionary parents, but entered the Episcopal Church in her teens. Her upbringing included two extended trips to Europe; she later recalled having heard Renan speak, and reading about the Catholic social reformers Montalembert and Lacordaire. Ruskin's final lectures at Oxford made a lasting impression on her in the 1880s. Her mature spirituality blended a Protestant sense of freedom and rationality with an attraction to Catholic symbolism, history, and unity.[24]

In 1887 she joined the faculty of Wellesley College. Over the next five years, she deepened her involvement in urban settlement work and the labor movement. She also deepened her focus on spiritual life: in 1889, she joined the Society of the Companions of the Holy Cross, a nonresidential community of Episcopalian women devoted to prayer and activism. As time went on, she participated in a number of Christian and secular socialist organizations, including the Socialist Party.

Her socialism was somewhat different from that of Rauschenbusch. Where his central concerns were the capitalist system and unearned wealth, Scudder's was the wage system—that is, the exchange of labor for wages. According to Marx and others, wages never represent the full value of what workers produce, so the wage system is inherently exploitive. Scudder also supported consumer cooperatives as an economic alternative—a recurrent idea in American life—and she drew clear distinctions between voluntary and involuntary poverty. During the 1920s she became increasingly committed to pacifism, like many serious Protestants of the time.[25]

In her autobiography, Scudder says that Francis was a longtime presence in her life. She first visited Assisi in the 1890s, but she marked the year 1901 as a particular turning point. In that year she spent sustained time in Assisi recovering from a breakdown and illness. There she met Sabatier, who had a residence in the city and gathered pilgrims around him. She must have made a strong impression: they corresponded until his death, and, through her influence, the Boston Public Library subsequently acquired his book collection.[26]

Scudder claims that she postponed sustained work on St. Francis until after she retired in 1928. But in fact he was a reference point for much of her tremendous body of work, beginning with her first book in 1895. And he carried a more or less consistent set of meanings for her throughout her life. Her main concerns were what Francis himself represented, what happened to the Franciscan movement after its first idealistic flowering, and the tension between the ideal and the real in the modern world. The sense of place at Assisi, too, figures frequently in her work, as we shall see later on.[27]

What Francis represented to her was the purest and most absolute expression of Christian faith. He signified radical poverty, sacrifice and self-giving, and also a divine madness, a "heavenly anarchy." All of this, she said, welled up from unlimited love. Thus Francis imitated Jesus and made Jesus visible to us. Like her contemporaries, Scudder associated Francis with other saintly and heroic figures, but hers were the saints of social action and alternative economics: Ruskin, Tolstoy, Kropotkin, and John Woolman.[28] At the same time, Scudder's thought was shaped by modernist Protestantism. She emphasized Francis's freedom and his engagement with the world, in contrast to cloistered monastics. She also noted that modern people would appreciate his love of nature.[29]

Her main concern in writing about Francis, however, was the tension between the ideal and the real. For example, this tension is a theme of her early novel *A Listener in Babel*, published two years after her encounter with Sabatier in Assisi. Scudder's semi-autobiographical heroine rejects several attractive career opportunities, choosing instead to live and work in a settlement house. Her struggle over this decision is set in Assisi. Eventually, however, the young women in the settlement house all reach a state of what today would be called burnout. They resolve the dilemma by exchanging radical communitarian life for more moderate commitments to simplicity and socially beneficial vocations.

Other works are similar. In *Socialism and Character* (1912) Francis is the archetypal representative of religious commitment. Yet Scudder ultimately concludes that religion alone cannot provide a practical structure for society. In the novel *Brother John* (1927), the hero—a "mouthpiece of Vida Scudder," according to one critic—struggles between the Franciscan ideal and the survival and unity of the brotherhood. *The Franciscan Adventure* (1931) reflects on art, scholarship, ownership of property, and obedience to authority, all of which the Franciscan orders eventually embraced.[30]

The tension between real and ideal was also a personal issue for Scudder. Reflecting on her middle years, she later wrote, "St. Francis had touched the springs of my life. The call of Lady Poverty rang clear, I longed to make an ultimate surrender." Yet she hesitated because she loved teaching and writing. "I hated my salary," she continued, yet she took responsibility for supporting her mother and aunt as well as herself. Thus she was attracted to St. Francis—as well as to poverty and to radical politics—and yet was never able to be wholeheartedly Franciscan.[31]

Neither, of course, was Rauschenbusch or Jones. But they do not seem to have been so troubled by it. Despite her many achievements, it was Scudder who recognized a gap between unreserved commitment—her "divine anarchy," Rauschenbusch's utter dependence on God—and the compromise and moderation of ordinary Christian life. There is much that we could say about this, but for now the most important point is that Scudder articulated an inherent tension in people's devotion to St. Francis. As we shall see, it recurs in every age.

The critic C. F. G. Masterman put it another way. In an essay on "Chicago and Francis" in 1902, he mused about the temptation of wealth. It was so easy, he thought, to admire Franciscan poverty while avoiding it in one's own life. Well-meaning Christians argued that they could help more people if they had more wealth, or that wealth was not harmful as long as one did not treat it as ultimate, or that God created all good things to be enjoyed. He implied, though, that they were deceiving themselves. "For long after Chicago and Birmingham . . . have become the habitation of bats and owls," he said, "men's hearts will still turn with longing towards the little brown cities of Italy." This brings us to the question of St. Francis and place.[32]

Place and Pilgrimage

In 1904 the Congregationalist pastor Ozora S. Davis wrote: "The person who would understand Francis must have access to two classes of sources. One is literary, the Fioretti, the Mirror of Perfection, and Sabatier's great work. . . . The other source is the land in which Francis lived. . . . The land interprets to an unusual degree the man."[33]

Davis was an influential minister and writer, later president of Chicago Theological Seminary. He was not alone in his views: a surprising number of non-Catholic voices, beginning in the nineteenth century, have insisted that it is impossible to understand Francis without having seen Assisi. On the face of it, this is a surprising claim. What do Francis's example and message have to do with any particular place? Poverty, imitation of Christ, and devotion to God would seem to be placeless—practices that one could carry out anywhere. And if Francis is understood to be a universal figure, or even a universal Christian, he should be even less connected to place. These non-Catholic writers often say that what they encounter in Assisi is the "spirit" of St. Francis. But again, we might think they would encounter his spirit in living by his example. Of course, an emphasis on spirit also serves to defend Protestants against idolatry by keeping material things at a distance. Yet for many of them, spirit seems to be especially bound to, and revealed in, a very material sense of place.[34]

In recent years, scholars in many academic disciplines have explored the idea of place. In this discussion, "place" is not just a geographical location, but a location to which people have ascribed meaning and value. In other words, a "place" is a human construction. Its meaning is usually tied up with memory—with narratives about something that happened there. "Place is space which has historical meanings," says the biblical scholar Walter Brueggemann. "Place is any space that has the capacity to be remembered and to evoke what is most precious," says the theologian Philip Sheldrake. It is also important to note that the sense of place may not be entirely a human invention. Several scholars have argued that physical places, especially natural features, are themselves participants in the discussion. Physical places and geographic features "have a kind of agency and power in shaping the way people imagine and make use of them," as historian Brian Campbell put it. The landscape around Assisi is a good example. By Euro-American standards of natural beauty it is breathtaking; no wonder it evokes a feeling that something special must have happened here. It also evokes a desire to make meaning of the view, in this case by connecting it with the historical person who is the visitor's reason for being there. This tendency—to associate history and spirituality with place—seems to be very common, if not universal. As Sheldrake observes, "Human memories, whether individual or collective, are often localized in landscapes."[35]

Place is often linked to pilgrimage. In broad terms, pilgrimage is a journey to a sacred place in hope of spiritual benefits of some kind. A classic anthropological description calls pilgrimage a transformative, "liminal" experience, a symbolic movement into some new phase of life. This movement is not only inner or spiritual, but is enmeshed with human community and material things. Natural sites, buildings, relics, pictures, and statuary focus the experience; tokens, medals, and natural objects like stones help the pilgrims carry the experience home. Thus pilgrimage is linked with place—and also merges into tourism, with its journeys and its souvenirs.[36]

Protestants as a group have been skeptical about both place and pilgrimage. As we noted earlier, the first Protestants rejected pilgrimage, and their descendants have generally downplayed the importance of physical space and material objects, affirming instead that true faith must be free of worldly attachments. For Protestants, "pilgrimage" has traditionally been a metaphor for an interior journey.

During the nineteenth century, though, Protestants began to explore the language and practice of pilgrimage, just as they explored Catholic heritage and European travel. By mid-century, places like Plymouth Rock had become travel destinations with many layers of sacred meaning. As we have seen, non-Catholics used the language of "shrine" and "pilgrimage" for artistic and cultural destinations. And by the 1890s, mainstream Protestants such as Methodists and Presbyterians were cheerfully making "pilgrimages" to sites that were important in their own history. Still, non-Catholics continued to use the word "pilgrimage" ambiguously, even ironically, trying to distinguish the reverence they felt toward a place or object from "true," spiritual religion. High-church Anglicans were the exception, with their frank embrace of their Catholic heritage.[37]

What did it mean, then, for American non-Catholics to say that Francis could only be fully known through place? Ozora Davis tried to make it a matter of old Protestant values. He thought that the church buildings and many artworks in Assisi misrepresented Francis as "the official head of an ecclesiastical institution." The "real" Francis, he said, is found in the simple, rough places where he lived and walked. These places show who Francis really was—"a restorer of religion to its true place as an experience of the soul, a champion of freedom in the face of tyranny, and a prophet of the true Christian order." Yet Davis could have made this argument on the basis of written texts alone. The physical place reinforced his point, but added nothing new.[38]

Davis's reactions do, however, resemble those of Holy Land pilgrims. Popular tours to the Holy Land began in the late 1860s; Mark Twain famously used the term "pilgrims" for one such group in 1869. And Davis's remarks echo then-familiar Protestant language. Guidebooks and travel narratives insisted that the spirit of Jesus was not to be found in elaborate churches or liturgies, but in the unspoiled countryside and villages through which he had walked. Protestant visitors routinely disparaged the "gorgeous decorations, costly shrines, and superstitious ceremonies" at sites like the Church of the Holy Sepulchre, but expressed deep pious emotion at hillsides, gardens, and lakes—sites that seemed to them unchanged since Jesus' time. As an 1859 author put it, "the Land and the Book . . . constitute the entire and all-perfect text, and should be studied together." These tropes may have influenced responses to Francis and Assisi.[39]

A deeper account of the meaning of place comes from Vida Scudder, who also referred to herself as a "pilgrim." Her essay about Assisi, "Footprints of St. Francis," won a prize in a "vacation experiences" contest sponsored by the liberal *Outlook* magazine in 1903—another instance of the overlap between pilgrimage and tourism. As an Episcopalian, Scudder was more open to material expression of religion than free-church Protestants would have been. Still, her account of the meaning of Assisi is revealing for all. Her description illustrates many dimensions of the relationship between land, memory, and spirituality.

First, for Scudder, the land itself is sacred. "Why is it that different landscapes seem to possess distinctive spiritual qualities?" she asks. "There could be no better witness to this indubitable fact than Umbria." It is also a focal point for holy power. Fourth-century monastics or hermits (legendary perhaps) came to stay there: "Then, as later, it was evidently a land recognized as in some peculiar sense fit for devotion."[40]

The land also generates holiness. It produced St. Francis and expresses itself in his life. The country "blossomed into spiritual expressiveness . . . in the lovely life of St. Francis and his first companions."[41] On the other hand, St. Francis makes the land holy. "We are looking over the country consecrated by the feet of St. Francis," she says. Particular places, too, such as buildings, have been made sacred by Francis's presence: for example, she writes about "the rough chapel of the Portiuncula . . . sanctified forever by the labors of the hands of Francis."[42]

Francis also found God in the landscape. He went to the Carceri when he needed "fellowship with God in nature." And people match the landscape; the place expresses itself in its human inhabitants. The friars at the remote, rugged mountain monastery of the Carceri "appear to be of a more spiritual type than those whom one meets in the monasteries of the fat plain below."[43]

In Scudder's account, we experience Francis in a particular way through place. "One may stand in the square where the Saint threw his garments in his father's face . . . may wonder with what eyes he viewed the hoary columns of the Roman Temple of Minerva." Elsewhere, "we may tread in his very footsteps," or follow the road "worn by his feet . . . ." One may even "feel his presence at one's side as one kneels in the old Cathedral of San Rufino." Simply being where Francis has been is enough to evoke his presence.[44]

There is continuity between past and present, both in the town and in the church. Assisi "bears an aspect that would be strange to these simple holy ones, yet even here many features remain unchanged." The elaborate church might "be not only strange but repellent to the lover of rudest wayside shrines," but processions bearing the Blessed Sacrament are the same as in Francis's day. Since these processions are characteristically Catholic practices, Scudder here draws the reader's focus to tradition rather than reform.[45]

At the same time, there is discontinuity between the church and the natural world. "One can get nearer to Francis," she reminded the reader, "than beside the church dedicated to his honor; the wide country under the open heavens was the home of the Little Poor Men, and this abides." Here she repeats the familiar distinction between elaborate church and unspoiled countryside.[46]

The friars, however, provide continuity. They imitate Francis physically, in their posture and silence and waiting, on the physical spot where Francis received a vision. They are, she says, a "visible memorial." This is a resonant choice of words. In many Protestant theologies, "memorial" describes communion—the communion service is a memorial, a commemoration of Christ, not the "real presence" affirmed in other theologies. In this sense a memorial is different from real presence. In present-day academic usage, though, "memorial" means nearly the opposite—an act of remembering that brings the past into the present and keeps it alive. So the monk as a "visible memorial" can be read either as distancing Francis from the present, or as bringing him closer.[47]

Scudder was far from alone in her sense of place. Throughout the twentieth century and into the twenty-first, visitors to Assisi have expressed again and again the sense that Francis is present there, or that they know him better for having been there, and that the place itself is sacred. In 1981, for example, the Catholic theologian Eric Doyle wrote, "Besides the writings of St. Francis and the early written sources of his life and message, there remains still one more source: the city of Assisi itself. . . . The spirit of St. Francis pervades its every inch. . . . Its medieval buildings, holy places and Giotto's frescoes reveal dimensions of St. Francis' person and life that no written source can possibly hope to communicate."[48]

Scudder's older contemporary Henry Adams also responded strongly to Assisi. Adams was a scion of Boston Unitarianism, the descendant of two presidents and himself a historian. He is remembered mainly, though, for the reflective writings he produced toward the end of his life. His *Mont-Saint-Michel and Chartres*—privately printed in 1905 and published in 1913—is an extended meditation on the Middle Ages. Adams reflected on the dialectical movements between unity and multiplicity, scholasticism and mysticism, intellect and primal energy, and especially, the masculine and the feminine. His spiritual ideal was the Virgin—a feminine religious principle that was nonrational, close to nature, and full of love. Of the many saints he considered, Francis alone approached the status of this ideal.

To understand Francis, said Adams, "one must wander about Assisi with the 'Floretum' or 'Fioretti' in one's hand;—the legends which are the gospel of Francis as the evangels are the gospel of Christ, who was reincarnated in Assisi." He suggested, in other words, that one cannot approach Francis through historicism, as nineteenth-century writers tried to do. Instead he evoked Renan's old argument that the historically questionable legends give a true account of Francis's character, and he reminded the reader that the Gospels are also distant in time from the life of Jesus. Above all, the encounter with Francis—and by extension, with Jesus—was for him intertwined with the sense of place. Assisi, as we saw in chapter 1, was indeed the city of St. Francis—and an alternative to the modern world.[49]

"The Real St. Francis": The Catholic Critique

Roman Catholics did not fail to notice the rise in Protestant interest. "At the moment," said Father Paschal Robinson in 1903, "a new race of pilgrims is wending its way towards the Umbrian towns." Catholic thought and practice had, of course, never turned away from the saints as Protestants had, so there was already a body of Catholic literature about Francis, drawing on a more continuous tradition. And Catholic academics were familiar with scholarly works by non-Catholics. In the 1890s, though, Catholics began to develop a more deliberate response to the Protestant vision of St. Francis. Popular magazines published critiques and rebuttals of works by Sabatier and others, and biographies of Francis with a Catholic agenda began to appear after the turn of the century.[50]

At its heart, this discussion was an argument over the "real" St. Francis. That was the title of an early essay, but it is also a much larger cultural argument that continues into the twenty-first century. Who is the "real" St. Francis? What is "real" in the many stories about him? In the early 1900s, Catholics began to construct a St. Francis who could speak to the modern age, yet was neither a Protestant nor a socialist.

The broad outlines of the Roman Catholic argument remain the same down to the present. As we noted earlier, many documents that are attributed to Francis, or to the early Franciscan movement, clearly affirm Catholic orthodoxy. They express loyalty to the pope, obedience to superiors, reverence for priests, and devotion to the sacraments. Non-Catholic authors, with some exceptions, have generally minimized the importance of these statements. Many have simply ignored them. Others, following Sabatier, have dismissed them as lip service, a kind of boiler-plate material that Francis and his followers had to include in order to placate the authorities. Still others have argued that they belonged to Francis's historical and religious context but need not belong to ours. Roman Catholic critics, however, have typically taken the statements at face value and have argued for their legitimacy.[51]

Father Paschal Robinson, OFM, author of *The Real St. Francis of Assisi* (1903), found the growth in Protestant interest strange but true. He acknowledged the nineteenth-century literature—Arnold, Renan, Ozanam, Ruskin, and Mrs. Oliphant—and he spoke well of Canon Knox Little's lectures. He even noted increased Protestant sympathy toward Catholicism, and toward the idea of sainthood. Yet, in the end, he was skeptical. "We fear," he wrote, "that not a little of what is being written nowadays about 'Sweet St. Francis' must be set down as mere sentiment." Or, if not that, Robinson argued, then as academic study or reductionistic social activism. "Does St. Francis stand for nothing more than universal peace, brotherhood, and the appreciation of the lowly?" Robinson asked. He was particularly scathing on the International Society of Franciscan Studies, "an emanation of the brain of Sabatier."[52]

A few years later, Johannes Jørgensen produced a more complete biography. Jørgensen based his narrative on primary sources and on a 1903 "pilgrimage" to Assisi. Perhaps he was there at the same time as Henry Adams, Ozora Davis, or the travel writer Edward Hutton. He had certainly met Sabatier. Jørgensen was a Danish poet and writer who converted to Roman Catholicism in 1896, in the context of a romantic cultural and religious movement not unlike the American one we encountered in chapter 1. On the whole, his story of Francis did not depart drastically from the usual telling, but he highlighted elements of Catholic commitment and doctrine. He devoted sections to relations with Rome, the Portiuncula indulgence, and other issues particular to Catholics alongside discussions of Francis's "vivid feeling for nature" and "love of nature." But he quoted Sabatier sympathetically, if not always in perfect agreement, and he even went so far as to compare Francis offhandedly with Tolstoy. His book influenced Catholic social activists and is still widely available today. A prominent Catholic reviewer, writing in the *New York Times*, said that "Sabatier's voice is out of tune, while Jørgensen sings true."[53]

Father Cuthbert, in *The Life of St. Francis of Assisi* (1912), confronted Protestant interpretations more directly. While he agreed that the medieval church needed reform, he argued throughout for Francis's orthodoxy. A Capuchin Franciscan, Cuthbert was a scholar and prolific writer and at this time had just become principal of the Franciscan House of Studies in Oxford. He was later a Minister Provincial and president of a Franciscan college in Assisi. Cuthbert argued that there had been no "adequate" biography written in English, although, he says, Canon Knox Little provided a useful character study. Sabatier's biography he damns with faint praise as "a delightful piece of literature," adding charitably that research has progressed since 1894.[54]

The differences between Cuthbert and Sabatier are particularly clear in their interpretations of Francis's "Testament." As we saw earlier, this text is a short account of Francis's conversion and faith and of his vision for the brotherhood. Both Cuthbert and Sabatier quote it in full—but they give it very different meanings. There are also differences in translation.[55]

In the Testament, as we saw earlier, Francis gives a brief description of his conversion through the encounters with lepers. He then mentions his simple faith in churches and his confidence in priests, the latter because they make Christ available through the sacrament. He urges readers to keep the holy books in "decent" or "becoming" places, and to respect theologians and preachers. There follows a long description of the friars' way of life, including poverty, worship, work, and begging. He then forbids the brothers to request any "letter" or "bull" from Rome, and he calls for obedience to ecclesial superiors. He discusses heresy within the order. He insists that the Testament is not "another rule," but says that the brothers should still follow its precepts. The Testament concludes with a blessing.

Cuthbert provides marginal notes to help the reader remember important points. These are oriented in a churchly direction: "His belief in the service of lepers [;] in churches, in priests and the Roman church. That priests must be reverenced; as also the mysteries of the altar, and the Names and Words of God; and theologians and ministers of the Divine Words. His belief concerning the Rule in the life of the fraternity. That the brethren must be Catholic; and that heretics must be delivered up," and so on.[56]

By contrast, Sabatier uses the Testament as further evidence for the primacy of conscience. He begins by quoting: "No one showed me what I ought to do [said Francis], but the Most High himself revealed to me that I ought to live conformably to his holy gospel." Sabatier contends, "The genesis of [Francis's] thought here shows itself to be at once wholly divine and entirely personal. The individual conscience here proclaims its sovereign authority." He continues, "For him . . . when there is conflict between what the inward voice of God ordains and what the Church wills, he has only to obey the former." Finally, Sabatier notes that the Testament forbids glosses or commentary. For him this means that any interpretations that softened the demands of poverty, or that strengthened ecclesial authority, were invalid.[57]

In other words, Cuthbert passes quickly over themes of poverty, simplicity, manual labor, homelessness, and dependence on God. But he does insist on Francis's Catholic context. And, as we shall see, Catholic interpretation later became more sympathetic to the practices of poverty. Sabatier, on the other hand, passes over the material about church order, insisting on individual conscience and direct communion with God. Each maintains that his is the "real" St. Francis.

So it is interesting that a minor work of this period was called *Everybody's St. Francis*—an implicit answer to the question of which Francis is "real." It was a simple book, probably aimed at older children. Its author, Maurice Francis Egan, was a Roman Catholic. He had been a professor of

English and a popular writer, but when the book was published, he was serving as U.S. ambassador to Denmark. It seems likely that his book was inspired by Jørgensen's, which was then available in Danish, and which Egan's narrative follows in several respects. In general, it is a conventional retelling of Francis's story, only adding low-key explanations of Catholic teaching here and there. In other words, a Catholic diplomat, posted to a Protestant country under a Protestant president, draws on the work of a Protestant convert to Catholicism in order to present to the rising generation a St. Francis who is for "everybody."[58]

Francis at the Center

In the early years of the twentieth century, Francis stood at the center of cultural tension about true Christianity and at the center of personal ambivalence about Christian commitment. A prosperous, confident culture constructed a St. Francis who was popular, well known, and for everybody. At the same time, this culture produced social criticism in the form of a dissenting Francis, the friend of the working man, the poor anticapitalist. A different dissenting voice insisted on Francis as a Catholic rather than a proto-Protestant. All the participants invoked history, yet interpreted it freely; they were not entirely bound to it. They also began to locate history, spirituality, and Francis himself in place and landscape. In so doing, they associated him more closely with nature and the material world, but also with the intangible experiences of memory and transformation. This Francis is both "real" and surprisingly elusive—a shadowy, almost transparent figure through whom all these cultural currents flow.

CHAPTER THREE

Between the Wars
Peace, Play, and Protest

The year 1926 marked the seven-hundredth anniversary of Francis's death. It was the occasion for a new spate of interest in Francis, though not for groundbreaking new material. There were biographies, reassessments of research, spiritual reflections, and festivals. Leading scholars published an essay collection with an introduction by Sabatier. The *New York Times* and other sources reported large numbers of pilgrimages to Assisi—repeating familiar phrases about the sense of place as they did so. *The Congregationalist*, a denominational magazine, devoted an issue to the anniversary. Two years later, Earl Marlatt included Francis among "Protestant saints" in a book of that title. Although Marlatt's agenda was to argue against some recent Roman Catholic decisions that limited ecumenical relationships, few Protestants would have objected to his characterization of Francis.[1]

What was new in this period was a freer, more imaginative way of interpreting Francis. It was as if, now that everyone knew his story, people could reflect on it and play with it a little bit more. Some of the most important works from the 1920s dwelt on foolishness, irony, reversals, and inversions. What was also new was an effort to "practice" Francis—to internalize, enact, and identify with him in a variety of embodied ways.

The pace of publication dropped markedly after 1926, and most of the religious essays that appeared during the 1930s concentrated on Francis's mysticism or spirituality. These essays spoke to a rising interest within the Protestant churches. They were generally cautious in approach, adding little new material to the conversation about Francis. We might have expected more focus on poverty, but it is not there. The only major biography published in that decade devoted part of a chapter to poverty, but avoided prescriptive social comment. Indeed, the author insisted that Francis's "Religion, his Order, was not to Francis an economic system." A dissertation focused on the issue of poverty had little impact. The churches did not say much, nor did the radical religious journals. The Great Depression-era writers and photographers gave little attention to religious figures, with the exception of James Agee, who seems to have had a private fascination with Francis.[2]

Those who did focus on poverty were located largely on the margins of the mainstream—Protestant socialists, antiwar activists, and, on the Catholic side, the new Catholic Worker movement. In a sense they carried forward the theme of foolishness, placing their faith in small-scale, everyday commitment rather than in systemic or governmental solutions. Pacifists used this time to develop a new narrative of Francis as peacemaker, a model for their own embodied practices.

There were also significant explorations of Francis in professional theater and dance, another mode of enactment. The modernist composer Paul Hindemith collaborated with the choreographer Léonide Massine on a ballet about St. Francis. Ted Shawn, a pioneer in modern dance, created a solo piece about Francis in 1931 and performed it regularly over the next three decades. Shawn was particularly concerned with the place of men and masculinity in dance, but his St. Francis was meditative and "lyrical" rather than forceful. In the fine arts, as we shall see, there was a public outcry over sculpture in the late 1930s.[3]

World War I is often regarded as a watershed, as a breaking point between one era and another. In many ways this is true: the war meant the end of the Gilded Age, the end of an aristocratic social world, the end of nineteenth-century aesthetics and of lavish excess. The age of the free-wheeling robber barons gave way to an age of corporations. By some measures the war also marked the end of the Progressive Era in American politics and activism. In another sense, though, the 1920s represent the high point of modernity, the culmination of cultural processes that had been developing since the Civil War. The 1920s brought wider prosperity and new technologies, new freedom for women and the hope of world peace. The Scopes trial over evolution was a high-water mark in the growth of religious liberalism; many thought (erroneously) that its triumph would be permanent. Modernist art changed the visual landscape. On the other hand, as in the nineteenth century, the confident embrace of progress was accompanied by nostalgia for a simpler way of life. The decade of the 1920s is also known for the "lost generation" of writers and artists, exploring disorientation and nihilism. And Europeans, having lived through the war, were far more skeptical than Americans about human progress and power.[4]

At the end of the decade, the stock market crash marked another cultural watershed. The Great Depression brought widespread poverty and dislocation, especially after the Dust Bowl drought of the early 1930s. Struggles between labor and industry were fierce; the radical Left became an energetic force in politics. Around the world there were changes and crises: the rise of fascism, ethnic nationalism, and a new wave of imperialism.

American Protestantism reflected these wider trends. Following the war, the 1920s saw renewed confidence, wealth, and expansion in mainline churches. The Depression era and the approach of the second war brought a darker mood. There was a revival of social criticism and protest, following the general outlines of the earlier Social Gospel movement. At the same time, there was an inward turn, manifested as interest in mysticism and spiritual life. Church architecture and decoration turned away from the Gothic, still a popular form in the 1920s, toward the modern. Academic theology began its shift toward what is loosely called neo-orthodoxy—a reaction against the modern tendency to see the work of God embedded in culture, and against the idea of continual progress, in favor of an emphasis on the otherness, mystery, and power of God. In this context, constructions of St. Francis were both continuous and discontinuous with what had gone before.

This chapter will look briefly at some of the continuities and then turn in more depth to some examples of imaginative, ironic expression, which included practice as well as literature. It will then turn to the 1930s and the ambivalent connection of Francis with real poverty, as well as the pacifist narrative. Three other forms of expression that also emerged during this period—a hymn, a prayer, and a garden statue—will be the subject of the next chapter.

Francis Upside Down

Against the wish to make St. Francis a Protestant, or a modern man, against the wish to explain away the miracles, against the wish to find the "real" St. Francis by differentiating historical fact from legend, G. K. Chesterton (1874–1936) set out to show that Francis's life was all of a piece. But he thought it was a life of reversals, foolishness, and irony.

Chesterton is something of a crossover figure in religious terms. When he published his book on Francis, he had recently entered the Roman Catholic Church after a long period of hesitancy. But he was already a well-known writer with a broad audience. *The Congregationalist* commented, "Though an intense Catholic, it can hardly be said that he has written predominantly from the Roman Catholic standpoint." For similar reasons, although he was English, I include his book here because of its wide influence in North America and its importance as a marker of changing perceptions. First published here in 1924, it is frequently referred to and is still in print.

Chesterton criticized modernizers, such as Renan and Arnold and their intellectual descendants, for dismissing the darker parts of Francis's story as outmoded or superstitious. But he also criticized narratives that focused on premodern preoccupations, such as painful stigmata or ascetic self-denial. These, he said, are "unintelligible" without context. One problem, Chesterton thought, is that modern critics treat religion as a philosophy or theory, while it is really more like being in love. Think of Francis as a medieval troubadour, a wildly emotional lover, he said, and "the whole . . . modern puzzle disappears." Chesterton also rejected the notion of separating the "historical" or "factual" from the superstitious, legendary, or supernatural. His Francis, then, was emphatically not modern.[5]

Chesterton first looked for consistency of character. By his account, Francis was always quick, impetuous, and a man of action. He had never understood money, either when he had plenty of it or had none. His strong sense of equality was not political or philosophical, but came from an inability to see distinctions. For Francis, everything was equal and equally significant. Chesterton insisted that Francis was not a "nature lover," because he did not see an undifferentiated, abstract entity that we can call "nature." Instead, he encountered each particular tree, dove, or lamb individually. For the same reason, it is wrong to call him a lover of "humanity"; rather, he encountered and cared for particular human beings.[6]

The heart of Chesterton's book reflected on Francis in images of reversal. As a young man, he wrote, Francis is confined in a dungeon with "the whole world . . . on top of him"; he falls from his war horse, both physically and metaphorically; he begs for stones instead of bread when he rebuilds a church, reversing a familiar biblical image (Matthew 7:9). Later, he comes to see the world from an upside-down perspective. That world is not powerful or enduring, but dependent—dependent in the sense of hanging, like a "vast crystal" that could fall at any moment. Francis is changed by seeing the world, in Chesterton's memorable phrase, "hanging on a hair of the mercy of God." From this perspective, formerly important things become unimportant, and solemn things become humorous. Asceticism becomes joyful, a gift to God. Knowing his infinite debt, Francis responds with everything he has, throwing poverty, hunger, and cold into "a bottomless pit of thanks." Most of us, said Chesterton, think we are too modern to understand asceticism, but in fact we are too stingy—"We are not generous enough to be ascetics."[7]

Chesterton's was a different kind of Catholic critique from those we have seen before. However, he did argue that Francis's life is proof of the church's continuous authority. Francis could not have mirrored the life of Christ so well, he said, if the church had not maintained the spirit of Christ continuously through the centuries. He also argued against those, like Sabatier, who regarded the Franciscan movement as true Christianity and dismissed the church as corrupt and repressive. Christianity needs the whole church, he said, for its comprehensiveness, its history, and its learning. Although the Franciscan movement provided an essential witness and critique, it would be narrow and limited on its own. The Catholic Church can include Franciscans, he argued, but the Franciscan movement cannot include the whole church.[8]

Enacting Francis

Reversals, subversion, and irony appeared in another transatlantic resource, one that moved beyond reading and reflection to embodiment. In 1947 Rufus Jones asked, "How can we ever pay the debt we owe to Laurence Housman for his 'Little Plays'? He and Paul Sabatier have done the most in modern times to make this dear saint known to the world in general." Laurence Housman's "Little Plays of St. Francis," the first of which were published in the early 1920s, entered imaginatively into the mind and spirit of St. Francis. Although Housman came from a background of involvement in social concerns, he disavowed any great concern with the issues of poverty and wealth. Instead, he claimed that his deepest interest, when writing about Francis, was in irony and foolishness.[9]

Laurence Housman (1865–1959) was born in Worcestershire, England. Raised as an Anglican, he drifted away from the church as an adult. He was, however, active in a number of social reform movements, notably women's suffrage and, in a minor way, gay rights. In 1920 he was resident at the progressive Brookwood Community School, later Brookwood Labor College, in Katonah, New York. After World War I, he gradually adopted pacifist convictions. He also grew increasingly involved with the Society of Friends (Quakers), although he did not formally join a Friends Meeting until 1952. Housman worked as an artist and writer in various capacities, but he never became as famous as his older brother, the poet A. E. Housman. In 1945 he cofounded Housmans Bookshop, a project of the then-flourishing Peace Pledge Union.[10]

Though they probably were never performed professionally, the Little Plays drew a grassroots following. Indeed, Housman noted ironically that the plays about St. Francis made more money for him than any of his other works. He wrote the first one in 1916, and the first collection, eighteen plays, was published in 1922 in London, Boston, and New York. New collections appeared every few years until 1935, when all the plays—a total of forty-five—were gathered into a set. This was reprinted regularly through the 1950s and occasionally thereafter.[11]

By 1927, according to Housman, there had been over a thousand performances of the Little Plays, chiefly in "amateur dramatic societies, schools, colleges, and church congregations." Settlement houses, peace groups, and other admirers also adopted them, then and later. One play was performed in Canterbury Cathedral as part of the observance of the 1926 anniversary of Francis's death. Paul Sabatier was the featured speaker at the same event, and he had written appreciatively to Housman about the first group of plays. He wondered, though, how Housman could capture the spirit of St. Francis so well without having been to Assisi.[12]

Taken together, the sequence of plays constitutes a life of Francis and a series about his followers. Each drama is self-contained, but many of them incorporate allusions to earlier events and conversations. While most of the material is derived from the Franciscan sources, Housman uses it freely, putting unrelated stories together or inserting familiar anecdotes into imagined contexts. "What most attracted me to St. Francis," Housman wrote, "was not his exalted piety or his practice of holy poverty, but his artistry in human nature . . . whereof Juniper the fool is the standing example." This "artistry," in Housman's presentation, often hinges on the reversal of presuppositions or values.[13]

A good example is his first play, *Sister Gold*. Although Housman said he wrote it in reaction to World War I, it is essentially a meditation on wealth. The play is a very free interpretation of some existing stories about St. Francis and robbers. Its plot is, essentially, that Francis persuades three robbers to give up the gold they have stolen. As the play opens, Francis and his companion, the foolish Brother Juniper, discover the robbers' stash in the woods. Francis gives little attention to it: he rambles on about Sister Night and Brother Bread. Three robbers then appear on the scene to claim the gold. In conversing with them, Francis makes gold a metaphor for poverty and want—it has brought the robbers conflict and fear instead of peace and friendship. And because they are hungry, he can persuade them that Brother Bread is more precious than gold.[14]

Gold, like bread, is personified, and she is female. Francis notes the beauty of Sister Gold and her resemblance to the sun. God created her good, he says, but humans have spoiled her beauty. In fact, he implies, "man" has prostituted her. When in use, she is tossed around and fought over; abandoned on the forest floor, she is naked, cold, and captive. He urges the robbers to return her to Mother Earth and peace.

Shifting the metaphor again, the play meditates on burial. We are reminded that human beings "go to God" by way of burial. Mortals must leave their gold behind. Gold itself should be buried because it is a dead thing. Yet it can also go "back to God" through burial, to be transfigured in the heavenly kingdom.

So Housman uses his imagined Francis to subvert conventional values, but he does it in a poetic and playful way. Gold is worthless in human terms, good in divine terms. It has been abused, deserves rest, and can be transfigured. Like other natural things, it can be personified as our "sister." And the author also makes ironic fun of this tendency: when Francis asks for a mouthful of Brother Bread, Juniper complains, "O Father, why do you always make us feel it's murder to eat anything?"

Housman's plays continued to reflect on Brother Juniper and foolishness. Juniper was originally a character in the *Little Flowers*—a fool who took figures of speech literally, failed to think through the consequences of his actions, and generally lacked good sense. In Housman's plays, he at first serves as a foil for Francis, an earthy and fallible counterpart. Later, he becomes a Francis figure himself—in his simplicity of soul, he is one of the few brothers who remains steadily faithful to Francis and his ideals.[15]

One final point: Housman also explored themes of peace and pacifism, a subject to which we will return later on. In the early play *The Revellers* (1922), for example, the young Francis makes a speech about the wastefulness of war that would not have been out of place in the Vietnam era. *Gate of Death* (1931) and *Brother Sun* (1922) frame Francis's journey to the sultan of Egypt as peacemaking rather than mission. The late plays *Holy Disobedience* (1931) and *Holy Terror* (1934) suggest the changing sensibilities of the peace movement in the 1930s—broadly speaking, a shift in emphasis from optimistic reformism to lived nonviolence. In *Holy Disobedience*, Brother Juniper refuses to obey an unjust superior after Francis's death. He confesses willingly, faces punishment patiently, and affirms the ultimate value of love. In *Holy Terror*, Clare calmly deflects a group of infidel mercenaries who seek to invade her convent.

So the plays imagine the mind of Francis, subvert conventional values, and express social ideals. But they have a very different purpose as well— to embody and enact Francis. Recent scholarship in religion and other fields has focused attention on the idea of "practice"—which in this sense means not only the ritual or moral actions that we usually associate with religion, but all the things that people do. Practice is embodied. It locates and expresses meaning through everyday actions. David Morgan has written about the practice of looking, for example, and Margaret Bendroth has proposed a practice of remembering.[16]

Practice, joined with imagination, is a way of meditating closely on Francis. In this way it resembles classical Christian devotions like Ignatian prayer with scripture, or following the stations of the cross—ways of projecting oneself imaginatively into Gospel scenes. In the Little Plays, not only the playwright but the actors could project themselves into Francis's mind and character, or could be close to him, among his followers. Audiences would participate vicariously. All would "become" Franciscans without going through official formalities, just as John Ruskin, in an earlier age, "became" a Third Order Franciscan through his dream. In one way they returned to a pure, uncorrupted past. But in another way, they used the past to reimagine the present. During the 1930s, the embodiment of Francis took new forms.

St. Francis and the Depression

We might think St. Francis, with his devotion to poverty, would be a saint for the Great Depression. But in fact, relatively few people made that connection. The connection between Francis and poverty was drawn chiefly in a sort of rearguard action among American Protestant social activists, in the pacifist community, in the nascent Catholic Worker movement and, occasionally, in a "plutocratic version of the Social Gospel" among people of wealth, which we will discuss further in the next chapter. Here, too, are the roots of St. Francis as the icon of 1960s antiwar protest and subsequent antimaterialism.[17]

While it is always risky to try to explain why something didn't happen, it would be reasonable to say that the most active advocates of reform did not see poverty as a positive good. The labor movement, the Socialist and Communist parties, the documentary journalists and photographers, and other critics were more interested in protesting and relieving poverty than in embracing it. The New Deal was among other things a massive antipoverty program. But the people who were drawn to voluntary poverty were often those who had material resources to give up, together with spiritual conviction and perhaps a hunger for "authentic" experience. Many of them also realized that voluntary poverty was different from the involuntary kind.

There is one other possible reason for subdued attention to St. Francis in the 1930s, which is that Benito Mussolini had by then claimed him as the patron of Fascist Italy. "Italy has become Franciscan," wrote the journalist Anne O'Hare McCormick in 1926. "The virtues of the Little Poor Man of Assisi are proclaimed as a formula of national salvation." Mussolini invoked all the familiar characteristics of Francis. Poverty, sacrifice, self-denial; a distinctive Italian identity; a sense of brotherhood and mission; and faithfulness to the church were all consistent with the Fascist program by this account. During the week of the seven-hundredth anniversary, which was celebrated throughout Italy, citizens made a "three-fold profession of faith"—in the church, the nation, and Mussolini. The government also supported restoration and rebuilding of Assisi in time for the anniversary—so that, ironically, the "place" we encounter today was shaped in part by Fascist-era restoration.[18]

Still, the people who made a connection between Francis and poverty in the 1930s call for our attention for several reasons. They are significant in the history of interpretation: they thought deeply about the meaning of Francis the poor man in a time of economic distress. They are also significant in the history of practice, since they all explored ways of enacting and embodying Francis—although they tended to be earnest and serious more than playful. Moreover, they sustained a long American tradition of dissent that linked economics, war, and peace. Most of them favored the foolishness of pacifism over the pragmatism of war. In all these ways, they imagined Francis as an alternative to their own society.

"St. Francis and Today"

In 1933 Vida Scudder and Edwin P. Booth organized a "Franciscan Institute" at a retreat house near Boston. "Institutes" were a common practice, a way of gathering a group of people for a week or two of intensive study. Under the rubric "St. Francis and Today," and using the Social

Gospel language of the "Commonwealth of God," this institute discussed issues of poverty, property, work, and peace. The institute extended over six days, with plenary addresses, devotions, and "round tables," or working groups.[19]

Booth (1898–1969), a Methodist clergyman, had been teaching church history at Boston University since 1924. The hosting organization was the Society of the Companions of the Holy Cross (SCHC), the laywomen's order to which Scudder belonged.

Some seventy-five or eighty people attended the institute. A seminary dean gave the opening address, but most of the speakers were younger scholars or members of the SCHC. Among the former was Richard Gregg, who, as we shall see, would soon be famous in pacifist circles. (A Miss Gregg, apparently his sister, was a member of the SCHC; possibly she invited him.) The Franciscan scholar Father Cuthbert sent good wishes, but his superiors forbade him to participate.

The round tables were really the heart of the institute. These groups struggled valiantly, discussing long lists of questions and writing multiple drafts of their statements. Yet they ended with compromise, or at best with very nuanced positions. The tension between the real and the ideal, which we encountered earlier, was a very concrete problem for them. Few of the participants—including Scudder herself—were really willing to advocate or practice radical poverty. They agreed that it might be a spiritual ideal for the individual, yet they admitted that property was sometimes necessary for a "practicable modern way of life." Ideally, they would have liked to advocate a complete separation of work from wages— work should be a gift to the world, and everyone deserved adequate support. Yet they were reluctant to impose their requirements on others, including the unemployed of their day. Thus they reached a convoluted conclusion: followers of Francis should not demand reward for themselves, but they could demand it for others in the name of love. Fair wages and "social security" were practical necessities, though not Franciscan ideals. Similarly, like others in their time, they recognized connections between war and economic systems, but they could not agree on the precise requirements of absolute pacifism. The one dissenter from all this was "Mr. Haroutunian," probably the historian Joseph Haroutunian (1904–68), then of Wellesley College. Speaking at a panel discussion, he said skeptically that the conference participants were trying to "eat our cake and have it too." They were willing to be Third Order Franciscans, he thought, but not to give up everything as the first friars did.[20]

The conference also heard reports—apparently solicited by Scudder—about Franciscan-style groups around the world. These included some of Toyohiko Kagawa's followers; two Anglican ashrams in India, neither of them approved by the official church; a brotherhood that worked with homeless men in England; and an Italian sisterhood led by a Franciscan nun who had "chafed under the restrictions of the formal order." None of these groups was very large, and as far as I know, none survives today. But they represent some cross-denominational attempts to reinvent the Franciscan ideals of poverty, service, and freedom, with a modern anti-institutional sensibility.[21]

An interesting sidelight on the institute is the work of John S. Hoyland, a British Quaker with some American connections. Hoyland's thinking drew on both Protestant and Catholic sources—Sabatier, Father Cuthbert, Scudder, Chesterton, and Laurence Housman, along with some of the Franciscan texts. A version of the "prayer of St. Francis," which we will discuss later, serves as epigraph to his 1935 book on Franciscan practice. He thus reflects a number of cultural currents and interpretive strategies.

Hoyland was particularly skeptical about money. In the Indian villages where he had once taught, barter had been a stable and equitable system, he said. But the introduction of money brought debt and exploitation. And in his projects with the unemployed in Britain, money led to unequal power. He also recommended that social-service organizations not pile up endowment funds. Rather, volunteers should pay their own way by soliciting donations (as in Franciscan begging), and by living frugally. Thus Hoyland, with Scudder (and later, Dorothy Day) argued that work should be uncoupled from reward. Hoyland was also interested in "Franciscan service to the dispossessed." Among his exemplars were C. F. Andrews, a pro-Indian missionary and educator, and the French pacifist Pierre Cérésole, who developed a well-known volunteer service corps.[22]

Both Scudder's group and Hoyland blended Francis's embrace of poverty with socialist ideas to construct a model of lived poverty for their time. Their direct impact was minimal—Hoyland's book was reprinted only once, most of the published references to the institute are Scudder's own, and neither generated much Franciscan practice. But both were connected to large networks through which their ideas percolated—teachers, professors, the student Christian movement, adult students and audiences, activist women in the SCHC, and the informal community of pacifists and social reformers.

Peace and Poverty

Scudder's group and Hoyland's readers would have had considerable overlap with the American midcentury peace movement, in which mainline Protestants and Quakers figured centrally. In the 1930s, American pacifism was in the midst of a transition from a confident, modernist, progressivist approach to a more marginalized and sectarian one. Throughout, it was rooted in the Bible as read through a modernist lens. Many of these Protestants also rediscovered an earlier tradition known as nonresistance—the peaceful acceptance of suffering and refusal to fight back, based on directives in the Sermon on the Mount. Over the course of the 1930s, pacifism gradually shifted from confident optimism to a set of alternative visions and lifeways. With Gandhi as their chief inspiration, pacifists explored nonviolent direct action as a mode of public resistance and witness. Most maintained a hopeful liberal theology that emphasized spiritual experience, the moral example of Jesus, and faith as a way of life. From socialism and the Social Gospel, they carried forward an emphasis on economic alternatives, including voluntary poverty and cooperative living. Above all, they sought "consistent living."[23]

It is not hard to see how this culture might have felt drawn to Francis. But we can also trace the pacifist adoption of Francis more directly. Paul Sabatier wrote in 1903 that Francis had "conspicuous affinities" with the modern peace movement—although his 1893 biography had not made this connection. A more direct influence probably came from a longtime pacifist spokesman, John Haynes Holmes. In *New Wars for Old*—published in 1916, in the midst of World War I—Holmes argued for the nonresistant position and presented Francis and Franciscans, along with other historical figures, as models of nonresistance. Holmes, a Unitarian clergyman, was a founding member of the Fellowship of Reconciliation in the United States, as well as the ACLU and the NAACP. He was a frequent lecturer, a writer, and an editor.[24]

Several prominent peace advocates connected Francis with pacifism during the postwar peace movement—notably the National Council for Prevention of War, the Quaker Rufus Jones, and the "social evangelists" Sherwood Eddy and Kirby Page, who also made explicit connections between peace and poverty. In 1930, a major history of pacifism—Devere Allen's *The Fight for Peace*—simply took it for granted that Francis had been a pacifist. Within the next few years, references to Francis were appearing in popular peace venues such as study programs, school plays, and spiritual writing.[25]

In addition to this grassroots adoption, two groundbreaking thinkers of that era presented Francis as a heroic pacifist model. Richard Gregg's work was a major catalyst in the pacifist turn toward nonviolent direct action. His book *The Power of Nonviolence* (1934) translated Gandhian thought and practice into a usable guide for Western activists, while his 1937 pamphlet *Training for Peace* was a manual of community building and spiritual practice. Here he advocated meditation on "great heroes and exemplars of non-violence," including Francis.[26]

A. J. Muste offered Francis as an example in his *Non-Violence in an Aggressive World* (1940), a manifesto of Christian peacemaking. Muste was the leading pacifist theorist and theologian of his time. A tireless activist, he had spent much of his early adulthood as a labor leader and socialist. He returned to Christian faith and ministry in the late 1930s, devoting his energy to pacifism and related causes. Although his religious thought took account of critiques from the neo-orthodox direction and elsewhere, he remained firmly convinced that pacifism was the way of Jesus.[27]

By 1940, pacifists were developing cooperative farms as alternative lifeways, and even here, the itinerant St. Francis was a model. Perhaps the most thoroughgoing example was St. Francis Acres, organized by the longtime activist David Dellinger (1915–2004) and his wife, Elizabeth. As a young man, "rejecting his heritage" and bumming around, Dellinger had identified with Francis as poor and outcast. Later, in the 1950s, the cooperative tried to renounce money and ownership entirely. They wrote a deed turning over their property to God. "They print [on their private press] for people for money, but feel that they are forced to, since they feel that the monetary relationship is basically wrong," said one description. In this they echoed an earlier Protestant socialism.[28]

Francis left no explicit statement opposing war or violence. But activists read the Franciscan texts in such a way as to support the position they already held. Already acquainted with Francis through general literature and church life, they used the documents and stories to construct a sacred figure for pacifist culture. First was the way his life mirrored that of Jesus. Francis's guiding idea, said Holmes, was "that of reproducing . . . the exact pattern of the life of Jesus . . . it is not surprising, therefore, to learn that . . . he was a scrupulous non-resistant." "His only weapons were love and humility," said Eddy and Page. Rufus Jones argued that Francis overcame evil with good, fear with love.[29]

Pacifists also noted Francis's active peacemaking. By some accounts, he reconciled warring factions in Assisi and in Bologna. A more beloved story, though, was the legend of St. Francis and the wolf of Gubbio. The story says that this fierce animal had been terrorizing the townspeople, but Francis called him "Brother Wolf" and persuaded him to leave them alone. In exchange, they agreed to feed him, and all lived in peace thereafter.[30]

Some claimed that the Third Order—the lay order whose members followed Franciscan ways in their ordinary lives—was originally forbidden to use or carry weapons. This claim is controversial. The Earlier Rule for the friars, attributed at least in part to Francis himself, implies a kind of nonresistance. It says that they should not resist evil and should remain vulnerable to persecution if they visit "Saracens." But these directives do not stand alone in the text; they are subsumed under discussions of poverty and Christian witness.[31]

Nevertheless, pacifists also found fresh implications in the story of Francis's visit to the sultan of Egypt during the Fifth Crusade. The sources say that Francis went on foot to see the sultan, hoping to convert him to Christianity and thereby conclude peace. For nineteenth-century readers, this event showed Francis's dedication to missionary service, as well as his willingness to be martyred. Many pacifists, however, saw it as a peacemaking mission, carried out according to the principles of nonviolence. Francis sought a face-to-face meeting, he traveled unarmed through hostile territory, and he returned safely, protected only by his trust in God and by the power of love.

The legend of St. Francis and the three robbers, which we encountered earlier, was read in a similar way. In the Franciscan texts, the point of the story is the robbers' repentance, but pacifist interpretations emphasize the way Francis returned good for evil. And the happy ending of the story supported the optimistic side of pacifism—the side that insisted nonviolence was powerful and effective.[32]

There is, in the end, one almost direct statement in the tradition. It concerns the beginnings of the Franciscan brotherhood, when Francis had only a few followers. According to an early source, the bishop of Assisi was not sure they could survive without possessions. But Francis said that possessions led to conflicts and therefore diminished one's love of neighbor. And what is more, "If we had possessions we would need arms for our protection." Here is a clear statement against weapons and conflict. And it also links conflict, once again, with property.[33]

The Catholic Worker

For one group, the connection between Francis and poverty was foundational. This was the Catholic Worker movement. Of course, the Franciscan orders themselves originated in a similar impulse—to embrace a life with the poor—and they were still active. The Catholic Worker, however, was rooted in the twentieth century, and particularly in the Depression. For this reason it offers instructive comparisons to Protestant movements.

The story of the Catholic Worker's beginnings is familiar by now. Dorothy Day (1897–1980), journalist and Catholic convert, and Peter Maurin (1877–1949), a "peasant philosopher-intellectual," founded a newspaper in 1932 and a "house of hospitality" in 1933, on principles of Catholic social teaching. A network of urban houses and rural cooperative farms soon followed and is still active.

The mythology of the Catholic Worker tends to treat the movement as a unique phenomenon, but in fact, many of its ideals and practices have had counterparts in other movements—Protestant, secular, and interfaith. Urban intentional communities, cooperative farms, and forms of personalist theology are not uncommon in North America and Europe. Often, these movements have common roots in biblical teachings and a broadly Christian culture, and some share intellectual resources as well. Still, the Catholic Worker was unusually successful at integrating Franciscan ideals into its corporate life and practice.[34]

Marc H. Ellis has shown how Peter Maurin was influenced by his studies of St. Francis. Always something of a seeker, Maurin arrived at his deepest convictions and his life work in the late 1920s. The Franciscan anniversary in 1926 was part of his transformation, and Pope Pius XI's encyclical *Rite expiatis* on Francis in that year was particularly influential. Maurin developed a lived critique of modern industrial society, giving up possessions, money, and a settled residence. He devoted himself to serving the poor and to spreading his message. For sustenance, he relied on others' hospitality and on manual work—although he preferred to work for free when possible.[35]

Thus far, he was in agreement with Scudder's Institute about the individual path. But on social systems, he took a different direction. Maurin believed that a Franciscan way of life could lead to a renewal of society if enough people adopted it—that the way to change the world was to live differently. Maurin's Franciscan way was communal as well as individual: he envisioned something like a small brotherhood or a village. If everyone were willing to give up property and possessions, to become poor, then paradoxically everyone would have enough, he thought. For this reason, he was not especially sympathetic to the labor movement or to the New Deal.

Dorothy Day, like Maurin, had doubts about the "wage system," just as did Scudder and Hoyland. Both Day and Maurin thought—at least some of the time—that wages should be uncoupled from work, that people should be paid according to their needs, not their jobs. Recalling the history of the movement in 1953, Dorothy Day remarked, "To work without wages! Here was the saying that made people turn away."[36]

But Day stopped short of believing that Franciscan life was the way to a new social order. She did not argue that the poor, the unemployed, and the dispossessed should embrace their poverty. In the early years of the Worker, she actively supported the labor movement and did not object to New Deal policies, although she grew more ambivalent after about 1937. Catholic Worker communities, however, took a variety of positions, including pro-labor activism.[37]

In other respects, Day's writings suggest a multidimensional, nuanced relationship with St. Francis. She was interested in him even before her conversion, and she read and wrote about him regularly throughout her life. Among other things, she saw him as a model of the reluctant leader: the person who is unwillingly placed in a position of leadership and must learn to handle it with humility and detachment. She also recalled Francis when she thought about craving material things, about embracing death, about practice and experience in the religious life. And she knew about St. Francis and the birds. An acquaintance later remembered a homeless man who fed "horrifying" pigeons on the city streets with garbage from the Catholic Worker kitchen—"foul, foul stuff." "And she would see St. Francis in this," he concluded.[38]

It was not only the founders who turned to Francis: he was embedded in the thinking and practice of the whole Catholic Worker movement. Early Workers read the *Little Flowers*, the significant Catholic books about Francis (Cuthbert, Jørgensen, Chesterton), and the papal encyclicals. The *Catholic Worker* newspaper regularly referred to and reflected on St. Francis, in illustrations as well as in text. In the course of time, several Catholic Worker houses were named for him—although he was not unique as a namesake or as an inspiration.[39]

The Catholic Worker also identified Francis with peace. Peace was a concern very early on and, in January 1942, following the bombing of

Pearl Harbor, Dorothy Day announced the continued "pacifist stand" of the Catholic Worker on the front page of the paper. Her article was illustrated with a small, simple image of St. Francis, accompanied by the words "peace without victory." The same image had appeared in the December 1941 issue with the "Peace Prayer"; presumably the editors simply reused it the next month. The prayer appeared without attribution: whether it came from a Catholic source or from its increasingly widespread cultural distribution we do not know.[40]

Catholic and Protestant constructions of Francis, then, had much in common by 1941, at least on the margins. But the image of Francis as a saint for the Depression was most fully worked out in the Catholic Worker. This image overlapped, however, with the concerns of Protestant socialists and pacifists, as well as with those of mystics, playwrights, and polemicists.

Embodiment and the Arts

In 1938 a controversy in San Francisco received nationwide attention. The eccentric sculptor Beniamino Bufano proposed to build a statue of St. Francis, some 180 feet tall, on the top of Twin Peaks overlooking the bay. Bufano had long been devoted to St. Francis, eventually producing over twenty statues of him. The first of these—made in France after a visit to Assisi in 1926 or 1927—won considerable critical acclaim (see figure 4). For the city of San Francisco, he wanted to make a different version.[41]

Bufano was a modernist sculptor given to a large-scale works with heavy forms and minimal detail. His sculpture of Francis was no exception. Designed in stainless steel, it showed him as a standing figure with a rounded upper body, wearing a robe that fell in symmetrical straight lines. Francis's arms were raised almost vertically above his head, presumably in blessing. He wore a tight-fitting cap or cowl and a bemused smile on his elongated face. And he was originally supposed to have had a birdbath on his head.[42]

In San Francisco, reactions to the proposal varied. But it became national news when the syndicated columnist Westbrook Pegler published a scathing critique of the proposal and declared that he could make a better St. Francis statue himself. Bufano bet him he couldn't, and the two traded insults for a while, with the national press looking on. In the end, Pegler produced a strange figure with a cornucopia, a baby or doll, and a mouse. Bufano essentially won, but was never able to have his statue funded and constructed.[43]

FIGURE 4 Beniamino Bufano's first statue of St. Francis, ca. 1926–27, shown at the Church (now National Shrine) of St. Francis of Assisi, San Francisco, August 1955. Today it stands near Fisherman's Wharf. © Barney Peterson/San Francisco Chronicle/Corbis.

What is striking here is that Pegler and his allies thought they knew what St. Francis should look like. Of course, this was not the only cause of the conflict: in part it was about modernist art and abstraction. The sympathetic journalist Heywood Hale Broun wrote of Bufano's design, "In time we may even learn to appreciate the brave beauty which lies in [its] simplicity"—but the public did not fully appreciate it yet. In part, too, the conflict was over public space and display. But it was also about Francis. An expressionless modern sculpture did not capture his spirit. It was not recognizable, visually or emotionally. "A great public monument," said a Franciscan superior, "should speak its message not only to the esoteric few but to every man on the street."[44]

Bufano's modernist vision did survive. Several of his other sculptures of Francis are now much-loved San Francisco landmarks—including his first one, which finally arrived there in 1955. In the next chapter we will look at some of the other visual forms that were emerging around this time. They proved to be equally enduring and far more popular.[45]

CHAPTER FOUR

Hymn, Prayer, and Garden

If a Protestant church today has any kind of outdoor statuary, chances are it will be an image of St. Francis of Assisi. Most probably, birds will be involved in it somewhere, perched on his outstretched arms or at his feet. There may be a birdbath or a bird feeder. It is not likely that a Protestant church will have a Virgin Mary grotto or an image of St. Jude—although it may have a live Nativity scene at Christmas, also associated with St. Francis. Inside the church, the congregation will most likely be familiar with the hymn "All Creatures of Our God and King," a paraphrase of Francis's Canticle of the Sun. There might even be a wall plaque or a greeting card with a familiar prayer that begins, "Lord, make me an instrument of thy peace."

Familiar as these artifacts are, they are fairly recent developments. All of them settled into American religious culture around the beginning of World War II. All of them seem to have been composed or initiated in the early twentieth century, to have emerged in the 1920s, and to have become widely popular or mass-produced in the late 1930s. By the late 1940s, they were well known and offhandedly recognized. Most of them were embedded most firmly in a handful of subcultures: mainline Protestantism and unaffiliated or secular cultural contexts.

Instruments of Peace

During the 1930s the now-famous "prayer of St. Francis," or "peace prayer," was beginning to circulate in English. There is no evidence that St. Francis composed this prayer. It does not appear among known Franciscan documents, and there is no record of its existence before the twentieth century. Still, although some publications note carefully that it is "attributed to" St. Francis, many others simply name him as author, even today. People who use it will often say that it reflects the spirit of St. Francis, even if the exact words are not his. The prayer circulates in variant versions, but one very common form is this:

Lord, make me an instrument of thy peace;
where there is hatred, let me sow love;
where there is injury, pardon;
where there is discord, union;
where there is doubt, faith;
where there is despair, hope;
where there is darkness, light;
where there is sadness, joy.
O Divine Master, grant that I may not so much seek
to be consoled as to console;
to be understood as to understand;
to be loved as to love.
For it is in giving that we receive,
it is in pardoning that we are pardoned,
and it is in dying that we are born to eternal life.

The prayer first appeared in French Catholic sources: a 1913 magazine and a prayer card that can be dated between 1912 and 1916. The Vatican newspaper printed it in Italian in 1916. But Protestants in continental Europe were using it by 1922, and it was available in English by the late 1920s. The first appearance of the prayer in the United States that I can identify was in a liberal Quaker magazine, the *Friends' Intelligencer*, in early 1927—just after the 1926 anniversary.[1]

For the next ten years, though, the prayer in English seems to have circulated mostly in Great Britain. Perhaps Quakers had a role in its dissemination: John Hoyland used the prayer as the epigraph to his book on Francis in 1935, and in the same year, it appeared in a "peace portfolio" of woodcuts published in London by a Quaker committee. But researchers have also found it in more ecumenical sources: the British Broadcasting Corporation prayer book of 1936 and a "devotional card" that circulated around the same time.[2]

In 1937, however, the Episcopal Diocese of Massachusetts included the prayer in a small devotional book for the Church Service League, an umbrella organization for laypeople's ministries. Earlier editions of this book did not include the prayer. As we have seen, the *Catholic Worker* used it in 1941. In 1942, the American Friends Service Committee placed it on the inside front cover of its *Handbook for Peacemakers*. Kirby Page was quoting it by 1944, and Dorothy Day said she was "reciting it daily" in 1949.[3]

And it must have reached a much wider audience, because in 1942 it appeared in a collection titled *Best Loved Prayers*, compiled by a generalist author. Then it left the categories of church and prayer to appear in an editorial in *House and Garden*. The editor, Richardson Wright, used the prayer to end a Christmas editorial in 1944, the dark days of World War II. The text was accompanied by an illustration of a Nativity scene such as a family might put on a mantelpiece—conventional figures of Mary, Joseph, and baby Jesus—with a huge military tank looming in the shadows behind them. This was in an otherwise ordinary issue of the magazine, without any noticeable sense of wartime crisis. Wright was an Episcopalian with an active interest in religion, though not an especially countercultural one. But he handed this prayer to his well-to-do, domestic audience—culturally Protestant, but outside any formal "religious" context. Thus by the 1940s, the prayer was clearly available to mainstream American culture. We will encounter it again.[4]

And what does this text say to its culture? For the 1930s and 1940s, and in later times, it emphasized peace in a time of international tension. But it is more interpersonal than international, and more intimate than large scale. It implies a very direct kind of peacemaking: repairing injury, replacing despair with hope. It emphasizes personal transformation as the way to peace: seeking to understand, to love. For peace activists, these emphases were quite consistent with the turn toward spiritually based nonviolent action. For others, they set the prayer free from political implications—it was open to free interpretation and personal appropriation. Giving, pardoning, and dying into eternal life are all personal concerns. The prayer is also closely connected to practice. We will think more about those implications after the next section.

"O Praise Him"

The early twentieth century also saw the appearance of the now-beloved hymn "All Creatures of Our God and King." This is a free translation of Francis's Canticle of the Sun, in a rhymed and metered form suitable for singing.

> All creatures of our God and King,
> Lift up your voice and with us sing
> Alleluia! Alleluia!
> Thou burning Sun with golden beam,

Thou silver moon with softer gleam!
O praise him, O praise him!
Alleluia! Alleluia! Alleluia!

Thou rushing wind that art so strong,
Ye clouds that sail in heaven along,
O praise him! Alleluia!
Thou rising morn, in praise rejoice,
Ye lights of evening, find a voice!
O praise him . . .

Thou flowing water, pure and clear,
Make music for thy Lord to hear,
Alleluia! Alleluia!
Thou fire so masterful and bright,
Thou givest man both warmth and light!
O praise him . . .

Dear mother Earth, who day by day
Unfoldest blessings on our way,
O praise him! Alleluia!
The flowers and fruits that in thee grow,
Let them His glory also show!
O praise him . . .

And all ye men of tender heart,
Forgiving others, take your part,
O sing ye! Alleluia!
Ye who long pain and sorrow bear,
Praise God and on Him cast your care!
O praise him . . .

And thou most kind and gentle Death,
Waiting to hush our latest breath,
O praise him! Alleluia!
Thou leadest home the child of God,
And Christ our Lord the way hath trod.
O praise him . . .

Let all things their Creator bless,
And worship Him in humbleness,
O praise him! Alleluia!

Praise, praise the Father, praise the Son,
And praise the Spirit, Three in One.
O praise him ...

This hymn has appeared in "virtually all English hymnals" and in virtually every American mainline Protestant one since the mid-twentieth century. It is also included in hymnals of conservative denominations like the Christian and Missionary Alliance and the Southern Baptist Convention; of at least one historically black denomination, the National Baptist Convention; of liberal denominations like the Unitarians and Friends General Conference, and in Mennonite hymn books; in several Roman Catholic collections; in hymnals put out by Christian publishers such as Eerdmans and Hope; and in those of liberal groups like the Cooperative Recreation Service.[5]

The outlines of the hymn's origins are known, although some of the details are missing. The Reverend William Henry Draper (1855–1933) wrote the hymn for a children's Pentecost festival sometime around 1910. Draper was a priest in the Church of England. At that time he was rector of Adel, a small parish in Yorkshire, now part of the city of Leeds. He was already the author of several books and a number of learned translations, and he ultimately wrote over sixty hymns. Few of these are well known in the United States, although he is remembered in England for his commemorative hymn "In Our Day of Thanksgiving" and others.[6]

The exact date of its composition is uncertain. Various hymnals cite 1910, 1913, or even 1926. The musician and editor Percy Dearmer wrote in 1933 that Draper wrote the hymn in Adel, where he served from 1899 to 1919, but that he "does not remember" the exact year—implying that Dearmer had been in touch with Draper directly. Nor do we know how it reached the hands of a publisher. Since it was first performed at a city festival, it was most probably heard beyond the little parish of Adel. Perhaps it circulated among musicians or was passed along to a hymnal editor. Or Draper himself may have submitted it for publication, as he had done with other hymns.

In Britain, it first appeared in print in the *Public School Hymn Book* in 1919. This widely used collection expressed a reaction against Victorian sentiment and World War I nationalism, instead emphasizing creation, earthly life, and human equality. The hymn was then published in *Songs of Praise* (1931), a revision of the innovative *English Hymnal* of 1906. Dearmer's introduction suggests this hymnal's agenda: "The deadest of all dead things is a hymn that has sprung from a dead theology; and perhaps nothing is so deadly to religion as the practice of singing such hymns."[7]

We also do not know who set the text to the tune "Lasst uns erfreuen," to which it is almost always sung today. The music was relatively new to English hymnody at that time; it had first appeared in the *English Hymnal*, revised from a seventeenth-century German Catholic melody by Ralph Vaughan Williams. It is easy to imagine a frequent writer of hymns inspired by a new melody—or, equally easily, to imagine a busy pastor, confronted with an upcoming event, hastily setting lyrics to an existing tune instead of trying to compose a new one.[8]

It is also possible that the text was not written for this tune at all. Without the alleluias and the repeated phrase "O praise him," the hymn consists simply of verses in a conventional meter, though a rather stodgy one. Some of the lines do seem to require the refrain, but other stanzas stand alone very well. "Lasst uns erfreuen," however, adds interest to the text with unexpected patterns of rhythm and emphasis.[9]

The hymn spread quickly through North America. The early years of its transmission have a clear shape: up to about 1935, it is found mainly in youth hymnals and Canadian hymnals. Its first North American publication was in 1928, in the *American Student Hymnal* of H. Augustine Smith, a well-known modern liturgist and educator. Five other youth and children's hymnals printed it between 1930 and 1935, and four more by 1940. Meanwhile, in 1930 it also appeared in two Canadian hymnbooks, one for children and one for adults. It continued to be popular for children's and student hymnals through the 1960s and occasionally later.[10]

By 1935, however, the song was beginning to make its way into denominational hymnbooks in the United States. In that year, it came out in the Unitarian *Beacon Song and Service Book*—not in the section devoted to children's hymns—and in the *Methodist Hymnal*, a joint publication of northern and southern Methodists and the separate Methodist Protestant Church. Thus Unitarians and southern Methodists agreed on its suitability. The Methodist Episcopal Church, South, included it in its own hymnal in 1938 as well, and southern Presbyterians picked it up in 1940. At the same time, the YMCA's forward-looking Association Press published it in 1939. The liberal Quakers of the Friends General Conference, who worshiped in silence but sang in Sunday schools and community gatherings, first included it in their hymn collections in 1940 and 1942. From the northern mainline, a hymnal jointly published by Baptists and Disciples of Christ included it in 1941, as did the small Evangelical and Reformed Church. The wartime military also found it suitable: it appeared in the 1942 Army and Navy Hymnal—perhaps because of its reference to death, but surely without any perception of St. Francis as a pacifist.[11]

After the war, the hymn found its way to the evangelical Moody Press and to the Church of Jesus Christ of Latter-Day Saints. The Southern Baptist Convention and the Lutheran Church—Missouri Synod found it suitable for children. And so on: Presbyterians, Lutherans, and the National Council of Churches; the Salvation Army and the Ethical Culture Society; the Mennonites and the Congregationalists, and many more groups all incorporated it into their hymnody. The one anomaly, oddly enough, is the Protestant Episcopal Church in the U.S.A. (now known as the Episcopal Church), a direct descendant of the Church of England. Its *Hymnal 1940* did not include "All Creatures," and it was another forty-two years before the next official hymnal came out. That one did include "All Creatures."[12]

Revivalists and fundamentalists were also slower to appreciate it. With the exception of the Moody hymnbook, it did not appear in the "old-time" or "gospel" songbooks that proliferated during the 1930s and 1940s. Some of their descendants had adopted it by 1960. More recently, it has appeared in evangelical collections such as *Renew!* (Hope Publishing, 1995) and *Celebration Hymnal* (Word Music, 1997).

For Roman Catholics, hymn singing has never been as central in worship and spirituality as it has been for Protestants. Nor is there any single official hymnal. "All Creatures" had no noticeable presence in Catholic hymnals until after Vatican II. Since 1975, though, it has appeared in collections for youth, for folk and contemporary musicians, and for more formal liturgy from virtually every significant Catholic music publisher. In summary, this hymn has had a very wide reach. It is most deeply embedded in mainline Protestantism, but is hardly exclusive to it.[13]

Protestant hymnals commonly alter received texts to suit denominational agendas or ease of use. In recent years "All Creatures" has seen a number of editorial changes, most of them to update archaic words or to remove gendered language. In the 1930s and 1940s, though, most of the variants were omissions. Many hymnals—for adults as well as for children—left out the verse about death. Some omitted two or three verses almost at random, presumably to make the length more manageable. Unitarians and some ecumenists altered the trinitarian doxology.

A recent commentator observed dryly, "The Italian text praises God for his creation. Draper's translation calls on creation to praise God." The commentator is not quite right: Francis's text can in fact be translated either way. But Draper's choice does explain some of the hymn's appeal to the twentieth century: it invokes human response and human action. It is also important, clearly, for its praise of nature. It identifies humanity with creation and honors the human relationship with the natural world. "Nature" as an ideal was of course well established in American culture by this time, but Protestant religious expression offered few avenues to a relationship with nature. Here was a familiar mode of expression that met a felt need.[14]

It is also a reasonable reflection of the historical Francis, as far as we know. The overall tone of both words and music is joyful, but the hymn also reflects on forgiveness, pain, sorrow, and death. This Francis rejoices in nature but also attends to suffering and conflict. Still, the hymn softens his asceticism; it offers consolation and comfort in saying "Praise God and on him cast your care" and in its gentle depiction of death and heaven.

Both the hymn and the peace prayer are very open theologically. While they are not completely humanistic, they also do not insist on doctrinal particulars. Neither of them even mentions Jesus or Christ. They are open to interpretation by Christians and are free to move outside organized Christianity—as indeed they have done in later years.

The hymn and prayer also signify a different kind of practice from those we considered earlier. Theatrical performers imagined themselves into Francis's life; activists adopted voluntary poverty. But the people who prayed the prayer or sang the hymn embodied Francis in a different way—by speaking in his voice. They prayed in his words (as they thought) and sang his Canticle. These practices might be private or communal, but in either case, they call for participation from each individual person. They are intimate and personal ways of enacting St. Francis.

In their intimacy and inwardness, the hymn and prayer are consistent with the mystical turn in the Depression-era mainline. And it was, and is, certainly possible to use them in a way that does not challenge culture at all—as purely private or even sentimental. Still, we should not underestimate their subversive capability. The person who sings or prays in Francis's voice is aligning himself or herself with a saint, an exceptional and sacred person. In "becoming" Francis in this way, the participant affirms interpersonal reconciliation, conversation with God, relationship with the natural world, and joy. Any of these actions can be deeply counter-cultural, as upside-down as Chesterton's generous ascetic.

In the Garden

In 1940, when America was barely out of the Depression, when Europe was already at war, when St. Francis was construed as a pacifist and a model for a new social order, an American magazine commented, "The vogue of St. Francis and the birds as a subject for garden ornaments grows steadily in popularity. Bird-baths, bird-houses and other garden objects now appropriately depict the saintly figure." This was not a magazine for social or religious activists, or even for ordinary people. It was a magazine for the very rich. It covered polo and horse racing. Its board of directors and advisory council included a Busch, a Vanderbilt, a DuPont, and a Mellon, as well as W. Averill Harriman. And yet, only thirteen years earlier, a book on garden statuary by the eminent designer Gertrude Jekyll—who was British but was widely read in America—had said nothing about St. Francis or indeed about any Christian figures. In 1928, a European historian noted that in American home gardens, "statuary of any sort is rare indeed." What happened in the interim?[15]

Statuary had been introduced into American gardens in the later nineteenth century, mostly in large-scale, professionally designed estate gardens. These gardens generally drew on European models, especially the Italian—with its balanced design and its patina of age—and the more informal English style pioneered by Gertrude Jekyll, as well as the very formal French model as at Versailles. In all of them, sculptures served as design elements and focal points. Most of this statuary was classical or Renaissance in style: sculptures of Greek and Roman gods, nature deities, noble human figures, putti, and animals accompanied classical columns and antique pots. American designers also explored ways to Americanize gardens, for example by reviving colonial designs or by focusing on indigenous plants and local landscapes. A self-consciously modern style, with abstract sculptures and organic lines, emerged around 1930.[16]

We know less about vernacular gardens. The land around modest houses has historically been working space, whether farmyard or ashcan alley. Those who could afford it have often devoted some space to ornamental gardens and lawns. Spaces expressly designed for outdoor living and recreation, however, are largely a twentieth-century phenomenon.

They developed alongside the ideals of home ownership, regular contact with nature, and privacy—and alongside indoor plumbing, which alleviated the need for outdoor privies. Garden ornaments were in use by the 1920s and became increasingly common after World War II.[17]

Francis did have a following among people of wealth. Some of the first St. Francis statues appeared at the summer estates of wealthy urbanites in the 1920s. In 1932, a "newsmagazine of society" from the North Shore suburbs of Boston featured an article on "Assisi in Boston" alongside a description of an estate, a reflection from a young debutante, and a piece on the Harvard-Yale yacht races. The writer noted that the Boston Public Library would be exhibiting facsimiles of European documents and artworks, among them items from Paul Sabatier's library of St. Francis literature. So those who could not afford to travel abroad that year, because of the economic downturn, might still have a vicarious experience of Assisi.[18]

In 1905 *Town & Country* reported on an estate in Pomfret, Connecticut, where the garden paths were named after saints. "Each has its own shrine," the article continued, "a picture painted on tiles made in Italy" and placed in a little shelter, modeled after Italian roadside shrines. One of these was dedicated to St. Francis, "preaching to the birds, with a rustic birdhouse." But he was not alone; the garden included tributes to saints Dorothy, Eustace, and others, and the house included an oratory with Christian artifacts from many different places.[19]

There is more evidence of garden statues of Francis in the 1920s. A statue of St. Francis—standing, in an archway—is recorded in 1924 in a garden in Pistakee Bay, Illinois, a favorite summer retreat of the Chicago elite. A few individual artists exhibited St. Francis birdbaths in the 1920s—in private galleries, which suggests that they expected to sell them.[20]

In 1926, the year of the St. Francis anniversary, Mr. and Mrs. Francis Kershaw had a "St. Francis Chapel" built at their summer estate, Meerwood or Merrywood, in Marlborough, New Hampshire. Mr. Kershaw was curator of Japanese art at the Boston Museum of Fine Arts, and Mrs. Kershaw (Justine Frances) was the daughter of Oscar Houghton, a founder of the Houghton Mifflin publishing company. The villages of southern New Hampshire at that time housed a number of artists' colonies and summer estates; the MacDowell colony, for example, was founded in 1908 in Peterborough.[21]

"Mrs. Kershaw," said a friend, "was a devout Episcopalian. Her favorite saint was St. Francis." And Mr. Kershaw designed the chapel himself, modeling it on European "peasant chapels." The Boston sculptor Frederick Warren Allen (1888–1961) later donated a bas-relief depicting St. Francis and the wolf, which was mounted above the front door. Although the Kershaws belonged to a "low-church" congregation in Cambridge, their personal tendencies seem to have been "high church" or Anglo-Catholic. They sponsored daily services at Meerwood, and there was always a resident priest among their many guests.[22]

At the same time that the chapel was built, the Kershaws also commissioned a St. Francis statue and birdbath from Allen (see figure 5). The graceful statue, one of the earliest of its kind, has since disappeared. The birdbath now stands outside the chapel, and most sources assume it has always been there. Early photographs, though, show it in a garden space—a circular lawn near the house, enclosed by hedges and woods. For the Kershaws, then, both chapel and garden were appropriate places to encounter St. Francis.[23]

Sadly, Francis Kershaw did not enjoy his chapel for long: he died in 1930. But Mrs. Kershaw had a long and active widowhood. She had always been involved in charitable causes, and she offered the estate for church retreats and summer programs. One such program, a fund-raiser for a Boston charity, included a performance of some of Housman's plays "in the St. Francis garden." During World War II, she housed over fifty refugees. She also took in other waifs and strays—such as a young high-churchman who turned Marxist—and lent or gave away some of her property. (Some was also sold to cover expenses.) By all accounts, she was generous and even profligate with her wealth. If she was not quite a "Social Gospel plutocrat" seeking to effect social change through philanthropy, she was also not a wealthy escapist. It appears that St. Francis had more than a nominal meaning for her.[24]

In about 1930, a gardener in the next town, Dublin, also installed a St. Francis statue and birdbath. This was Mrs. Frederick Brewster (1884?–1963) of New Haven, Connecticut. A gracious but strong-willed woman, Margaret Brewster was a skilled amateur gardener; she was later vice president of the Garden Club of America, and her New Hampshire estate garden was photographed for national publications. In accordance with the fashion of the times, it included a number of "little gardens" or "garden rooms." The smallest and most distant from the house was "the sanctuary"—a quiet space enclosed by shrubbery and housing a birdbath and a statue of St. Francis. The basin was Etruscan, and the statue was a

FIGURE 5 Frederick Warren Allen. St. Francis statue and birdbath, for Francis and Justine Kershaw, Marlborough, N.H. Statue ca. 1926–30, now missing; photographer unknown. One of the earliest of garden statues, this is an original sculpture, not mass-produced.

"rare" artifact from Siena. At her death, the gardens were let go and the property and furnishings were sold.[25]

The Brewsters were also Episcopalians—members of Trinity Church in New Haven, Connecticut—but surviving records say nothing about their piety. We also do not know whether they knew the Kershaws, their fellow church members in the town next door. So we are left to wonder what St. Francis meant in the Brewster garden—a borrowed idea or a shared spiritual sensibility? An expression of Christian commitment or of proper and conventional religiosity? A meditative space or an attempt to keep up with the Joneses?[26]

But these were private efforts. Mass production came a little later. In 1932, the English weekly *The Spectator* mused on the need for better statuary: "How fitly a Gilbert White [a famous naturalist] or a St. Francis or a Ceres might preside over a bird bath and table in the midst of the English lawn." In 1934, Richardson Wright—a garden writer as well as an editor—said nothing about St. Francis in his book on home garden design, even though he did mention a couple of other saints. Vida Scudder, in 1937, referred to "the little penthouse shrines of St. Francis projecting from our window-sills, where his picture presides over a bird-seed banquet." It is not entirely clear what she is describing here—homemade shrines or commercial products, a single picture or many.[27]

But in 1938, *House and Garden* featured a figure of St. Francis with a birdbath from Malcolm's House and Garden Store in Baltimore (see figure 6). This was, of course, the same year in which San Francisco was arguing over Bufano's proposal. In 1940, *Country Life* identified the "vogue" for St. Francis statuary. The following year, *Designs for Outdoor Living* published a picture of Mrs. Brewster's St. Francis garden, describing it as a "bird sanctuary"—"for anyone who wants the maximum pleasure of the little garden retreat with a bit of water in it." Advertisements for St. Francis birdbaths appeared regularly after the war (see figure 7), and at least two preeminent manufacturers—Frederick Lynch and Sons and Erkins Studios—included multiple variations on the theme in their 1950 catalogs. None of these ads treats a St. Francis statue as anything remarkable.[28]

Virtually all of these statues share an iconographic style: a standing St. Francis with birds—in his hands, on his arms or shoulders, or at his feet. This was different from Catholic iconography, which typically showed him gazing at a crucifix or a skull, as in figure 8, or gazing heavenward with his arms crossed. Familiar as the non-Catholic iconography is today, though, its origins remain unclear. The earliest examples seem to

be the garden statues of the 1920s and 1930s. Perhaps the artists meant to allude to Giotto's picture of St. Francis with birds, in which Francis is standing, but is not actually touching or holding the birds. Perhaps, also, they borrowed his standing posture from Catholic statuary, but replaced the cross with birds. They seem also to have adapted his face and figure to accord with the change in meaning.[29]

In 1942, a Congregational church near Boston set up a St. Francis shrine in its garden (see figure 9). There was a birdbath and a small statue of Francis in a little wooden shelter, along with a rustic cross and Communion table. St. Francis was not unknown in other kinds of church imagery, such as stained-glass windows, by that time. But Protestants were, and remained, somewhat suspicious of statuary, with its potential for veneration and idolatry. However, a commentator in the *Missionary Herald* wrote about the garden approvingly. It was a quiet, meditative space, and was also suitable for children, who would "visit [the garden] in the spring to learn about the flowers, birds, and the good St. Francis." Five years

FIGURE 7 "St. Francis in Your Garden." Advertisement from Erkins Studios, in *House and Garden*, November 1946. A different image of Francis, from the beginning of the prosperous postwar era, with suggestions about how it might be used.

FIGURE 8 St. Francis of Assisi. Zinc sculpture with Francis holding a crucifix, 1941. From *Creations in Ecclesiastical Art* (Daprato Statuary Company catalog), 1941, 22; also reproduced in Grissom, *Zinc Sculpture in America*, 610. The catalog lists similar works dating back to 1921. The crucifix and skull are characteristic of Roman Catholic iconography.

later, a Congregationalist guide to church arts published a photograph of the shrine and noted the "priceless value" of such a garden. It seems to have been an original idea; for example, a contemporary Episcopalian guide to church decoration mentions gardens and birdbaths, but not St. Francis. Since then, it has become popular.[30]

We have little testimony about what these statues of St. Francis meant to the people who installed them in the 1920s and 1930s and early 1940s.

FIGURE 9 St. Francis shrine. Bethany Church (Congregational), Foxboro, Mass., 1942. Probably the first St. Francis garden at a Protestant church. Reprinted with permission from the United Church of Christ from the *Missionary Herald*, October 1942.

Were they nothing more than the latest fad—a fashion or vogue replacing Roman gods? Did they reflect some deeper piety or longing? The Kershaws' lives recall the "plutocratic Social Gospel" mentality, the use of wealth in the causes of social equity and reform. The simplest explanation, of course, is that people liked his connection with birds and nature and gave no further thought to his meaning.

A few references hint at more. The 1938 advertisement, when such statues were still relatively new, suggested an appropriate use: "St. Francis and the Birds provides a beautiful theme for a quiet corner of the country garden." The church Sanctuary Garden was said to "[inspire] meditation and prayer," offering "an effective pathway into the presence of God." St. Francis is frequently associated with "secluded" space and "rest and thought." He is described as "gentle" or "good St. Francis." But the same gardeners were making use of humorous frogs, unadorned arches and birdbaths, art sculptures and Italian urns. All of this suggests a very open construction of Francis: kind to animals, close to nature, and helpful to quiet meditation, but with little assigned meaning beyond that.[31]

On the other hand, the choice of St. Francis over a Roman god or a secular image suggests a wish to profess Christian faith (insofar as the garden is public) or to express it (in one's private meditations). It echoes Matthew Arnold's contrast between Roman religion and Franciscan Christianity. It also suggests a wish to place a historical rather than mythical or fictional figure in the garden—to remind the viewer that human beings like him- or herself might also be mystically close to nature. Any gardener who had read Thoreau or John Muir or Gilbert White might find this meaningful.

The garden statue helps to define the space as meditative, and perhaps as powerfully sacred. Gardens are liminal spaces, a shifting middle ground between public and private, home and outside world. Enclosed by hedges or walls, the garden is a private space for family and invited guests. Within the garden, a hidden corner or enclosed space may form an individual retreat, private even from the family. Yet the garden (or yard, or estate) also forms part of a larger landscape and social system. The garden is outside the "sacred space" of the home, outside the daily round of work and obligations, and also outside the church. Liminal spaces are particularly open to a sense of the sacred. As private space, the garden is particularly open to individual reflection.[32]

As David Morgan has observed, Protestants respond to pictures of Jesus with a kind of double-mindedness. When he studied the uses of Warner Sallman's *Head of Christ* in Protestant devotion, his informants took pains to explain that they knew the picture wasn't "really" a picture of Jesus, and to say that they didn't worship it. Yet the pictures did somehow mediate the presence of Jesus to them. Not only were they reminded of him in a rational or cognitive way, they experienced emotion and felt his nearness when they looked at the picture. Tanya Luhrmann's recent work on some evangelicals' imaginative relationship with God suggests a similar sensibility. And the *New York Times* has reported on sensible, secular Europeans engaging in phone conversations with a stone angel.[33]

Perhaps we can attribute a similar sense of presence to statues of St. Francis in the garden. They were locations of presence and memory, both personal and collective. Like the prayer and the hymn, they were open to individual interpretation; unlike them, they were not statements of identification with Francis, but of nearness to him, perhaps conversation with him. In this they were closer to the experience of place than to the practices of enactment. Like the prayer, they could be private; like the hymn, they could be used in a small community. And gardeners constructed a St. Francis who was especially present in nature—the forerunner of the "patron saint of ecology" of the 1970s and beyond.

Not all Christians have been radicals, and the question of whether or not they should be is a question for theology, not history. The turn to prayer, song, and garden statuary could, of course, be read as retreat or even hypocrisy. But it equally suggests an alternative use of wealth, the spiritual uses of presence and intimacy, privacy and community, and a different kind of embodied practice. The anxious times of the Depression and the war give us the saint of radical poverty, placed in the garden and surrounded with birds. He embodies and refracts the tensions and paradoxes of the time.

CHAPTER FIVE

Postwar Prosperity
Embrace and Resistance

Sometime in the late 1940s, a Brownie Girl Scout troop in New Canaan, Connecticut—a town named for Puritan ideals—made a visit to a local bird sanctuary. At the entrance to the sanctuary was a little statue of St. Francis, with a birdbath at his feet and birdseed in his hands. "These Brownies stopped to explore every detail of it," wrote their leader. "They liked the idea of the birds eating out of St. Francis' hand, where the seeds were put each day, and of the bird bath at his feet." The girls also "wanted to know what was inscribed on the back of the statue. It read, 'Lord, make me an instrument of your peace. Where there is hatred let me sow love.'" After examining the statue, the girls went on to explore the nature sanctuary.[1]

Over the course of the year, as the seasons passed, these same girls and their older sisters made Christmas gifts and Easter decorations—most of them festive and seasonal but not explicitly theological. When the Brownies "flew up," or graduated to the Intermediate level, they reflected upon their duty to God (as in the Girl Scout promise) and even held a part of their ceremony in the church on the town common. But there was no minister or churchly rite involved.[2]

They were, in short, part of the "consensus culture" of the post–World War II era, from about 1945 to about 1963—the middle-class, optimistic, generally patriotic, not very critical, kindly and generous culture that most people believed to be the American mainstream. The consensus culture assumed that religion was a good thing in general, and assumed that the typical American religion was a kind of generic Protestant Christianity. St. Francis had a place in this culture as nature lover and as nonpolitical peacemaker, signified by statues and birdbaths and the "peace prayer."

But he was also beloved by dissenters and outsiders, who did not disappear during this period of apparent harmony. Social activists and Catholic Workers, followers of Eastern religions, novelists, and intellectuals of various stripes adopted Francis for their own and insisted that there was more to him than generic goodness.

Conformity and Change

Many historians have described the postwar period as a time of contradictions. On the one hand, it was a period of unprecedented prosperity and power in American life. The nation felt itself to be at peace. Income and purchasing power rose. The "consensus culture" valued domesticity and social harmony, along with the old liberal values of optimism and progress. One critic described it as an era of "consumerism, capitalism, and conformity." Worldwide, American power was consolidated by its war victories and by its wealth, as well as by the popular culture it was exporting in increasing quantities.[3]

On the other hand, it was an "age of anxiety," as the poet W. H. Auden put it. America's peace and power were due, in part, to the devastating use of the atomic bomb. Close on its heels came knowledge of another kind of devastation, the Holocaust. The 1950s opened with the Korean War and the anti-Communist hysteria of Joseph McCarthy and others. American power required a higher level of global entanglement—at its best, hardheaded political realism; at its worst, spying and corruption.[4]

And there were also signs of the social-change movements yet to come. Catholics and Jews were entering the socioeconomic mainstream. African Americans and their supporters challenged segregation—for example, with the integration of the armed forces in 1948 and the *Brown vs. Board of Education* decision in 1954. By 1963, with the publication of Betty Friedan's *The Feminine Mystique*, the women's liberation movement was stirring. Around the world, European colonialism was breaking down.[5]

Religious life reflected similar contradictions. On the one hand, there was growth across the board in all the major religions: in membership, wealth, building, and publishing. In addition, public figures spoke more frequently about religion, and the phrase "under God" was added to the Pledge of Allegiance. In academic theology and religious studies, there was an enlivening ferment of new ideas. Within this general revival, the Protestant mainline was usually taken for granted as normative—as representative of the cultural consensus. Protestants were in fact a numerical majority and enjoyed considerable cultural power.[6]

Yet the old religious boundaries were breaking down. Within Christianity, the ecumenical movement that had begun at the turn of the century was at its height. It sought to modify doctrinal differences and to build Christian unity through institutional structures and social action. Meanwhile, popular religion was ecumenical in a different way: it was more concerned with piety and emotion than with rules or doctrines. Evangelical Protestantism, marginalized after the Scopes decision, was beginning to reassert itself, and many minority faiths flourished on the margins.[7]

Contemporary observers disagreed as to whether this broad revival of religion was genuine. Did numerical growth really mean much? People were flocking to churches and synagogues, but were they really serious about their faith? Was consensus religion intellectually shallow? The historian James Hudnut-Beumler proposed that there were actually three different types of religion in this era. Popular religion was accessible through the general culture, without necessarily a formal commitment. It tended to be generous and tolerant, but also private and personal. Ecclesiastical religion was "lived out within a formal institutional setting," with recognized membership, rites, doctrines, and the like. And elite religion was the province of "professional scholars and religious practitioners, and sometimes educated amateurs"—those who valued systematic thought and its far-reaching implications for practice. There is, of course, overlap among the three types: popular religionists went to church, for example, and congregational leaders learned from academic theologians. But the typology provides a useful framework for understanding this period.[8]

Images of St. Francis in this era reflect the contradictions of the age and different meanings of "religion." In popular materials and mass media, Francis appears most often as a gentle lover of nature. He is generally not the gritty, difficult, radically poor St. Francis that earlier generations recognized. This is the Francis of consensus culture and of popular religion.

At the same time, many voices pointed out in many different ways that the popular St. Francis was not entirely the true one. Most of these were the elite voices of established authors and scholars; a few belonged to social outsiders and marginal religions. Both groups were critics of the consensus. Ecclesiastical religion, when it said anything at all about St. Francis, mostly stood in the middle ground—approving of the popular adoption of this saintly figure, yet aware that there was something more to him.

In this chapter, we will first look at the Francis of consensus culture and of popular religion, as encountered in the general-interest press and in garden statuary. Then we will look at ecclesiastical religion as represented in hymn singing, prayer, and church decoration. Next, we will consider the works of elite critics—novelists, scholars, and a few others. We will then turn to some cultures on the margins, outside the consensus, including social activists and minority religions. Finally, we will look at the paradoxical St. Francis of Bernard Malamud—St. Francis as a Jew.

St. Francis and Consensus Culture

As we have seen, a version of St. Francis was already out in the garden by this time. A "fad" for St. Francis statuary was already active in 1940, and he had appeared in church gardens by 1942. By 1950 he was well established in home gardens, in forms that are familiar today. The statuary firm Kenneth Lynch and Sons says that all of its current models of St. Francis were in the catalog by that year. Customers of this firm have typically been fairly well-to-do, and most of the mid-century evidence for statuary reflects this class location. But St. Francis did make a brief appearance in the Sears, Roebuck catalog in 1961, reaching a much wider and less wealthy clientele.[9]

Francis was also familiar in the popular press. In 1945 the *Reader's Digest* published an article on Francis with the title "Everybody's Saint." Its author was a well-known nature writer, Donald Culross Peattie. But the article is not primarily about nature. It is "a tribute from a Protestant . . . to a saint of the Catholic Church beloved of all regardless of creed." For the most part this article repeats the usual Protestant tropes, such as Francis's humanness and his resistance to greed, and it soft-pedals the supernatural, the ascetical, and the radical. It does, however, mention Francis's ability to engender trust in animals. But it refers to these animals as "pets," whereas earlier sources had said only that Francis tamed or befriended them. This Francis sounds domesticated, not wild.[10]

Francis also appeared in two popular collections of "familiar" poetry and prose, Ralph Woods's *Treasury of the Familiar* (1942) and his *Second Treasury* (1950). The first volume included a version of the sermon to the birds. The second contained the Canticle of the Sun and the peace prayer. But Woods wrote that the second volume incorporated many texts requested by readers—their own "familiar" favorites. It seems likely, then, that it was readers who requested the Canticle and the prayer.[11]

Reader's Digest printed the "peace prayer" in 1949 as part of an inspirational series "Words to Live By," which was first published in *This Week* magazine. "Of all the selections published in *This Week*," said the caption, "none brought as great a response as this simple prayer." A contributor wrote, "That prayer hit me between the eyes. . . . I read it over and over, and finally put it to a test. I lived by those words for one brief week and found the most tremendous joy and peace. I am still living, gloriously, by them." The prayer also ran prominently in *Life* in 1955 and in *House Beautiful* in 1962. *Life* accompanied the prayer with a generalized theological statement about divine love, Christian duty, and blessing, following a photo essay about Christmas and Easter in the Holy Land. In *House Beautiful* it was part of a two-page spread headed "Christmas is love."[12]

The New Yorker aimed for a more sophisticated audience, but shared the popular perception of St. Francis. In 1949, this magazine ran a short piece about a night watchman at a botanical garden who kept a bird feeder. It was offhandedly titled "Saint Francis of the Bronx," with no further explanation, implying that everyone knew who St. Francis was—and that he was associated with birds.[13]

This connection seems firmly established by the postwar era. Visual images outside Catholicism typically included birds. An amusing photo in *Life* showed a statue of St. Francis with live doves nesting in the saint's hands, and its caption mentions that he preached to the birds. A 1955 advertisement in *House and Garden* offered "St. Francis for your garden, that birds may flock to the bowl at the feet of their Guardian Saint for their baths all year around." Images of St. Francis in neo-Gothic cathedrals, such as the Riverside Church and Washington National Cathedral, usually depict him with birds as well; we will return to these images later on. And birds were very significant in popular children's books about Francis.[14]

But these visual images were not necessarily connected to any focused religious commitment. Instead, they suggest once again a generic, nonspecific Francis. The *House and Garden* advertising pages in the 1950s, for example, offered St. Francis alongside "Bless This House" trivets, ornaments representing signs of the zodiac, and hitching posts in the form of black servants.

Still, this is a St. Francis who transcends creeds, who is friendly and gentle, who loves birds and nature. Indeed, he himself is now "lovable." A 1952 movie reviewer called him, without explanation, "one of the most lovable holy men who ever lived." The writer J. D. Salinger also called him lovable, although he did not mean it as a compliment, as we shall see later on. A writer in *Time* magazine even called Francis "sickly sweet."[15]

Perhaps the archetypal St. Francis for the consensus culture of the suburbs appears in Robert Lawson's *Rabbit Hill*, an award-winning children's book. *Rabbit Hill* was published in 1944, won the prestigious Newbery Medal in 1945, and was in its fifth printing within a year. A "chapter book" for elementary-age readers, *Rabbit Hill* is told from the point of view of small wild animals who live in the fields and woods around an old house in Connecticut. A rabbit family (not surprisingly) is the center of the story, and their neighbors include a woodchuck, a skunk, field mice, and more distantly, a fox and a buck deer. (As is typical for the era, there are very few female characters in the book.) The plot revolves around the arrival of new people in the derelict house and whether they will ultimately prove beneficial or harmful to the animals on the hill.

The animals are delighted at the prospect of new vegetable gardens, which they regard as a food source for themselves. And the humans at first appear to be kindly toward small animals—for example, they direct a stonemason not to disturb the woodchuck's burrow when rebuilding a wall. But the animals' fears and suspicions are aroused when a rabbit child is injured by a passing car and is taken into the human household. They imagine all sorts of horrors, especially as a new stone structure is built near the garden (a dungeon?) and a large crate arrives (traps and guns?).

The climactic scene occurs on Midsummer's Eve. By this time the mysterious building project is finished and is covered with a tarpaulin. The humans sit on a garden bench as the animals quietly draw near. There they find the rabbit child, now healed. Then the humans remove the tarp. The blind mole asks a field mouse to describe what he sees:

"Oh, Mole," he said. "Oh, Mole, it's so beautiful. It's Him, Mole, it's *Him*—the Good Saint!"

"Him—of Assisi?" asked the Mole.

"Yes, Mole, *our* Saint. The good St. Francis of Assisi—him that's loved us and protected us Little Animals time out of mind—and, Oh, Mole, it's so beautiful! [*sic*] He's all out of stone, Mole, and his face is so kind and so sad. He's got a long robe on, old and poor like, you can see the patches on it.

"And all around his feet are the Little Animals. They're *us*, Mole, all out of stone. . . . And His hands are held out in front of him sort of kind—like blessing things. And from his hands there's water dropping, Mole, clear, cool water. It drops into a pool there in front of him . . . It's shallow like, so the Birds can bathe there. . . ."[16]

The mouse goes on to describe a stone ledge around the pool where food is set out for the animals. There is an inscription on the stones: "There is enough for all." The animals enjoy the feast and afterward decide that they will leave the humans' lawn and garden alone—they will find their food elsewhere. The book concludes with two local handymen wondering why their poisons and traps are ineffective against small animals while this unfenced, open garden remains unmolested.

Although this is a very individual and particular story, it also reflects the culture of its time. The social location of the human characters, for example, reflects contemporary assumptions. When the humans move in, the animals observe that they are "quality Folks"; they have nice things and good mahogany furniture. They subsequently invest in upgrading the property. In addition, they have a servant—a black cook who is depicted with the casual racism of the time. Within that context, though, these are cultivated people: they have a lot of books and are often seen reading. Thus the statue of St. Francis is linked to the affluent, educated middle to upper class.[17]

The statue that Lawson's field mouse describes is consistent with the emerging garden iconography of St. Francis. The saint is standing, his hands are extended, and there is a pool of water at his feet, some of it designed for birds. Lawson adds animals, as many later designers would do. At the same time, Francis is abstracted from any kind of historical or ecclesiastical context—once again, he is generic. And he is only barely connected to the human context. He is directly known only to animals, and his primary function is to care for them.[18]

The animals' instant recognition of St. Francis is a curious feature of the story. It is as if they had unmediated knowledge of him through some cosmic or spiritual connection. Indeed, he is a divine figure to them, a kind of God or Christ, as the capitalized "He" and "Him" indicate. It is also interesting that the animals' colloquial speech suggests a lower class location than the humans'. When Lawson does allude, briefly, to Francis's "poverty" and "sadness," perhaps he is thinking of animals as the poor.

Lawson never gives us a detailed drawing of the statue. There is a back view on the endpapers, within a drawing of the whole landscape. In the text, though, the only illustration is a distant view of the shrouded statue. Lawson was an illustrator long before he was a writer, so it is interesting that he chooses to describe his St. Francis statue in words. Perhaps a verbal description enables writer and reader to dwell on the image longer: a reader may glance at an illustration and turn away, but two pages of text demand sustained attention. The written text also enables the author to make the animals' reactions and emotions explicit.[19]

It is hard to overstate the reach of this book. It won two awards besides the Newbery and appeared on many lists of recommended reading for children. In print through at least 2007, it has also been recorded, filmed, and issued as an e-book. Lawson's idea of St. Francis must have influenced the thinking of several generations of children.[20]

More broadly, *Rabbit Hill* spoke to postwar America through its emphasis on peace and prosperity and its grounding in the American rural past. Lawson's biographer Gary Schmidt notes that animals, humans, and land are closely connected in the story. "The human presence in this world is complementary, not adversarial ... It is a world with no real threats." In other words, an intimate, harmless relationship between humans and animals is here transferred to an archetypal American landscape—an antique house in New England—and is summed up in the statue of St. Francis. St. Francis as patron of nature and animals here becomes Americanized.[21]

The Ecclesiastical St. Francis

Ecclesiastical religion occupied a space between popular religion and elite criticism. While it shared in both kinds of discourse, it was often closer to the popular end of the spectrum. Churches seem to have encouraged a familiar, accessible idea of St. Francis, though ecclesiastical sources did retain some awareness of his more complex features.[22]

The most vivid and widespread site of Francis's presence was the hymn "All Creatures" in the numerous new hymnals of this era. Here St. Francis becomes clearly embedded in Protestantism through the practice of hymn singing and the spiritual expressiveness that it brings. The hymn, as we noted before, emphasizes the joyful side of Francis and his love of nature, but in its fullest form does not overlook sin and death. As we have seen, not every hymnal used the fullest form. The "peace prayer" was also known in church circles, of course.

Anecdotal evidence suggests that many churches of the postwar building boom included images of Francis in their stained-glass windows and garden statues. Non-Catholic images of Francis usually included birds, of course, and Francis often appeared alongside other "saints." In the Cathedral of Saint John the Divine in New York City—mentioned approvingly in a 1955 history of religious architecture—St. Francis appears twice: as a representative of the Italian heritage in America and as an evangelist, alongside St. Paul, Shakespeare, and Abraham Lincoln. In the Cathedral of Saints Peter and Paul (Washington National Cathedral) in Washington, D.C., St. Francis is represented in a "humanitarian" grouping, along with the twentieth-century favorites Father Damien, Albert Schweitzer, and William Booth. The Community Church of New York, of Unitarian origin, moved in the direction of religious diversity. It placed St. Francis in a peace chapel, describing him as "a Christian of universal sympathies and spirit" and adding a statue of Gandhi.[23]

But even the more conventional images were not without nuance. For the Washington Cathedral, the building committee commissioned a figure of St. Francis from Marian Brackenridge, a well-known working sculptor, in about 1958. The sculptor accepted the commission with "enthusiasm," and she knew, or soon learned, a good deal about St. Francis. She was careful about historical accuracy in such matters as his appearance (according to the description in the *Little Flowers*) and the shape of the robe he might have worn. She repeats familiar tropes, hoping that the figure "expresses the sensitive, nature loving spirit of St. Francis." And her design builds on familiar iconography: a standing St. Francis holding a bird.[24]

Yet the artist also wished to innovate. In her sculpture, St. Francis is not feeding the bird but releasing it. His hands are open and he leans slightly forward. Brackenridge cited stories that told how Francis "used to go to the market place, buy birds, and set them free." An earlier version of her design had involved an open cage. Brackenridge wrote, "I think that the releasing of the bird makes a new subject in the representation of St. Francis." The supervising architect, Philip Hubert Frohman, agreed: "[The figure] adjusts the traditional conception of St. Francis and yet is not shown in the more usual activities—feeding the birds or receiving the *stigmata* [*sic*]." The committee approved the design despite what appeared to be some technical difficulty for the stone carver. So this ecclesiastical St. Francis is familiar but not clichéd, recognizable but not tied down to stereotypes. Like his bird, he is almost free.[25]

Criticism of the Consensus: Literature and Film

Just as consensus culture and consensus religion had their critics, so did the consensus idea of St. Francis. Critical voices came from fiction, literary nonfiction, film, scholarship, and social activism.

Criticism of the popular St. Francis garden statuary appeared as early as 1948. In *The Living Church*, the flagship magazine of high-church Episcopalianism, a book reviewer praised a new collection of early texts about St. Francis. The selections, said the reviewer, "will correct any tendency one has to see [Francis] as a sort of proto-John Burroughs or fit subject for birdbath statuary." (Burroughs was a turn-of-the-century naturalist.) He added that the selections "will also correct the modern tendency to see him as the first socialist . . . or the model for Evangeline Booth." In other words, he objected not only to garden statuary, but to images of Francis as nature lover and social reformer, whether liberal or evangelical—images that went back to the nineteenth century.[26]

But the most significant criticism came from more substantial works. Most of their authors were European, with the notable exceptions of J. D. Salinger and Bernard Malamud, whom we shall discuss later on. We shall review the European works because they were widely read in the United States and because they introduce new interpretations of St. Francis. And we should note that most of the critics, European and American, admired St. Francis or felt an attachment to him; what they resisted was a shallow or one-sided notion of Francis.

Nikos Kazantzakis added Francis to his world of agonized, sensual heroes. As a reviewer in the *Christian Century* said, "This St. Francis . . . does not belong inside those benign statues seen in many suburban gardens." Instead, he dances on the edge of the abyss and calls God "the Insatiable, the Merciless, the Indefatigable, the Unsatisfied." Kazantzakis (1883–1957) was a Greek novelist who became an international celebrity in the 1950s, after he was twice nominated for the Nobel Prize. Two of his books have been made into Hollywood movies (*Zorba the Greek*, 1964, and *The Last Temptation of Christ*, 1988). His work was well received by educated readers, although critics and academics have been more ambivalent.[27]

Kazantzakis's Francis bears a striking resemblance to the author's other protagonists, such as Zorba the Greek and Jesus. Most probably, this is because Kazantzakis's fiction was an expression of his philosophical vision, which incorporated elements of Nietzsche, Bergson, and Greek Orthodox Christianity. Kazantzakis's Francis is torn between his spiritual potential and his limited capabilities. His God is endlessly demanding, and Francis pushes farther and farther in response to his demands. Abuse, violence, humiliation—it is never enough. "When the Almighty seizes a man," says the narrator, Brother Leo, "He no longer has any mercy, but tosses the victim from peak to peak even if he break into a thousand pieces." Francis rejects his family, kisses the leper, retreats for prayer and fasting. "'Not enough!' That is what He screamed at me," says Francis.[28]

A particular temptation—as in Kazantzakis's other works—is sex. The narrator announces very early that Francis was strongly attracted to Clare, although the attraction remained pure and unconsummated. Indeed, before her conversion, she taunts him for rejecting the life of a "real man" and says that "real women" are interested in love. Still, Francis affirms the goodness of the natural world in every particular, even as he tries to transcend it. Indeed, he affirms the right of the wolf of Gubbio to express its true nature, which is to eat sheep. This is no pacifist vision.[29]

Elizabeth Goudge could hardly have taken a more contrasting approach. She interprets Francis's life through the lens of classical Christian prayer disciplines. Goudge (1900–84) was a prolific and well-respected novelist, though not a groundbreaking one. The daughter of a prominent Church of England clergyman, she remained a pious Anglican all her life. Most of her works incorporate religious themes or ideas. Her life of St. Francis, *My God and My All* (1959), attracted modest public attention with a dozen or so reviews that described it as "warm and understanding" or "reverent and poetic."[30]

Goudge's framework is a traditional Catholic (and Anglo-Catholic) understanding of the spiritual journey, a process of conversion, purgation, progress, struggle, and ultimately union with God. Chapter 2 thus begins with a little discourse on conversion as the process of being drawn to God. Goudge says that the first thing Francis had to do was to learn to pray—not to repeat words or formulas, but to give himself up to the will of God. She alludes to the common experience of dryness and struggle in prayer. Even Francis's continuing sense of sinfulness is an indication of his growing nearness to God, she says, because it means he is increasingly aware of his human unlikeness to God. Francis's mystical experiences are signs of a deeper growth toward union. Goudge reflects on them often, with the most extended discussion in the chapter on Mount Alvernia and the stigmata.[31]

Her accounts of Francis with animals accord with her spiritual emphasis. The sermon to the birds, she says, is not just a pretty story but a sign of Francis's spiritual growth. Having first seen God in human outcasts such as lepers, he has extended his ability to discern God so that it now extends to animals in creation.[32]

One other critical view of the sentimental St. Francis comes from a 1950 movie, Roberto Rossellini's *Flowers of St. Francis (Francesco, giullare di Dio)*. The film reflects Rossellini's "neorealist" approach to filmmaking, an almost documentary style that emphasizes ordinary people and real places. It was little more than a series of separate scenes or vignettes, most of them taken from the *Little Flowers*, and most of the performers were Franciscan brothers from an Italian monastery.

In 1952, when a subtitled version of the film was released in the United States, it was "ignored" and was a "commercial flop," but it has remained steadily in the public eye in a small way. It has periodically been revived and reassessed—notably during the centennial of Rossellini's birth, 2006—and is still available.[33]

It is true that those who were looking for a familiar or sentimental version of Francis were able to find it in this film. For example, a commentator in the *Boston Globe* compared the movie to flowers presented to "a favorite saint in a wayside shrine." Writing in 1956, she described it as "a reverent, joyous, tender story of a great goodness," filled with "soul peace and love of beauty that transcend the narrow dogma and religious rivalries of the formalized church."[34]

But more typical assessments call the film elegiac and "starkly genuine." Rossellini himself said that he wanted the film to show simplicity, innocence, and delight, together with the freedom of "absolute detachment from material things." Some critics have also suggested that, in the wake of World War II, Rossellini was nostalgic for a pre-Mussolini Italy, or was trying to revive interest in an earlier Italy. Rossellini's daughter Isabella later said that he made this film to show the world that Italians were "nice people." In these respects it was part of a reassessment of American-Italian relationships after World War II.[35]

The American writer J. D. Salinger was also critical of the stereotypical Francis. The novelist Donna Tartt wrote in 2005 that she first heard of St. Francis in Salinger's novella "Zooey" (1957), where he was called "more loveable [sic] than Jesus." Intrigued by this reference, Tartt found in Francis a refreshing alternative to the kind of Christianity she had grown up with, which she described as "suffocating and humorless . . . evangelical bullying." *Franny and Zooey* refers only briefly to Francis. Yet it reflects a contemporary cultural construction of Francis and also makes him a foil for social criticism.[36]

As the story opens, Franny, a college student, has taken up using the Jesus Prayer, a mystical practice popularized from Russian Orthodox spirituality. She is also depressed and disillusioned; she sees college as bleak, little more than a place for professors and fellow students to gratify their egos. Her older brother, Zooey, thinks she is misusing the prayer as escapism.

He also thinks she misunderstands Jesus—and he sets up St. Francis as a contrast to Jesus. Jesus, he says, was intelligent and unsentimental, the only biblical figure who understood that "there is no separation from God." He was a "supreme adept" on a "terribly important mission." But Franny, like most of the Christian world, is trying "to turn Jesus into St. Francis of Assisi to make him more 'loveable.'" Francis was "endearing," says Zooey, and had a "consistently winning personality." He cannot have had an important mission if he had "enough time to knock out a few canticles, to preach to the *birds* . . . ." Franny, says her brother, is looking for a "sticky, adorable divine personage" to comfort her—"St. Francis and Seymour and Heidi's grandfather all wrapped up in one." (Seymour was their deceased older brother; the grandfather was a character in Johanna Spyri's classic novel *Heidi*.)[37]

Here the Francis of postwar consensus culture is front and center. What isn't quite clear is whether Salinger himself really believed this stereotype. There is no question that he was critical toward the culture in general, and the Francis of birds and sweetness made a convenient foil for his criticism, a proxy for the culture. But Salinger hints at a more nuanced view when he equates "Heidi's grandfather" with the lovable, endearing Francis—because the grandfather was not lovable or endearing either. He was gruff and distant until little Heidi slowly reawakened his softer emotions. It is not clear whether Salinger knew this, but if he did—and if he knew that there was more to St. Francis—then he was ironically skewering Zooey as well as Franny.

Criticism of the Consensus: Scholarship

Critiques of the consensus culture came from another direction as well—scholarship. A considerable body of new work on Francis appeared during this period, but as with fiction, most of it originated in Europe. The history of scholarship is not my primary concern in this work, but a few texts are important for understanding the interpretation of St. Francis.

The historian Raphael Brown commented in 1964 that English-speaking scholars had not really kept up with St. Francis scholarship. (One exception was John Moorman, whom we shall discuss later on.)

Brown, with his co-author Ignatius Brady, edited and augmented a biographical study by the historian Omer Englebert, which was first published in French in 1950 and revised in 1956. The English version was a benchmark work because of Brown's extensive scholarly apparatus. He provided a new introduction, an exhaustive research bibliography of works published since 1939, and appendices on basic subjects like chronology and genealogy. Brown also included "a footnote on a lately popular apocryphal item: the so-called Peace Prayer of St. Francis."[38]

One particularly striking discussion concerns place. Brown reviews a long-running controversy over the location of Francis's birth and childhood home, reminding us of the importance of place in the popular memory of Francis. The question engendered considerable discussion from 1939 through 1943, and it was revived in 1948 and again in 1959. Two sites in Assisi could make reasonable claims to represent Francis's birthplace, and both claims were based in part on legend. Brown thought the family might actually have lived in both at different times, but the question was by no means settled.[39]

Another scholarly critique came from the English historian John Moorman. Beginning in 1940, Moorman produced a lasting and significant body of work on the Franciscan movement, notably a history of the order and a collection of documentary sources. He was also an Anglican priest (a bishop from 1959) and, oddly enough, had grown up in the little church in Adel where the hymn originated. In 1950 he published a short biography of Francis for nonspecialists. Like Hoyland's 1935 book, Moorman's was published by the Student Christian Movement (SCM) Press and was clearly intended for the SCM's audience—students, seminarians, and serious laypeople. While it probably did not attract a huge readership, it had some sustained appeal—it was reprinted in 1963 and again in 1976 by two different publishers.[40]

Moorman of course rejects the sentimentalized Francis. He reminds his prosperous readers of Francis's poverty and insecurity. Yet he also argues against anticapitalist activism for its own sake. Francis's life was grounded in prayer and nearness to God, he says, and everything else flowed from that.[41]

Moorman also objects to the depiction of Francis as cheerful, friendly, and antidogmatic—the stereotype that Salinger invokes. Modern people, he says, like to think of Francis talking to the birds, preaching a simple gospel of love, and "doing whimsical things." But, while St. Francis's love of nature was "very attractive to the modern mind," Moorman thinks that the sermon to the birds is really incidental in Francis's story. Moreover, Francis was dirty and shabby and (by implication) diseased. Far from being friendly to all, he tried to avoid women. He freely reproached people for their sins and called them to repentance. "There is something frightening about him," says the author, "about his absolute standards about his uncompromising teaching." On the other hand, Moorman, like Goudge, is sensitive to the limitations on Clare's calling. While the mendicant life was "not really possible" for women in her time, he wonders whether she longed for more and suggests she was "born out of her time."[42]

Most strikingly, Moorman reminds us that Francis loved unattractive things as much as beautiful ones—bugs and lice as well as birds, lepers as well as healthy people. "Artists should take note of this," he says. "They should include in their pictures not only doves and squirrels, but rats and toads and even bugs and lice." If Francis could choose his own stained-glass window, "he would certainly choose one which depicted him surrounded not by birds and butterflies, but by the sick and the lepers, by cripples and tramps, by all the dregs of society whose life he so bravely shared and whose souls he so dearly loved." This is surely a countercultural idea.[43]

Criticism of the Consensus: Social Activism

Some voices from the margins remembered the tramps and lepers. Pacifists, a small minority in this era, continued to associate St. Francis with alternative economics and consistent living. David Dellinger's farm, which we discussed in an earlier chapter, is one example. And the "peace prayer" appeared not only in *Life* and *House Beautiful*, but also in the left-wing magazine *The Nation*, in 1950. It appears to have been sent in by a Jewish reader: the credit line acknowledges Blanche Ittleson (1875–1975), an innovative social worker and philanthropist. In the early 1950s Alcoholics Anonymous adapted the prayer for use in its Twelve Steps, where it serves as an introduction to prayer and meditation for hesitant beginners. A collection of peace stories for Quaker youth concluded with the peace prayer, which had not appeared in any of its predecessor collections.[44]

Francis also remained a steady beacon to Dorothy Day and the radical Catholic Worker movement. Day wrote about using the St. Francis prayer in the context of community and poverty. "All this week," she wrote,

"Irene and Helen making scenes, wanting to be loved rather than to love, to be appreciated, etc. My turn next. I had better watch for self-deceit." But it was only one of her resources; at that time she was also reading John of the Cross and Frederick Faber.[45]

Some years later (1959) she recalled the "perfect joy" story. The community had suffered frequent vandalism: "All our windows have been broken across the front of the house." An outdoor painting of Christ was defaced; garbage was left in the doorway. Good neighbors complained about the Bowery men who came to the house. Here again, the St. Francis story seemed to apply to the situation.[46]

The Protestant educator Margueritte Harmon Bro, a Congregationalist and pacifist, had similar concerns. In her book *When Children Ask,* which teaches parents how to listen to children and teenagers, she posed an apparently fictional problem. Suppose a young girl—a little older than the Brownie Girl Scouts we met earlier—is attracted to the example of St. Francis. She wants to imitate him in her own life. So she decides to give up some of her possessions and clothing; she wants no more than the poorest children in her class have. She goes on to argue that we can only understand hunger and need by experiencing it, and that we must rely on inner rather than outer motivations. This girl's distracted mother laughs off the girl's earnest questions. How might a parent respond differently?[47]

It is not clear whether this story is based on fact or is entirely imagined. But in either case, Bro here maintains the old activist idea of consistent living—the idea that religious beliefs must be lived and enacted, not only professed. She resists generic belief and consensus culture. Her young girl embraces poverty more than birdfeeders, the darker and more challenging side of Francis. We are a long way from Robert Lawson here.

So Francis inspired Christian activists, Protestant and Catholic alike. For them he was a model of authority, a guide to everyday committed living, and a preacher of peace.

Pluralism

In 1958 a hobbyist printed a little book in letterpress as a Christmas gift for his friends. It was a collection of prayers for peace, a theme he thought appropriate to the Christmas season. One of them was the St. Francis prayer. The others, if his attributions are correct, are Hindu, Taoist, Jewish, Japanese Buddhist, and Navajo, along with two other Christian prayers. St. Francis, then, appears here in the context of consensus culture—Christianity and the popular celebration of Christmas—but also in a multifaith context.[48]

As early as the nineteenth century, religious seekers suggested that Francis transcended religious boundaries. But he emerged as a clearly pluralistic figure in the paradoxical postwar era. Most notably, he was adopted as a Hindu and as a Jew—in both cases Americanized.

In 1945 a group of California spiritual seekers put out a book called *Vedanta for the Western World*. Vedanta, briefly stated, is a nineteenth-century interpretation of Hinduism with a missionary element that includes both outreach and social action. Leaders of the Vedanta movement reached out to the West, beginning with the World's Parliament of Religions in 1893. Many Americans found the movement attractive: it offered a mystical spirituality, a universalistic worldview, and a way to incorporate elements of other religions into its thought and practice. But Vedanta remained a very small movement in America until the postwar era. The 1945 book—a selection of essays from a magazine—was reprinted many times and was influential in spreading Vedantist ideas. Among those who were drawn to Vedanta was J. D. Salinger.[49]

In the book is an essay comparing Ramakrishna, Vedanta's founder and "greatest human exemplar," with St. Francis. Its author was Guido Ferrando, a retired professor of Italian and head of a Theosophical school in California. Although he argues that both Francis and Ramakrishna were exemplars of a single universal religion, the essay in fact presents Francis primarily in Hindu terms. In Ferrando's view Francis was not just a reformer. Rather, he revived "Eternal Faith" in a God who could be "realized in our earthly life." Poverty removed obstacles to spiritual progress. It was not merely renunciation but the *"negation of all desire* for worldly honor or bodily comfort"—a Hindu concept [italics mine]. Similarly, obedience brought "freedom from the illusion of our ego." And having negated desire, removed obstacles, and abandoned illusion, Francis did in fact attain *samadhi*—spiritual union with the ultimate Reality.[50]

Ferrando also draws parallels between Francis and Ramakrishna. For example, both attracted followers and established lasting religious orders. Both had the personal qualities of childlike purity, intellectual simplicity, and spiritual intelligence. Both were "supreme religious artists," expressing ecstatic joy through poetry and music. Ferrando quotes a poem by Ramakrishna and declares, "Francis would have loved this beautiful song."[51]

A universalized idea of Francis was not new. Nor was the argument over whether or not "spiritual union" meant the same thing for Hindus (as in Ferrando's Vedantist formulation) and for Christians (as in Goudge's interpretation). What was new was that Ferrando used Francis—a figure familiar to American Christians and to American culture—to make Vedanta accessible. His universalized construction of Francis was slanted more toward Vedanta than toward Christianity, and he presented Francis persuasively in Vedantist Hindu terms.

Bernard Malamud, in his 1957 novel *The Assistant*, suggests that Francis was more like a Jew. The story revolves around Morris and Ida Bober, Jewish immigrants who run a small, not very successful grocery store in a mostly Gentile neighborhood, and their adult daughter Helen, who would have liked to go to college but must work as a secretary to help support her parents. One night a pair of thugs attacks Morris and robs the store. Shortly afterward, a young Gentile man appears in the neighborhood and asks Morris for work. He is willing to help out for nothing, just to learn the retail trade. His name is Frank. In an early scene, he discusses a magazine picture of St. Francis with a Jewish retailer.

Gradually, Frank takes a larger role in running the store. Business improves on his watch, but at the same time, he is pilfering food and cash, and the store seems to be a losing proposition in any case. Meanwhile, he and Helen experience a growing attraction to each other. As their relationship intensifies, they occasionally allude to their differences without drawing any firm conclusions. But it all ends abruptly when Frank loses control and assaults Helen. She calls him, significantly, an "uncircumcised dog." At the same time, it is becoming clear that Frank was one of the original two thieves. Through the rest of the novel, Frank struggles to redeem himself and to assist the family, even while they reject him. In the end—with almost no explanation—he converts to Judaism.[52]

Images of St. Francis are woven through the narrative. In the first episode, Frank stares at a magazine picture of a barefoot monk in a brown robe with his arms "raised to a flock of birds."

"He looks like some kind of priest," [the Jewish shop owner] said cautiously.

"No, it's St. Francis of Assisi. You can tell from that brown robe he's wearing and all those birds in the air. That's the time he was preaching to them. . . ."

"Talking to the birds? What was he—crazy? I don't say this out of any harm."

Frank then says that St. Francis was a great man, not only because he had the "nerve" to preach to birds, but because he gave away his possessions.

> "He enjoyed to be poor. He said poverty was a queen and he loved her like she was a beautiful woman."
> Sam shook his head. "It ain't beautiful, kiddo. To be poor is dirty work."[53]

One night, early in their acquaintance, Frank and Helen are walking in the park. Almost at random, Frank tells Helen the story of St. Francis making a wife and children out of snow. "After," says Frank, "he felt a whole lot better." Later, Helen reflects on their encounter and wonders, "Who was he making into a wife out of snowy moonlight?"[54]

Not long afterward, birds appear again:

> Coming up the block, Helen saw a man squatting by one of the benches, feeding the birds. Otherwise, the [traffic] island was deserted. When the man rose, the pigeons fluttered up with him, a few landing on his arms and shoulders, one perched on his fingers, picking peanuts from his cupped palm. . . . The man clapped his hands when the peanuts were gone and the birds, beating their wings, scattered.[55]

And near the end of the book, Frank is in the grocery store—and incidentally still trying to make it profitable. While he waits for customers, he reads the Bible.

> As he was reading he had this pleasant thought. He saw St. Francis come dancing out of the woods in his brown rags, a couple of scrawny birds flying around over his head. St. F. stopped in front of the grocery, and reaching into the garbage can, plucked the wooden rose out of it [a rose that Frank had carved for Helen and she had rejected]. He tossed it into the air and it turned into a real flower that he caught in his hand. With a bow he gave it to Helen, who had just come out of the house. "Little sister, here is your little sister the rose." From him she took it, although it was with the love and best wishes of Frank Alpine.[56]

Half a page later, we read that Frank is circumcised and becomes a Jew.

Malamud was part of a flowering of American Jewish literature in the 1950s and 1960s. With Saul Bellow and Isaac Bashevis Singer, and the second generation of Philip Roth, Grace Paley, and others, this postwar Jewish voice emerged as an important stream of American literature. It is all the more remarkable that a Christian figure like St. Francis figures so prominently in a novel of Jewish identity.

As a biographical question, it is not clear why Malamud was interested in St. Francis. There are hints—his wife was Italian-American, a "lapsed Catholic"; they visited Assisi in 1956. Malamud admired Dostoevsky, Tolstoy, and Flannery O'Connor, all of whom worked with Christian themes. But a definitive answer remains to be uncovered.[57]

The Assistant has attracted extensive critical attention. Its meanings are ambiguous and many layered. It explores everything from the American dream to the meaning of self-sacrifice. The novel has been both praised and scathingly criticized for its identification of Jews with suffering. "I bet the Jews could make a suit of clothes out of it," thinks Frank toward the end. And when he becomes a Jew, he embraces suffering—in the physical act of circumcision, and in taking on the tiny store, which the novel symbolically identifies with imprisonment. Malamud even associates suffering with atonement: at one point Morris tells Frank calmly, "I suffer for you."[58]

Western literature also identifies voluntary suffering with Christ, of course, and one commentator called *The Assistant* Malamud's "Christian book." Malamud rejected this characterization. He was not overly concerned with boundaries. For him, "being too Jewish for some Americans or too Christian for some Jews was not a problem." He once wrote, "As for the Christian elements in Judaism, ideas flow forwards and backwards." Nor was Jewishness itself clear-cut. A scene near the end of the book depicts Morris's funeral, where a rabbi who doesn't know him must preach a funeral sermon. Because Morris neglected many religious practices, the rabbi struggles with the meaning of true Judaism: "Shall we say that just because he doesn't keep kosher and doesn't go to synagogue, he's not really a Jew?" In all these ways, Malamud worked in a middle ground. In an early draft of the novel—and later, in interviews and comments—Malamud said, "Everybody is a Jew but they don't know it."[59]

Including, presumably, St. Francis. Frank is a St. Francis figure. He shares the saint's name and his iconography—especially in the scene in which he feeds the birds. He is also poor and mendicant, humble and ultimately self-abnegating. His only wife is made of insubstantial snow. Toward the end he is dressed in brown rags.

Malamud's identification of Frank with Francis is not absolute, however. Frank is clearly not altogether saintly: he pursues sex and money, he knows he was not "born good" like Francis. And in the visionary episode near the end, Francis accomplishes what Frank himself cannot. Critics have interpreted Francis as representing the best in Frank, the "truth of his life," or the spiritual longing that demands fulfillment. Or, in an alternative reading, Francis might signify that part of Frank that embraces poverty and suffering.[60]

But all of these interpretations point in the same direction. Whatever it is in Frank that draws him to Judaism, it is the part of him that resembles Francis—whether it is his embrace of suffering, or the best in him, or his spiritual longing, or indeed the whole of him. The inevitable conclusion is that Malamud gives us St. Francis as a Jew. This is a stunning turn in St. Francis interpretation.

Insider, Outsider

In the postwar era, St. Francis was widely recognized and firmly embedded in consensus culture. He signified peace, love, and a connection with nature, generally in a benign and unchallenging way. He was certainly recognized as a religious figure—in a context in which "religion" implicitly meant moderate mainline Protestantism—but, like popular religion generally, he eluded clear boundaries and doctrinal definitions. Indeed, his image was elaborated in many directions. Creative writers and serious thinkers found a more subtle Francis—though sometimes as a projection of their own agendas. Left-wing dissenters continued to claim him for their own. He was also recognized as a religious figure beyond Christianity.

CHAPTER SIX

The Hippie Saint
Counterculture and Ecology

A young pastor is preaching to a loose congregation of hippies, street people, and students. The world around them is in turmoil. Old truths and social structures are crumbling. Everything is being called into question—from business success to popular music to the existence of God. The preacher says:

> Let me run it down to you about this cat from Assisi! Like he had super-advantages. His family had all the bread they needed. His mother was cool. His father was a straight businessman with cloth for sale: respectable, leading citizen in the community. [Note that "straight" at this time meant conventional and sober. "Bread" meant money.]
>
> As a teen-ager he was like super-straight too. He was gifted, promising, with a successful career before him in the family business . . .
>
> His case history shows no signs of like turning-on with drugs but he began to act, much of the time like he were on a "trip," withdrawn, and experiencing visions and hallucinations . . .
>
> His actions became increasingly bizarre. Like he insisted nothing mattered but love and brotherhood. He made it with the Peace scene too, and openly advocated total integration.
>
> But what really blew the minds of the straights was that he turned against education and urged the runaways and drop outs who flocked to share his pads to stay away from books . . .
>
> The cat claimed he was trying to live like Jesus . . . [1]

This sermon was preached in a experimental Protestant ministry in Berkeley, California, in 1967. It reflects a time when Francis was imagined as a hippie, not just a dropout but a harbinger of a purified faith and a new world. The most vivid statement of this vision was a 1973 movie, *Brother Sun, Sister Moon*, that would influence popular spirituality for decades to come. At the same time, Francis was central in the early conversations about ecology.

A Search for Authenticity

"The sixties" were a watershed period in American life. These years of turmoil introduced divisions in American society that continue to shape us. The assassination of President Kennedy, in late 1963, was a blow to the nation's trust in social order and American goodness. The civil rights movement brought nonviolent mass protest and sweeping changes in race relations that proved both beneficial and unsettling. Above all, the Vietnam War generated bitter division as it pulled increasing numbers of young men into military service in a morally ambiguous undertaking.[2] Although the period of upheaval did not coincide exactly with the decade from 1960 to 1969, the term "sixties" is a convenient shorthand.

Doug Rossinow has argued that the left-wing culture of the period generated a "politics of authenticity." Like the Victorians who sought an alternative to modernity, many young adults of the 1960s longed above all for authenticity in their lives and experiences. But they did so for twentieth-century reasons. Drawing from existentialist philosophy, they identified the problem of the times as alienation—from self, from community, and, for religious people, from God—and its result as anxiety. Authenticity, a real and natural self in society, was the solution to the problem, they thought. Unlike the Victorians, they believed that their goals were attainable and that they would issue in a truer, more authentic democracy. What is more, this politics was initially cultivated in student Christian groups, especially the YMCA and YWCA, whose members "brought the legacy of the earlier social gospel movement into the Cold War era."[3]

In early 1967, *Time* magazine's "man of the year"—it was not yet "person"—was the younger generation of Americans, those aged twenty-five and under. Most of them had been born during the postwar baby boom, and although there was considerable breadth and diversity among them, almost all had grown up in relative affluence, in a generally peaceful world, with educational opportunities and a range of life choices available. But the article focused mainly on those who were rebellious and different. Change was in the air. The success of the civil rights movement had encouraged activism in many directions. More students were choosing majors in the humanities and asking large philosophical questions. They distanced themselves from established institutions like the church. They were even more distant from their elders when they pursued sexual freedom, hallucinogenic drugs, and new music.[4]

In the middle of the era "flower children" and "hippies" appeared—young adults who expressed their resistance to mainstream culture by trying to create an alternative culture and community. They made "peace" and "love" the watchwords of the day. At the same time, antiwar protest was growing. Beginning with demonstrations in Washington and New York in 1965, the movement quickly evolved toward draft resistance and civil disobedience. Tens of thousands of people participated in "teach-ins" and demonstrations.[5]

By the late 1960s, the atmosphere was becoming harsher and more confrontational. The federal government, the military hierarchy, and many traditionally minded Americans resisted the protests. The watershed year was 1968, with two assassinations and a violently suppressed protest at the Democratic National Convention in Chicago. Around the same time, the Black Power movement renounced nonviolence and rejected the goal of racial integration. Soon afterward, the women's liberation movement took shape, building on the earlier movements, but also reacting against their sexism.[6]

American religion was also changing rapidly. For Roman Catholics, the 1960s were marked by the Second Vatican Council, which ran from 1962 through 1965. Pope John XXIII was interested in *aggiornamento*, "updating," or "opening the windows" to let in fresh air. To this end, he called together church officials from all over the world—as the Roman Catholic Church had done periodically in the past—to consider the state of the church in the modern world. The council reviewed everything from liturgy and piety to political and economic power structures. Among its many changes, it affirmed a "preferential option for the poor" in all the church's decisions. Vatican II generated tremendous reforming energy—and considerable resistance as well. Some effects were felt immediately, such as changes in worship and music. Others took longer to resonate through this worldwide institution.

Protestant theologians, meanwhile, were exploring "radical religion." Building on an earlier idea of "religionless Christianity," radical theologians declared the "death of God" in the early 1960s. What they meant was that the modern world had displaced and outgrown the ancient myth of an all-powerful deity and all its trappings. Christianity, they argued, offered primarily a way to live in this world, a model for holy and righteous action. Theology offered only "provisional statements," not eternal truth—and this provisional quality was "cause for hope and optimism." A touchstone work of the era was Harvey Cox's *The Secular City* (1965).

Cox argued that urbanization and secularization were the realities of the age—and they were not threats but "epochal opportunities to be embraced." Modern people now had to speak and conceive of the divine presence in secular terms. As Robert Ellwood wrote of the all too earthly city of Chicago, he thought that "despite all appearances, this place was real, was holy, was the future, was where real life had now to be lived."[7]

One source of this theology was existentialism, which reintroduced, in a new key, the idea of personal authenticity. Existentialist philosophies and theologies varied, but they agreed that the most important reality was individual existence in the present. So the highest moral value was to live out that existence as truthfully and courageously as possible, even in the face of despair and meaninglessness. Protestant forms of existentialism deemphasized tradition and the prospect of an afterlife in favor of authentic living in this world. They also made a case for radical social change, arguing that modern social structures caused alienation from the self and from God. Through colleges and seminaries, these ideas made their way into student populations.[8]

But theological challenges were not the only ones to confront the Protestant mainline during this era. These churches, so recently part of consensus culture, found themselves in a rapidly changing religious landscape. The Vietnam War caused internal tensions and uncertainty over direction. Beginning in the middle of the decade, church membership declined slowly but steadily, with most of the losses occurring among young adults. Meanwhile, new religions and offshoots of Asian traditions burgeoned. Evangelical Christianity, which had been slowly building strength, returned to the public scene with great energy in the early 1970s. By 1975, when American forces finally left Vietnam, the public mood was turning inward; in 1976 the journalist Tom Wolfe began to write about "the 'me' decade." In the same year, a southern evangelical, Jimmy Carter, was elected president.[9]

St. Francis was the man for the antiauthoritarian, antiestablishment 1960s. He was imagined in this age as a barefoot hippie rejecting materialism and as a peace lover. He was a model for those seeking religious alternatives—Christian and otherwise—and for the newly emerging "ecology" movement. Above all, he signified authenticity. To a youth culture suspicious of hypocrisy, seeking to live fully in the present, Francis was one who lived out his belief and was personally authentic, fully himself in God. He overcame his alienation. He rejected materialism, artificiality, and conformity. All of these were pressing concerns for the youth movement and its sympathizers.

In the Background

New work about Francis was scanty in the early 1960s. It seems most likely that the Francis of consensus culture had simply settled into the cultural and religious landscape. The texts and images of earlier periods continued to circulate. The hymn "All Creatures," for example, was available to the thriving Sunday schools of the baby boom era, still far from over. The novels and biographies of the postwar period were still being reprinted. The peace prayer reappeared in such varied forms as a meditation by the South African antiapartheid writer Alan Paton and a sticker to seal one's personal mailing envelopes. A movie about St. Francis covered familiar ground and made little impact. But all these constructions of Francis remained available in the culture for new uses by the hippie and antiwar movements.[10]

Among serious studies from this period, perhaps the most notable are the translations and editions of early documents. For English speakers, the Franciscan Marion Habig compiled a collection of translated texts from a variety of sources. First issued in 1973 by a Roman Catholic press, this volume was widely used for many years and is still in print. At the same time, the German scholar Kajetan Esser was at work on an authoritative compilation of early Franciscan sources, the fruit of all the research since Sabatier. This was published in final form in 1976. Raphael Brown's biographical work, of course, was still new on the scene in the 1960s.[11]

Biographers were still looking for the "real" St. Francis—not a new idea, of course, but one that they recast for their own time. Garden statues with birds were common enough by this time to symbolize popular misconceptions about Francis. As a 1967 biography put it, he could not be reduced to "mass-produced shoddy statuary." A journalist similarly argued that Francis's attractions were not obvious to "purpled bishops and the heavily propertied . . . though they honor him with insipid statuary in birdbaths [sic]." The historian Lawrence Cunningham referred to a common "tendency to view Francis as a sort of charming, medieval 'nature freak' . . . [with] innumerable statues of St. Francis with a dove perched on his shoulders gracing innumerable gardens of believers and nonbelievers alike." Instead of these popular images, mainstream writers and rebels alike claimed to have found an authentic Francis and his "meaning for today."[12]

Most of these biographies have not stood the test of time, but they carried forward some traditions about Francis and added a few new concerns. The sense of place continued to be important. Pacifism, oddly enough for this era, often went unmentioned. In keeping with the age, however, most biographers speculated about Francis's sexual behavior before his conversion.[13]

One important biographical treatment appeared in Sir Kenneth Clark's blockbuster television series *Civilisation* (1969). This series was a sort of early multimedia course, offering accessible lectures on European history, integrated with period art and music. Its audience numbered approximately 2.5 million viewers in England and 5 million in the United States, in addition to readers of a best-selling book version. Clark, an art historian, devoted a substantial amount of space to Francis: twelve minutes of a fifty-minute segment on the Middle Ages. He presented Francis as "a religious genius—the greatest, I believe, that Europe has ever produced." While the camera panned across works of art and Umbrian scenery, Clark discussed Francis's place as a bridge figure between chivalry and capitalism. Along the way, he managed to review the story of Francis's life and to mention the most famous texts and stories, such as the Canticle of the Sun, the *Little Flowers*, and the sermon to the birds. He had tactfully covered birds in an earlier program, arguing that they symbolized artistic and spiritual freedom in medieval art. He thought that there was a nearly universal belief, across religious traditions, that spiritual life required shedding worldly possessions. Francis, he said, made this "truth . . . part of the European consciousness." Yet he implied that voluntary poverty was no longer a realistic way of life—that Francis belonged to an earlier time.[14]

Morris Bishop's biography of Francis also received more notice than most. Published just after his death in 1973, the book is derivative and generally undistinguished. Bishop was popular as a writer, though, and *Horizon* magazine—an educational general-interest publication—published an excerpt from the book along with an appreciative memorial notice.[15]

Bishop echoed nineteenth-century material. He revived Protestant language: Francis wanted freedom from the "set formulas of the church" and its corruptions; medieval pilgrims to Assisi indulged in "hysterical ecstasies of penance." Bishop even called Francis a "revivalist," comparing him to Russell Conwell (1843–1925) and to the Jehovah's Witnesses. And he resurrected the notion of Francis as the source of Italian poetry, paraphrasing Matthew Arnold.[16]

For his own time, Bishop leaned toward the conservative side. He affirmed the right of property, and he insisted that Francis was only interested in the "deserving" poor. Francis's father, he said, was just trying to be a good businessman and a responsible parent. While Bishop followed his contemporaries in inquiring about Francis's sexual behavior, he drew the startling conclusion that "the influence of Francis on [Clare] was total . . . He taught her the joy of submission."[17]

Summer of Love

The American story of St. Francis in this era really begins in 1967, not in the political watershed year of 1968. The year 1967—an *annus mirabilis* for Francis imagery—saw the birth of the hippie and of the underground church, the Summer of Love, and a widely published article that proposed St. Francis as the patron of a new discipline—ecology.

The word "hippie" came into widespread use in 1967. It seems to have had several sources, but in that year it was suddenly everywhere. Hippies were young adults and teenagers who dropped out of mainstream society in search of a life that was less materialistic and more loving, less connected to institutions and more free. Many tried to be simple and peaceful. Others were harshly critical toward the mainstream or were advocates of revolution. Hippies resisted the draft and the Vietnam War, sometimes by active protest, more often simply by dropping out of sight. They further expressed rebellion in their material culture and in the way they built relationships and communities. Many experimented with hallucinogens as a way to expand imagination and spiritual awareness.[18]

San Francisco—the city of St. Francis—was the epicenter of the movement. It was rooted in several intertwined social networks and energy centers: the Haight-Ashbury neighborhood, with its young adult residents and alternative businesses; the *San Francisco Oracle*, an experimental newspaper; and the Communication Company, which printed broadsides and street posters. The Communication Company was associated with the Diggers, a group named for a radical religious movement of the seventeenth century (and perhaps also for the slang term "dig," meaning to appreciate and to be hip). The Diggers set out to subvert the established order in all its dimensions. One of those was money: they provided free food to all comers and at one point staged a theatrical "death of money" procession. The parallels to St. Francis are clear, if only implicit thus far. Meanwhile, mainline Protestant churches were surprisingly supportive of hippies—though not universally or without controversy. All Saints Episcopal Church on Haight Street, for example, allowed the Diggers to use office space in the church, which in practice meant that they spread out through much of the building. Glide Memorial Church, a Methodist congregation in the Tenderloin district, hosted a hippie festival that ended in chaos. Other mainliners also reached out, and within the next few years, some Bay Area churches began to develop alternative models of Christianity for the times, as we shall see. Evangelicals, meanwhile, were also beginning to develop alternative forms of church. A handful of Haight-Ashbury drifters planted the seeds of the 1970s "Jesus movement," and many of their concerns—authenticity, true Christianity, resistance to materialism—mirrored those of the counterculture. But Francis was not significant for them until much later.[19]

Early in 1967, a coalition of hippies and political radicals sponsored an event they called a "Human Be-in" in Golden Gate Park. Thousands of young adults gathered to celebrate—as they thought—the beginning of a new society. There was music, poetry, and LSD. There was also a new religious consciousness. The event began with a Hindu blessing ritual and continued with chants to Shiva and to the Buddha. A Zen leader meditated on stage all day. The ethos was authenticity—experience, free exploration, and resistance to Western culture.[20]

The Be-in was the catalyst for the Summer of Love. Another coalition, including the Diggers, issued a statement in May in which they invited everyone, across the nation, to come to San Francisco and celebrate love and freedom. It was not meant to be an organized event but a summer-long spontaneous festival and an alternative way of life. Perhaps 75,000 young adults passed through San Francisco that summer—most of them with few resources and no direction. But the event was a cultural benchmark for the youth movement.[21]

The May 1967 press release of the Council for a Summer of Love invoked the name of St. Francis. Not only that, the announcement was framed to a surprising degree in religious terms. "This summer, the youth of the world are making a holy pilgrimage to our city," they wrote. The new culture in Haight-Ashbury was "a small part of a worldwide spiritual awakening," temporarily focused on the city of San Francisco: "This city is alive, human, and divine." Food and housing would be prepared. There would be festivals and meditation hours and celebrations of universal values. Religious leaders and gurus would be invited to join in the festival. There was a plan to carry a statue of St. Francis from Marin County to Golden Gate Park (apparently never fulfilled). Above all, the pilgrims would be "met with Love," which was the "will of God."[22]

"And so I would like to recall to you," the statement concluded, "that Saint Francis of Assisi is the Patron Saint of the City of San Francisco, and that therefore Saint Francis is the Patron Saint of the Summer of Love." St. Francis, then, was here associated with the new world of the 1960s: love, youth, freedom, sharing (food and housing and company), and a new direction for humanity. This new world went beyond the boundaries of Christianity. The statement associates Francis with universal spiritual values, with "all gurus, and all men of enlightenment and good will," and with "God within."

The council also printed a poster (see figure 10). It depicted a stigmatized St. Francis on a background of psychedelic colors: red, hot pink, and deep yellow. Francis stands with his arms extended, with the stigmata clearly visible in his hands and feet. His face is obscured by an irregular inkblot. The only bird is a dove, and a wolf sits to Francis's left. On his right is the familiar peace prayer.

The artist has explained that the poster was meant to address the "growing tension" between the hippies and other city residents. "All San Franciscans could embrace St. Francis as a nonthreatening symbol," he says. The wolf signified the fears that St. Francis could tame, as he tamed the wolf of Gubbio in the story. The dove and peace prayer reinforce the message, and Francis's outstretched arms suggest blessing and peace.[23]

Clearly this poster departs from conventional non-Catholic iconography of Francis. It does, however, offer an interesting visual parallel with Bufano's first statue, although the artist intended no such reference. This statue had arrived in San Francisco in 1955 and had attracted considerable public attention before it was installed near Fisherman's Wharf in the early 1960s.

The peace prayer seems to have been widely known in Haight-Ashbury. For example, it appeared on an undated flier issued by the Communication Company consisting of the prayer, in informal hand lettering, and a drawing of St. Francis receiving the stigmata. This drawing, too, departs from conventional iconography. In most images, a winged seraph imposes

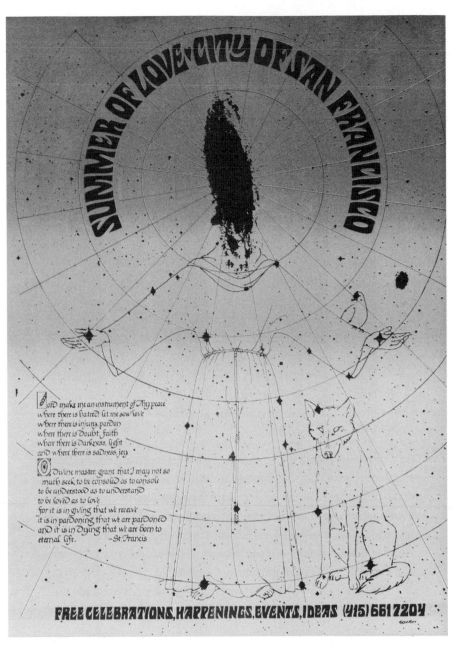

FIGURE 10 Bob Schnepf (Raphael Schnepf). Summer of Love poster. *San Francisco Oracle*, June 1967, reproduced in facsimile edition, 1991. The original was printed in bright psychedelic colors: red at the top, hot pink in the middle, and mustard yellow in the lower half. Image by Bob Schnepf which originally appeared in the *San Francisco Oracle* provided courtesy of the estate of Allen Cohen and Regent Press, publishers of the SAN FRANCISCO ORACLE FACSIMILE EDITION (Print & Digital Versions) available at www.regentpress.net.

the stigmata. But the flier shows a human-like figure—perhaps Christ or a divine messenger—and a large bird with outstretched wings.[24]

It is worth noting here that the peace prayer also figured in the wider antiwar and youth movements. It is hard to overstate the intensity of personal feeling about the Vietnam War at that time. Within and beyond the mass protests, virtually every young man had to confront the possibility of military service because of the draft. Perhaps half of these men accepted the traditional view of patriotism and service to the nation. For the rest, it was a profound struggle with conscience over serving in a war whose aims and methods they believed were morally wrong.

Far away from San Francisco, in New Haven, Connecticut, St. Francis was given credit for a student's decision for unlawful war resistance. This student turned in his draft card, thereby signifying resistance to the draft, the war, and the government. The occasion was an antiwar rally with the Reverend William Sloane Coffin as a speaker. Coffin was then chaplain at Yale University and was a leader among a new breed of activist Christian clergy. Like others on the cutting edge, Coffin was influenced by contemporary movements toward church involvement in the world and saw the Vietnam War as the pressing issue of the time. These clergy were, of course, only one part of a very large antiwar movement that drew on the knowledge and leadership of the older pacifist traditions. Thus there was considerable cultural transmission alongside innovation.

Coffin's biographer writes:

> In November 1968, Coffin spoke at a New Haven antiwar rally and concluded with the prayer attributed to St. Francis of Assisi, "Lord, make me an instrument of thy peace." Exceptionally moved, a young man who had driven down from Hartford with a group of friends, stood, held out his draft card, and said, "My name is Gordon Coburn and I'm a sophomore at the University of Hartford and I'm doing this because I'm a Christian."
>
> . . . The next day Coburn telephoned his parents, who hit the ceiling.

Coburn told the biographer that the experience changed his life—and that the St. Francis prayer was particularly influential. When Coffin, years later, told Coburn he hadn't done much, Coburn countered that he had "recited the prayer." "Well," said Coffin, "let's give St. Francis credit then."[25]

In San Francisco, the peace prayer was also the occasion for a more sinister use of St. Francis. An undated Communication Company broadside argued for "turning people on" to LSD without their knowledge or consent. "You can't explain it to them," it said. "DO IT TO THEM. . . . Rape every mind and body you can reach. Put it in their coffee & booze & water. . . . Make every water cooler an instrument of your peace." Here the familiar, available cultural reference was subverted and its meaning reversed, another sign of the harsh edges of the hippie movement.[26]

Undoubtedly, hippie consciousness changed after the Summer of Love. St. Francis was not forgotten: for example, the August 1967 issue of the *Oracle* emphasized the "City of St. Francis" in its cover design, and a later memoir noted the irony of city officials' anxiety about vagrants "in the city of St. Francis." December's *Oracle*, the "City of God" issue, devoted two pages to an illustrated passage from the biblical book of Revelation (21:9–27). But it was only one of many religious texts in that issue. Asian religions increasingly dominated the San Francisco conversation.[27]

And, by summer's end, the once spontaneous hippie movement had become the object of media scrutiny and commercial exploitation. Hippie clothing became fashion. The Haight was a tourist attraction. People with a cruder interest in sex and drugs began to flood San Francisco neighborhoods. Problems of homelessness and health grew out of control.[28] Thus, in the fall, the Diggers proclaimed the "death of the hippie" with a wake in All Saints Church. But the nationwide youth movement was still growing, and images of the hippie Francis would continue for a long time, as we shall see.[29]

The Alternative Church

The Summer of Love was interreligious, but it was also the impetus behind a new kind of Christian community for the times—not an evangelical but a radical one. Once again, the year was 1967. Young travelers were turning up not only in San Francisco, but in the nearby city of Berkeley, around the university campus. As the summer approached, the mainline churches—still the dominant religious presence in the neighborhood—grew concerned. In May they inaugurated the "South Campus Community Ministry" as a social-service project.[30]

The Berkeley churches were not alone in their concern. Loosely speaking, this ministry was part of a "radical" or "underground" church movement that was stirring in the mid-1960s. It was widespread but always a minority. Campus ministries, too, were reshaping themselves in response to the times, with experiments ranging from coffeehouse Communion services to "Freedom Seders." There were new denominational and interdenominational bodies concerned with renewal and outreach to youth. But the Berkeley alternative church was a forerunner and a model. It is an especially clear illustration of the place of St. Francis in these ministries.[31]

The Berkeley group hired Richard L. York, a young Episcopalian minister just out of seminary, who became the central charismatic figure of the new organization. In 1968 two more staff members joined him: Anthony Nugent, a young Presbyterian clergyman, and John Pairman Brown, a former seminary professor. Something of a rebel, Brown had just lost his teaching contract at Church Divinity School of the Pacific. In the new community he functioned as "theologian in residence." His voice and York's gave shape to the thought, practice, ritual, and performance of the group.[32]

By August the project was calling itself the Free Church of Berkeley. "Free" was a code word for "hippie" but also signified liberation in a broader sense. The Free Church saw itself as Christianity for the times— grassroots and ecumenical, a natural movement away from denominational divisions and bureaucracies, flexible and able to respond quickly to contemporary concerns. It developed a loosely organized congregation, a network of like-minded groups, and a series of new liturgies. These dramatized religion and sacralized protest—a kind of practice that the influential Berrigan brothers were also exploring, though in different ways.[33]

Within a year of its founding, Berkeley's "hippie church" was receiving national attention. York's ordination to the priesthood was covered by *Time* magazine and by national wire services. York himself was, ironically, "in demand on the suburban church speaking circuit." More substantively, the Free Church was a leader in the national "underground church" movement that was stirring in many different quarters. Small groups, rethinking Christian practice and theology, looked to the Berkeley church as a model.[34]

For a while it looked promising. The church fed, housed, and counseled hundreds of people. It confronted draft boards, city authorities, and ecclesiastical bureaucracies. It developed community ceremonies and blessed rebellions. By 1971 its directory of the "liberated church" listed 835 contacts—though it construed the notion of "church" very broadly. By that time, though, it was also struggling with internal tensions and lack of funding.[35]

This church of the hippies embraced St. Francis wholeheartedly. The homily about the "cat from Assisi" was one of York's first. St. Francis was also central in the church's "liberation prayer book." He was the first named in the litany, a long ritual invocation of saints and sacred figures. He was the last named in the prayer book, where a version of his canticle concluded an "Earth Rebirth" liturgy. The church's Communion service—the "Freedom Meal"—opened with the peace prayer attributed to Francis. And both Francis and Clare were invoked in shorter prayers.[36]

The prayer book was published in 1971 as *The Covenant of Peace*. Issued by an official church publishing house, it was the last of the Free Church's publications and perhaps a summation of a sort. Its introduction is a concise statement of the church's intentions. The authors present themselves as reformers, not breaking away or founding a new institution, but calling an old one back to its truest self. "We feel an overwhelming urgency," they wrote, "to put together texts that will point a wandering Church back toward its Pole Star." Speaking to the present age, they still grounded their speech in sacred texts and in theological tradition.[37]

The texts—and the book itself—borrow their shape in many ways from the Book of Common Prayer, the Anglican worship book. There is an annual calendar of holy days and commemorations, a litany for use in many different ceremonies, and a collection of prayers. There were rites of passage, such as initiation and marriage, and a separate section devoted to the "freedom meal," a form of Communion.

The theology of the city, too, echoes through these texts. The authors claim that they drew on the voices of ordinary people and the needs of street ministry. Although many of the street people were not so much the "ordinary" poor as hippies and social rebels who had deliberately chosen their way of living, the church was confident that all had common interests and could work together to build a new world—not unlike Francis and his early followers working alongside the involuntarily poor. In reality, the authentic voices of street people may have been filtered or adapted, since many of the church's decisions were channeled through the staff. Still, the authors went far beyond mere sloganeering. They sought to put "the words together into that right order whose highest name is Poetry." In many ways they succeeded.[38]

Their vision of Francis permeates this work. "What we could not improve upon in the tradition, we kept," says the introduction—and Francis's canticle is the first example it names. Their use of the Francis traditions is complex, however. The litany alone invokes several different meanings of Francis. "Bridegroom of poverty, our brother Francis, follower of Jesus and friend of the creation, stand here beside us," it says. The notion of Francis as bridegroom, instead of poverty as bride, is innovative. Here also are the traditions of the animal lover, the imitator of Christ, and the poor Francis. The peace prayer, placed at the beginning of the Communion rite, here evokes freedom and community along with peace. The authors also strengthen its emphasis on peace by rewriting the traditional line "where there is injury, pardon" to read, "where there is violence, let us sow forgiveness."[39]

Their version of the canticle carries their interpretive energy a little farther. While the praises of the natural world stay close to Francis's wording, the later verses on forgiveness and death turn toward a social-protest interpretation. "[God,] be praised by all who pardon, / And who suffer in harassment," they say. Here, Francis's original language—approximately, "all who bear infirmity and tribulation"—becomes "suffer in harassment," a more focused reference to political struggles. "Blessed are all who witness/In peace their lives conducting," it continues, recalling the pacifist ideal of whole-life commitment. The original says more generally, "Blessed are those who endure in peace." Finally, the Free Church version pronounces "woe to all that died in violence," not "mortal sin," as in the original. In this community, violence *is* mortal sin.[40]

In the litany, Francis leads a varied company of holy figures. The litany calls upon pacifists and political radicals, poets, musicians, prophets and church reformers, holy innocents and martyrs. A few transcend categories, like "Madman in America, Johnny Appleseed." Others shake up traditional conceptions: "Unwed mother, blessed Mary;" "inductee of Africa, Simon of Cyrene." Like the litany, the calendar of "saints" includes contemporary and historical figures, some of the latter with fresh interpretations. There we find the traditional "Mark, evangelist"; the thought-provoking "John Wesley and Charles Wesley, street ministers"; and the very recent "Norman Morrison, confessor in flames."[41]

Francis had, of course, appeared on lists of modern saints since the early twentieth century. Unlike these earlier lists, though, this one was not framed as a set of twelve disciples or ten lectures. Instead, it drew on a tradition closer to Catholicism, with space for hundreds of saints in a whole year's calendar. There is a political agenda to this list, but also a breadth of vision and language. Its complex theology was able to incorporate both Karl Barth and Karl Marx.

Like most grassroots movements, the Free Church was unstable. Within a few years, tensions surfaced among its three main goals: social service, political action, and Christian commitment. Nugent left the Free Church in 1970 to develop a different network, the Submarine Church. Even then, the Free Church, like the early hippie movement, was coming undone, struggling with internal conflict over its style, purpose, direction, management, and organization. By 1972 it was effectively defunct. Richard York later wrote that they made the mistake of expecting an imminent revolution, even an eschatological moment. No one was expecting to build an institution. Neither, of course, did St. Francis.[42]

Brother Sun, Sister Moon

It was only then, in the early 1970s, that the mainstream press began to associate St. Francis with hippies. True, there had been a few earlier hints: René Dubos, a scientist and popular writer, mused in 1968, "Was not Francis one of the rebellious youths of his time . . . ? Francis, like Buddha, spent his early years in ease and luxury but rejected bourgeois comforts in search of more fundamental values." The English theologian Norman Pittenger remarked in 1969 that the flower children reminded him of the "little flowers" of St. Francis. "I felt in those odd young people," he wrote, "something of the simplicity, the desire to care, the urgency to love, which characterized followers of the Poverello many centuries ago."[43]

In 1971, however, a popular weekly magazine explicitly declared Francis "the hippie saint." *Look*, a competitor to *Life*, used this title for a piece by its frequent contributor Joseph Roddy, which was quickly picked up for a 1972 anthology. Roddy compared Francis to the young people trying to build a counterculture in "hippie communes"—"the unchurchable young discovering that the owners are themselves fatally owned." He contrasted Francis especially with people of wealth and status—the "success-mongers" and "organization men" of his own time. A writer for the Readers' Digest reiterated these themes as late as 1975.[44]

The 1972 anthology was the same one whose criticism of birdbaths we have already seen. Its editor, the Catholic historian Lawrence Cunningham, reflected on the parallels between Francis and the youth counterculture. Francis rebelled against his businessman father, the wealth and comfort of his upbringing, and social conventions. He adopted "unkempt clothes . . . a life of wandering, a refusal to get a decent job and settle down, and a vague yet determined idea that he could save the world by . . . love and forgiveness." More important, both Francis and the hippies were concerned about the natural environment and skeptical about wealth.[45]

Others were more critical, though. Cunningham himself went on to say that Francis was far more than just a medieval hippie—that he could not be reduced to a "medieval prototype of the 'now' generation." John Holland Smith, a biographer, tossed a few snide remarks about hippies into his life of Francis. For example, he compared the young Francis with affluent twentieth-century youth whose parents are proud of them—"until the day when they drop out, and become flower people, or beautiful people, following cults of their own exhibitionist protests against the world that has given them the best it knows." Such comments were not unusual in the 1960s and 1970s, and Smith was not interested in inventing a conservative Francis, but he both saw and denied the hippie connection.[46]

The ultimate popular-culture expression of Francis as hippie was the 1973 movie *Brother Sun, Sister Moon*. The director, Franco Zeffirelli, intended it that way. "Francis had everything from the Establishment . . . [but he] didn't want any part of all this," he explained. And elsewhere: "The words Francis says to his father are echoed by many young people to their parents nowadays, in Italy, Europe, America . . . ." Indeed, he and several early collaborators had initially wanted to engage the Beatles for the film, with Paul McCartney starring as St. Francis. Although that plan fell through—perhaps fortunately—they claimed that the Beatles "were fascinated with the figure of St. Francis, whose philosophies struck a deep chord with them." In the end, Zeffirelli chose young, little-known actors for the leading roles. Although the movie was not an American expression, the script was in English, and the film was widely seen and reviewed in North America.[47]

Most critics panned it. Gary Arnold of the *Washington Post* called it "kitsch," and Vincent Canby of the *New York Times* called it "a big, absurd doodad . . . that makes saintliness look like an extreme form of Asian flu." For Kevin Kelly of the *Boston Globe*, it was "an outrageous pop-religion tract." A summary in the *Times* counted one positive review, four mixed ones, and nine negative ones.[48]

On the other hand, audiences loved it and still do. In the current Amazon.com reviews of the DVD, people say things like "Beautiful film" and "I saw it for the first time in 1973 and it stayed with me all these years." The Order of Ecumenical Franciscans, founded in 1983, cites it as a reason people seek them out. A prominent writer on animal theology cites it as an early influence. The title of the film has also entered into popular discourse: two different children's books have used it, and a 1986 environmental conference alluded to it.[49]

At least two influential activists found the movie transformative. Philip Mangano, director of the Federal Council on Homelessness for the George W. Bush administration, called it "a spiritual experience" that changed his life. "I just sat there, sobbing," he said later. Mangano was then a successful, "hard-ass" executive in the Los Angeles music industry, but he went on to read more about Francis and eventually returned to his native Boston to serve the homeless poor at a Franciscan shelter.[50]

Jim Wallis gave a deeper testimony. Wallis is well known as a boundary-crossing evangelical, conservative in theology but progressive on many social issues. He is a founder of the Sojourners community, the long-time editor of *Sojourners* magazine, and a prominent speaker and writer. In 1981—around the time of the eight-hundredth anniversary of Francis's birth—he described his early, "shallow impression" of "St. Francis of the birdbath." Sometime in the late 1970s he saw the Zeffirelli movie. "I was completely unprepared for my first meeting with the saint," he wrote. "I left the theater stunned and speechless. On the way home in the dark car, I quietly began to weep. Never before have I encountered a life so consumed with the gospel. . . . His utter obedience to Christ was radiant in exposing the places where my commitment was still compromised. . . . I cried that night because my faith seem so small and weak when compared to his." It appears, then, that the public's reaction was not the same as the critics'.[51]

Whatever its artistic strengths or weaknesses, this film is a thoughtful treatment of Francis's story. Unlike Rossellini's simple realism, Zeffirelli's approach is lavishly visual. The lead actor resembles Cimabue's portrait of Francis, and he is occasionally posed in attitudes that recall Cimabue or Giotto. There are lush landscapes, knightly processions, and richly adorned churches. Canby in fact noted the irony of Zeffirelli's spending millions to represent poverty. But the visual representation is not always pretty: we also see bare feet, dirty skin, and ragged robes. We see the beauty of nature and its harshness in snow and rain; the ruined stone church of San Damiano and the ruined bodies of the poor. Toward the end, we see Francis's bare foot with a wound in it—though the film makes no comment about whether it is a stigma or only an abrasion.

As a "hippie" film, it alludes to a number of contemporary themes. Francis seeks personal freedom and a deeper spiritual freedom. He drops out of mainstream society and lives simply. He and his followers rely on love instead of competition or exploitation. Flowers are a recurring image; nature serves as a metaphor for freedom and honesty. The young men live communally in the countryside. Francis's way of life causes conflict with his parents and with civil and church authorities. The experience of a war is a turning point for young men—in this case Francis himself and also his first follower, who goes crusading in search of glory, but comes home weary and disillusioned with killing. (This character has a historical name, but the story is fictitious.) Perhaps the greatest contemporary theme is youth itself: Zeffirelli uses very young actors, and they sometimes look like a group of hippies with long hair and shabby clothing. Though these Franciscan hippies are privileged dropouts, they also labor in the fields, beg in the streets, and endure suffering. Figure 11 illustrates the encounter of youth with authority and of simplicity with pomp.

Where it most reflects hippie sensibility is in Francis's resistance to materialism and money. The film invents a narrative in which Francis gradually learns where his father's wealth came from—the spoils of war and the exploitation of impoverished workers. Dressed in gray, he wanders among lengths of newly dyed fabric, gradually taking the colors upon himself. In subsequent scenes, color becomes a symbol of wealth. Finally Francis begins flinging lengths of finished fabric out of the tower window to the street below. It is a joyful gesture; he is happy as he shouts, "Throw it away! You don't need this!" "This won't make you happy!" This theme—"throw it away; it won't make you happy"—sets the tone for the rest of the film.

Like other works of fiction, then, this film seeks to present the "essence" or "spirit" of St. Francis. For Zeffirelli, this essence is poverty and joy. While the poverty is made visual, the joy is enacted: an actor can convey a happiness that is, perhaps, easy to miss in written texts. Not only an enactment, but the sense of place is important in the film's understanding of Francis: many of the symbolically charged outdoor landscapes were filmed in Umbria. The film also includes a number of biographical allusions for those who know about them—for example, Francis's weak com-

FIGURE 11 Francis and the brothers meet Pope Innocent III. Still from the film *Brother Sun, Sister Moon*, 1973. The young brothers, in simple garb and bare feet, contrast with the age, wealth, and institutional power in the papal court.
© Paramount Pictures. All rights reserved.

mand of Latin, the problem of establishing a rule, and a pun on the name of Pope Innocent.

Theologically, the film is more interested in true Christianity than in universalizing Francis. Despite their conflicts with authority, the characters articulate their vision in Christian and Catholic terms. Francis has a vision of Christ in the course of his conversion, and Pope Innocent III has a vision of Christ during his encounter with Francis. When Francis must explain himself to a bejeweled bishop who berates him about the "established order," Francis quotes the Gospel of Mark about leaving his father, mother, and fields. The film makes clear that the institutional church has lost its way, yet in a moment of trouble, Francis affirms his obedience and seeks counsel from Rome. Once there, however, he throws away—again—a carefully prepared Latin speech provided by a friend. Instead he recites the Sermon on the Mount. Indeed, he essentially performs it, as if it were a spontaneous expression. Clearly the filmmaker— who had relatively recently been "reconverted to Catholicism"—is making a point about the true meaning of Christ and Christianity. If it is not an entirely new point, it is at least realized in a new way.[52]

Ecology

In the *annus mirabilis* 1967, an article appeared in the academic journal *Science* and, in slightly different form, in *Horizon*. It was based on a paper presented in late 1966 at the annual meeting of the American Association for the Advancement of Science by the historian Lynn White. White argued that the "historical roots of our ecologic crisis," as he called it, lay in Western Christian thought and culture—beginning with the biblical commands to "subdue" the earth and to "have dominion" over it. Toward the end of the paper, he speculated about cultural alternatives and role models for the modern West. "I propose Francis," the paper concluded, "as a patron saint for ecologists."[53]

White's argument was a turning point in the discussion of ecology, religion, and American culture. One contemporary source noted that "this article has aroused widespread discussion. It has echoed through academic publications. It has come to the ears of the world at large and is to be found discussed in the pages of such diverse journals as *The New York Times* and the *Oracle*, the latter a . . . hippie newspaper." It was the first selection in the first Earth Day handbook, a 400-page compendium, in 1970. One witness remembers its being passed from hand to hand among Harvard students. It was reprinted often in the early 1970s and has reappeared regularly since then.[54]

White began by tracing the growing awareness of the environment and the science of ecology since the publication of Rachel Carson's *Silent Spring* in 1962. He argued that the key factor in ecological destruction was the marriage of science and technology. Each had a long and complex history—science as an intellectual exercise, technology as a practical necessity. The key was their union. White argued that this happened in the global West and not elsewhere because of the way Christianity shaped Western thought and culture. Central among these cultural underpinnings was the idea that humanity has the authority to "subdue" the earth and the power to name the creatures. In addition, Latin Christianity emphasized moral action, as opposed to the emphasis on contemplation in Eastern Christianity. Thus the stage was set; and White argued that technological change spread through Western Europe with the spread of Christianity. Centuries later, the consequence is environmental degradation.

We need, then, a different worldview, said White. Zen Buddhism might be a possibility, but he doubted its staying power in the West.

St. Francis, however, "proposed what he thought was an alternative Christian view of nature and man's relation to it." The most important feature of this alternative was humility, White argued: Francis rejected human dominance and recognized the equality of all creatures. In other words, White offered an alternative worldview and attitude that were nonetheless rooted in Christian Europe—and were therefore authentic, not artificial or grafted on, for European and North American society.

White was off base in some respects. Most historians today would reject his claims that Francis was a heretic and that he believed in the "animal soul." White also speculated needlessly about connections between Francis and the Cathar movement. But his points about humility and equality are reasonable, and his interpretation of Francis was a very far-reaching one.[55]

"Ecology" was a relatively new concept. For most of the twentieth century, the dominant model for nature lovers and policymakers was conservation. As practiced by well-established organizations like the Audubon Society and the Sierra Club, it was largely an upper-class concern with little popular following. By the early 1960s, though, perceptions were beginning to shift. Prosperity and the hopeful Camelot era coincided with a growing awareness of pollution and exploitation of resources. *Silent Spring* was quickly followed by the Leopold Report on the decline of wilderness. A reform-minded Congress passed the Wilderness Act easily in 1964.[56]

At the same time, a generation of children raised on outdoor recreation for youth—Scouting, the suburban outdoors, and summer camps—was coming of age. Later observers even saw a connection between the environmentalist movement and *Rabbit Hill*—not too surprising, perhaps, if we consider the generation who grew up reading it. "Lawson outlines an early message of ecological interdependence," said editor Anita Silvey. Biographer Gary Schmidt concurred: Lawson's vision, he says, reflects "an empathetic relationship with the natural world." Characters, roles, and setting "all point to the union of the human and animal, union made possible by the recognition that there is enough for all."[57]

In Christian circles, environmental discussion was already under way. Since the early 1960s, a group of mostly younger theologians had been meeting as the Faith-Man-Nature Group to explore the issues. Several of the members went on to be significant theologians of science, nature, and ecology, among them Ian Barbour, Richard Baer, and Paul Santmire. But White's article moved the discussion into high gear. The group's conference in November 1967 was its most energetic yet, and it issued three essay collections over the next five years. It also shifted its focus from conservation to ecology and crisis.[58]

These theologians, and others, brought environmental concerns into theological discussions. Richard L. Means, a Faith-Man-Nature member, noted in 1968 that the radical theology of the day—the existentialist and Death of God theologies—mostly ignored nature. We now need to fill that "vacuum," he wrote. In early 1969, Richard Baer called conservation "an area for the church's action." The word "ecology" appears quite suddenly in the indexes of the *Christian Century* in that year. And in 1970 Ian Barbour proposed an "ecological ethic," pointing to theologians who emphasized the "organic interdependence of all creatures," such as Alfred North Whitehead and Teilhard de Chardin. Much of this discussion sounds familiar in the twenty-first century.[59]

Although many of these works mention St. Francis, he remains in the background. This is largely because the authors—like many progressive Protestants of their day—were more interested in the formal domains of theology and ethics than in piety or spirituality. It is also because Francis was, as Richard Baer put it, an "isolated figure." "Whom else can we point to?" he asked, perhaps bitterly.[60]

We should also note that White's article generated criticism, defensiveness, and soul-searching among Christian thinkers. They questioned his biblical scholarship, his sweeping thesis about Western civilization, and, not least, his understanding of Francis. The theologian John B. Cobb thought Albert Schweitzer was a better contemporary exemplar than St. Francis, while the scientist René Dubos preferred St. Benedict's model of stewardship to Franciscan "identification with nature" and "worship of nature." Roger L. Shinn noted Francis's distrust of the body and sexuality, hardly an affirmation of nature. As Eugene Hargrove put it fifteen years later, "the general response to White's position was overwhelmingly defensive" and ultimately ended in stalemate.[61]

Perhaps the most significant treatment of Francis was a groundbreaking book by the young theologian H. Paul Santmire, *Brother Earth: Nature, God, and Ecology in Time of Crisis*. This provocatively titled volume was one of the first book-length efforts to develop a Christian ecological theology. Influenced by Reformation and neo-Orthodox thought, Santmire proposed an "ethic of responsibility" guided by a vision of the Kingdom of God. Santmire rejected not only exploitation and manipulation of nature but also romantic nature worship and the "cult of the simple rustic life."[62]

In this context Santmire both affirms and criticizes ecologists' devotion to St. Francis. He agrees with these colleagues that Francis is almost unique in Western history. And yet, he says, "Francis remains unreal." He continues, "No one in his right mind would preach to the birds today. Few of even the most passionate nature-lovers truly consider the sun and the bears and the ants to be truly their brothers and sisters." Santmire proposes a Kingdom of God theology that would allow us to "salvage" some of these "Franciscan motifs." This theology would recognize that humans are a part of nature, and at the same time that they transcend it—through their divinely ordained power, creativity, wisdom, and wonder. Santmire is almost more Franciscan than Francis here: he rejects the term "Mother Earth," which Francis himself used, because it implies too strong an identification of humans with nature. But to call the earth "brother," as Francis called the sun and other natural things, is to imply the balance of unity and transcendence that Santmire advocates.[63]

Santmire also evokes Francis by challenging wealth. "Do we need all those power-hungry air conditioners for example?" he asks. "Do we need that air-poisoning second car? What about the first car?" We should "remember St. Francis today, not only as the one who called all his fellow creatures brother and sister, but also as the one who, following Jesus, shaped his life by poverty." He asks whether we can say "Brother Earth" without also saying "Lady Poverty" and concludes, "That is a question every affluent disciple of Jesus must ponder today." And it remains a familiar question in the twenty-first century.[64]

Perhaps the end of this trajectory, a coda to the Christian theological discussion, was the assertion that Francis was a "nature mystic." This is an idea that still survives. Edward Armstrong, an ornithologist, first made the case for it in 1976. He argued that Francis was a genuine nature mystic—a person who experienced and expressed love of God through nature—and by extension, that Christian nature mysticism was possible.[65]

Most of Armstrong's text is a close reading of the stories about St. Francis and animals. Indeed, Armstrong is most compelling when he writes as a naturalist, briskly assessing the accuracy of the legends in terms of real animal behavior.[66] Less convincingly, he searches for parallels to the legends about St. Francis in earlier Christian folklore and hagiography.

Most of his examples come from Celtic sources, which are only tenuously connected with Francis and Italy. Armstrong himself seems uncertain about what was transmitted through folklore, as distinct from universal patterns of human thought. In the end, he simply affirms the popular view of Francis as "a warm and lovable personality" whose "loving sympathy for all aspects of creation invigorated his insight."[67]

Earth Day and Beyond

The first Earth Day took place with widespread participation on April 22, 1970. It was intended to be "the first national environmental teach-in"—a creative effort in mass education. To that end the organizers compiled the *Environmental Handbook*—a collection of articles, directories, and suggestions for action, finally issued by a trade publisher. It covered topics as diverse as wilderness preservation, overpopulation, recycling, car travel, and a proposed supersonic aircraft. "A year ago," observed one contributor, "hardly anybody in the United States knew what ecology meant. Today almost everybody has at least a sense of it."[68]

Lynn White's article—with its critiques of Western civilization, Christianity, science, and technology—appeared near the beginning. His proposal of St. Francis as patron of ecology cannot have gone unheard, given the wide reach of this book. The rest of the book barely mentioned either Francis or religion, however, focusing instead on the need to change civilization. The only significant exception came from the Berkeley Ecology Center, which supplied a list of helpful "social and religious forces." Christianity was conspicuously absent, except for Quakers and "Teilhard de Chardin Catholics." In 1970, the groundswell of religious interest was turning elsewhere, even as the Christian theological discussion of ecology was just beginning to heat up.[69]

The major nature writers of the era, too, all seem to have drifted away from the conventional Christianity of their childhoods. Aldo Leopold, Rachel Carson, Wendell Berry, and Edward Abbey were all raised in some form of American Protestantism, but none continued to practice it, although its traces can sometimes be discerned in their work. Abbey did refer directly to St. Francis, but treated him more as a common cultural figure than as a personally meaningful one. A character in a semi-autobiographical Abbey novel mentions Francis alongside Mahatma Gandhi and Mother Teresa as saintly figures to whom he can't measure up. The peace prayer serves as the epigraph to Abbey's memoir *One Life at a Time, Please*, but readers are left to discern its meaning for themselves, as he never mentions Francis again.[70]

Across Generations

Everyone—the novelists, the historians, the science commentators, the hippies—knew by now that Francis was not just garden statuary. The private garden and the carefully preserved conservation lands continued to be important. But in this period, American culture added an ecological sensibility—a sense of systems, interactions, and relationships—whether these were interpreted scientifically or more intuitively. Those who thought about St. Francis reinterpreted him in the environmentalist mode. Along with the Audubon Society, the vision of Francis began to make the transition from conservation to ecology. As Paul Santmire put it, "The patron saint of modern devotees of nature is St. Francis." In the 1980s, as we shall see, that devotion took on a new dimension—the "animal turn" in intellectual disciplines and the "blessing of the animals" service in popular religious practice.[71]

For American society in the sixties, Francis functioned as a sign of authenticity across generations. He was a known and beloved figure who could also be called upon to justify change; he stood both within and against the received tradition. For hippies, he embodied liberation and love, a new society, past and present; for older adults, he explained what their children were up to. For dissenting churches, he was evidence of their claim to true Christian heritage. For early ecologists, he offered an authentic critique of Western civilization because he came from within the tradition, and an authentic alternative because he stood outside it.

CHAPTER SEVEN

Blessing the Animals

In 1985 the Cathedral of St. John the Divine celebrated the feast of St. Francis. The music for the service was the *Missa Gaia*, or *Earth Mass*, written in 1982 by jazz composer Paul Winter. It opened with a version of St. Francis's Canticle of the Sun, in place of the usual Gloria, and went on to blend traditional texts of the Mass with world music and the recorded sounds of wild animals. The service ended with the St. Francis peace prayer. Then the celebrant called for silence. The great bronze cathedral doors—until then opened only on Christmas and Easter—swung open to admit a procession of animals, domestic and wild, local and exotic, to be blessed at the altar. In the pews, dogs and a few other pets sat with their humans. These animals were individually blessed in the church precincts afterward.[1]

The "blessing of the animals" service has since become a fixture in American religion. While St. John's was not the first, it was the most spectacular and surely had the biggest impact among non-Catholics. It built on well-known cultural conceptions of St. Francis, on the environmentalist movement, and on a rising cultural interest in animals, and it went on to generate a widespread practice. Recently, Jews, Buddhists, and secular charities have also offered animal blessings—often detached from references to Francis.

Beyond the blessing of animals, the period from 1980 onward has seen extensive interest in St. Francis. Publication patterns have followed the pattern of events. The year 1982 was widely observed as the eight-hundredth anniversary of Francis's birth. As with the earlier anniversaries, the occasion generated numerous articles, books, art exhibits, and other reviews of his life and meaning, as well as gestures like a U.S. postage stamp. Through the next decade and a half, there was a slow but steady stream of historical works, personal reflections, and interfaith explorations, both within and outside the United States. In a later chapter we will look more closely at events after the mid-1990s.[2]

The trends of the 1980s established patterns that continued into the twenty-first century. Ideas about Francis followed developments in

Christian thought, practice, and affiliation. Interfaith and post-Christian constructions became more important. The image of Francis as a saint of nature and the environment evolved in a number of different ways. Americans explored counternarratives about gender, power, and material display, as well as irony, humor, and joy. These and other tendencies are reflected in the blessing of the animals—perhaps the most significant innovation of the era.

American Culture in the Late Twentieth Century

After the exhaustion of the Vietnam era, and the inward turning of the late 1970s, the election of Ronald Reagan in 1980 ushered in a new period of American conservatism. Economic policies brought a new wave of prosperity, even extravagance, which did not outlast the decade. The American public grew increasingly polarized on both political and social issues, breaking along roughly the same lines as it did during the Vietnam era.

In American Christianity, the evangelical resurgence of the 1970s proved to be a long-term trend. After 1980, evangelical churches and communities continued to grow. They developed strong political networks and became an established presence in the American cultural scene. Pentecostalism also grew in size and influence, both in the United States and around the world. Mainline denominations, meanwhile, slowly but steadily lost members and institutional power, although their long-term influence on American society is still being assessed. At the same time, there was a growing openness between Protestants and Catholics. Vatican II had opened the Catholic Church to ecumenical contact. Evangelicals were developing a growing interest in history, and they also found a culture-war ally in the Catholic Church. Liberals found fresh ideas on social witness and spiritual life.

Christianity grew and changed on the left as well as the right. In theological circles, the most significant movement was liberation theology, which emerged from Latin America Catholicism but attracted wide interest in the global North. It built on the stirrings of liberation movements worldwide—far beyond the liberationist hippie church of the 1960s—and on the reforms of Vatican II, but above all, on the everyday reality of poverty and social dislocation. At the same time, lay Christians renewed their interest in "spirituality"—in the inward and experiential side of faith.

Growing numbers of Americans also turned away from organized religion altogether, identifying themselves as "spiritual but not religious," or as having no religion. "New Age" spirituality blended many old and new influences with common themes of personal spiritual experience, harmony with the natural world, and the ability to shape events through spiritual practices. Americanized forms of Buddhism exerted increasing influence in liberal circles, though the numbers of formal adherents were relatively small. Increasingly, individuals pieced together their own beliefs and practices out of diverse sources, whether or not they maintained a formal religious affiliation.

The Last Hippies

The 1980s began with the last remnants of the hippie era. Adolf Holl's resonant title *The Last Christian*—and his idea of St. Francis—could well have been "the last hippie" or "the last liberal." His Francis is one who rejects his parents, the bourgeois mentality, and indeed the very "forces of modernity." In the anniversary year 1982, the radical Bread and Puppet Theater dedicated its large summer festival to St. Francis—a Francis who preaches to the potatoes, discusses draft resistance, and "tells us that the sun is our brother and the toothbrush is our sister." He shows us the way out of "a domestic mud puddle of gigantic proportions."[3]

Sojourners, Jim Wallis's progressive-evangelical magazine, observed the anniversary with a special issue that also recalled hippie critiques. "It's so easy to be a 'radical Christian' in America," Wallis wrote. "Here the church is so affluent, so comfortable, so lukewarm, that the most basic kind of discipleship or the simplest acts of justice, mercy, and peace seem extraordinary by comparison." Quoting the story about "true and perfect joy"—in which Francis imagined being thrown out into the cold—Wallis suggested that Francis could speak to our confusion of obedience with success, "a particularly American affliction." In another article, the historian Glenn Hinson insisted on Francis as peacemaker. Using familiar pacifist language, he claimed that Francis "fought against war and its causes" and, again, valued faithfulness over success. Tellingly, most of the remaining essays in the special issue were written by Roman Catholics, including the popular singer John Michael Talbot and the Benedictine writer Joan Chittister. Richard Rohr, a popular Franciscan writer today, invoked the usual anti-institutional shibboleths of theology, ideology, denominations, judgment, and worshiping Jesus instead of "being" him.[4]

Evangelicals

Wallis was not alone. Around 1980, the evangelical world was beginning to embrace Francis. College students had seen Zeffirelli's movie. "All Creatures" was making its way into conservative hymnals. In the early 1980s, *Christianity Today*, the flagship evangelical magazine, published two articles about Francis, apparently for the first time in its history. Twenty years later, a conservative Christian publisher issued a biography of Francis written by Mark Galli, then the magazine's editor. Later, in 2006, a novel presented Francis as an alternative model for a burned-out megachurch pastor. The persistent thread throughout these works is the vision of Francis as a person who truly lived his Christian faith—a vision much like that of early mainliners and liberals.[5]

The *Christianity Today* articles suggest that evangelicals were already encountering Francis in church and in the wider culture. The first article, in 1982, began by noting that everyone knows the peace prayer, and added, "His hymn text for 'All Creatures' is sung in churches everywhere." But the writer adds, "Few, however, know much about" Francis. This article covered a popular one-man play about Francis performed by a Catholic actor who seems to have been inspired by the movie, since he "dances through the fields, welcoming Brother Sun and Sister Moon." The actor made a somewhat different comment: Francis, he said, "is a fundamentalist in the true sense of the word." The second piece, in 1985, was about John Michael Talbot, a famous figure in Christian pop music. Talbot had explored evangelicalism in the 1970s, but had ultimately converted to Roman Catholicism and founded a Franciscan-style intentional community. One of his earliest songs was a setting of the peace prayer. Talbot's reach as a popular musician was such that thousands of people knew of his neo-Franciscan life, and the photograph accompanying the article showed him in his brown robe, playing the guitar. The article glossed over his Catholicism, though, focusing instead on his biblical perspective and his vision of the church as community. Both of these stories present Francis as an acceptable model for evangelicals because of his unrestrained commitment to the Gospel.[6]

Within two decades, Francis was familiar enough to evangelicals that Mark Galli could set out once again to find the "real" St. Francis. "Everyone loves Francis," Galli began. "His statue (usually with a bird on his arm) is found in gardens all across the world. His example is touted as much needed in our day. Francis, the patron saint of ecology. Francis, the peacemaker. Unfortunately, in our attempt to make Francis relevant, the man we have come to love resembles only a distant relative of the real Francis." This Francis, then, was neither a birdbath nor a liberal.[7]

Galli's was, however, a fairly conventional account of Francis, built on standard historical sources. Notably, he did not insist that Francis was a proto-Protestant; he was careful to show how Francis was embedded in his Roman Catholic world. But he provided signals that would speak to his evangelical audience, using the language of Bible, mission, and obedience to God. He wrote, for example, that nature was not an abstract idea for Francis: "he took his cues from the Bible." Francis engaged in "evangelization of pagan lands" and "foreign missionary work." "Spiritual experiences" such as visions, on the other hand, mattered less than service and obedience to God. "The real St. Francis," Galli concluded, "makes every age a tad uncomfortable."[8]

Music

Evangelicals, Catholics, and mainliners all contributed to new musical expressions in this era. By far the most significant classical work was Olivier Messiaen's opera *Saint François d'Assise* (1983), a long and difficult composition devoted to contemplation more than to drama. In the mainline churches, there was movement toward gender-inclusive, non-hierarchical language, and this generated at least two new paraphrases of the hymn "All Creatures."[9]

But the peace prayer became a crossover phenomenon, among Christian churches and outside them. It was adapted for singing in at least two popular versions, both of which have appeared in evangelical, mainline, and Roman Catholic collections across the English-speaking world. Both originated outside American Protestantism: "Lord, Make Us Servants," by the Scottish Jesuit James Quinn (1919–2010), and "Make Me a Channel of Your Peace," by Sebastian Temple (1928–97), a Third Order Franciscan from South Africa. While Quinn's version is constructed like a hymn—four stanzas with the same meter and melody—Temple's is more like a pop ballad, with three stanzas and a "bridge" variation. Written in the late 1960s, they have appeared in printed hymnals from 1979 onward.[10]

These adaptations have also been widely recorded and performed for the general public. Temple's version was sung at the funeral of Diana, Princess of Wales. British pop star Susan Boyle and rebellious Irish singer Sinead O'Connor—a vocal critic of the Catholic Church—have also recorded it. In addition, the Canadian singer-songwriter Sarah McLachlan released her own musical setting of the prayer text in 1997.[11]

Roman Catholics and Post-Christians

In 1980 an account of Francis's life appeared in a new form—a Marvel comic book. Marvel was one of the foremost producers of "superhero" comics, aimed primarily at adult audiences. At the initiative of several Franciscan leaders, the publisher agreed to produce a comic book in honor of Francis's anniversary. Roy Gasnick, OFM, a communications specialist for the Franciscans, and Marvel's writer Mary Jo Duffy prepared the text; Marvel's staff provided illustrations and distribution. The final product—*Francis, Brother of the Universe*—drew considerable attention. *Publisher's Weekly* claimed that "European publishers were mesmerized."[12]

The Francis of the comic book takes another step away from the "hippie Francis" of the previous era. Unlike hippie imagery, the book's visual language is distinctly masculine-gendered—that is, it draws on and refers to social constructions of maleness and masculinity. It opens with an image of a craggy-faced Francis praying in agony before a rocky cliff, and it dwells on scenes of battle and danger. In a climactic image, the stigmata "are transmitted from the figure on the cross *zzzaapp*! to Francis—who, like comic-book heroes everywhere, exclaims, 'Uuhhh!' " The rough wooden cross and the muscular Christ add to the masculine impact. The imagery also speaks of power. Strong, laser-like rays connect the two heroic figures, with points of contact resembling explosions or electric shocks. Francis is fully awake, not lost in ecstasy (see figure 12). In all these ways, the comic book implicitly draws the reader away from the imagery of the hippie Francis—the San Francisco mystic devoted to love and universal spirituality, or the young, sweet-faced brother of the 1973 movie.[13]

But some influences of the 1960s continued to unfold. In the early 1980s, Leonardo Boff offered a serious new reading of Francis. Boff was a major figure in liberation theology, an important Roman Catholic movement that also attracted the attention of American Protestants. Developed by Latin American theologians, liberation theology was an effort to "do theology" by beginning from the standpoint of the poor and integrating thought with practice. Like Progressive-era Christian socialists, these theologians analyzed systems and structures and critiqued the disparities in wealth that capitalism produced. What emerged was a

FIGURE 12 John Buscema and Marie Severin. Francis receiving the stigmata. This heroic image is from the Marvel comic book *Francis: Brother of the Universe*, 1980. © Marvel Entertainment, 1980. Used by permission.

guiding ideal of liberation—as a biblical theme, as an image of Christ, and as a life goal.

Boff (1938–), a Franciscan priest and seminary professor, argued that Francis modeled many of the practices of liberation. He identified with the poor and with the marginalized, not just "helping" them but sharing their lives. In so doing he identified with Christ, who became poor by choice. Francis also refused to dominate, to place himself above anyone or anything. In this very personal way, he resisted power structures, including human domination of nature. Boff's Francis did not want to overturn or leave the Catholic Church. But he did refuse its material and spiritual power. He remained firmly situated in his "base"—the community of the poor—which was marginal and nonconformist. Boff observes insightfully that Francis did not receive a vision of Christ until he had lived with the poor, and he did not sing the Canticle of the Sun until nearly the end of his life of self-giving. "To begin where Francis ended," he writes, "is a disastrous illusion."[14]

At the same time, a different kind of Roman Catholic was attracting a popular following among non-Catholics. This was Matthew Fox, then a Dominican priest, who was developing what he called "creation-centered spirituality." In place of the orthodox framework of sin, fall, and atonement, Fox proposed a narrative of creation, blessing, and mystical experience. This narrative offered a way to incorporate into Christian faith many changes of the previous twenty years—Earth Day, feminist spirituality, Catholic ecumenical outreach, and, not least, accessible psychotherapy that affirmed one's personal goodness. In many ways, of course, Fox was restating the "seeker" ideas that resurface regularly in American spiritual life. Still, many restless Christians found his intuitive and nonlinear voice appealing.[15]

For Fox, Francis was second only to Jesus. He showed this most vividly in a chart that ranked historic figures on a scale of 1 to 5 for the "fullness" of a creation-centered spirituality. Francis, Meister Eckhart, and Hildegard of Bingen each got four stars. Jesus got five. No one else ranked above 3.5. But this is Jesus—and Francis—as seen through the lens of Fox's creation spirituality. Thus the Canticle of the Sun is "a celebration of the ancient cosmology and its physics of earth, air, fire (light), and water." It arose from a mystical "empty space deep within" Francis, and incorporates themes such as divine motherhood, male-female balance, and healing. Fox, no historian, argues that Francis was a panentheist and that he was influenced by both Celtic and Sufi traditions. He later wrote that "we" had denied Francis's sense of cosmic unity by "locking him up in birdbaths."[16]

Fox's "creation-centered" idea of Francis pointed toward a post-Christian construction of Francis. Of course, the idea of Francis as a figure who transcended Christianity had a long history, as we have seen. But in this era, it appeared more frequently and consistently. Religious pluralism was increasing, and the New Age was flourishing. So it is not too surprising to find, in 2000, the evangelical Tony Campolo describing a new kind of "spiritual revival" for readers of the progressive Jewish magazine *Tikkun*. This was not a traditional revival, he said, but a postmodern, anti-institutional spirituality encompassing "mystical environmentalism" and a "personalistic rapport with nature." Campolo offered Francis as one of its exemplars. Similarly, Adrian House's 2001 biography of Francis carried a foreword by Karen Armstrong, an advocate for interfaith action and antiauthoritarian skepticism. She emphasized Francis's broad appeal—both spiritual and secular. These visions of Francis continued to develop over the next three decades.[17]

Environmentalists

In the late twentieth century, the environmentalist movement both "matured" and fragmented. From the unified wave of enthusiasm that came with the first Earth Day, and the first wave of recognition of the problem, the movement spread out in multiple directions, including legal action, radical disruption, and organic farming. The movement encountered significant challenges during the Reagan era, both from the federal government itself and from a broader backlash against environmental regulation. Yet events repeatedly called for a new focus on the environment, from the Love Canal chemical leaks in 1980 to the Exxon *Valdez* oil spill in 1989. The threat of global warming was first identified in 1988. Bill McKibben's seminal work *The End of Nature* came out the next year. So by 1990, with the twentieth anniversary of the first Earth Day, the movement was gathering new strength.

By this time the connection between Francis and environmentalism was firmly cemented. Pope John Paul II officially declared Francis the patron saint of ecology in 1979. An American naturalist launched an international effort to save the birds of Assisi in 1983. Other institutions and publications carried the work forward; for example, the National Council of Churches started an "Eco-justice working group" in 1983.[18]

In 1986, when a British conservation organization decided to enlist religion in environmental action, it invoked sense of place: it organized an international conference in Assisi. Though the conference had few direct effects, it attracted worldwide attention and served as a benchmark for religious environmental activists. It clearly constructed Francis as an environmentalist. The American journalist Lis Harris, writing in *The New Yorker*, observed that nearly every speaker at the conference mentioned Francis's Canticle of the Sun "as if it were a kind of ecological catechism." She found this "dispiriting," as the participants' real interests seemed to be bureaucratic procedures and official statements. Far more inspiring, she thought, were the ragtag "pilgrims" who arrived on foot with banners and posters in the rain—and who were rather coolly received. The conference ended with a ceremony in the basilica that was intended to be interfaith, though with limited success.[19]

Not long afterward, the historian Roger Sorrell reconsidered the question of Francis and nature. His 1988 book *St. Francis of Assisi and Nature*, a landmark work, went far beyond Armstrong's early effort in this area. Sorrell tried to trace all possible sources for Francis's thought and practice and to understand what Francis did that was original or innovative.[20]

Interestingly, he argued that the most significant documents were the old favorites, the sermon to the birds and the Canticle of the Sun. He proposed that they brought together a number of influences: Francis's own love of creation, older traditions descended from hermits and ascetics, biblical texts that call on creation to praise God, and an evangelistic impulse. Sorrell's understanding of the canticle depends on reading the crucial word "per" as "for" rather than "by" or "through"—as in, for example, "Be praised, my Lord, *for* Sir Brother Sun." This is not only an admonition to human beings, he argues, but is also an early ecological statement. It points to the intrinsic value of the world as created by God, apart from human needs. In turn, this valuation of the world shaped Francis's innovative mysticism—a kind of threefold communion of nature, humanity, and God. Sorrell's linguistic point is controversial. If he is right, though, it would mean, among other things, that Draper's hymnic paraphrase is all wrong.

The canticle continued to be an important touchstone for environmentalists. It served as an epigraph for the *Green Bible* of 2008. And it began and ended Paul Winter's musical setting for the blessing of the animals ceremony.[21]

Another Environment

In 1987 a very different interpretation of Francis and nature attracted a crowd in San Francisco. In that year the Los Angeles designer Tony Duquette (1914–99) purchased an abandoned synagogue and remade the whole interior in honor of St. Francis. "Pull open the malachite doors set in the Byzantine mosaic and you have arrived," Duquette wrote. "Inside the Duquette Pavilion . . . awaits a world of wonder and mystery based on the Canticle of Creatures of St. Francis of Assisi. Needing a permanent home for my massive 25 foot tall angel sculptures and being inspired by the legend of St. Francis, I decided to design and build a 'celebrational environment' to honor San Francisco's patron saint."[22]

One commentator called the main space "the Hall of Dropped Jaws." The ceiling light was a forty-foot-diameter gold sunburst. "Pillars, towers, standards and stupas shimmer everywhere," Duquette later wrote. "Brother Sun is radiant in the dome, and the great angels come and go as the lighting changes." Another sunburst, transformed from the pipes of the synagogue's organ, was suspended above a human-sized statue of St. Francis, clothed in green leaves and accompanied by trees full of ceramic birds. At the entrance, a double-tailed mermaid with a filigree skin held a convex mirror. Nearby were doors glittering with crushed abalone shell. The design incorporated natural objects like shells and tree roots, along with found objects like golf balls, salad servers, and "a dozen plastic bedpans, sliced in half and painted gold."[23]

Clearly, this is a very different vision of Francis from that of Bread and Puppet or the Assisi conference. In one respect, of course, it is simply the expression of one man's personal devotion and aesthetics. "I've always been totally involved with St. Francis," Duquette told a reporter. A visual thinker, he was especially drawn to Francis's canticle and its "evocative 'Brother Son, Sister Moon' reference," as a colleague put it, echoing the movie title again. He also thought of Francis as "the first hippie." Baptized a Catholic, Duquette had long had a universalistic spirituality, and he loved mystery, splendor, and wonder. The style of the pavilion is typical of his work, a large opus of interior and stage design. Perhaps it also appealed to the extravagant materialism of the 1980s.[24]

In another sense, Duquette's pavilion is the far extreme of the cultural construction of Francis as a saint of nature. The operating symbols are sun, moon, cosmos, birds, natural objects. There is no poverty, no stigmatization, no sacrament or church: the intent is brotherhood and oneness with the universe. Even the use of nature has a constructed quality, and a bit of ironic humor, because most of the natural objects are crafted, worked, gilded, painted, or otherwise altered.

But perhaps the most distinctive feature of this work—and a surprisingly uncommon one—is the element of joy. Duquette describes the pavilion in words like "beautiful," "magical," "radiant," "thrilling," "splendor," "festive," and "smile." According to the *Los Angeles Times*, tens of thousands of people saw the pavilion in its first few months, and they, too, called it "magic" and "celestial." If it did not capture Francis's poverty, it did capture—and embody and express—his wholeheartedness and generosity. G. K. Chesterton might have approved.[25]

Blessing the Animals

The Blessing of the Animals is a short novel for older children published by a mainstream house in 2000. It tells the story of a lonely Jewish boy whose Roman Catholic friend invites him (and his dog, of course) to a blessing of animals on St. Francis's day. "He [the Jewish boy] certainly knew about St. Francis—how could anyone not know about St. Francis?" says the narrator. "All his neighbors in the country even had figurines of the saint in their yards." The invitation is the occasion for the boy to explore larger questions of faith and identity. In the end, after much soul-searching, he decides not to go to the Catholic service. This story is interesting for several reasons. It suggests that St. Francis is generally known and that animal blessings are a familiar practice. But it is especially striking because the blessing of animals here plays the role once taken by the Christmas tree—the tempting Christian attraction that threatens to draw the Jewish child away from his people and heritage.[26]

The "blessing of animals" service has become commonplace since the 1980s. Listings on Lexis-Nexis, for example, show only 33 animal blessings between 1985 and 1990, but over 150 in 2013 alone. These are not complete lists of events, of course, but they give a rough idea of how the popularity of the blessing service has grown. More qualitative measures tell the same story. The Web site eHow, built on users' contributions, includes a section on how to hold an animal blessing. Numerous recent books offer guidelines and sample liturgies. Offhand references to animal blessings assume that the reader is acquainted with the practice.[27]

Few animal-blessing services are as extravagant or extensive as the one at St. John the Divine. More typical Protestant congregations are likely to offer short services in a traditional style. They will usually include Bible readings and prayers; they may add a hymn or two, a short sermon, a litany, a responsive reading, or a general blessing; and there is usually an individual blessing for each animal (see figure 13). The biblical text is likely to be one of the many that speak of creation—whether the divine act of creation or the created world of land, water, plants, and animals. Many services are devoted specifically to pets, while some are careful to refer to all kinds of animals.[28]

Interfaith services are more variable. They may include readings from sacred or secular sources, various types of prayers and invocations, and perhaps music or performance. One account of a blessing ceremony— held in October, near the feast day of St. Francis—mentions an indigenous Central American rite and a prayer of Albert Schweitzer. A popular sourcebook for animal blessings concentrates almost entirely on the logistics of the event, remarking vaguely that a "spiritual leader" usually offers the words of blessing.[29]

The origins of animal-blessing services are not entirely clear. Their present form owes a great deal to the service at St. John the Divine, and it is entirely possible that St. John's staff came up with the idea independently. But there were earlier precedents.[30]

To begin with, Roman Catholics have long had a practice of blessing practical things, such as buildings, tools, and vehicles. Roman Catholics have also historically blessed animals—but on the feast day of St. Anthony Abbot, not of St. Francis. In 1820, an English traveler said of Rome, "Not only every Roman, from the Pope to the peasant, who has a horse, a mule, or an ass, sends his cattle to be blessed at Saint Anthony's shrine, but all the English go with their job-horses and favorite dogs; and . . . get them sprinkled, sanctified, and placed under the protection of that worthy personage, who . . . preached to the fish." (Here she confuses Anthony Abbot with Anthony of Padua. The January date of the service clearly pertains to the former.) Later travelers also described this festival in Italy and Spain. Even in Assisi today, animals are blessed on St. Anthony's day, not St. Francis's. This festival is also widely observed in Mexico, and Olvera Street, a Los Angeles tourist attraction, holds an annual blessing of animals in the spring that claims to reproduce Mexican custom. Some sources have claimed that animal blessings go back to the Middle Ages, but without clear evidence.[31]

Outside these traditions, there were other precedents for the 1985 service, though the records show no very consistent pattern. An Episcopal church in Virginia caused some raised eyebrows when it offered a blessing of the animals in 1957. A Roman Catholic priest blessed pets in Golden Gate Park in San Francisco in 1961, apparently in connection with a new movie about Francis. Although the blessing was associated with "St. Francis day," it took place not in October, but on July 7, close to the feast day of his canonization. Two other blessings—one Episcopalian and one interfaith—were connected with rogation days, a spring agricultural festival in some Christian traditions. An Episcopal church in Connecticut held an animal blessing at Christmas, apparently a British custom; a New York rabbi and priest cooperated on a blessing for "Be Kind to Animals Week" in 1981. There were October blessings of animals, associated with St. Francis, in 1979 in Toronto and in 1984 at a Roman Catholic basilica in Washington, D.C.[32]

But the event at St. John the Divine caught the public eye. It was covered annually in the New York Times in its first few years. Attendance was up to 6,000 people—enough to fill the cathedral—by 1989. The idea soon spread to other big-city Episcopal centers: in 1987 Grace Cathedral in San Francisco picked it up; by 1991, the National Cathedral in Washington, D.C., had followed, and in 1992, the Cathedral of Saint Philip in Atlanta. In Roman Catholic circles, the popularity of these services and their association with St. Francis appears to date from the 1980s.[33]

At this writing, blessings of animals appear to take place mostly on the East and West Coasts, in cities and suburbs, and in a range of mainline and Roman Catholic congregations. Those held in rural areas or interior states are most often in Episcopal churches. Most of Laura Hobgood-Oster's sources, in a pioneering study of animal blessings in 2002, were Catholic and mainline churches, including Methodist, Disciples of Christ, and Lutheran congregations. Some were located in the American South or Southwest, where mainline congregations may lean toward evangelicalism. But she found no blessings of the animals in independent evangelical churches or networks, Pentecostal churches, or predominantly African-American churches. The demographic picture looked similar in 2013.[34]

Eastern Orthodox churches, though, are beginning to take up the practice. Because Francis is not in the Orthodox calendar of saints, some Greek churches associate the blessing with St. Modestos of Jerusalem instead. At least one congregation of the Orthodox Church in America has embraced St. Francis: the monastery of New Skete, which is known for its work with dogs.[35]

And, despite the children's book, even Jewish congregations are blessing animals these days. One rabbi said humorously, "I figured if it was good enough for St. Francis, it was good enough for me . . . so I stole it." Jewish congregations—mostly Reform—in New York State, Florida, Ohio, Michigan, and California have held animal blessings since at least the early 2000s. Many of these services take place in late September or October in connection with the story of creation or of Noah's ark, which are traditionally read at that time of year. Outside organized religion, numerous secular venues offer blessing services—often, though not always, on the first weekend in October. A few such events have even taken on commercial overtones, with vendors and fundraising.[36]

Why has this practice spread so rapidly? The speed of transmission through the news media may be one factor. Clergy and church members also share ideas through informal channels. But these mechanisms do not account for its emotional appeal. What is clear is that it caught the right cultural moment. The 1980s and 1990s were the age of the "animal turn" in American society. All over the developed world, humans' relationships with animals have changed in the last half-century. Mechanization, urbanization, and suburbanization mean that we have less everyday contact with animals. The mass production of food means that animals have been commodified, treated simply as products or as producers. Wild animals meanwhile are threatened by expanding human populations and can also threaten them. At the same time, human social connections have become more tenuous, and families are smaller.

All these factors contribute to the changing human-animal relationship. It seems likely that human beings need contact with animals. The human-animal bond is undoubtedly real. But in the absence of routine interaction, our attitudes change. We become both more affectionate and less realistic toward animals. We may romanticize them, attribute human qualities to them, or rely on them as substitutes for secure human community. Or we may fear them unduly, or deny the realities of their death or exploitation. As Katherine Grier has argued, Americans simultaneously depend on animals, dominate them, and recognize our differences from them. While we live with this tension, she says, we have no clear cultural or ritual ways to express it.[37]

Alongside these social shifts, the academic world saw an "animal turn" in the last quarter of the twentieth century. The benchmark work was philosopher Peter Singer's *Animal Liberation* (1975), which gave rise to extensive discussion about animals' personhood, consciousness, and rights. Theologians quickly joined the conversation, beginning with Andrew Linzey's *Animal Rights* (1976); we will return to that discussion shortly. Historians began to recognize animals as another "hidden," unnoticed set of historical actors, like women or colonial subjects. By the 1980s, the field of "animal studies" was emerging alongside other cross-disciplinary fields like women's studies and black studies. Scholars in anthropology, sociology, psychology, and other fields began to look at animals and at the human-animal relationship in fresh ways.[38]

New political movements also emerged. Activists began to recognize animal rights as a category different from conservation or humane care. An animal liberation movement, analogous to other liberation movements, gave rise to new organizations like the radical Animal Liberation Front and the durable People for the Ethical Treatment of Animals.

Pets have taken on a vast new importance. Americans have a deep attachment to their companion animals. Some evidence of this is economic: the pet industry is a rapidly expanding multibillion-dollar business. In 1994 it was worth about $17 billion, in 2004 some $34 billion; in 2012, according to an industry group, $53 billion. Veterinary care has expanded. Pet products like food, bedding, toys, clothing, and videos increasingly resemble those offered to humans, as services like babysitting and "hotel" accommodation gradually replace kennels. On a more personal level, studies show that 50 to 70 percent of Americans consider animals part of their family. Over 80 percent of dog owners refer to themselves as the animal's "mommy" or "daddy."[39]

So it is not surprising that there has been increasing interest in the question of animals and religion. The British Anglican theologian Andrew Linzey, whose first work appeared in 1976, has continued to be a leading voice in an ever-widening conversation. Although Linzey, unlike Singer, does not affirm moral equivalency between humans and animals, he argues that animals are part of the biblical covenant alongside humans, that their rights are grounded in God, and that "dominion" does not mean dominance. More recent works have turned specifically to the question of pets. In his seminal work *On God and Dogs* (1998), the Christian theologian Stephen Webb contended that animals can be channels and images of divine grace in their capacity for love and self-giving. Laura Hobgood-Oster, in *The Friends We Keep* (2010), reflected on the goodness of creation, the relational nature of God, and the divine call for compassion. She also discussed St. Francis and other animal-friendly saints in Christian tradition—and Lynn White as well. She suggests that the blessing of animals at St. John the Divine, with animals and humans together awaiting the word of grace, is an icon of a better world.[40]

Practitioners, not necessarily listening to theologians, have begun integrating pets into religious life. There are dozens, if not hundreds, of religious texts and objects dedicated to animals—prayers, greeting cards, Christmas ornaments. There are several reports of dogs wearing yarmulkes at Jewish services, which include "pet mitzvahs" as well as blessings. A few churches offer worship services at which pets are welcome, though typically not on Sunday morning. An unaffiliated chapel in Vermont, designed by a folk artist, is devoted entirely to the spirituality of the human-canine relationship. Its stained-glass windows depict dog angels, and the pew armrests are shaped like dogs' heads. Visitors are encouraged to post photos and letters about their deceased canine companions.[41]

There is also extensive conversation in popular culture about the death and afterlife of pets. St. Francis is sometimes invoked in this context as a friend to animals, and his legacy has been at the center of a recent controversy. Authorities at the National Shrine of St. Francis of Assisi, a Roman Catholic church in San Francisco, proposed in 2013 to build a formal repository for the cremated remains of pets and service animals. The response was enthusiastic. Many people felt that a church of St. Francis was an especially appropriate place to remember animals, and the clergy were careful to provide a theological framework for the decision. Others, however, have argued that animal burials are contrary to church teaching, and that Francis was in any case not interested in them. There are, of course, larger questions at issue about doctrine and sacred space. But the debate suggests the extent to which St. Francis is intertwined with popular perceptions about the place of animals in religion.[42]

Not only were the 1980s the right cultural moment for animals, they were also the right cultural moment for the act of blessing. Unlike Roman

Catholics, Protestants did not have long-standing practices of blessing utilitarian things. There are exceptions—both Lutherans and Methodists have historically blessed houses, for example—but for the most part, Protestant worship books have taken little account of blessing. For example, the *Book of Common Worship* of 1932—an ecumenical collection of model services—has no blessing rites at all. A Congregationalist handbook from 1948 includes only the blessing of a civil marriage. In the Methodist Church worship book for 1945, a few services invoke God's blessing, but their main focus is on human acts of dedication and commitment. More recent sources are similar: Presbyterians, Episcopalians, the United Church of Christ, and others have offered, at most, brief blessing rites for a handful of occasions. The Lutheran worship book *Occasional Services*, in 1982, seems to have been the first to provide a "general order of blessing." By contrast, the *Catholic Encyclopedia* of 1907–12 says, "Inanimate things that subserve the equitable needs and conveniences of society may receive from the Church the stamp of her benediction." Among the many "things" that may be blessed, animals—which of course are not inanimate—constitute a category of their own. The text clearly assumes that they are working animals, not pets. The Catholic bishops' 1989 *Book of Blessings* includes a much broader blessing of animals. It makes no connection to St. Francis.[43]

But in the 1980s and 1990s, a number of historical currents came together to enable the practice of blessing to take hold among non-Catholics. Mainline Protestants by that time felt less of a need to define themselves in opposition to Catholicism, and perhaps their sense of a particular identity as Protestants was itself softening. A significant 1968 study of the biblical practice of blessing influenced theological circles. In the 1970s and 1980s, feminist spirituality on the one hand, and Pentecostal and charismatic movements on the other, emphasized practical actions like healing and blessing. Matthew Fox's books helped to popularize the idea of blessing. Another factor may have been the controversial movement toward acceptance of gay partnerships: sympathetic religious communities offered formal blessings of relationships when they could not legalize them, and in the process they made the practice of blessing more familiar. So barriers to blessing fell, the concept circulated, and the practice became visible. In recent years, Protestant churches have blessed bicycles, backpacks, and chainsaws, among other things.[44]

There were also deeper currents at work. Animal blessings met an emergent need and desire. As animals came to provide important and meaningful relationships to humans, people wanted to recognize their animal companions in sacred space and time. The desire probably came first, the religious warrant afterward. That is, the need for recognition of pets generated a search for biblical backing, theological justification, and a patron saint, who of course is Francis.

Blessings of the animals also provided an attractive way to reach out to the public, especially for mainline churches. As we noted earlier, by the late 1980s these churches had realized that their numbers were in steady, not temporary, decline. They found aggressive evangelism off-putting, however, and so did the people they most wanted to reach. Blessing services were an appealing way to invite people in.

The blessing phenomenon also suggests a transactional view of religion, which is consistent with the consumer revolution of the last few decades. A blessing is a single act at a specific moment. Unlike membership or commitment, which are long-term and generalized, a blessing is particular and circumscribed. The participant need not belong and barely has to believe. So it is a way for churches to make something available to a cautious or suspicious public.

In addition, services of blessing are a way to resolve collective ambivalence about animals. As Hobgood-Oster observes, an important function of ritual is to act out an ideal world. The present world is less than ideal for animals, and participants in a blessing service probably know that. They themselves may go home and eat meat or kill mice. But the ritual action they are performing is the expression of an ideal, not yet attained, in which all animals and humans will live in a divinely sanctioned peace.[45]

Finally, blessings of animals are a way to bring nature into Christian religious life. As we have seen, theologians and laypeople had been looking for ways to integrate the two since before the first Earth Day. For many people, too, pets are the closest and most immediate contact with nature that they have. Many of the liturgies connected with animal blessings say as much about the natural world as they do about St. Francis.

St. Francis and the Blessing of the Animals

But what do they say about St. Francis? I would suggest that there are two main streams of interpretation: St. Francis as Earth Saint, and St. Francis as Patron of Pets. Both interpretations can move beyond Christianity or stay within it. Both are multilayered symbols. Both can call for moral action or can veer toward sentimentality. Of course they include some ambiguity and overlap, and there are some exceptions. But most blessings of animals follow one of these patterns.

Earth Saint is the vision pioneered by the Cathedral of St. John the Divine. In this vision, Francis is the patron of ecology and of the environment as well as the patron of animals. He is the symbol of a kind of spirituality that incorporates the earth and its creatures. Depending on the participants, this outlook may imply inward "creation spirituality," radical "eco-justice," or interfaith "deep ecology." It may also imply Christian environmental advocacy, and it brings nature into Christian worship. It may even include an affirmation of human cultural diversity, as in Winter's mass, which draws on the "earth-power of African and Brazilian percussion."[46]

The *Earth Mass*, especially, makes these connections explicit. It connects Francis with environmental awareness by adapting the Canticle of the Sun to contemporary sensibilities. Although the first stanza in this version stays fairly close to Francis's original wording, the second stanza introduces new animals and other elements. Whale and eagle can be construed as biblical references, and "Brother Wolf" is associated with Franciscan tradition. But Sister Loon, Brother Tiger, and Brother Seal are not traditional at all. They bring to mind the endangered or threatened creatures of our own time. Moreover, both stanzas end with a more generalized statement than is in the original: "praise to those who live in peace." The implication is peace between animals and humans, and between humans and ecosystems.

The *Earth Mass* is also linked with images of St. Francis in the wider culture. The choral pieces at the beginning and the end include a repeated chant, "Brother Sun, Sister Moon." Although these words are extracted from Francis's text, they also echo the movie title once again. And the canticle concludes with an unrelated line: "Ask of the beasts and they shall teach you the beauty of the Earth," which is repeated with "trees" and "flowers" in place of "beasts." This is a loose paraphrase of a text from the biblical book of Job (12:7–8a). In the Internet age, however, it is widely attributed to St. Francis.[47]

Other communities share the vision of Francis as Earth Saint. Many participants, both clergy and lay, frame the meaning of animal blessings in the terms of St. Francis and creation. "We observe St. Francis's day in this way because Francis was particularly aware of the unity and the power and the oneness of all God's creatures and all of God's creation," said the celebrant at an Atlanta service. Others say that the festival "celebrates

God's gift of creation" or recalls our "stewardship" of the earth. Some of Hobgood-Oster's informants drew connections with creation, human responsibility, and divine love. This construction of St. Francis is focused on public and social concerns.[48]

But there is a second stream of interpretation: Francis as the patron of animals, especially pets. Many, if not most, blessing services are directed toward pets. This vision of Francis finds some justification in the tradition: although there is certainly no suggestion that he kept permanent pets, there are several stories about his affectionate care for individual animals. Other tales tell of his releasing animals that could have been killed for food. (According to the sources, Francis ate meat when it was offered. He did not call for vegetarianism, only for poverty.) Most people, of course, know about the sermon to the birds and the story of the wolf.[49]

As Patron of Pets, Francis himself is mostly relegated to the background. To take an example, one service I attended—an ecumenical Protestant event—provided background descriptions of Francis in its printed leaflet, but did not mention him at all during the blessing itself. Another example comes from an ecumenical Christian manual on animal care. Debra Farrington's *All God's Creatures* offers unusually extensive and thoughtful suggestions for rituals of blessing, notably including confessions of sin along with the usual prayers and readings. But the materials are almost all focused on God, creation, and animals. In some twenty-one pages of resources, the peace prayer and two hymns are the only texts that refer to Francis. Even the early October date is recommended as much for the good weather as for the feast day.[50]

Participants, too, focus on pets, while Francis stays in the background. "I just feel good having my dog blessed," said a layperson in St. Paul, Minnesota. A participant in Atlanta similarly said, "She's a real soulmate. It just seems appropriate that she should come and get a blessing." "It's interesting that we can get [our pets] kind of baptized," said a New Yorker. A Duke University chaplain refers to the "sacred role of pets." Others hope that the blessing will help to heal their animals' illnesses or behavior problems. Still others are even less specific: the service is "just nice." When Hobgood-Oster asked her respondents about the meaning of the blessing service, she received "rather short, and in general vague" answers. Some respondents said there was "no deep significance" to the service, or said that its main purpose was outreach to non-churchgoers. Perhaps the most striking answer was "?"[51]

There are exceptions—notably a service attributed to the (Episcopal) church of St. Paul and the Redeemer in Chicago, in which the texts focus mainly on Francis. For the most part, though, these blessings are about animals. Francis as Patron of Pets is essentially a symbolic figure, or even a token figure. His presence indicates the church's approval of animals or affirms that animals have a legitimate place in Christianity. This stream of tradition is focused on private and domestic concerns.[52]

Both streams of interpretation run the risk of sentimentality and emotional excess. Even though the Earth Saint has a more urgent sense of purpose than the Patron of Pets, there is always the possibility that rallies and rituals, music and spectacle can simply be exercises in feeling good, displacing more substantive forms of action. Creation spirituality, with its emphasis on the nonrational, can also slide into sentimentality. On the other hand, the Patron of Pets image, while often sentimental, can sometimes stand for a broader purpose: perhaps a concern for helpless or suffering creatures, or a search for a thoughtful theology of animals. But it may also reflect only a wish to have one's emotions affirmed, or to have the church bless one's everyday way of life, regardless of whether it might call for a critique. Each of these interpretations arises out of specific cultural circumstances and responds to cultural needs. The blessing of the animals can stop there, as an affirmation of cultural conventions and private emotions—or it can offer an alternative vision.

Perhaps the blessing of animals will eventually take the symbolic place of birdbaths. Some recent garden statues of Francis incorporate an animal that looks more like a dog than a wolf—an interesting development as Francis becomes more closely associated with pets. And we are already beginning to hear critics say that St. Francis is not just about blessing animals.

CHAPTER EIGHT

Living Voices

A professor of literature prays on his porch in the morning with his dog at his feet and a plaque of Giotto's St. Francis within sight. A young veterinarian prays to St. Francis about "situations I cannot control" with respect to the animals in her care. An evangelical pastor appreciates Francis's "advocacy and ministry to the poor, his creation care ethic, and his commitment to loving neighbor and enemy alike."

In the summer and fall of 2013 I surveyed living Americans about their relationships to St. Francis—by which I mean their knowledge, understanding, feelings, practices, spiritual sensibility, and more. A copy of the survey appears in the appendix. I based my approach loosely on that of David Morgan in his groundbreaking work *Visual Piety*, but on a smaller scale, closer to that of Laura Hobgood-Oster's survey on animal blessings. Like theirs, this is a qualitative survey, not a statistically representative sample. I placed advertisements in the *Christian Century* and in *Christianity Today*, the flagship periodicals, respectively, of mainline and evangelical Protestantism, both of which draw wider audiences as well. The ads ran in print and online. I set up a Facebook page. I also invoked my personal network of colleagues, friends, and family, and asked them to pass it on. The survey questions were available in an online SurveyMonkey format, on the Facebook page, and on paper, and I maintained a post-office box and a separate e-mail address.[1]

I received forty-two responses, a number comparable to Hobgood-Oster's. They constitute a collection of very revealing, open, personal testimonies that can tell us much about the personal and spiritual meanings of St. Francis today. These testimonies show a surprisingly wide range of responses. They are especially significant for the subtlety with which they appropriate common cultural signs and symbols. Many of them are tender and deeply felt, and I've tried to discuss them with the respect they deserve.

I numbered the surveys and have used those numbers to document direct quotes. Any names I have used are pseudonyms.

Many Meanings

Familiarity with St. Francis, and attachment to him, varied widely. A lapsed Protestant probably spoke for many people when he said, "He doesn't mean much to me. A nice guy who loved animals" (23). On the other end of the scale, "He is the most beloved saint"; "He is perhaps my favorite saint" (2, 15, 34). One respondent is a historian who has read extensively in medieval biographies and sources. A Third Order Franciscan has an extensive library and years of study and devotion behind her. But another source says, "All I know of him is that he blesses the animals, and I love animals" (7).

Some respondents were concerned about the problem of myth and historicity. One said, "If everything said about him was true, the truth has long since been covered up in myth" (9). But another writes, "I am aware [that] much of what I find moving about him owes more, perhaps much more, to myth than to the facts of his life, but that doesn't diminish my devotion" (6). For the first respondent, "myth" seems to imply something that is not true, while for the second, it implies a story that conveys meaning. But both make a distinction between history and interpretation.

No single meaning of Francis dominates the responses. Some people focused on his care for animals, creation, or environmental issues. Some were more drawn to his humility and simplicity, his care for the poor, and his own poverty. He is "an important antidote to so much consumerism and prosperity gospel"; "his rejection of material well-being is a reproach" (26, 17). Several mentioned his lived critiques of the church: "Of most significance is Francis' response to hearing the voice of Jesus say 'repair my church'" (29). "I think he offered a prophetic witness to the church in his time when he reclaimed a simple lifestyle as one appropriate for a follower of Jesus" (12). His personal qualities were important for some respondents. One quoted an early source on his "extreme natural sweetness" (6). Another respondent sees him as "compassionate, caring, loving, understanding beyond any limits" (5). He had "courage and vision"; he signifies peace and love; he involved himself with the shunned and outcast. "What's important to me is his radical willingness to follow God, however difficult the path" (13, 4).

Admiration and knowledge, however, did not always imply a sense of a relationship. When I asked, "How do you engage with St. Francis?," almost half of respondents said they did so minimally or not at all. "I don't"; "Very little. I'm familiar with one of his prayers"; "Not much. [I] think of him when I'm outdoors"; "Not at all," they wrote (8, 21, 24, 16). A music student had encountered him chiefly in the Messiaen opera—and also in intellectual debates about religion. A Jewish respondent calls Francis a "spiritually powerful historical figure" (13). Others, though, are more personal: "I say the prayer often," says one; "[I] talk to my children about his names for 'Brother Moon' and 'Sister Sun'," says another. "I try to live simply, be a good steward of God's creation," reports a third (19, 25, 29). We will hear from some more deeply involved respondents later on.

The ways people first learned about St. Francis varied with age. For younger adults, the first encounter was often a "blessing of the animals" service, typically a happy and important memory. "I remember bringing pets to the Sunday service for St. Francis to be blessed. It was my favorite service of the year when I was quite young because it was lively, full of community, and who doesn't love playing with animals?" (5). For older respondents, the source is more likely to be garden statuary, children's books, or religious life. Some Protestants say that they rarely or never encountered Francis in church, but learned about him in college, seminary, or elsewhere.

Cultural "osmosis" was the source for many respondents (20). Awareness of Francis "seeped in from who-knows-where," said a former conservative Protestant (17). Several respondents couldn't remember or thought they must have learned about Francis through some cultural reference or the media. Others named garden statues, not all of them with the same degree of certainty. Art, music, church life other than blessing services, and family and friends figured prominently. Books, movies, summer camp, travel, the names of hospitals and buildings, and the environmental movement were other sources. One person mentioned a movie that seemed to present Francis as the "original hippie" (4). Another said, "In school when studying the Middle Ages" (11). A third, a European, first encountered him as a child on a visit to Assisi with her parents (28).

Cultural osmosis also figured in respondents' further learning about Francis. While about a quarter of respondents simply said they had not pursued additional information, several reported running across references to Francis in the ordinary course of things. Some had read a book or two but were not sure of titles or authors. Others were more specific. Three respondents mentioned Kazantzakis's novel; others named books by Julien Green, Lawrence Cunningham, and Murray Bodo, and collections of "lives of the saints." Several respondents, of varying ages, relied on Internet sources for information. And, as in earlier times, people learned about St. Francis by traveling to Assisi—five respondents mentioned visits to Assisi as sources of information.

The question about images produced more extremes than any other. The opening inquiry ("Do you own or use any images of St. Francis?") generated more flat-out "no" answers than any other question, as well as several qualified noes—for example, "I don't [but] my parents have statues of him" (2). On the other hand, for some people, images are primary—early memories, for example, or central elements of their spiritual lives. One respondent, reflecting on Francis, turned first to a mental picture: "I know relatively little about St. Francis. . . . I have an image of him in a painting surrounded by wild animals, perhaps a bird or a squirrel on his shoulder, a halo around his head, dressed in a monk's robes. . . . I'm not sure where I saw the picture or how often, but I do have a strong image . . . in my mind" (35). For others, a physical picture of Francis mediates a powerful sense of his spiritual presence. Still others use images as reminders or as teaching tools but deny any sense of presence. We'll discuss these testimonies more fully in the next section.

Those who use images integrate them into their lives in a number of different ways, which we'll also discuss more fully later on. To take a few examples, a Roman Catholic priest keeps a picture of Frances in his prayer book. A Unity Church member in California has a bas-relief of Francis "in the meditation area of my garden" (23, 14). A few have collections of images, distributed through the house or posted near a desk. For several people, the images are primarily reminders, either of Francis's life or of a person who made or gave the image. In this context they have no particular power of their own. Several people mentioned San Damiano crosses with varying levels of significance. These are copies of the crucifix from which Francis is said to have heard Jesus' call to rebuild the church.

The evidence about prayers and songs is as much historical as devotional. The most widely cited texts were the familiar ones: the hymn "All Creatures" (six respondents) and the "peace prayer" (fourteen, plus two that were unclear). Several respondents mentioned musical settings of the prayer, and one person noted a recent "inclusive" version of the hymn. But the responses showed no age gap in musical tastes: both younger and older people spoke of using the classic hymn and the newer settings of the prayer. There were also scattered references to other songs and texts, including the original Canticle of the Sun.

Concerning the peace prayer, one typical response was, "I like it and say it often" (19). A different but also representative response was, "I wouldn't say I 'use it,' but I have prayed it with others . . . and certainly find it significant and moving" (21). One respondent connected it with social justice, another with peaceful resistance.

For many people, it has remarkable personal resonance. A young woman in Colorado wrote that the prayer was a revelatory moment for her. "It was the text to a hymn that I remember from when I was probably ten or eleven," she writes. "It was the first time that the idea of self-less love made sense to me." Although she learned Christian ideals during her mainline church upbringing, it was the words attributed to St. Francis that generated her "first memory of understanding what selfless dedication and love mean" (5).

For a middle-aged Lutheran pastor from Vermont, the prayer is embedded in practice. " 'Make me an instrument' is one of my short-hand prayers (saying [the] first words implies [the] whole thing," she wrote. The prayer was the "theme of my ordination service—including bulletin cover, liturgical dance, [and] banner." Her seminary classmates and colleagues composed the dance and an original musical setting of the prayer (26).

A retired woman in Massachusetts keeps a copy of the prayer in her wallet. When she was a social worker and teacher, she said, she knew what her role was. Now, without that role, she finds it too easy to "get caught up in stuff, to take sides." The prayer reminds her of the way she wants to be in social interactions (33).

In Depth

Following are a half-dozen personal stories that describe some individual relationships with Francis more fully. What is most important about them is their complexity. All are multidimensional, incorporating personal histories and sensibilities as well as material from formal religion and culture. None reflects a narrow or stereotypical vision of Francis. Yet each is a different interpretation. Each has different points of connection. We will turn to some broader interpretations at the end of the chapter. The names I use are pseudonyms.

Eric, a middle-aged professor of literature, describes a relationship with St. Francis developed over many years. "On my porch is a wooden plaque, with gilt edges, representing the Giotto (or pseudo-Giotto, I suppose) fresco of St. Francis preaching to the birds. On summer mornings, early, I sit on the porch listening to the birds, with my dog at my feet. During my prayers, I sometimes look up at that plaque and think about St. Francis." Eric notes that he does not pray "to" St. Francis but "with" him. The quiet presence of the dog enhances this relationship. And he adds, "Julien Green says that perhaps God uses birdsong as a means of calling our attention back to him."

Eric has known of St. Francis since childhood through various sources, from garden statues to a St. Francis hospital. He has also read about Francis in some depth and has seen films—not *Brother Sun*, but Rossellini's *Flowers* and a less well-known American movie from 1961. What he most appreciates about Francis is his "gentle character." Francis's relationship to nature and the "poetry" of many of the stories about him are also meaningful. "More recently," Eric says, "I have started to think a lot about the concepts of poverty and simplicity."[2]

Among prayers and songs, the hymn "All Creatures" is especially significant; he sometimes shares it with friends who have lost an animal companion. Images are also important. Eric retains an early memory of the statue of St. Francis that his mother owned, which "fascinated me as a child." Today, his own garden statue provides a spiritual focus: "I always take an extra second to look at it and 'say hello' to St. Francis." He has a San Damiano cross and a St. Francis medal. This openness to visual spirituality is consistent with his identity as a high-church Episcopalian.

A garden statue is also a focal point for Bella, a mainline Protestant in her thirties. She doesn't claim to know much about saints, but she tentatively names Francis as her favorite. "I know he is the patron saint of animals and by association with nature/the environment (which is part of why I like him)." He is also, for Bella, intimately associated with family. "Growing up, my grandfather (who was Catholic) had a small statue of St. Francis in his garden .... I associate St. Francis with my grandfather (who I love very much)." Later, in her own garden, her small daughter played with another St. Francis statue. "She used to talk to him and sometimes move him around . . . which made me happy."

Bella's garden statue was full of meaning for her. One part of the meaning was his connection with nature: "I liked to feel like he was looking over my small patch of the earth here and all my plants and the wildlife that I co-exist with." Another part of the meaning was emotional or spiritual: "I think he had a calming effect. He reminded me . . . that I am small in the grand scheme of nature," a peaceful feeling for her. When the statue broke, she was "devastated." The image of Francis thus carries a web of associations—with a beloved grandparent and child, with the intimate and personal space of a private garden, and with the way the garden connects more broadly to nature and the earth. It is a focal point for significant concerns.

A young veterinarian, Jennifer, writes that she discovered Francis in a new way when she was "grieving the loss of a patient." Although she had known about Francis before, it was then that her fiancé, a Roman Catholic, encouraged her to pray to him. Now she prays to Francis often—especially "when I feel sorrow for a situation I cannot control involving one of my patients or my own pets." She writes, "I see St. Francis as very loving, generous, and nurturing. He is a protector and he is willing to help in times of need. He is important to me because he cares for the innocent creatures who have no voice of their own." St. Francis is a spiritual support and companion in a concrete and challenging daily practice, working with animals. Her picture of St. Francis is embedded in everyday activity, located not in the garden, but on the refrigerator.

Melinda, an Episcopal priest, associates Francis with nature in a different way. "I think of him [Francis] as an archetype of what *can happen* to a person who lives very closely with the natural world—who sees deeply into it, as a person of prayer, discovering the presence of the divine in the natural world. To me, it's about the evolution of consciousness." This is a spirituality that is oriented toward the cosmic, the mystical, and universal mythic patterns. The story of St. Francis and the wolf, for example, Melinda interprets in psychological terms, as a myth about making peace with one's "inner wolf."

Francis first caught her attention through her concern with environmental issues. "I was reading a book on faith and the environment," she recalled, and "in passing, it said Francis could be called the patron saint of ecology." This sounds like another echo of Lynn White. Francis, she believes, had a mystical consciousness and knew himself to be at one with the universe. For her, Francis represents an "ancient perception" in which God is "present in every aspect of creation, and he is known to be thus present."

Visual images are important for Melinda. Like Eric, she prays on her porch with an image of Francis—in this case a garden statue. "I use it inwardly as a friend," she says. "I can weep in the presence of Francis."

Another time, she was preparing to preach to a less than sympathetic congregation about an act of civil disobedience related to oil drilling. "I remember sitting there [in the church] looking at the stained-glass window of St. Francis and thinking that he would know what I'm talking about," she said. But the most important image for her is a copy of a contemporary painting by Nancy Earle, SMIC (see figure 14). In the center of the image is a somewhat abstracted, two-dimensional Francis with seven circular medallions or windows in his body. In them, or through them, elements of the natural world are visible. Francis stands within a larger circle with earth to his right and water to his left, each side filled with creatures. Some are animals traditionally associated with Francis: wolf, rabbit, and bird. But the artist also adds a whale, a lotus, a snake, and other symbols representing current concerns and non-Christian religions. Above the circle, the sun forms a halo around Francis's head. A translucent crossbar suggests a Tau cross, a symbol associated with Francis.[3] For Melinda, this image recalls what the Buddhist teacher Thich Nhat Hanh calls "interbeing." "Everything is interdependent, nothing exists on its own . . . the created world are our kin!" This Francis can be read as transparent to nature or as bearing nature in his body. He may be Christian but surely transcends Christianity.

Lewis, a middle-aged man from a mainline Protestant church, grew up in a suburban Roman Catholic congregation where "Francis was just part of the culture." He remembers active Franciscan friars and priests in local parishes during the lively ferment after Vatican II. His own brother seriously considered entering the Capuchin order. One friar in particular was "very cool" and among other things organized a trip to see the film *Brother Sun, Sister Moon*. Later, Lewis visited Assisi with this friar, at one point walking the streets "singing with young Catholic socialists."

Lewis argues that most pictures of Francis are "too soft." "His life practice is a big challenge to us, a tough example," he says. "His communion with nature is powerful, and seems demeaned by the birdbath thing. His way is too hard for most people." One of the few images he finds significant is a scene from the movie. Francis is in church with his parents, dressed in rich clothing, and he starts "panicking" as he recognizes the disparity between himself and the poor in the back rows. "It is a powerful image of discontent," he says. Recognizing these deep challenges, Lewis began in later adulthood to think about alternative models, such as other saints and the mystical writings of Richard Rohr.

FIGURE 14 Nancy Earle, SMIC. "Brother Francis: A Canticle to Creation."
Giclée print from a painting, early twenty-first century. Richly colored in the
original, this image incorporates many natural elements and religious signs
into Francis's body and being.

Analogous thoughts about Francis's challenges come from Adam, a young mainline pastor, who says, "His way of life calls us to a more radical expression of Christianity . . . which if I'm honest, I'm not yet willing to commit to." He admires Franciscans for "their solidarity with those in poverty and their work with those who are in poverty." He also connects the "peace prayer" with social-justice issues: "It resonates with me in its honesty about participation in systems larger than us, both calling to action and trusting the work to God." So he recognizes the way Francis represents an alternative to the dominant culture—and how difficult the alternative is.

Sandra, an Episcopalian in her early sixties, is a Third Order Franciscan. She describes an attraction to St. Francis that began with a "stirring," a gradual and persistent pull that deepened with time. Early on, St. Francis seemed to be "an important person, someone associated or near God." Now, "for the last thirty years or so, St. Francis has become an example of someone who loves God so much, and finds God in everything, that his entire being is tuned in to God at all times."

Growing up in the Protestant mainline, Sandra encountered a familiar range of St. Francis references. Her childhood church had a stained-glass window, and the children's choir sang a version of the Canticle of the Sun. A book of children's prayers placed the canticle on its endpapers. A more vivid impression came from summer camp: she recalls a St. Francis garden at a girls' camp in New Hampshire in the Monadnock region. She also visited a St. Francis garden at a camp counselor's home.

Nevertheless, Sandra experienced her relationship with Francis as her own discovery. She began to read about him as a young adult and remembers that when she first discovered him, she read the same biography three or four times. She also read more extensively, particularly in the library of Adelynrood, Vida Scudder's spiritual home. In 1986 she entered the Third Order. Since then she has visited Assisi, amassed a library, and collected a number of images.

This engaged spirituality is expressed in a rule of life according to the vows of the order—"to serve our Lord Jesus Christ . . . and to live joyfully a life of simplicity and humble service after the example of St. Francis." But she also expresses it in love of nature. "Most of all, I believe I share with St. Francis a joy of the created world and God's presence in everything. It is an incarnational theology." Nature and creation, then, are integrated with a more formal Franciscan commitment.

New, Old, and Creative

These stories suggest, in a fine-grained way, some of the ways in which contemporary Americans relate to St. Francis. On the one hand, common cultural materials are certainly in use. Ideas and imagery are shaped by these materials—from academic history to movies and animal-blessing services—and draw on general knowledge and concerns. On the other hand, Francis continues to signify an alternative to the surrounding culture. These stories reflect on economic simplicity, environmental action, and cultural tensions around animals. Moreover, even though people draw on materials available in the wider culture, they appropriate these materials in deeply personal and creative ways. Their responses are not predetermined.

There are also signs of a new and significant critique emerging. Many of these voices speak of Francis in terms of quiet, stillness, focus, and meditation. This quiet, centered Francis represents a powerful counterpoise to the busy, hurried, and noisy quality of contemporary American culture.

Many of the personal responses to Francis reflect traditional spiritual practices, whether consciously or not. When Eric takes a moment to "say hello" to St. Francis in the garden, he is practicing a form of recollection, refocusing the soul. When Jennifer prays to Francis, she is asking for his intercession, revising this traditionally Catholic practice for her own non-denominational spirituality. Those who engage imaginatively with Francis recall to us the Ignatian way of imaginative engagement with scripture. Reading, prayer, and singing are practices with a long history in Protestant spirituality. Several witnesses tell of examining their consciences, surely a deeply rooted religious discipline. And Sandra's rule of life is explicitly connected to Franciscan tradition.

All of this suggests that contemporary relationships with Francis, or with other saints, have rich and nuanced meanings. Their meaning and character also transcend traditional Catholic-Protestant boundaries and, to a considerable extent, other religious boundaries as well. The saint is a human figure, a model and example, but is also a holy figure, a locus of transcendence and beneficent power, and a social figure, one who holds people in community through family, history, or moral commitment. We will have more to say about the meanings of sainthood in the epilogue.

CHAPTER NINE

Into the Future

"Isn't it always a sense that something is wrong, even though we don't know quite what, that leads us out of our usual habits and haunts?" asked the writer Gretel Ehrlich in the year 2000. She was thinking about Francis, who has continued to signify a call toward something different, an alternative to what contemporary culture offers.[1]

Any historical assessment of the 1990s and the early 2000s has to be tentative, since this period is still so close to us. In this brief chapter, though, I want to point to three trends that began in the 1990s and seem strong enough to continue for a while. One trend brings Francis into the postmodern age. One explores his relationship with Islam. The third is a new kind of folklore about Francis.

In the background is the continual interest in Francis since the 1982 anniversary, along with several new events. In 1997 a major earthquake struck central Italy, including Assisi, drawing new attention to the buildings and works of art associated with Francis—and most especially, once again, to the sense of place. In 1999, Regis Armstrong and colleagues published the first volume in a comprehensive English-language collection of Franciscan sources, with new translations and commentary. The events of September 2001 generated new works on Francis's visit to the sultan of Egypt as a means of exploring Christian relationships with Islam. Since then, there has been a notable increase in the number of biographies and personal reflections on Francis. These recent works seem to circle around his meaning for the fragmented, unstable, uncertain postmodern age.

Francis, the Postmodern Man

By the 1980s, the United States was entering upon the postmodern era. There are many ways to define postmodern, but perhaps the simplest is to say that it is an age with no single master narrative. In contrast to the modern age, there is not much sense that history is moving toward a recognized goal or making steady upward progress. Society is not certain that clear and definite truth can be uncovered by means of scientific study or rational thought. Institutions are fragmented: both large ones like nation-states and organized religions, and small ones like the family. Subordinated groups like racial minorities and women have insisted that their own stories differ from the dominant narrative. We have seen the long engagement of modernity with Francis. This new era brings some changes.

For the postmodern world, Francis is appealing because he can be nonlinear. He can offer action and practice in place of reasoning. He does not want to build an institution; even the Franciscan orders ultimately disappointed him. For non-Christians, he can be appropriated without the master narrative of a Protestant America. Postmodern thinkers may also see Francis in terms of social construction and deconstruction. By rejecting the values of his society—specifically wealth and security—Francis exposes the discourses of power, the hidden, socially constructed agreements about what matters.

The liberation theologian Leonardo Boff, in fact, thought Francis modeled an alternative for the postmodern age. For postmodern people, everything is in flux, in "objective change, negotiation, disguise, falsification." Money, he says, is the purest example of this flux and change, an unstable and illusory substance. Francis rejected money—in favor of usefulness, concreteness, human freedom, and human community. Boff concludes, "Francis of Assisi, more than an idea, is a spirit and a way of life [which] are made manifest in practice, not in a formula, idea, or ideal." As a postmodern alternative, Boff's Francis resembles the premodern and antimodern ideals of an earlier time.[2]

Valerie Martin's 2001 novel about Francis, *Salvation*, is quintessentially postmodern: it is told in fragmentary episodes and proceeds mostly backward through time. Another novel, Ian Morgan Cron's flawed but popular work *Chasing Francis*, explored a postmodern form of evangelicalism. In this story, an exhausted and alienated megachurch pastor discovers Francis and builds a new ideal of "church" on his example. Many of his discoveries essentially reinvent earlier liberal ideals—simple living, solidarity with the poor, active peacemaking, following the Sermon on the Mount. But in this instance, the work seems designed to appeal to the "emerging church"—a loose movement that has been described as a "self-consciously postmodern" effort to blend conservative theology, contemporary concerns, historical resources, and transcendent experience. This movement has found much to appreciate in Francis.[3]

But Gretel Ehrlich probably said it best. She found in Francis a companion for the road.[4]

Ehrlich is known for writing about nature, travel, and adventure. In 1999 and 2000, respectively, she published two very similar essays about a journey on foot from Assisi to Gubbio—one in the *New York Times Magazine*, the other in the American Buddhist magazine *Shambhala Sun*. In both stories, she frames St. Francis as a walker, one who loved to be in motion. Her guiding metaphor is the path. And what is more, "the path moves." It is not solid or certain. There are no certainties any more. The path is also "a flesh wound . . . in the foot of the walker"—implicitly, a stigma.[5]

The act of walking is also uncertain. "To walk is to unbalance oneself," she reflects. "Between one step and the next we become lost. Balance is regained as the foot touches earth, then it goes as the foot lifts." Because of all this, she says, "what we are, and where we are going, and the way we've chosen to get there, remains directionless; the traveler is forever wounded and lost. Pain, discomfort, and groundlessness are the seeker's friends." One could hardly ask for a better statement of the postmodern condition.[6]

Ehrlich's Francis is more imagined than historical. He wanders the road singing "Lord, make me an instrument." He is also a pantheist: "Bird, human, river, mountain—they were all God," she says. Much of her description of Francis uses the language of Buddhism, a natural connection with the images of change and flux. "From emptiness came compassion," she remarks, and Francis moved toward "the truth of the human condition, which is suffering." He is, as well, very twentieth century. He "hated the hypocritical moroseness of formal church life with its tomb-like cathedrals and its common assignment of sin and guilt," she claims. "He could well have been a 60's radical."[7]

Still, this Francis is a guide through postmodern anomie. "I was perched on the head of a pin at century's end and didn't know how to proceed," Ehrlich wrote. "The medieval European mind was fixated on eternity and driven by notions of sin and mystery. Now, at the end of the twentieth century, we had traded in linear time for the ever-present Einsteinian time. Our weak link is not a Christian tragedy we are powerless to escape, but the nihilism of living in the ever-present Present. To find the path through a continuum takes another kind of imagination and tenacity." Francis shows us how to do this.[8]

Francis for the postmodern age, says Ehrlich, encompasses and transcends all human religions, all master narratives. He is steadily in motion on the open road, which is itself directionless and fluctuating. Though

Ehrlich did not mention it, imagery of the road appears with striking frequency in this era. It was a central feature in the first American staging of Messiaen's opera—an elevated ramp winding across the stage. A newly edited version of Sabatier's biography was titled *The Road to Assisi*, and a travel book followed his journeys "on the road." Valerie Martin's novel ends with a chapter called "A Rich Young Man on the Road." What Francis has done, says Ehrlich, is to find the path through a continuum, to learn to inhabit change. In this he speaks to us in our uncomfortable, wounded, and ungrounded condition.[9]

Francis and Islam

Postmodern American culture has looked toward Islam with a new kind of interest—and anxiety—since the late twentieth century. The Muslim world, rejecting colonial narratives, began to assert itself in a new way with the Iranian revolution of 1979, and Americans began to realize how little they knew. Popular introductions to Islamic religion and society appeared in print and on television. Universities expanded their course offerings in Islamic studies. Interreligious dialogue broadened—and so did hostility. All of this intensified, of course, after the attacks of September 11, 2001. Confronted by this new set of challenges, Americans looked for guidance in exemplars from the past. Once again, they found one in Francis.

Francis, of course, was said to have visited a Muslim leader under conditions of war. He sought peace in some sense, and he returned unharmed. In some accounts, he offered to walk through fire to demonstrate God's faithfulness and challenged the Muslim clerics to do the same.[10]

As historian John Tolan has shown, in his *St. Francis and the Sultan* (2009), every age has reflected on the encounter between Francis and the Muslim leader. For the early Franciscans, the episode proved that Francis desired holy martyrdom. In the sixteenth century, European Protestants, facing a real threat from the Ottoman Empire, derided him as a fool. Catholic religious orders saw him as a model for mission. Many in the nineteenth century presented Francis not only as a missionary but also as "a European civilizer of barbarous Arabs, precursor to the European colonizers of modern times." In the twentieth and twenty-first centuries, Francis became above all a model of various forms of peacemaking— pacifism, political diplomacy, interreligious dialogue, and pluralism. Although Tolan traces the emergence of this peacemaking vision primarily through Franciscan and other Roman Catholic literature, many non-Catholic sources take the same view.[11]

There were other kinds of reflection on Francis and Islam before 2009. Universalistic thinkers have speculated since at least the 1960s that Francis was a sort of Sufi. And in 1976, Anthony Mockler, a military historian, set out to explain a gap in the historical record after Francis's visit to the sultan. He proposed that Francis had spent that time studying Islam. The records are silent, he said, because Francis's interest would have been too embarrassing for his followers to report. Mockler's idea does not seem to have had much traction, but it foreshadows the later interest in Francis's relationship with Islam. Other historians have considered the question occasionally, with a more cautious approach to sources and contexts.[12]

But the idea of Francis as a proponent of interreligious dialogue appeals especially to postmodern America, with its interfaith and post-Christian voices. Constructed in this way, Francis remains a professing Christian but becomes a very open-minded one. Not long ago, the journalist Paul Moses focused on Francis as an early exemplar of dialogue and pluralism. His book *The Saint and the Sultan* argued that Francis presented Christianity by example more than by instruction. He approached the sultan respectfully, lived side by side with Muslims in his court, and engaged in thoughtful, good-natured debate and discussion with him. "The contemporary concept of interreligious dialogue didn't exist at the time," Moses noted, "but this was nonetheless a dialogue—a peaceful exchange of ideas about two competing religions." Moses is far from alone in this angle of vision, although his statement is the most extensive and the most popularly oriented. Tolan quotes a Jesuit theologian, an Italian journalist, and a "spiritual" peace organization to this same effect.[13]

This encounter has also entered into contemporary iconography. Robert Lentz, a Franciscan artist who is well known for his creative icons in Byzantine style, produced one of Francis and the sultan sometime after 2000. The image blends Islamic with Eastern Christian imagery. Stylized figures of Francis and the sultan embrace before a flat gold background and a circle of flame. According to the artist, fire signifies divine love and is also used in Islamic art to signify holiness. Especially, it serves to "disarm" the story in which Francis challenged the Muslim clerics to a trial by fire. In an age of renewed Christian engagement with Islam—accompanied by anxiety and sometimes violence—the icon constructs Francis as a guide to peaceful coexistence.[14]

"If Necessary, Use Words"

Sometime in the 1990s, an aphorism began circulating in popular religious culture. While its exact wording varies, it says essentially, "Preach the Gospel at all times. If necessary, use words." It has already become folklore—a text with many variations and no clear source, circulating by informal means. In fact, the variations appeared almost as early as the saying itself. It is universally attributed to Francis, but there is no evidence that he really said it. Still, as with the peace prayer, those who use it seem to feel that it expresses his spirit. It began to appear in print in the mid-1990s, and in the short span from 1994 to 1997, it was quoted in evangelical, liberal Protestant, and Roman Catholic sources.[15]

Other spurious quotes have also emerged. We have already seen how a biblical verse came to be credited to Francis by way of Paul Winter's liturgical music. More recently, a poem, "Wring Out My Clothes," has circulated under Francis's name. Its central image is of the saint "wringing out the light" from his clothing after standing outdoors. Its author is not Francis, though, but the popular poet Daniel Ladinsky, who published it in a collection of mystical verse in 2002. Ladinsky presented the texts in this collection as "translations" from twelve poets of diverse religious traditions, but the Francis poems, at least, are entirely his own inventions. Ladinsky may have meant that he was translating divine inspiration or interpreting Francis's spirit—it is not entirely clear—but many readers understandably take the texts as authentic to Francis.[16]

A blessing attributed to St. Clare is also recent. "Live without fear! Your creator has made you holy . . . Go in peace to follow the good road," it says. Appealing though they are, these are contemporary sentiments: Clare's known writings are far more concerned with holy poverty and service than with personal blessing. This text is in any case not among them. It seems to have received a boost from the Episcopal Church, where it appeared in an officially sanctioned collection of worship materials in 1998.[17]

But why has the aphorism about "preaching the Gospel" taken hold in the public imagination? In part because it is witty, of course, but, more significantly, because it suggests that actions are more important than words. For liberal Christians, it may imply a subtle critique of aggressive verbal evangelism. Yet, as we have seen, evangelicals as well as liberals appreciate Francis especially for his actions. More darkly, Mark Galli cited the aphorism as evidence of the "postmodern assumption that words are finally empty of meaning."[18]

Because it emphasizes action, the saying is open to interfaith as well as to Christian constructions. "Action was devotion," said Ehrlich of Francis. It also resonates with the conversation about Francis and Islam. Moses and others suggest that Francis enacted his faith for the Muslim armies—and that he demonstrated a better kind of Christianity than the Crusaders did. And, finally, the saying arose as theories of practice and performance were developing in the academic world.[19]

The adoption of this aphorism also suggests some interesting things about Americans' relationship to history. Before the modern era, it was common for writers and lecturers to attribute a text to an important historical figure in order to give it authority. Modern people are supposed to prefer reliable sources and solid evidence over authority figures, but it appears that they sometimes do not. Perhaps we are closer to the premodern age than we might think.

On the other hand, all authority is relative in postmodern thinking. And postmodern scholars argue that we should work with texts as they stand, regardless of source or authority. Yet the authoritative attribution to Francis still seems to matter to those who use this aphorism.

Then again, perhaps it is devotion to the saint that generated the saying. Devotees of Francis may have been looking, consciously or unconsciously, for fresh ways to present his message. And since this summation sounds as if he could have said it, they made the short leap from "could have" to "actually did" or "would have if he had lived in our time." The same thing, of course, would be true of other quotes like "wringing out the light" or "asking the beasts."

Yet this tendency, too, suggests that the past still means a great deal to us, and so does the connection with spiritual forebears. The texts do not circulate as anonymous proverbs or blessings—they are presented as quotations. It isn't enough, in other words, simply to say that it would be a good idea to preach the Gospel by one's actions, or even to say so in a clever aphorism. Instead, the saying survives and is passed along largely because it is connected with St. Francis. Even as these spurious quotes offer visions and interpretations for their own time, they still reach back to the past for their validation.

Epilogue

Since about 2000, there has been a new surge of interest in Francis. Sabatier's life of Francis was reissued in 2003. A television documentary and an accompanying book came out in the same year. New biographies have appeared throughout the early 2000s, with two major historical treatments in 2012. An academic publisher has recently issued a "companion" volume, surely not the last. A movement of "new monastics" within the emerging church has found inspiration in Francis. And there is much more.[1]

Francis is equally visible in the popular realm. In print, references range from a book for children by the public figure Robert F. Kennedy Jr. to Elizabeth Gilbert's best seller *Eat, Pray, Love*. As we have seen, spurious quotations surface with some frequency. A Google search for "Francis of Assisi" generates well over 3 million hits in half a second. Musicians post their performances of the peace prayer on YouTube. New visual images, like the anonymous statue in figure 15, appear frequently. In 2013, the Speaker of the House of Representatives of the United States, at the height of tension over a possible shutdown of the federal government, opened a contentious meeting with the peace prayer.[2]

Perhaps the single greatest impact has come from the pope elected in 2013, born Jorge Bergoglio, who made the unprecedented gesture of taking Francis for his papal name. As the Catholic theologian Hans Küng put it, "no previous pope has *dared* to choose the name of Francis" (emphasis mine). Why? "The expectations seem to be too high." Pope Francis, at this writing, has spoken often and publicly about shifting the focus of the church to the needs of the poor. He has addressed world economic leaders in the same terms. In addition, he practices material simplicity, if not absolute poverty. He presents himself as an ordinary human sinner, and he seems to delight in mixing with ordinary people. Pope Francis has drawn intense interest within and outside the church.[3]

FIGURE 15 Garden statue with blended iconography. Found outside a Roman Catholic gift shop, this statue adds birds to the traditional Catholic iconography of cross and skull, suggesting an influence from non-Catholic culture. Newtown, Pa., 2013. Photo © Margaret Holladay.

St. Francis of America

The story of Francis of Assisi is very well known, yet is usually known only in part. Each time and culture constructs Francis in the terms that it knows. The version of Francis that seems obvious today is not the one that seemed obvious fifty years ago, or one hundred, or even twenty. And yet, even though culture shapes the understanding of Francis, each culture also discovers a Francis who is an alternative to its own limitations. The alternative may take the form of nostalgia and longing, of paradox and tension, or of a driving force for action and change. Even when images of Francis seem to be fully domesticated, he rarely stays that way.

Nineteenth-century Protestants rediscovered Francis through the genteel, cultivated channels of art, continental travel, and historical studies. They accepted him as a true follower of Jesus and a proto-Protestant harbinger of freedom. Yet he also stood for the forbidden and suspect energies of Catholicism and, even more, for a lived alternative to the constricting forces of modernity and capitalism.

At the turn of the twentieth century, Francis, largely as conceived by Sabatier, was constructed as an exemplar of true Christianity and a broadly available cultural reference point in a confident, prosperous, modernizing society. Yet this same idea of Francis was a central force in social criticism and reform. The Francis associated with sense of place subtly questioned the traditional Protestant emphasis on word and spirit rather than material things. An argument about the "real" St. Francis had already begun.

By the 1920s, the thoroughly familiar figure of Francis was the occasion for celebration and for new discovery. There was a deepening appropriation in the form of enactment—in amateur plays, in a popular hymn and a prayer, and in alternate lifeways. At the same time, irony and images of inversion reflected the weariness and cynicism of the post–World War I generation: culturally conditioned and culturally critical. During the Depression a minority revived the tradition of social criticism, especially with respect to war and money.

The hymn "All Creatures" and the peace prayer enabled participants to identify with Francis by speaking in his voice. Both expressions could be domesticated, treated as private and personal, emphasizing tranquility and happiness. But they could also be, and were, used against the cultural pressures that led toward self-interest, war, despair, and fear. In their theological openness, they could move beyond the boundaries of Christianity.

The garden statue, created largely in the 1920s and commodified by the 1950s, has become a cliché, a symbol of a trivialized idea of Francis. And yet it is far more complex than that. Garden statues may mediate Francis's presence, signify intimacy, evoke emotion and relationship, or suggest an alternative use of money. As symbols for children, they simplify Francis but introduce some of his meanings. Radical poverty in the private garden was a site of paradox.

The consensus culture of the 1950s was also an age of anxiety. The churchly and popular uses of Francis at first seemed to domesticate him. Yet arguments about the "real" Francis continued, and dissenters and outsiders of all kinds appropriated him. Among other things, Francis was imagined as a poor Jew.

The cultural stresses of the 1960s produced new images of Francis. Hippie culture—the counterculture, the alternative—pointed to Francis to justify change in search of authenticity. Voluntary poverty, rejection of money, and the ideal of true Christianity took on new forms. Meanwhile the ecology movement, with Francis as its patron saint, was culturally generated—by science, research, theology, the press—and at the same time resistant to cultural business as usual. And a commercial film, surely a mainstream cultural production, produced spiritual transformations and changed lives.

The living voices are all people of our time. In one sense it is easy to see how they, and we, are conditioned by culture: we know where our images of Francis came from, what we were taught, and what we had to figure out on our own. But in another sense, seeing our own cultural conditioning is the hardest of all. We can see, I hope, how the long history of interpretation of St. Francis outlined in this book has fed into the understanding that each of us carries around of him. For some people, he is just a familiar figure in the cultural landscape. Others are shaped by Sunday school, protest movements, or Scout troops. Yet those who engage deeply with Francis do so in very personal and meaningful ways. Though shaped by culture, these kinds of engagement are not wholly predetermined; we are not robots. As one historian put it, "we neither passively receive nor naïvely challenge" images of the past in popular culture, but instead "negotiate" between those in our own past and our own subculture.[4]

The ferment since the 1980s has been shaped by culture in many different ways: by new religious movements, by the environmental crisis and reactions to it, by Hollywood extravagance. Francis again inspires religious alternatives. Joy and foolishness are also countercultural gestures.

The rise of the "blessing of the animals" practice responds to the "animal turn" of the late twentieth century, which affected everything from the academy to the pet-supply store. The movement between affirming and challenging culture is especially clear in this practice. It can focus on pets almost to the exclusion of St. Francis and his cultural critique. It can become transactional or can function as marketing for churches. Countercultural messages can be muted by an atmosphere of celebration. Yet these ceremonies can also ritualize a vision of a better world, and can propose the alternative lifeways of honoring animals and living in peace with the natural world.

In recent times, postmodernity casts doubt on any master narrative or general truth. Words become untrustworthy; stories are told in fragments. In this context Francis becomes a person who lives by action, who is constantly in motion on the road. But this same Francis shows us a way through postmodern instability, because he keeps his balance and transcends traditional boundaries. At the same time, American confrontation with the Islamic world brings another kind of attention to Francis the traveler. His deliberate encounter with Muslims again signifies an alternative: dialogue and peacemaking rather than conflict.

Why Francis?

One of the stories about Francis tells how a brother once murmured, "Why after you?"—that is, why did people follow Francis? Francis's answer was that God could find no one more sinful than he was to show that all good things come from God. For contemporary Americans the issues are a little different. I want to consider two interlocking questions: why were Protestants and other non-Catholics drawn to St. Francis? And what did sainthood mean for them?[5]

To begin with some background, Protestants, early in their history, rejected many aspects of the Catholic cult of saints: veneration, intercession, miracles, and official canonization. They feared idolatry, and they insisted on the spiritual equality of all human beings, as against the idea that some were given special spiritual powers or status. They also rejected the practice of pilgrimage as a means of gaining spiritual merit. They have been a little more uncertain about holiness—about whether or not powerful figures in Christian history have been unusually near to God in some way. For non-Christians, the questions are slightly different: what a Christian sacred figure means in a non-Christian context, and whether his religious affiliation matters.

When I ask people why they think Francis is so popular, many think the answer is obvious: because of the birds, or because of nature and ecology, or because of his kindness. In the short term, they may be right. Presented with a saint who loves what we love, we may simply embrace him and go no further. But I think there is more to his popularity.

First, Francis is human and historical. No matter how uncertain the historical details may be, it is beyond dispute that there was a Francis of

Assisi who did, for the most part, what we think he did. Because he was human and historical, he was "real." Historicity gives him a concrete reality that myth and fiction do not have. Humanness means he was a lot like us, a person we might meet on the street. These claims—humanness and historicity—are often made for the human Jesus, of course, but Jesus is far more distant from us historically than Francis, less well-documented, more shrouded in myth, and therefore more elusive. Francis can feel much closer. The fact that he comes from a real place that we can visit, and which is relatively little changed, adds to the sense of his reality and concreteness.

Second, Francis has many dimensions. If this study tells us nothing else, it shows how many different ways people can find to understand, relate to, and depict St. Francis. Artist, poet, clown; traveler, camper, farmer; leper, street person, prisoner: the list goes on and on. A columnist has recently written sensitively about Francis as a returning soldier. Most of these images and constructions have at least some warrant in the sources or in Francis's historical context; they are not purely invented. Few other saints have such rich stories with so many vivid details.[6]

But the attraction is not just to a historical figure with many dimensions. Francis also appeals to the religious imagination. As the historian Jaroslav Pelikan and others have observed, Francis is of all saints the one who seems most fully to imitate Jesus, to do what Jesus did. Francis offers inspiration and encouragement to those who want to do the same, especially if they are not certain it can be done.[7]

And there is still more to it. He also offers purity to those who—for any of a number of reasons—are weary of Christian hypocrisy or half measures. Unlike so many professing Christians, Francis followed literally the commands to give up his possessions and take nothing for his journey. Francis also appeals to those who want to separate Jesus from churches, institutions, and organized religion, who may or may not themselves be Christians. Modern people have found it fairly easy to distinguish Francis from the church, regardless of what Francis's own convictions may have been. Equally, though, he appeals to those who resist such separation: those who would argue that the imitation of Jesus is consistent with the church in its historical continuity and its teaching.

And yet, not very many of the people who admire Francis (or Jesus) really do give everything up and take to the highways. They place a statue in the garden, perhaps—or convene an institute or write a book—and hope to do better someday. In this sense Protestant devotion to Francis is after all not so different from the Catholic kind. Here, the saint is qualitatively different from the ordinary Christian; he is someone we can admire or perhaps emulate in some small measure, but whose full stature we do not try to attain.

Is imitation necessary? As I said at the outset, it is not my intention to offer a spiritual program for readers to follow. The question of *imitatio* has been debated many times in Christian history, leaving aside non-Christians for the moment. Radical reformers from the Roman Empire to the twenty-first century have criticized the larger church for failing to practice what it preaches, failing to live up to the ideals it proposes to believe. Francis, for all his joy and music, offers the same critique, a profoundly important one. There is always a danger that a selective reading of Francis will overlook that critique entirely.

Still, human relationships are infinite in their variety, and they do not always involve imitation. We may love, admire, appreciate, dance with, or pray with someone who is very different from ourselves, without trying to become the other person. If Francis (or Jesus) is a fully human, historical figure, then presumably any of those varied human relationships is open to us. At least they are open to us in imagination or in a spiritual dimension, since neither person is available to us in the flesh. Here, we are approaching metaphysical and theological questions that I cannot address: in what way a deceased person is or is not available to us, and what the communion of saints means. The deepest theological question, and one with a long history of debate, is what kind of a life Christians are obligated to live.

One scholar has observed that the field of religious studies has never come up with an adequate definition of "saint." Virtually all religions have some kind of historical holy figures. In Western Christianity, sainthood was not formally defined until the Middle Ages. It was instead a matter of custom, practice, and popular acclaim. By that measure, Francis clearly is the functional equivalent of a saint for Protestants and for many non-Christians: a human figure widely recognized by the people as having some special degree of holiness.

Moreover, moderns and postmoderns seem to need saints. Modernity, says one critic, rejects the excess and marginality of sainthood, but people keep seeking it out. Saints think outside socially normative patterns, offering "intensification" and access to the supernatural. This is not so different from Victorian antimodernists' hunger for "primitive energies."

A religious journalist says that people who "cold-shoulder ecclesiastical structures . . . all embrace the saints. They *love* the saints." Another critic, reflecting on recent biographies of Francis, concluded that contemporary people are looking for sainthood whether they give it that name or not. And so they turn once again to Francis.[8]

The Uses of History

Finally, I turn to one of my first and last questions in this study. What is the relationship of history to religious devotion? I mean the term "devotion" broadly, to encompass all kinds of admiration and relationship. Clearly, the people who have been drawn to St. Francis over the years have not all been historians, and they do not relate to Francis as an object of academic study. Of course, we could also ask what motivates historians to study Francis. We would probably find that it is seldom a purely rational intellectual interest.

In any case, lay devotees of Francis are looking to the past for resources for faith, spirituality, and everyday living, and also for ethics, social criticism, and responses to world events. When they find these resources, they engage with them in all kinds of ways—imaginatively and materially, in the conventionally religious modes of prayer and hymnody and moral action, and also in storytelling, gardening, woodcuts, social practice, and countless other ways. What does history mean in this context?

It seems to me that there is a continual dialogue with the past. Perhaps the best analogy is the work of public history, which can be defined as professional history that interacts with and serves the general public, as in museums or at historical sites. Often, public history begins with questions about a particular place, community, or event, rather than with scholarly questions about large-scale historical processes or theoretical issues. In a similar way, any interest in St. Francis obviously begins with a particular person and story, and perhaps with a place as well. Some devotees will then turn to history—to sources and historical studies—to deepen their knowledge. History will provide correctives and broadened perspectives, as it did for me when I first encountered Francis the devout Catholic. History will also raise the question of what is true—not answer it necessarily, but raise it. It will also suggest new kinds of interpretation—again, not necessarily better interpretations, but different ones. Yet the appropriation of Francis always goes beyond historical thinking, whether the appropriation is socially constructed or individually imagined or privately experienced. Appropriation is cultural, spiritual, and embodied. History is its basis and its corrective.[9]

There are times in the appropriation of Francis when the past seems to function only as a resource to be mined for consumer satisfaction or personal gratification. In Van Wyck Brooks's famous phrase, people seek a "usable past"—and sometimes, the meaning of "use" can lean toward exploitation or very narrow selection. As I said at the outset, I am not going to make an argument about the "real" St. Francis, but I think it is fair to affirm that Francis enacted a difficult and demanding way of life, and that he offered a social critique for his own time, and plausibly for ours as well. History, then, does set some boundaries on interpretation. It sets a limit on speculation and on the promotion of particular agendas, left wing and right wing, institutional or not. At its best, history also offers growth and new insight.

There is a growing literature today on the ways ordinary people make use of and relate to the past. One essential point in this complex subject is the idea of memory rather than history: the idea that people and groups engage actively in the process of remembering—for example, by telling stories, building memorials, or collecting artifacts. They make choices about what is important in the past, and they also reject or "forget" parts of it. As a social process, these practices build a community of memory whose self-understanding may be articulated in its texts, enacted and performed, or expressed concretely in bodies, places, and material things. When pilgrims travel to Assisi and look for St. Francis there, they are joining in such a community.

Individuals also remember, of course. And the practice of remembering Francis is as often individual as it is communal. It is also, in the broadest sense, spiritual: the ways in which people relate to Francis are not only remembrance, but relationship in the present. As we have seen, they seek from Francis inspiration, guidance, or support in very immediate concerns. These relationships resemble classical spiritual practices, particularly the Ignatian tradition of participation through imagination. They are also not so distant from traditional Roman Catholic relationships to saints as heavenly friends who offer intercession and spiritual intimacy.

I would hope that historical criticism would continue to provide a moderating force in speculations about Francis. And yet he can never be reduced to incontrovertible facts. Nor should he be. Where would we be without the St. Francis who comes "dancing out of the woods," throwing a wooden rose up in the air and catching a real one? Francis stands "here beside us" in street protest, waits quietly in the green garden, preaches to the potatoes, and sings alleluias. Though undeniably a historical figure and a human being, he remains elusive, still upside down and laughing in amazement at the world.

Survey

You and St. Francis

This two-page survey contributes to research for a book. It is open to everyone, and you may respond anonymously if you wish.

Some of the survey questions are open-ended; please think of them as starting points for your own reflections, and feel free to add extra comments or pages.

What does St. Francis of Assisi mean to you? How do you feel about him? What is important to you about St. Francis?

How do you engage with St. Francis? What place does he have in your life?

How did you first learn about him? Some possibilities: through your family, religious community, Sunday school, formal education, recreational reading, seeing birdbaths or statuary, art, movies or other media. Or some other way?

When did you first hear of him? For example, in childhood, adolescence, young adulthood, older adulthood?

Have you ever tried to learn more about St. Francis? If so, how? Please name the most significant books, artworks, or other sources.

Do you use any prayers or songs associated with St. Francis? Please name the most important ones.

Do you own or use any images of St. Francis—pictures, statues, medals, garden figures? Where do you keep them and how do you use them? How important are they to you? (For instance, a picture hanging over your bed is probably more important than a postcard in a box in a closet.)

Do you own or use any other things related to Francis—books, DVDs, etc.?

May I quote your words in the finished book? If so, would you like them to be anonymous, or may I use your name?

Demographic information (optional but much appreciated)—your age, sex/gender, the city and state where you live (or at least state), your country if outside the United States, your religious background, and your current religious affiliation and/or practice. Also optional: your name.

Notes

Introduction

1. When I say "Francis's own writings," I mean those that most scholars agree are probably authentic to Francis. Most of these documents survive only in later copies with numerous variations, and many were edited.

2. A few shorter works have considered the questions of Francis's rediscovery and reinterpretation in some depth: Seton, "The Rediscovery of St. Francis of Assisi"; Cunningham, *Saint Francis of Assisi*, 109–30; and Vauchez, *Francis of Assisi*, 229–43. Seton focused on the nineteenth century, primarily on European and scholarly works. His essay contains some inaccuracies. Cunningham surveyed twentieth-century fiction and spiritual writing, and the Catholic critique, as well as the nineteenth-century revival. Vauchez emphasized nineteenth-century romanticism and also noted the mid-twentieth century Italian revival. He framed Francis as a figure of modern myth which calls for (sympathetic) deconstruction.

3. Tartt, foreword to *Life of St. Francis* by Bonaventure, v.

4. The translations appear in Armstrong, Hellman, and Short, *Francis of Assisi: Early Documents*. Sabatier's biography was reissued in 2003 as *The Road to Assisi*, edited by Jon M. Sweeney. The 2012 biographies are Vauchez, *Francis of Assisi*, and Thompson, *Francis of Assisi*. On Islam, see Tolan, *St. Francis and the Sultan*, and Moses, *The Saint and the Sultan*. On literature and art, see Ho, Mulvaney, and Downey, *Finding St. Francis in Literature and Art*. On evangelicals and the "emerging church," see, for example, Cron, *Chasing Francis*, and Claiborne, *The Irresistible Revolution;* on Catholics, see Cunningham, *Francis of Assisi*; for Buddhist allusions, see Ehrlich, "On the Road with God's Fool" and "Walking with St. Francis." Children's books include Kennedy, *St. Francis of Assisi*, and Rosen, *The Blessing of the Animals,* among many others. On rock and punk, see Enzo Fortunato, *Vado da Francesco* ("I am going to Francis"), 2014, described in Pullella, "Rockers in the Sacristy." The chapters that follow discuss many of these works, and other sources, in more detail.

5. Wadding, *Annales Ordinis Minorum*, 8 vols. (Leyden, 1625–54), and his *Scriptores Ordinis Minorum* (Rome, 1650).

6. None of these was in any sense unbiased, of course; in particular, all reflected political agendas for the future of the Franciscan Order and authority within it. For fuller bibliographic history, see Moorman, *A History of the Franciscan Order*, 593–613; Armstrong and Brady, *Francis and Clare*, 6–10, 245–46.

Chapter One

1. Blewitt, *Hand-book for Travellers*, 265; Hutton, *Cities of Umbria*, 23. The 1905 *Guide to Italy and Sicily* said, "The town . . . owes its celebrity and interest entirely to St. Francis" (53).

2. Franchot, *Roads to Rome*. Peter Williams described a similar ambivalence in his "A Mirror for Unitarians." Arnstein, *Protestant Versus Catholic in Mid-Victorian England*, provides useful background.

3. Franchot, *Roads to Rome*, 5, 202–3, 256; Ryan K. Smith, *Gothic Arches, Latin Crosses*, 8, 15, 123.

4. Lears, *No Place of Grace*, xiii, 142–44, 151–54, 161. Lears's agenda was deeper than mere description, connecting antimodernism with class structures and cultural power in the later twentieth century.

5. See, for example, Richard Fox, *Jesus in America*, 283; on "seekers" see Leigh Eric Schmidt, *Restless Souls*.

6. For detailed historical and theoretical discussion, see Albanese, *Nature Religion in America* and *Reconsidering Nature Religion*.

7. The idea of corrupt Franciscans predates Luther: see Chaucer's "Friar's Tale" in his *Canterbury Tales*, for example. On American Protestant impressions see, for example, Paul R. Baker, *Fortunate Pilgrims*, 170–74.

8. Church history remained controversial, however: it was not fully incorporated into Protestant seminary curricula in the United States until the late nineteenth century.

9. Stephen, "St. Francis of Assisi," *Edinburgh Review*. The article was reprinted as "[Life of St. Francis]" in *Littell's Living Age*, as "St. Francis of Assisi" in *Eclectic Magazine of Foreign Literature and Art*, and as "Saint Francis of Assisi," in the book *Essays in Ecclesiastical Biography*. The biographies were Malan, *Histoire de Saint François d'Assise*, and Delecluse, *St. François d'Assise*. Stephen was later Regius Professor of Modern History at Cambridge and was the grandfather of Virginia Woolf. L. S. [Leslie Stephen], "Stephen, Sir James"; Gordon, "Woolf [née Stephen], (Adeline) Virginia."

10. Stephen, "St. Francis of Assisi," *Edinburgh Review*, 1–2.

11. The general histories were Hase, *A History of the Christian Church*; Milman, *History of Latin Christianity*; and Montalembert, *Les moines d'Occident*, published as *The Monks of the West* in Edinburgh and Boston. Milman was probably a source for other English-language writers; some later magazine articles use almost direct quotes from his history. His section on Francis was not changed in the revised edition of 1903. Abbé Migne's magisterial *Theological Encyclopedia* was also in progress; Arnold and Sabatier referred to it (see discussion below), but few others did. Hase's life of Francis was *Franz von Assisi: Ein Heiligenbild*. One American source mentioned another biography, Daurignac, *Histoire de St. Francois d'Assise* ([Gage], "Saint Francis of Assisi," 57). Joseph von Göerres published *Der heilige Franziskus von Assisi: Ein Troubadour* in Strasbourg in 1826 (cited in Armstrong, Hellman, and Short, *Francis of Assisi*, 1:22); Candide Chalippe's *Histoire de St. Francois d'Assise* (Paris, 1728) was translated in 1853 by the eminent churchman Frederick W. Faber

(cited in Moorman, *A History of the Franciscan Order*, 598). Neither occasioned much notice among non-Catholic general readers.

12. On the Reformation: Stephen, "St. Francis of Assisi," *Edinburgh Review*, 40–42. On "the mission and the pulpit": Stephen, "St. Francis of Assisi," *Edinburgh Review*, 41; "Saint Francis of Assisi," *Lend a Hand*, 283; and see also [Adams], "St. Francis and His Time," 399. On resistance to Rome: [Adams], "St. Francis and His Time," 382, 371; see also Caldwell, "The Mendicant Orders," 255–56, and "St. Francis of Assisi," *Littell's Living Age*, 515–17, 520–21, which claims to be a reprint from the *London Quarterly Review*. On preaching: Caldwell, "Mendicant Orders," 256; see also "St. Francis and the Franciscans," *American Journal of Education*, 400, and "Saint Francis of Assisi," *Lend a Hand*, 280. On comparisons with Protestants: "St. Francis of Assisi," *Littell's*, 522; "[St. Francis of Assisi]," *Quarterly Review*, 10–11, 22; Heath, "Crown of Thorns that Budded," 843. Heath also, however, associated Francis with "Soul" and the sacredness of the universe (838, 847). Philip Schaff's standard-setting encyclopedia in 1882 devoted one sober page to Francis, but gave twice as much space to St. Patrick, emphasizing his role as a missionary (Schaff, ed., *A Religious Encyclopedia*, s.v. "Francis of Assisi, St.," "Benedict of Nursia," and "Patrick, St.").

13. McClintock and Strong, *Cyclopædia of Biblical, Theological, and Ecclesiastical Literature*, s.v. "Francis of Assisi." Even James Stephen himself called the figure of Francis "cheerless and unalluring"; he thought that Francis had faith, but lacked peace and hope ([Life of St. Francis], 363).

14. Stephen, "St. Francis of Assisi," *Edinburgh Review*, 1; "St. Francis of Assisi," *Littell's*. On Protestant attitudes, compare Davis, "Catholic Envy," 108–9, and Franchot, *Roads to Rome*, 234, which minimize this active engagement.

15. In 1865 some 40,000 Americans traveled to Europe, while in 1891, 90,000 Americans returned from abroad through New York alone (Brendon, *Thomas Cook*, 105; Bradbury, *Dangerous Pilgrimages*, 180). On meanings of travel, see Bradbury, *Dangerous Pilgrimages*, 7, 145–47, 155–57, 188; Paul R. Baker, *Fortunate Pilgrims*, 3–4, 202–24; Buzard, *The Beaten Track*, 7; Stowe, *Going Abroad*, 19 and passim. Baker is particularly helpful on the meaning of Italy for Americans; Buzard introduces the idea of "anti-tourism," the search for authenticity in "unspoiled" places.

16. Paul R. Baker, *Fortunate Pilgrims*, 60; Buzard, *Beaten Track*, 47–49; on railway line, *Umbria*, 97; John Murray, *A Handbook for Travellers in Central Italy*, 255; Henry James, *Transatlantic Sketches*, 332. "Baedeker" is a reference to a popular series of travel guides.

17. John Murray, *Handbook*, 257. Nathaniel Hawthorne took a similar view in 1858 (*Passages from Hawthorne's Note-Books in France and Italy*, vol. 1, 257–61). David Morgan discusses the evolving role of clergy and religion in art appreciation (*Protestants and Pictures*, 290, 317–19).

18. Jameson, *Legends of the Monastic Orders*; Jameson, *Legends*, 2nd ed.; references to Stephen, xvi, 5, 246, and elsewhere (2nd ed. xv, 235, and elsewhere); quotes, xiii, xvii (2nd ed., xiii, xvii). Like Margaret Oliphant (see below), Jameson supported herself and a number of family members by writing. She lived independently, apart from a brief unsuccessful marriage. She produced significant work in travel

writing and women's rights as well as in art history, her primary field (Barwell, "Jameson, Anna Brownell," 221; *Oxford Dictionary of National Biography*, s.v. "Jameson [née Murphy], Anna Brownell," 752–54; Maugham, *The Book of Italian Travel*, 95).

19. Jameson, *Legends* (2nd ed.), 227–38, 239–69, and introduction; xiii, 269; 261–62; see also xxii–xxiii, 263–69. On monasticism see, for example, Calvert, *Scenes and Thoughts in Europe*: "The fictions of the Catholic Church are mostly unsuitable to the Arts; nor can martyrs or emaciated anchorites be subjected to the laws of Beauty" (172). Jameson urged the reader not to be led astray by the vogue for medieval art: "Ugliness is ugliness; the quaint is not the graceful" (Jameson, *Legends*, 2nd ed., xviii).

20. Nineteenth-century art critics associated "medieval" qualities with religious and political movements and, increasingly, with St. Francis; see, for example, Taine, *Italy: Florence and Venice*, 21. For an overview of the Giotto controversy see Creighton E. Gilbert, "Giotto," 691–96. John Ruskin had doubts about the attribution to Giotto (Bradley, *Ruskin and Italy*, 53).

21. Jameson, *Legends*, xxii; Crowe and Cavalcaselle, *A History of Painting in Italy*; Thode, *Franz von Assisi*; "Francis of Assisi and the Renaissance," 350, 361. See also Taine, *Italy: Florence and Venice*; Caldwell, "Mendicant Orders," 252–53; Heath, "Crown," 848; Darlow, "M. Sabatier's Life of St. Francis."

22. Peter Williams, "Mirror for Unitarians," 79, 224.

23. Ozanam, *Les poètes franciscains*; Jameson, *Legends*, 2nd ed., xii, 228–29; [Gage], "St. Francis," 62–63; Matthew Arnold, "Pagan and Mediæval Religious Sentiment," 224. The essay was first published in *Cornhill* under the title "Pagan and Christian Religious Sentiment" and appeared in the collection *Essays in Criticism* (1865 and many subsequent editions).

24. The 1932 edition was Arnold, *Essays in Criticism, First Series*.

25. Arnold, "Pagan and Mediæval Religious Sentiment," 224–25. There are many different English translations of the Canticle. More recent versions typically address God directly as "you" and name the creatures directly, as, for example, "Sir Brother Sun." See, for example, "The Canticle of Brother Sun," in Armstrong and Brady, *Francis and Clare*, 38–39.

26. On Unitarians, note Longfellow and Norton; and see [Gage], "St. Francis"; C. Farrington, "St. Francis of Assisi"; and Bradley and Ousby, eds., *Correspondence of Norton and Ruskin*, 320. On Arnold, see apRoberts, *Arnold and God*, 77–79, 104–9. *Imitatio Christi*, or *The Imitation of Christ*, was a fifteenth-century guide to personal devotion and spiritual life, emphasizing humility, detachment from the world, obedience to God, love, and the Eucharist. Modern readers have tended to appreciate its personal and practical focus while sitting loosely to some of its theology.

27. C. Farrington, "St. Francis," 164; cf. [Gage], "Saint Francis of Assisi," 50; Milman, *History*, 269–70; [C. K. Adams], "St. Francis," 395.

28. Schaff, *History of the Christian Church*, rev. ed. (New York, 1890), vol. 1, 853–60, 862–63, cited in Penzel, ed., *Philip Schaff*, 188–89; Renan, "Saint François d'Assise." The references that follow are to the English translation (Renan, "Francis

d'Assisi and the Franciscans, a.d. 1182," 108–27). The enduring value to liberals of Renan's book is suggested by the Modern Library edition of 1927, reprinted in 1955, with an introduction by John Haynes Holmes, a prominent Unitarian minister, editor, and pacifist.

29. Renan, "Francis," 116, 122.

30. Renan, "Francis," 116, 117, 118, 122. Heath made a similar argument about deprivation and freedom ("Crown," 855).

31. Raised as a Scottish Nonconformist, Margaret Oliphant Wilson Oliphant ultimately found orthodox theology inadequate. Her husband died while their three surviving children were young. An artist, he had never had a large income. Margaret Oliphant supported not only the children—none of whom survived her—but at various times, her mother, a distant cousin, two brothers, and several nieces and nephews. Her unfinished autobiography and her letters reveal profound struggles with questions of faith and meaning (Merryn Williams, *Margaret Oliphant*, 89, 91–97, 139–40; Jay, *Mrs Oliphant*).

32. Oliphant, *Francis of Assisi*.

33. Oliphant, *Francis of Assisi*, 14–15.

34. Oliphant, *Francis of Assisi*, xi–xii, xv, 304.

35. The preceding discussion draws on Hilton, *John Ruskin*; Wheeler, *Ruskin's God*; and Alexander Bradley, *Ruskin and Italy*. On community, see Hilton, *Ruskin*, 2:145; Merryn Williams, *Oliphant*, 90, 96. Both Ruskin and Margaret Oliphant took an interest in Laurence Oliphant (distantly related to the latter), who promoted an American utopian community called the Brotherhood of the New Life, founded by Thomas Lake Harris. On the portrait, see Hilton, *John Ruskin*, 2:280. Hilton cites Van Akin Burd, ed., *Christmas Story: John Ruskin's Venetian Letters of 1876–1877* (Newark: University of Delaware Press, 1990), 102, 105. Burd reproduces a copy of the image, titled "St. Francis; study from Cimabue's *Madonna with Angels and St. Francis*" (1874). Walter Seton claimed that Ruskin wrote about the Third Order in *Deucalion*, but this appears to be an error (Seton, "Rediscovery of St. Francis," 252).

36. [Adams], "St. Francis and His Time," 394; Tulloch, "St. Francis, Part II," 49; Richards, "A Sunbeam from the 13th Century," 151. Tulloch was a friend of Margaret Oliphant and disapproved of Matthew Arnold's theology (Tulloch, "Amateur Theology").

37. Two other significant books of this period were Arsène de Chatel, ed., *Saint François d'Assise*, and Bonghi, *Francesco d'Assisi: Studio*; the second edition of Bonghi's book included an introduction by Paul Sabatier, whom I discuss below. Henry Wadsworth Longfellow also weighed in with "The Sermon of St. Francis," first published in 1875 (Samuel Longfellow, ed., *Final Memorials*, 434) and reprinted in 1877 (Henry Wadsworth Longfellow, *Poems of Places*, 71) and 1908 (in Schauffler, ed., *Through Italy with the Poets*).

38. Sabatier, *Vie de S. François d'Assise*; Sabatier, *Life of St. Francis of Assisi*. The French edition was reprinted in 1931, the English edition in 1938. The most recent reissue was Sweeney's edited version in 2003 (see introduction). For biographical information, see Sabatier, *Life*, xii, xvii; *New Catholic Encyclopedia*, s.v. "Sabatier, Paul"; Rawnsley, "With Paul Sabatier at Assisi." (Sabatier refers to " '89," the

founding year of the Second International, and says that "the mendicant orders were . . . a true *International*.") On the Vatican Index, see Englebert, *Saint Francis of Assisi*, 32. On travel, see Baedeker, *Italy: A Handbook for Travelers*, 71; Blashfield and Blashfield, *Italian Cities*, 87; and chapter 2 of this volume. On Tolstoy, see Steele, "Sabatier's Life of St. Francis," 96; Warfield, "M. Paul Sabatier's Life of St. Francis of Assisi," 159.

39. Butler, "Francis of Assisi, St.," in *Encyclopædia Britannica*, 939; Moorman, *History of the Franciscan Order*, 596, 598; Thompson, *Francis of Assisi*, 155–61, quote from 157; "Francis of Assisi, St.," in *Oxford Dictionary of the Christian Church*, 636. As late as the 3rd edition of the ODCC (1997), Hase and Oliphant were mentioned as important early biographers. See also Armstrong, Hellman, and Short, *Francis of Assisi*, general introduction, 1:22.

40. Armstrong, Hellman, and Short thought Renan's essay "undoubtedly attracted" Sabatier's attention, but they take little note of the wider context (*Francis of Assisi*, 1:22). Boase, *St. Francis of Assisi*, says Sabatier was "taught by" Renan (15).

41. The stumbling blocks that troubled earlier Protestant writers were red herrings, Sabatier thought. The cloth that Francis sold was his own, not his father's. Clare was an agent in her own decisions, not merely a victim of abduction. Relations between the brothers and sisters, he said, were spiritually intimate but entirely pure. He also made a somewhat strained case that the sisters were as active as the brothers except where they were limited by being cloistered (Sabatier, *Life*, 57–58, 62, 147–67).

42. Sabatier, *Life*, xiii. Compare with Oliphant, *Francis of Assisi*.

43. Sabatier, *Life*, 181.

44. Tinel, *Franciscus*; a review notes that the work was first performed in 1888 ("A New Oratorio by Edgar Tinel"). It was reviewed in New York in 1893 ("'St. Francis of Assisi' to be Presented by Oratorio Society"); Shaw, "Poor Old Philharmonic," in *Shaw's Music*. On the Salvation Army, see Douglas, *Brother Francis*, and A. P. Doyle, "St. Francis in Salvation Army Uniform," who mentioned "the twice-told tale of St. Francis" (760). Douglas was also the author of *George Fox, the Red-hot Quaker*. On Little, see his *St. Francis of Assisi* and his "The Last Days of St. Francis of Assisi"; on moderation, see also Smyth, "Recent Revivalism and the Franciscan Rule"; on Stephen, see n. 13.

Chapter Two

1. Crothers, *Pardoner's Wallet*, 199. For background on Crothers, see *Who Was Who in America*, 1897–1942.

2. Trenholme, "Saint of Assisi," 490. On travel, see Macquoid, *Pictures in Umbria*, xv, 171; Lina Duff Gordon, *Story of Assisi*, 63–64, 138n, 238, and elsewhere. Selincourt, *Homes of the First Franciscans*, has a preface by Sabatier, and the author says the book was undertaken at his suggestion (v, vii). On meetings, see Masterman, "Chicago and Francis," 188. See also "Woodbrooke Summer Settlement," 649.

3. David Hollinger and others have recently proposed the term "ecumenical" in place of "mainline." (Hollinger, "After Cloven Tongues of Fire," 4–5; see also

Hedstrom, *Rise of Liberal Religion*). I stay with "mainline" in this book because it implies a social as well as a religious location, and because the term "ecumenical" elides the strongly felt differences among denominations.

4. On the mainline, see especially Hutchison, "Protestantism as Establishment," 3–6.

5. Hutchison, *Between the Times*, preface, vii, and passim.

6. "Editorial notes," *New York Evangelist*; "Literature," *Christian Advocate*; Coe, "Studies in the Psychology of Religion"; Sheldon, "The Law of Christian Discipleship"; "Closet and Altar," *Congregationalist and Christian World* (September 17, 1900, and October 18, 1902); [Article 3], *Friends' Intelligencer*; Deacon, "Assisi," *Friends' Intelligencer*; "Woodbrooke Summer Settlement," *Friends' Intelligencer*; "The Meaning and Service of Silence in Worship," *The Friend*; "Connecticut Letter," *Watchman*; Hale, "Chautauqua Special Courses," *Chautauquan*; Alice Brown, "Little Windows into the World," *Harper's Bazaar*; "With the Corresponding Editor," *Harper's Bazaar*; "St. Francis of Assisi," *Overland Monthly and Out West*. The *Friends' Intelligencer* was Hicksite, *The Friend* was Orthodox. Sabatier's publisher advertised in *Christian Advocate*, *Congregationalist*, and elsewhere. General-interest periodicals included *Littell's Living Age*, *Macmillan's*, *Outlook*, *The Nation*, *The Critic*, *The Ladies' Home Journal*, *The Saturday Evening Post*, *Massachusetts Ploughman and New England Journal of Agriculture*; learned magazines included *The Academy* and *The North American Review*.

7. See, for example, Griggs, *Moral Leaders*, 49–89.

8. On McKinley, see Doane, "Anarchism and Atheism." On wildlife, see "Massachusetts Association Dinner" (listed as "Letter 3 —No Title" in the American Periodicals series database). On Duncan, see Sheel, "On with the Dance." For other comparisons, see "Among the New Books," *New York Observer and Chronicle*; "The Oscar Wilde Revival," *Current Literature*.

9. Martinengo Cesaresco, "Friend of the Creature"; Wood, "Auto-suggestion and Concentration"; Storr-Best, "Common Sense of Hypnotism"; "[Article 1]," *Catholic World*; Rufus M. Jones, *Studies in Mystical Religion*, xxvii–xxviii; William James, *Principles of Psychology*, 2:612–13. See also James, *Varieties of Religious Experience*, 14, 279, 491.

10. "Impressions of a Careless Traveler"; Crothers, *Pardoner's Wallet*, 219.

11. "Day of the Birds"; Barrett, "A Word About the Old Saints"; pieces in *Youth's Companion* included "Oddity" and "A New Voice in the House"; Jewett, *God's Troubadour*, 179–81, 183–85, illustrations facing pages 10, 60, 100, 82, 66, 70.

12. Many cathedrals and larger churches in the first half of the twentieth century included these window series. See, for example, Cook, "A Christian Vision of Unity," 164–67, on the Riverside Church in New York City.

13. Jefferson, *Things Fundamental*; Stone, "Joseph Barber Lightfoot"; Herron, "The Recovery of Jesus from Christianity," 14; "John Wesley Bicentennial in Boston." On mystics, see "John Wesley Bicentennial"; Hurlbut, "Inner Life of Mme. Guyon"; and "Article IV: Psychology and Salvation." On missionaries, see "Being a Brother"; Potter, "An Economic Asset"; and "Quest for Life." On social visionaries, see "Article IV"; "Being a Brother"; Willcox, "Tolstoi's Religion";

Birmingham, "Island of Saints"; Douglas, *Brother Francis*; and Herron, *Between Caesar and Jesus*, 180. On masculinity, see "Virility of Goodness." In British social-reform circles, however, Francis was "an exemplar of a new kind of masculinity" in the 1880s (Ross, "St. Francis in Soho," 847).

14. Hutchison, *Modernist Impulse*, discusses anxiety about the uniqueness of Christianity (111–32) but does not focus on this question of definition.

15. Hopkins, *Rise of the Social Gospel*, 131–34; Hopkins, "Walter Rauschenbusch"; Evans, *The Kingdom Is Always But Coming*, 104–10. Rauschenbusch's major works are *Christianity and the Social Crisis* (1907), *Christianizing the Social Order* (1912), *The Social Principles of Jesus* (1916), and *A Theology for the Social Gospel* (1917).

16. Hopkins, *Rise of the Social Gospel*, 131, 134. On Houghton and on Richard Heath, see "The Brotherhood of the Kingdom," *New York Evangelist*, 28–29. On studying Sabatier, noting that they also honored Mazzini, Tolstoy, Wycliffe, and others, see Woodruff, "Religious Intelligence: The Brotherhood of the Kingdom."

17. Rauschenbusch, *Social Order*, 84; *Social Crisis*, 76, 334; *Theology*, 116.

18. Rauschenbusch, *Theology*, 62, 272; *Social Principles*, 108.

19. Leigh Eric Schmidt, *Restless Souls*, 56; Hedstrom, "Rufus Jones."

20. On Sabatier, see Vining, *Friend of Life*, 53; Rufus M. Jones, *Flowering of Mysticism*, 2. On 1903 tragedy, see Rufus M. Jones, *Trail of Life in the Middle Years*, 124; Vining, *Friend of Life*, 100. On the visit, see Vining, *Friend of Life*, 226–27. On multiple matters, see Jones, *Luminous Trail*, 63.

21. Rufus M. Jones, *Studies in Mystical Religion*, 152, 156, 157; Jones, *Luminous Trail*, 68. Compare Eddy and Page, *Makers of Freedom*, 81–82; Rauschenbusch, *Christianizing the Social Order*, 87–88; and Rauschenbusch, *Christianity and the Social Crisis*, 93. On robbers, see (e.g.) *Little Flowers*, chapter 26.

22. Jones, *New Quest*, 100–105. Later still, in *The Luminous Trail*, Jones told Francis's story yet again. He concluded with the "true and perfect joy" anecdote but, like so many others, offered no explanation of it (78–79).

23. *Little Flowers*, chapter 35. Jones told the Brother Giles story in his *Studies in Mystical Religion*, 162; *New Quest*, 102–3; *Luminous Trail*, 71, and elsewhere.

24. Biographical information is drawn from *Notable American Women*, s.v. "Scudder, Vida"; *American National Biography*, s.v. "Scudder, Vida Dutton"; Corcoran, *Vida Dutton Scudder*; Scudder, *On Journey*.

25. Corcoran, *Vida Dutton Scudder*, 83; Scudder, *Socialism and Character*, 216–19; Scudder, *On Journey*, 338. "Programme of the Social Justice Committee of the S. C. H. C: Institute of Studies, 'St. Francis and Today,'" printed flyer; "Poverty and Property;" and "Work and Reward" in Franciscan Institute, [Statements], typescript, page [1], Franciscan Institute Records.

26. Scudder, *On Journey*, 198, 231, 239–40, 313–15, 320–21; Haraszti, "A Library," 275–76; Scudder, "Sabatier Collection," 218.

27. Scudder, *Life of the Spirit*, 172–75.

28. Scudder, *Socialism and Character*, 102–3, 216, 229; Scudder, "The Larks of St. Francis," 191.

29. See, for example, Scudder, *The Church and the Hour*, 32–35; Scudder, *Socialism and Character*, 100–101, 221, 222.

30. Scudder, *Socialism and Character*, 108–12, 218–35; Corcoran, *Vida Dutton Scudder*, 69.

31. Scudder, *On Journey*, 176–78.

32. Masterman, "Chicago and Francis," 187–89.

33. Ozora S. Davis, "Assisi," 192.

34. MacDonell, *Sons of Francis,* 6–7. Jewett concludes *God's Troubadour* with a poem about place, 183–85. On Rufus Jones's reaction to Assisi, see Vining, *Friend of Life*, 226–27. See also Buckley, "Two Newspaper Women Abroad"; Sabatier, preface to Selincourt, *Homes*, v; and Masterman, "Chicago and Francis," 187–89, among many examples.

35. There is a very large literature on the subject. I have relied here on Rhys H. Williams, "Creating an American Islam," 147; Sheldrake, "Human Identity and the Particularity of Place," 43, 51; Brueggemann, *The Land: Place As Gift, Promise and Challenge in Biblical Faith* (Philadelphia: Fortress, 1977), 5, quoted in Sheldrake, "Human Identity," 46–47; Campbell, "Religion and Ecology," 192–93; Ivakhiv, *Claiming Sacred Ground* (Bloomington: Indiana University Press, 2002), 235, cited in Campbell, 192; Brueggemann, introduction, 6–19. See also Gieryn, "A Space for Place."

36. The classic work is Turner and Turner, *Image and Pilgrimage*; see also Tomasi, "*Homo Viator*," among many critiques and updates. On materiality and tourism, see Stausberg, *Religion and Tourism*, 19–26, 53–71; Waller, "From the Holy Family," 72; Coleman and Elsner, "Pilgrimage to Walsingham," 191–94; Swatos, "New Canterbury Trails," 93–95.

37. On Plymouth Rock, see Seelye, *Memory's Nation*. On Protestant pilgrimages see, among others, B., "Epworth Pilgrimage," D., "Pilgrimage Letters," and "The New Jersey Pilgrimage." Useful background from a British perspective is found in Waller, "From the Holy Family," 79; Larsen, "Thomas Cook," 341; and Coleman and Elsner, "Pilgrimage to Walsingham."

38. Ozora S. Davis, "Assisi," 193.

39. Sherrard, " 'Palestine Sits in Sackcloth and Ashes,' " 88–90; Larsen, "Thomas Cook," 334–36. Sherrard cites William McClure Thomson, *The Land and the Book*, 1859, quoting page 1, and Edward Robinson, *Biblical Researches in Palestine*, 1838, as well as Twain, *The Innocents Abroad*, 1869. See also Stowe, *Going Abroad*, 18, on literary tropes for travelers.

40. Scudder, "Footprints," 322.

41. Scudder, "Footprints," 323.

42. Scudder, "Footprints," 322, 323, 325.

43. Scudder, "Footprints," 324.

44. Scudder, "Footprints," 325.

45. Scudder, "Footprints," 325.

46. Scudder, "Footprints," 325.

47. Scudder, "Footprints," 326.

48. Eric Doyle, "Select Bibliography," 74. Doyle was a British Franciscan theologian who also taught in New York. His 1981 book on the Canticle of the Sun was developed in part from "lectures to trainee yoga teachers" (Doyle, *St. Francis and the Song of Brotherhood*, vi). The introduction to Raphael Brown, *True Joy from Assisi*—a 1978 anthology about place—strikes some of the same notes as Scudder.

49. Henry Adams, *Mont-Saint-Michel*, 375.

50. Robinson, *Real St. Francis*, 5. The bibliographic history of this work is confusing. Robinson published an essay with this title in *The Catholic Mind* in July 1903. It was reprinted as a twenty-four-page pamphlet or book by the Messenger Press of New York, probably in 1903, according to a WorldCat entry. My copy is a small book, ninety-three pages, whose title page says "Reprinted from The Catholic Mind," with no other bibliographic data. A "second edition" of 112 pages came out in London in 1904. Citations here are to the 93-page book. On Catholic response to non-Catholic interest, see, for example, "Talk about New Books"; "Library Table," 73; E., "Non-Catholic Work in Franciscan Studies."

51. Among the many examples in the early documents are the Admonitions, especially chapter 3, "Perfect Obedience," and chapter 26, "The Servants of God Should Honor the Clergy" (Armstrong, Hellman, and Short, *Early Documents*, 1:128–37); and the Earlier Rule, especially chapter 19, "The Brothers Are to Live as Catholics" (Armstrong, Hellman, and Short, *Early Documents*, 1:63–86). Note that recent Protestant authors have been more likely to acknowledge Francis's Catholic faith; see, for example, Galli, *Francis of Assisi*, 7.

52. Robinson, *Real St. Francis*, 4–5, 6, 8–12, 13, 15–17, 19.

53. For biographical information, see Jørgensen's preface to his *St. Francis*, 3–5; *Encyclopædia Britannica*, 15th ed., s.v. Jørgensen, Johannes. On nature, see Jørgensen, *St. Francis*, 25, 254. On Sabatier, see, for example, 26, 287; on Tolstoy, 73. Citations are to the 1955 reprint. The review was Brann, "Francis of Assisi."

54. Biographical information from *Who Was Who, 1929–1940*, s.v. Cuthbert, Very Rev. Father. A revised edition of Cuthbert's *Life* appeared in 1913, with three more printings by 1917, and it is still occasionally cited. The first edition was published in New York as well as in London, as were many subsequent printings. Quotations from Cuthbert, *Life*, v. Page numbers here, and in subsequent references, are from the second edition.

55. Cuthbert, *Life*, 450–55; Sabatier, *Life*, 337–39. The problem of translation is complex: there are questions of original intent, meaning, and context, and how best to render that in another language for another time.

56. Cuthbert, *Life*, 450–54.

57. Sabatier, *Life*, 334–35, 336–37, 337–39.

58. Egan, *Everybody's St. Francis*; see, for example, 56, 90.

Chapter Three

1. Seton, *St. Francis of Assisi: 1226–1926*; Bush, "Simple Homages"; "All Italy Honors St. Francis of Assisi"; Marlatt, *Protestant Saints. The Congregationalist* 111,

no. 39, September 30, 1926, included an unsigned editorial, three articles, and a poem by Gertrude Huntington McGiffert, wife of the theologian Arthur Cushman McGiffert. In 1927 Lawrence Abbott characterized Francis as modern (Abbott, *Twelve Great Modernists*, 29–46).

2. On poverty, see Boase, *St. Francis of Assisi*, chapter 3, esp. 36–37, 42–49, quote on page 47. This was a British publication. See also Petry, "The Ideal of Poverty in St. Francis of Assisi"; and Petry, *St. Francis of Assisi: Apostle of Poverty*. On spirituality, see Wieman and Jones, "What Saints and Sages See"; Sperry, "The Little Flowers of St. Francis"; and Washburn, "Francis of Assisi." Even Washburn's treatment of Francis as philanthropist soft-pedals absolute poverty: see "Francis of Assisi," in his *Religious Motive in Philanthropy*. On the Depression era, see Colleen McDannell, *Picturing Faith*, 14–15, 17–18. On Agee, see Doty, *Tell Me Who I Am*, 51; and Wranovics, "Chaplin in the Art and Life of James Agee," 157. Biographical sources note Agee's Anglo-Catholic upbringing and his general ambivalence about religion.

3. García-Marquez, *Massine*, 262–65; Terry, "O, Brother Sun," 39; Jack Anderson, "Ted Shawn's Legacy"; "San Francisco's Saint."

4. Dumenil, *Modern Temper*, esp. 1–13; Dumenil, "Reinterpeting the 1920s," 5; Parrish, *Anxious Decades*, esp. ix–x, 183–203.

5. Chesterton, *St. Francis* (1923; reprinted New York: Doubleday, 1990), 11–16, 31.

6. Chesterton, *St. Francis*, 39–40, 44, 47, 86–89, 96–97.

7. Chesterton, *St. Francis*, 55, 57, 70, 72, 75, 78, 80. Chesterton was already exploring the theme of asceticism in 1902 in *Twelve Types*, 63–78.

8. Chesterton, *St. Francis*, 117–18, 149–52.

9. Rufus M. Jones, *Luminous Trail*, 64.

10. Biographical information is from Housman, *Unexpected Years,* and from *Oxford Dictionary of National Biography*, s.v. "Housman, Lawrence."

11. Bibliographic information is from Housman, *Unexpected Years*, 279; Housman, *Little Plays*, complete ed., 1:vi; *National Union Catalog, Pre-1956 Imprints*; and WorldCat.

12. Housman, *Little Plays Handbook*, 1927, ix; *Unexpected Years*, 280–87. Housman says professional actor Maurice Evans performed the plays in a settlement house early in his career. On Evans's interest, see "Money in Shakespeare" and "Ethel Barrymore in Premiere Here." On American amateur performances see, for example, the item headed "Mid-summer Fair at Merrywood" in "Table Gossip," and Peppeard, "Passion Sunday Sermons." The American Quaker teacher Douglas Steere recommended the plays for retreat settings (Steere, *Time to Spare*, 183).

13. Housman, *Little Plays*, complete ed., preface, vii–viii; Housman, *Unexpected Years*, 272–73.

14. Housman, *Sister Gold*, in *Little Plays* (1922), 173–96.

15. "In the foolishness of Juniper," says Housman, "the wisdom of Francis reveals itself" (Housman, preface to *Little Plays*, complete ed., x).

16. David Morgan, *Visual Piety*, 3–5; Bendroth, *Spiritual Practice*, esp. 5, 122–25.

17. On the "plutocratic" Social Gospel, see Vidich and Lyman, *American Sociology*, 132.

18. McCormick, "Fascism Takes Francis as Patron Saint"; Marshall, "Italians Profess Threefold Faith"; Bush, "Simple Homages Paid to St. Francis"; "All Italy Honors St. Francis of Assisi"; "Grey Friars Get Back Sacred Monastery."

19. Scudder, *On Journey*, 339–43; Scudder, "A Franciscan Institute," 427–28; "Programme of the Social Justice Committee of the S. C. H. C: Institute of Studies, 'St. Francis and Today,'" printed flyer, 1933; Social Justice Committee of the S.C.H.C., "Program of the Institute of Franciscan Studies: 'St. Francis and Today,'" mimeograph, 1933; "Reports of the Franciscan Institute, Adelynrood, 1933," typescript, 1933; all from Franciscan Institute Records, Vida Scudder Collection, Adelynrood, Byfield, Mass.

20. Franciscan Institute, [Statements], typescript, page [1–2]; "First Report on Findings of Roundtables," in "Reports of the Franciscan Institute," from Franciscan Institute Records, Scudder Collection. See also Haroutunian, *Wisdom and Folly*.

21. "Reports of Modern Franciscan Groups," in "Reports of the Franciscan Institute"; Scudder, *On Journey*, 342–48.

22. Hoyland, Administrative/Biographical History; Hoyland, *Way of St. Francis*, 30, 128, 133–34, 136, 149–56. See also Sweeney, "E. Stanley Jones, C. F. Andrews, Gandhi, and St. Francis."

23. Kosek, *Acts of Conscience*; Appelbaum, *Kingdom to Commune*.

24. Sabatier, "St. Francis and the Twentieth Century," 326; Holmes, *New Wars for Old*, 10, 191–93.

25. Among many examples are Sherwood Eddy, *A Pilgrimage of Ideas*, 103, 108, 217; Eddy and Page, *Makers of Freedom*, 81–82, an essay that also connected Francis with poverty; Rufus M. Jones, "Experiments in Heroic Love," 97–105; Allen, *The Fight for Peace*; Binyon, "St. Francis of Assisi"; Alden H. Clark, foreword to Laubach, *Letters by a Modern Mystic*, 5; "Peace Syllabus"; "Young People and a New World."

26. Gregg, *The Power of Non-Violence* and *Training for Peace*.

27. Muste, *Non-Violence in an Aggressive World*, 9, 81.

28. Dellinger, *From Yale to Jail*, 19–20, 145–51; *The Intentional Communities*, 22–24; quote, p. 22.

29. Holmes, *New Wars*, 192; Eddy and Page, *Makers of Freedom*, 81; Rufus M. Jones, *The New Quest*, 100, 105. Jones contrasted this view of Francis with the image of "an anaemic mystic who worked himself up to such a pitch of auto-suggestion that he finally produced the stigmata of nail prints in his hands and feet" (100).

30. Jørgensen, *Saint Francis of Assisi*, 196–97. The story of the wolf is chapter 21 of the *Little Flowers of St. Francis*.

31. The claim about the Third Order was based on documents that were always controversial and are now no longer considered authentic to Francis; see Moorman, *Sources for the Life of S. Francis of Assisi*, 12, 16; and Peterson, "The Third Order," 200. Sabatier, *Life*, cites the papal bull *Significatum est*, 1221 (267); Moorman, *History of the Franciscan Order*, discusses the supposed rule of 1221, which does not survive, and the rule of circa 1228 (41–44). See chapters 14 and 16 of "The Earlier Rule (the Rule without a Papal Seal)," 63–86, in Armstrong, Hellman, and Short, *Early Documents*, vol. 1, 63–86, esp. 72, 74–75.

32. Holmes, *New Wars*, 192–93; *With Children Leading*, 78–80.

33. See chapter 9 of "The Legend of the Three Companions," in Armstrong, Hellman, and Short, *Early Documents*, vol. 2, p. 89; and Rufus M. Jones, *Luminous Trail*, 71.

34. On common origins, see Piehl, *Breaking Bread*, 134–39; Baker, *"Go to the Worker,"* 46–47.

35. Ellis, "Peter Maurin"; Gneuhs, "Peter Maurin's Personalist Democracy," 49.

36. Dorothy Day in *Catholic Worker*, May 1953, quoted in Zwick and Zwick, *The Catholic Worker Movement*, 126–27.

37. Baker, *"Go to the Worker,"* 57–60; Heineman, *A Catholic New Deal*, 70, 122; Sicius, "The Chicago Catholic Worker," 349.

38. Day, *The Duty of Delight*, 30, 45, 59, 74, 118, 190–93, 210, 227, 253; Riegle, *Dorothy Day*, 90 (her informant was Tom Cornell).

39. Zwick and Zwick, *Catholic Worker Movement*, 117.

40. "Lord, make me an instrument" (untitled copy of prayer), *Catholic Worker*, December 1941, page 7; Dorothy Day, "Our country passes from undeclared to declared war: we continue our pacifist stand," *Catholic Worker*, January 1942, page 1.

41. Lewin, *One of Benny's Faces*, 146, 166, 183–91; Reddy, "Stormy Benny," 23, 94; Bess, "Sculptor Who Embarrasses San Francisco," 54; "World's Tallest Statue"; "San Francisco's Saint."

42. For a photograph of Bufano's maquette for the statue, see "San Francisco's Saint," 28.

43. "San Francisco's Saint"; Bess, "Sculptor Who Embarrasses San Francisco," 54–55; Reddy, "Stormy Benny," 22, 94–95; "Benny's Back"; "World's Tallest Statue"; "Bufano vs. Pegler" (photo of Pegler effort), 22–23; *Benezit Dictionary of Artists*, s.v. "Bufano, Benjamino" [*sic*].

44. Broun was quoted in "Bufano vs. Pegler," 23, and in Reddy, "Stormy Benny," 95.

45. "Benny Bufano Statues in San Francisco"; "Art and Architecture San Francisco: Bufano."

Chapter Four

1. On the origins of the prayer, see three articles in *Greyfriars Review*: Schulz, "The So-Called Prayer of St. Francis," 240, 242; van Dijk, "A Prayer in Search of an Author," 258, 259; and Poulenc, "The Modern Inspiration for the Prayer," 265–68. On 1927 publication, see "A Prayer of St. Francis of Assissi [*sic*]." The *Intelligencer* gave no source or attribution other than Francis.

2. Hoyland, *The Way of St. Francis*, 11; Langford Jones, *Peace Portfolio*, 12. On the BBC and the card, see Schulz, "The So-Called Prayer of St. Francis," 240.

3. *Prayers for the Church Service League*, 5th ed., 117; *Handbook for Peacemakers*, inside front cover; Page, *Living Abundantly*, 125; Day, *Duty of Delight*, 118. In Britain, it appeared in a classic collection, Milner-White and Briggs, *Daily Prayer* (1941). It does not appear in the 4th ed. of *Prayers for the Church Service League* (1930).

4. Milligan, ed., *Best Loved Hymns and Prayers*, 384–85; Richardson Wright, "Instruments of Peace," 40–41; *Who Was Who in America*, vol. 4 (1961–68), s.v. "Wright,

Richardson Little." Wright was also the author of *The Anatomy of Saints* (Morehouse-Gorham, 1946) and other collections, and a sampling of his editorial columns includes "The Cloud of Witnesses" (December 1931), "Wise Men from Afar" (December 1935), and "Plowshares into Swords" (March 1941).

5. The quote is from Brink and Polman, eds., *Psalter Hymnal Handbook*, 431. For hymnals, see notes 9 and beyond below. Much, though not all, of this research is based on the very helpful database at hymnary.org.

6. Watson, *Annotated Anthology of Hymns*, 44; Lightman, "The Reverend William Henry Draper"; Val Crompton, personal correspondence with author, 3 November 2011. Ms. Crompton says that until 2007, there were church members with living memory of singing "All Creatures" under Rector Draper's direction.

7. On early history, J. R. Watson, correspondence with author, October 22, 2011; on hymnals, see Dearmer, *Songs of Praise Discussed*, 234; Adey, *Class and Idol*, 229–33; Dearmer, *Songs*, xxii.

8. Dearmer, *Songs*, 102; Brink and Polman, *Psalter Hymnal Handbook*, 431. Ian Bradley, in *The Book of Hymns*, 12–13, errs in saying that "All Creatures" appeared in the *English Hymnal*. Dearmer, Shaw, and Williams, *Songs of Praise,* tried a new tune, "St. Francis" by G. W. Briggs (Hymn 439), but it has not stuck.

9. For example, the first line stresses the first, fourth, and eighth syllables and ends on a rising phrase. Musical notation and sound files can be found in the hymnary.org database.

10. For the sake of brevity, I have not included full bibliographic data in the next few notes. All of these hymnals can be identified through hymnary.org as well as through library catalogs. H. Augustine Smith, *The American Student Hymnal* (1928); *Oxford American Hymnal for Schools and Colleges* (1930); *The Chapel Hymnal* (1931); Stanley A. Day, *The Boys and Girls Song Series* (1932); Edith Lovell Thomas, *Singing Worship with Boys and Girls* (Methodist, 1935); Edward Dwight Eaton, *The Student Hymnary* (1937); *The Canadian Youth Hymnal* (United Church of Canada, 1939); William H. Crawford, *A School Service Book* (1939); *Hymns for Junior Worship* (Presbyterian, 1940); *The Hymnary of the United Church of Canada* (United Church of Canada,1930); *Songs for Worship* (Religious Education Council of Canada, 1930). Translations into French and German, dated 1929, appear in a later youth hymnal. The German translator was the eminent biblical historian Karl Budde (*Cantate Domino*, 1942).

11. *Beacon Song and Service Book* (Unitarian, 1935); *The Methodist Hymnal* (1935); C. A. Bowen, *The Cokesbury Worship Hymnal* (Methodist Episcopal Church, South, 1938); *Hymnal for Christian Worship* (Presbyterian, 1940); *Hymns for Worship* (YMCA, 1939); *A Hymnal for Friends* (Quaker, Friends General Conference, 1942); *Christian Worship* (Northern Baptist and Disciples of Christ, 1941); *The Hymnal, Authorized by the General Synod* (German Reformed, 1941); *The Army and Navy Hymnal* (1942).

12. *The Voice of Thanksgiving*, No. 5 (Moody Press, 1946); *Hymns, Church of Jesus Christ of Latter-day Saints* (1948); *Christian Youth Hymnal* (Lutheran, 1948); *Songs for Primaries* (Southern Baptist, 1948); *Songs for Christian Worship* (Presbyterian, 1950); *Church School Hymnal for Children* (Lutheran, 1961); *Fellowship Hymnal* (Na-

tional Council of the Churches of Christ in the USA, 1955); *The Song Book of the Salvation Army* (1953); *Our Hymns of Praise* (Mennonite, 1958); *Pilgrim Hymnal* (United Church of Christ, 1958); *The Hymnal of the Protestant Episcopal Church in the U. S. A.* (1940); *The Hymnal 1982* (Episcopal).

13. *Worship II: A Hymnal for Roman Catholic Parishes* (GIA, 1975). Among many locations are Theodore Marier, *Hymns, Psalms, and Spiritual Canticles* (BACS Publishing [Boston Archdiocesan Choir School], 1983); *Peoples Mass Book* (World Library Publications, 1984); *Rise Up and Sing* (OCP Publications, 1988); *Gather* (GIA, 1994); *Gather Comprehensive* (GIA, 2004).

14. Stulken and Salika, *Hymnal Companion to Worship*, 335. On translation, see Raphael Brown, "The Canticle of Brother Sun," Appendix 8 to Englebert, *Saint Francis* (441–58), 445.

15. "July in the Shops" (the manufacturer was Florentine Craftsmen); Jekyll and Husey, *Garden Ornament*; Gothein, *History of Garden Art*, 2:443; Sheehy, *The Flamingo in the Garden*, 17. A 1924 American article commented "Americans have an inherent dislike for sculpture in the garden" (Dean, "Fitly Furnishing," 272).

16. Many general histories trace this pattern, including Watters, *American Gardens, 1890–1930,* and Griswold and Weller, *Golden Age of American Gardens*. On statuary, see *Fauns and Fountains*; Jane Brown, *Art and Architecture of English Gardens*; Israel, *Antique Garden Ornament*.

17. Grampp, *From Yard to Garden*; Stickley, *Craftsman Houses*, 45–47, 82; Goldsmith, *Designs for Outdoor Living*, viii–ix, 3–4; Sheehy, *Flamingo*, 17–20, 68–72.

18. Munsterberg, "Assisi in Boston," 9, 33. The Boston Public Library acquired Sabatier's library after his death, largely through the mediation of Vida Scudder; see chapter 2.

19. "A Country House with a Private Chapel," 14–16. The owners were Mr. and Mrs. William V. Chapin.

20. "Furnishings That Bring Friendliness to Gardens," 299; "Miss E. Muntz's Sculpture," 381–82; Sheehy, *Flamingo*, 20.

21. William Eddy, *Stone Pond*, 4–5, 10; "Wallace Oliver: Meerwood," in Eddy, *Stone Pond*, 2–3; Rev. Richard Cassius Lee Webb, personal correspondence with author, March 20, 2012. The original name of the estate was Meerwood, which is engraved on the foundation stone of the house (Linda Ferranti-Nesbeda, personal communication). Some contemporary sources and personal memoirs refer to it as Merrywood, for reasons that are not clear ("Table Gossip"; Oppler, "Duchess of Stone Pond," 42).

22. Oppler, "The Duchess of Stone Pond," 43; Eddy, *Stone Pond*, 4–5; "Chapel of St. Francis and the Wolf of Gubbio"; "St. Francis Birdbath/Garden Statue"; Webb, personal correspondence, March 20, 2012.

23. Eddy, *Stone Pond*, 5; "St. Francis Birdbath/Garden Statue." Photographs suggest that the St. Francis garden was located in an open area southeast of the main house, toward Stone Pond, with Allen's statue in the center. Another house now stands on the site. The photos are in the private collection of the Ferranti family.

24. Eddy, *Stone Pond*, 4, 11, 28–29, 130; Oppler, "The Duchess of Stone Pond," 44–52; "Table Gossip" (the section about Mrs. Kershaw is headed "Mid-Summer

Fair at Merrywood" and describes a fundraising event including "Little Plays of St. Francis" and East Indian music along with the usual refreshments and games).

25. William Morgan, *Monadnock Summer*, 104; Tom Hyman, *Village on a Hill*, 315, 359; Brewster, "Factual History of Morelands," 2, 8. Mrs. Brewster says that pictures of the gardens appeared in E. I. Farrington, *Garden Omnibus*, 1938, and in Fitch and Rockwell, *Treasury of American Gardens*, 1956. *House and Garden* reported on it in June 1935 ("Varied Garden of Mrs. F. F. Brewster," 40–41); and the St. Francis statue was featured in Goldsmith, *Designs for Outdoor Living*, 301.

26. "Obituary: Mrs. Anna Heaton Fitch," 2; "Brewster Family History." Anna Heaton Fitch was Margaret Brewster's mother. "Flowers and Gardens in Art," a 1934 account of a Pittsburgh flower show, mentions a St. Francis statue alongside ornaments from significant private gardens (301).

27. "Country Life," 437; Wright, *The Story of Gardening*, 1934; Scudder, *On Journey*, 405.

28. "Shopping Around," 1938, 5; "St. Francis in Your Garden" (advertisement); "St. Francis and the Birds" (advertisement); Maria Lynch Dumoulin of Kenneth Lynch and Sons, telephone interview with author, February 17, 2012; Erkins Studios, *Garden Ornaments* [catalog], 3, 19.

29. An exception was an artist's St. Francis birdbath, in which Francis is depicted as a kneeling boy ("Sculpture by Elizabeth Muntz," 137; "Miss E. Muntz's Sculpture"). For a classic image of Francis with arms crossed, see Spagnoletto [Jusepe de Ribero], *St. Francis of Assisi* (frontispiece to Jørgensen, *St. Francis of Assisi*, 1912). I have been unable to identify any single statue, in Assisi or elsewhere, as a definitive source for non-Catholic imagery. Well-known sculptures of Francis in a standing posture include one at Saint Peter's in Rome, and one by Della Robbia at the Basilica of St. Mary of the Angels in Assisi. Both are Baroque, with a very different style of expression from the twentieth-century examples. Contemporary Italian and American Catholic statuary often incorporates birds and animals— sometimes with a cross or skull as well (see figure 15).

30. "A Sanctuary Garden," 26–27; Ritter, *Arts of the Church*, 35, photo facing page 53; McClinton, *Flower Arrangement in the Church*, 109–10.

31. "Fitly Furnishing"; "Flowers and Gardens," 301; "Shopping Around," 5; "Sanctuary Garden," 27.

32. On images defining space, see David Morgan, *Visual Piety*, 170. In gardens, the space is often designated meditative first; the image reinforces the existing definition.

33. Morgan, *Visual Piety*, 125, 156–57; Luhrmann, *When God Talks Back*; Tagliabue, "A Little Dutch Angel's Cellphone Number," A8.

Chapter Five

1. Bacon, *Come Along With Us* (1949) 71–72.
2. Bacon, *Come Along With Us*, 37, 47, 62, 67–68, 72; on flying up, 77–78; see also 122–23, on honoring God and on "spiritual" education.

3. Foertsch, *American Culture in the 1940s*, 28; Chafe, *Unfinished Journey*, 5–9, 105–39; Halliwell, *American Culture in the 1950s*.

4. Auden, *Age of Anxiety*. Useful general sources include Henriksen, *Dr. Strangelove's America*; Wagner-Martin, *Mid-Century American Novel*; Jones, McCarthy, and Murphy, *It Came From the 1950s*.

5. Classic works of the era about the changing religious scene were Herberg, *Protestant, Catholic, Jew*, and, in a different vein, Blanshard, *American Freedom and Catholic Power*.

6. Hudnut-Beumler, *Looking for God*, 31–40.

7. Hudnut-Beumler, *Looking for God*, 40–55, 79, 83; Gill, *Embattled Ecumenism*, 4–7, 23–28.

8. Hudnut-Beumler, *Looking for God*, 79–80.

9. Maria Lynch Dumoulin, Sales Manager, Kenneth Lynch and Sons, telephone interview with author, February 17, 2012. She noted that St. Francis statues are typically bought by the end user, not by the designer; they are "very personal."

10. Peattie, "Everybody's Saint," 63, 66.

11. Woods, *Treasury*, 139; Woods, *Second Treasury*, 641–42, 211, xii.

12. "Lord, Make Me an Instrument," *Life*, 168; "Lord, Make Me an Instrument," *House Beautiful*, 140–41. *House Beautiful* replaced the word "sadness" with "sickness," possibly a wrong transcription.

13. "Saint Francis of the Bronx."

14. "Bird Finds Friend in Statue of St. Francis of Assisi" (Erkins Studios advertisement).

15. "Flowers of St. Francis," *New Yorker*, a comment on Rossellini's movie; "The Claws of God," a review of Kazantzakis's novel.

16. Lawson, *Rabbit Hill*, 122–23.

17. Lawson, *Rabbit Hill*, 70.

18. Lawson's description of the statue with the "water dropping" from his hands recalls a sculpture from the Golden Gate International Exhibition in San Francisco in 1939 ("[Cora Babcock, dressed as the Goddess of Peace]," photograph). It is not clear whether there is any connection between the two.

19. On Lawson's career, see Collier and Nakamura, *Major Authors and Illustrators*, 1414–17; Mary Brigid Barrett, "Lawson, Robert," 252–53.

20. The other awards were the Lewis Carroll Shelf Award in 1963 (Collier and Nakamura, *Major Authors and Illustrators*, 1414) and the Fanfare Award from Horn Book magazine (Helbig and Perkins, *Dictionary of American Children's Fiction*, 422). Bibliographic data come from WorldCat. It is not clear what St. Francis meant to Lawson himself. There is no evidence that he participated in any religious community, although his mother was an active Roman Catholic and his father came from a Protestant background. Photographs of his Connecticut estate show a statue that may represent Francis. Interestingly, Lawson's birthday was October 4. Sharon McQueen, personal correspondence with author, December 10, 2012; Schmidt, *Robert Lawson*, 60, 62, 77.

21. On postwar culture, see especially Vidor, "Lawson, Robert," 417; for further analysis see Schmidt, *Robert Lawson*, 59.

22. Hudnut-Beumler, *Looking for God*, 80.

23. Short, *House of God*, 288–89; "The Ministers' Corner" [newsletter clipping], 1958; *Guide to Washington Cathedral*, 45. The Riverside Church in New York, constructed in the 1920s, also placed Francis prominently among humanitarians (Cook, "Christian Vision of Unity," 164–67).

24. R. T. Feller to Marion Brackenridge, June 30, 1958; Philip Hubert Frohman to John H. Bayless, business manager, August 29, 1958, quoting a letter from Brackenridge; both in Archives, Cathedral of Saints Peter and Paul, Washington, D.C.

25. Frohman to Bayless, August 29, 1958; "Comments by Mr. Philip Hubert Frohman about the photograph of the statue of St. Francis by Marion Bracken-ridge," September 5, 1958; unsigned letter to Brackenridge, December 16, 1958; Feller to Brackenridge, January 6, 1959; Washington Cathedral Building Committee—Check List, Statue of St. Francis of Assisi, June 1959; all in Archives, Cathedral of Saints Peter and Paul, Washington, D.C. The cathedral also kept a bronze of St. Francis outdoors until the second copy was stolen in 1970 (memo from Jack Fanfani to Feller, March 2, 1973).

26. Wilson, "Lore of Francis," 26. The book being reviewed was Otto Karrer's *St. Francis of Assisi: The Legends and Lauds* (Sheed & Ward, 1948). This review did not fully represent the magazine's editorial position: an article in the same magazine two months later had no problem with the idea that "St. Francis saw the revelation of God in all nature" and "almost single-handed . . . changed man's outlook on nature" (Nathan, "Religion in Art," 11).

27. Grundy, "Alien Holiness," 1136; Kazantzakis, *Saint Francis*, 118; Bien, "Nikos Kazantzakis," 1067–70; Kunitz, *Twentieth Century Authors*, First Supplement, 514–15.

28. Bien, "Nikos Kazantzakis," 1072–74; Kazantzakis, *Saint Francis*, 74–75, 109, 118, 220; quotes: 56, 118. On ideology, the critic Christopher Ricks commented sardonically, "This is less a novel than a tract" (Ricks, "Forgers," 330).

29. Kazantzakis, *Saint Francis*, 21, 112, 113, 224; on nature, 47, 167–68, 183–86.

30. Schlueter, "Elizabeth de Beauchamp Goudge"; Burger, "In the Field of Religion"; "My God and My All," *Booklist*.

31. Goudge, *My God and My All* (New York), 26–28, 189–90, 283.

32. Goudge, *My God and My All*, 160–61.

33. Carr, "Captivating Rossellini Film"; Wilmington, "'St. Francis' Breathes Life."

34. M. L. A. [Marjory Adams], "Rossellini Film at Brattle." *Time* took a similar view ("Flowers of St. Francis," Oct. 6, 1952).

35. Dunne, "Tribute to Christian Piety."

36. "Zooey" was published in *The New Yorker* May 4, 1957, and in book form in 1961 (Salinger, *Franny and Zooey*). Tartt, foreword to *Life of St. Francis*, viii–ix.

37. Salinger, *Franny and Zooey*, 169, 166, 171.

38. Englebert, *Saint Francis of Assisi: A Biography*, 2nd English ed.; quote, 15. Brady worked with Brown on the text and notes. An English translation by Edward Hutton was published in 1950.

39. Brown, "The Homes of St. Francis," appendix 5 to Englebert, *Saint Francis of Assisi*, 407–19.

40. Moorman, *Saint Francis of Assisi*, 1950. The later publishers were, respectively, SPCK and Franciscan Herald Press.

41. Moorman, *Saint Francis of Assisi*, 6, 33, 36–39.

42. Moorman, *Saint Francis of Assisi*, 77–78, 84–86, 59.

43. Moorman, *Saint Francis of Assisi*, 78. Moorman is also one of the few authors with a clear explanation for the "perfect joy" story: he thinks it was about humility (25–26).

44. "Prayer: Make Me an Instrument of Thy Peace," 635; on Blanche Ittleson, see Hyman and Moore, *Jewish Women in America*, s.v. "Ittleson, Blanche Frank," 681–82; on Quaker youth, see "Prayer of St. Francis," in Brinton, McWhirter, and Schroeder, *Candles in the Dark*, 248. *Twelve Steps and Twelve Traditions* has a complex bibliographic history. My citation comes from an edition copyrighted in 1952, 1953, and 1981, the 76th printing, 2011, pages 99–101. The introduction to this book claims that the book was first published in 1953 and has not changed since then (14), but bibliographic records are unclear and pagination varies across editions.

45. Day, *Duty of Delight*, 118.

46. Day, *Duty of Delight*, 252–53; Day, "On Pilgrimage," 1.

47. Bro, *When Children Ask*, 7–9.

48. [Attebery], "Prayers for Peace: Christmas MCMLVIII," [11].

49. Queen et al., *Encyclopedia of American Religious History*, s.v. "Vedanta Society"; Isherwood, introduction to *Vedanta for the Western World*, 26–28; Slawenski, *J. D. Salinger*, 286–87.

50. Isherwood, introduction to *Vedanta for the Western World*, 8–10, 15; Ferrando, "St. Francis and Sri Ramakrishna," 253, 255–56.

51. Ferrando, "St. Francis and Sri Ramakrishna," 253, 254, 256, 257–58.

52. Malamud, *The Assistant*, 168, 246.

53. Malamud, *The Assistant*, 30–31.

54. Malamud, *The Assistant*, 95, 102.

55. Malamud, *The Assistant*, 118.

56. Malamud, *The Assistant*, 245–46.

57. Smith, *My Father Is a Book*, 76, 165; Davis, *Bernard Malamud*, 127, 146.

58. Malamud, *The Assistant*, 231, 125. Among the most useful critical sources are Davis, *Bernard Malamud*, and Nisly, *Impossible to Say*. On suffering, see especially Philip Roth and Ruth Witte, cited in Davis, 137–38.

59. Davis, *Bernard Malamud*, 137–39; the "Christian book" comment came from Mrs. Gershom Scholem. Cheuse and Delbanco, *Talking Horse*, 86–87; Malamud, *The Assistant*, 229.

60. Davis, *Bernard Malamud*, 128; Nisly, *Impossible to Say*, 65–71.

Chapter Six

1. York, "Homily on St. Francis of Assisi, 4 October 1967," CRRE Historical Archives, quoted in Stelmach, "Cult of Liberation," 33–34.

2. Wuthnow, *Restructuring of American Religion*, esp. 12–13, 145–72.

3. Rossinow, *Politics of Authenticity*, 3–8.

4. "Man of the Year: The Inheritor."

5. Wittner, *Rebels Against War*, 282–92.

6. DeBenedetti and Chatfield, *An American Ordeal*, 228–29; Collins, *When Everything Changed*, 182–86.

7. Robert Ellwood, quoted in Allitt, *Religion in America Since 1945*, 74, 75: Allitt provides a useful survey of the movement. Bonhoeffer, *Letters and Papers from Prison*, 137, 362–63. The 1960s movement was inaugurated by Vahanian, in his *The Death of God*. For a general discussion, see "Toward a Hidden God"; Cox, *The Secular City*, xi, 211.

8. Rossinow, *Politics of Authenticity*, 4, 6, 85–114.

9. Wolfe, "The 'Me' Decade." Recent scholarship argues that the decline in church membership signaled a change, but not a decline, in cultural influence; see Hollinger, "After Cloven Tongues of Fire," esp. 18–20, and Hedstrom, *Rise of Liberal Religion*, 213, 221–22.

10. *Francis of Assisi*, film by Michael Curtiz; Paton, *Instrument of Thy Peace*; "Shopping Around," *House and Garden,* March 1969, 183.

11. Esser, *Opuscula*; Habig, *St. Francis of Assisi*; Brown's work appeared as supplements and appendices to Englebert, *Saint Francis of Assisi*.

12. Almedingen, *St. Francis of Assisi*, 54; Roddy, "Francis of Assisi: The Hippie Saint"; Cunningham, *Brother Francis*, x; Smith, *Francis of Assisi*, 2, 165.

13. Almedingen, *St. Francis of Assisi*, 32, 69–70, 79, 91, 106, 121, 162; Smith, *Francis of Assisi*, 1–2, 27, 68, 90, 94, 131. Smith's works and interests suggest that he was a Roman Catholic. Englebert devoted a lengthy footnote to this question, favoring the "purity thesis" (*Saint Francis of Assisi*, 56, 461–62n).

14. On viewers, see Hearn, untitled introductory essay, 4–17. Quotes from print edition: Kenneth Clark, *Civilisation*, 76, 52.

15. Bishop, "Song of the Creatures." Bishop (1893–1973) was a professor at Cornell, and an editor, biographer, and poet.

16. Bishop, *Saint Francis of Assisi*, 30–32, 57, 64, 73, 66, 71, 102, 110.

17. Bishop, *Saint Francis of Assisi*, 37, 47, 18–19, 48, 55–56, 92.

18. *Oxford English Dictionary*, s.v. "hippie"; Perry, *The Haight-Ashbury*, 5, 19; Didion, "Slouching Towards Bethlehem."

19. Perry, *The Haight-Ashbury*, 19–20, 76. The *Oracle* was also known as the *San Francisco Oracle* and the *City of San Francisco Oracle*. There were twelve issues, monthly at first, later bimonthly (*San Francisco Oracle*, viii–ix). The Diggers' free meals were dwindling by the spring of 1967 (Perry, *Haight-Ashbury*, 167; David Talbot, *Season of the Witch*, 38). On change, see Perry, *Haight-Ashbury*, 116, 159, 169; Williams and Mirikitani, *Beyond the Possible*, 49–63; on the festival (the "Invisible Circus"), see Cecil Williams, *I'm Alive!*, 85–95; on outreach, especially to runaways, see Talbot, *Season of the Witch*, 42–44. See further Miles, *Hippie*, 195–210. On All Saints Church, see Kinsolving, "A Rector, a Church and the Hippies." On evangelicals, see Eskridge, personal correspondence with author, October 28,

2013; Eskridge, *God's Forever Family*, 1–2, 10–53; Shires, *Hippies of the Religious Right*, esp. 96–98.

20. Miles, *Hippie*, 186–91; interpretation of ethos mine. Perry, *Haight-Ashbury*, 124–27; Talbot, *Witch*, 22–29.

21. Talbot, *Witch*, 31, 34–35; Perry, *Haight-Ashbury*, 171, 271, 275; Helms, "About This Event. . . ."

22. Council for a Summer of Love, "To sons, to daughters, to mankind. . . ." Several sources say that there was a press conference on April 5 (Perry, 171; Helms, "About this event . . .").

23. Cohen, "The San Francisco Oracle, A Brief History," xliii; Raphael Schnepf, personal correspondence with author, November 18, 2014. Schnepf, the artist, was known as Bob Schnepf at that time.

24. Communication Company, Untitled poster.

25. Goldstein, *William Sloane Coffin, Jr.*, 191–93.

26. Communication Company, "A Poem of Heroes," [5]; Anderson papers, folder 1, item 14.

27. On vagrants, see Grogan, *Ringolevio*, 439. On Revelation, see [*San Francisco*] *Oracle*, December [1967], 328–29 in 1991 facsimile ed. A 1967 Free City flyer also quoted Revelation (21:18, 25) ("Free City: And the City was Pure Gold"). A 1968 interreligious mandala used an uncommon biblical text, Luke 6:38 (*Oracle*, February 1968, 362–63 in *San Francisco Oracle*, facsimile ed.). The Vedanta movement, mentioned in chapter 5, was already past its heyday by then; to the 1960s counterculture, it "seemed old-fashioned" (Jackson, *Vedanta for the West*, 108).

28. Perry, *Haight-Ashbury*, 171; Roth, "Coming Together," 194.

29. Perry, *Haight-Ashbury*, 243–44; Miles, *Hippie*, 210; Coyote, *Sleeping Where I Fall*, 130.

30. For a good historical summary, see Finding Aid, Berkeley Free Church Collection, which is based on Stelmach, "Cult of Liberation."

31. On the movement in general, see Boyd, ed., *The Underground Church*; on campus ministries, see Hammond, *Campus Clergyman*, xiii, 11–13, and Friedlander, "Never Trust a God over Thirty." Evangelicals had been laying the groundwork for a youth-oriented movement, but were a bit later in establishing a presence on college campuses: see Shires, *Hippies of the Religious Right*, 48, 40, 47, 92–93, 96, 131–34, 135.

32. Finding Aid, Berkeley Free Church Collection; Stelmach, "Cult," 53–59, 83–84. Brown's theological treatise, *The Liberated Zone*, functioned as a handbook for the Free Church (Stelmach, "Cult," 91–92). York's classmate Glee Bishop, a social worker, worked closely with him, as did his then-wife (Stelmach, "Cult," 62–63, 93–94, 103).

33. Stelmach, "Cult," 30, 33, 50–52, 54; see also Shires, *Hippies*, 23–24, 33–34. Daniel (1921–) and Philip (1923–2002) Berrigan were Roman Catholic priests (Philip later married) who created dramatic visual and embodied forms of nonviolent antiwar protest. For example, during the Vietnam War they used napalm to set draft-board files on fire; during the anti-nuclear movement of the 1980s, they

"destroyed" nuclear weapons with hammers. Their thought and practice had far-reaching influence on peace activism.

34. On York, see Stelmach, "Cult," 85. For an early treatment of the underground church, see the essay collection edited by Boyd, *The Underground Church*. Brown contributed an essay. On the Free Church's role, see Stelmach, "Cult," 2, 17, 82–83.

35. *Win with Love!*, esp. 62.

36. Brown and York, *Covenant of Peace*, 33, 202, 121, 37.

37. Brown and York, preface to *Covenant of Peace*, 5–13; quote, 5.

38. The poetic voice is most probably Brown's (Stelmach, "Cult," 102). Along with his radical sensibility, he brought a deep respect for tradition, literature, and language. He had earlier urged York to remember the "old books" he had studied in seminary: "The time may well come when you find you haven't got any other anchor" (Brown, ordination sermon for Richard York, quoted in Stelmach, "Cult," 88).

39. Brown and York, *Covenant*, 7, 33, 121.

40. Brown and York, *Covenant*, 202. For the more typical translation, see Armstrong and Brady, *Francis and Clare*, 38–39.

41. Brown and York, *Covenant*, 33–35. Morrison immolated himself in front of the Pentagon in 1965, protesting the Vietnam War.

42. Richard L. York, *Radical Religion* 1, no. 1 (Winter 1973): 23–25, cited in Finding Aid, Berkeley Free Church Collection. They had earlier written, "We hope to have found the narrow way between sectarian withdrawal and harmless generalities" (Brown and York, *Covenant*, 12).

43. Dubos, *So Human an Animal*, 8; Pittenger, *The Christian Situation Today*, 20.

44. Roddy, "Francis of Assisi: The Hippie Saint"; Hauser, "Francis: A Saint for Today."

45. Cunningham, *Brother Francis*, introduction, ix.

46. Cunningham, *Brother Francis*, introduction, x; John Holland Smith, *Francis*, 28.

47. Curtiss, "Zeffirelli to Depict Life of St. Francis"; Napoleone, "A Passion for Art and for Life," 18, 54–56. On Francis and his father, see Pietroni, "Il mio Francesco," *Epoca*, 1971, quoted in Napoleone, *Franco Zeffirelli*, 421. Newspaper databases show screenings through the late 1970s and early 1980s.

48. Gary Arnold, "Kitsch with a High Gloss"; Canby, "Zeffirelli's Film Study of St. Francis" and "Which Flick Rates no. 14,684?"; Kevin Kelly, "Zeffirelli Film Outrageous"; Johnson, "Brother Sun, Sister Moon"; "The New Movies"; Andrews, "An Excuse for the Schmaltzathons." I am no expert on film, but I would agree with at least some of their criticisms. Most of Donovan's music was saccharine, some of Francis's longer speeches were didactic, and the implication of romantic attraction between Francis and Clare is something of a cliché.

49. Amazon.com reviews by Claudia McKinney and D.C., accessed July 19, 2013; "Considering the Franciscan life?" on Franciscans.com; Hobgood-Oster, *Holy Dogs and Asses*, 148. The title of the Zeffirelli film has been borrowed regularly (for example, Harris, "Brother Sun, Sister Moon"; Mayo and Malone, *Brother*

Sun, Sister Moon; Paterson, *Brother Sun, Sister Moon*; Terry, "O, Brother Sun and Sister Moon").

50. The sources disagree on the time sequence. It appears that Mangano returned to Boston sometime after 1978: Leonard, "Homeless Chief Faces Tough Task"; Reckdahl, "The Abolitionist"; Penn, "Giving It All Away," 176.

51. Wallis, "A Holy Jealousy": quote from page 3.

52. On reconversion, see Curtiss, "Next for Zeffirelli."

53. White, "The Historical Roots of Our Ecologic Crisis," 1203, 1205, 1207; see also White, "Man and Nature"; White, "Saint Francis and the Ecologic Backlash."

54. Spring and Spring, *Ecology and Religion in History*, introduction, 2–3; DeBell, *Environmental Handbook*, 12–26; Richard Cassius Lee Webb, conversation with author, July 2013. The environmental activist Bill McKibben noted in 2007 that the article "provoked storms of controversy" (McKibben, introduction, *American Earth*, xxxi).

55. Ayers, "Christian Realism and Environmental Ethics," 155–57; Bauckham, "Creation Mysticism," 199, 203–4, 209; Moorman, *Saint Francis of Assisi*, 25–30, 74–78.

56. Rothman, *The Greening of a Nation?*, 15–26, 52–54. See also Stoll, *U.S. Environmentalism Since 1945*, 9–12.

57. Silvey, "Rabbit Hill, by Robert Lawson"; Schmidt, *Robert Lawson*, 59, 67.

58. Dates and organizational structure are a bit unclear. Ian Barbour said that a group had been meeting since 1961, but it is not clear whether that was the same group (Barbour, introduction, *Earth Might Be Fair*, 2). Paul Santmire said that the Faith-Man-Nature Group began in 1963, while Richard Baer dated it to "1963 and 1964" (Santmire, "Struggle for an Ecological Theology," 275; Baer, personal papers, cited in Nash, *Rights of Nature*, 102). Others said 1964 (Stefferud, introduction, *Christians and the Good Earth*, 9–11). The group seems to have been related to a faculty seminar of the National Council of Churches (Santmire; Baer papers). Moreover, the first collection of papers the group published, in 1969, claimed to be based on their third conference, in 1967 (Stefferud, introduction, 9); but Santmire said that this was their first conference, describing earlier meetings as "seminars."

59. Means, "Man and Nature: The Theological Vacuum"; Baer, "Conservation: An Area for the Church's Action"; Barbour, "An Ecological Ethic."

60. Baer, "The Church and Conservation," 84. David and Eileen Spring agreed with Baer; see introduction, *Ecology and Religion in History*, 6. Among the articles that referred to Francis are MacQuarrie, "Creation and Environment," 34 (originally published in *Expository Times* 83 [1971]: 4–9); Brueggemann, "King in the Kingdom of Things"; Shinn, "Population and the Dignity of Man"; Kuhn, "Environmental Stewardship." Shinn, in Barbour's 1972 collection *Earth Might Be Fair*, which was based on discussions going on since 1961, also engaged the Francis idea (Shinn, "Science and Ethical Decision,"141–42). Barbour, in an essay in the same collection, mentioned Francis in passing, as one kind of Christian response to the natural world (Barbour, "Attitudes toward Nature and Technology," 150, 157).

Fackre and McHarg, in Barbour's 1973 collection *Western Man and Environmental Ethics*, both take Francis for granted as a good example (Fackre, "Ecology and Theology," 121, reprinted from a 1971 journal article; McHarg, "The Place of Nature in the City of Man," 175, reprinted from a 1964 article).

61. For general critiques see, for example, Ayers, "Christian Realism," 156; Wright, "Responsibility for the Ecological Crisis," 35–40; Derr, "Religion's Responsibility for the Ecological Crisis"; Brueggemann, "King in the Kingdom of Things." For specific critiques, see Cobb, *Is It Too Late?*, cited in Hargrove, preface, *Religion and Environmental Crisis*, xiv; Dubos, "Franciscan Conservation Versus Benedictine Stewardship," in *A God Within*; Shinn, "Science and Ethical Decision," 141–42; Hargrove, preface, *Religion and Environmental Crisis*, xiv, xvi–xvii. Susan Power Bratton has recently argued that the same "battle" is still "being repeatedly fought with very little new ground gained" (Bratton, "The 'New' Christian Ecology," 205).

62. Santmire, *Brother Earth*, 6–8, 132.

63. He takes this idea a step further in his mention of "brother death." Only when we accept natural death on the one hand, and transcendence of death in the Resurrection of Christ on the other, can we truly call death our brother (Santmire, *Brother Earth*, 175). Santmire seems to have forgotten that Francis called death "sister."

64. Santmire, *Brother Earth*, 186–87. He adds a severe admonition on romanticism and charity, 231, note 3.

65. Edward Armstrong, *Saint Francis, Nature Mystic*.

66. Armstrong also recounts several charming stories about Francis's admiration of honeybees, 150.

67. Armstrong, *Saint Francis, Nature Mystic*, 76, 95, 100, 218–19.

68. DeBell, *Environmental Handbook*, 5.

69. Berkeley Ecology Centre, "Four 'Changes,'" in DeBell, ed., *Environmental Handbook*, 331.

70. Indeed, Leopold, like Lynn White, looked for an alternative to the Genesis story in the tradition. He found it in the prophets Ezekiel and Isaiah (McClintock, *Nature's Kindred Spirits*). James McClintock thinks that Leopold's shift from conservation to ecology reads like a conversion experience. See also Lorbiecki, *Aldo Leopold: A Fierce Green Fire*, 175; and Meine, *Aldo Leopold: His Life and Work*. Lisa Sideris has argued that Carson retained a sense of reverence and mystery, as well as a sympathetic view of science, from her Calvinist upbringing (Sideris, "The Secular and Religious Sources," 232–50). See also McClintock on Carson; Abbey, *The Fool's Progress*, 219; Loeffler, *Adventures with Ed*, 50; Abbey, *One Life at a Time, Please*. On Wendell Berry, see, for example, Kroeker, "Sexuality and the Sacramental Imagination," 120; and Shuman, "Introduction."

71. Santmire, *Brother Earth*, 132.

Chapter Seven

1. Winter et al., *Missa Gaia—Earth Mass*, sound recording; see also Marini, *Sacred Song*, 166; Krulwich, "Blessing the Animals."

2. As noted earlier, it is not clear from existing records whether Francis was born in 1181 or 1182. Significant works after 1980 include Pelikan, *Jesus Through the Centuries*; Green, *God's Fool*; Robson, *St. Francis of Assisi*; Trexler, *Naked Before the Father*; Armstrong, Hellman, and Short, *Francis of Assisi: Early Documents*; Tolan, *St. Francis and the Sultan*; Moses, *The Saint and the Sultan*; Spoto, *Reluctant Saint*; House, *Francis of Assisi*; Galli, *Francis of Assisi and His World*; Murray, *A Mended and Broken Heart*; and see below. On the postage stamp, see Gail Ramshaw Schmidt, *Francis, a Saint We Share*, 2.

3. Holl, *The Last Christian*; see especially 173, 235–38; Bliss, "St. Francis at Bread and Puppet Circus," 1108.

4. Wallis, "A Holy Jealousy," 3, 5; Hinson, "St. Francis of Assisi: Divine Fool," 18; Rohr, "A Life Pure and Simple," esp. 14. See also Thompson, *Francis of Assisi*, 153.

5. Historian Larry Eskridge recalled a screening of the Zeffirelli movie at the evangelical Trinity College, now Trinity International University, in Deerfield, Illinois, around 1980 (personal correspondence with author, October 28, 2013). The "Jesus movement" was also active on non-evangelical campuses, where the movie was popular. On hymnals, see chapter 4 in this volume; on *Christianity Today* articles, see below; Galli, *Francis of Assisi and His World*; Cron, *Chasing Francis*.

6. Duin, "Freeing St. Francis"; Michael G. Smith, "Troubadour of the Kingdom"; Marini, *Sacred Song*, 240, 246–49, 253–62. On Talbot, see also his *Lessons of St. Francis*. Also in *Christianity Today*, writer Matthew Scully referred to Francis in reference to animal rights (Beattie and Scully, "Creating Discomforts," 57).

7. Galli, *Francis of Assisi and His World*, 6–7. Evangelical Wendy Murray also set out to find the "real" Francis, without complete success (*A Mended and Broken Heart*, xi–xiii, xxv).

8. Galli, *Francis of Assisi and His World*, 50, 117, 119–20, 125–27, 133, 156, 182.

9. Inclusive paraphrases: Miriam Therese Winter, "To You, O God, All Creatures Sing," in *New Century Hymnal* (United Church of Christ), no. 17; "All Creatures, Worship God Most High" in *Evangelical Lutheran Worship*, no. 835. The Lutheran text is marked "translation composite." For data on hymnals, see hymnary.org.

10. On Temple, see http://www.hymnary.org/person/Temple_S, citing hymns withoutwords.com, and http://www.ocp.org/artists/587 (Oregon Catholic Press). For texts, music, and publication data, see hymnary.org.

11. A search of YouTube videos easily turns up performances by Boyle, O'Connor, and the Westminster Abbey Choir, among others, as well as McLachlan's "Lord, Make Me an Instrument."

12. Duffy and Gasnick, *Francis: Brother of the Universe*. Background information on inside front cover of the book and in Pelc, "Saint Francis of Assisi . . . Superhero"; quote from G., "Francis of Assisi, Supersaint."

13. Duffy and Gasnick, *Francis*, 38; G., "Francis of Assisi, Supersaint."

14. Boff, *St. Francis*, 25–27, 39–40, 113–19, quote page 40; see also Cox, *The Silencing of Leonardo Boff*.

15. Fox, *Original Blessing*, esp. 11–26. On the "seeker" tradition, see Leigh Eric Schmidt, *Restless Souls*.

16. Fox, *Coming of the Cosmic Christ*, 63, 112–14; *Original Blessing*, 307–9; *Confessions*, 152. For a critical view, see Bauckham, "Creation Mysticism in Matthew Fox and Francis of Assisi."

17. Campolo, "The Coming Spiritual Revival"; Karen Armstrong, foreword, in House, *Francis of Assisi*.

18. Schwarzschild, "Earthwatch" and "Saving the Birds of St. Francis." See also Hargrove, *Religion and Environmental Crisis* (1986); and the *Religions of the World and Ecology* book series edited by Mary Evelyn Tucker and John Grim (Cambridge, Mass.: Harvard University Press, 1997–).

19. Harris, "Brother Sun, Sister Moon," 86, 89, 94. Commenting on the event, a writer in *Wilderness* magazine concluded that Hindus and Buddhists were better followers of Francis than Christians were (Meeker, "Assisi Connection," 63).

20. Sorrell, *Francis of Assisi and Nature*, which theologian Richard Bauckham called "the definitive study" (Bauckham, "Dominion Interpreted," 36n.). Vauchez, in *Francis of Assisi* (271–82), has also considered the question of originality, but with less detailed attention to the sources.

21. Sorrell, *Francis of Assisi and Nature*, 90; *Green Bible*, [I-3]; see also Clowney and Mosto, *Earthcare*, 45; Winter et al., *Missa Gaia—Earth Mass* [music score], 10, 90.

22. The description that follows is based on Duquette, "Fantasies by the Bay," 266, 268, 338; and on Goodman and Wilkinson, *Tony Duquette*, 15–27, 352–55, 359–60. Both sources include illustrations.

23. Roraback, "A Pilgrimage to the Duqal Palace"; Duquette, "Fantasies," 338.

24. Roraback, "Pilgrimage"; Hutton Wilkinson, personal correspondence with author, October 11, 2013; Keeps, "The Holidays' Magic Maker." See also tonyduquette.com.

25. Roraback, "Looking Back"; Wilkinson, personal correspondence with author; Rowlands, "Tony Duquette."

26. Rosen, *The Blessing of the Animals*, 4. Some of Rosen's details about Christian practice are inaccurate.

27. In the LexisNexis database I used the search terms blessing* animal*. In 2013 there were another fifty animal blessings held at some time other than St. Francis's day. Laura Hobgood-Oster found two hundred animal-blessing services on a public, voluntary list in 2004 (Hobgood-Oster, *Holy Dogs and Asses*, 120). Today, the same list, on AmericanCatholic.org, is spotty and heavily Catholic. A Google search in 2013 for the term "blessing of the animals" turned up an impossible 11,400,000 hits, with 46,000,000 for "blessing of the pets." Liturgies: Maroff, "How to Attend and Hold a Pet Blessing"; Linzey, *Animal Rites*, 32–43; Guerrero, *Blessing of the Animals*, 5–38, 111–12, and her blessingoftheanimals.com; Hobgood-Oster, *The Friends We Keep*, 183–91; Debra K. Farrington, *All God's Creatures*, 179–200.

28. A good selection of texts is found in Farrington, *All God's Creatures*, 187. Hobgood-Oster provides liturgies of blessing for farm and food animals and for endangered species, 187–90. Only her liturgy for pets is specifically associated with Francis.

29. Holak, "Ritual Blessings," 537; Guerrero, *Blessing of the Animals*, 111–12.

30. At least once they claimed to have invented it (Sack, "A Day When the Pews"). The cathedral staff did not respond to several requests for further information in 2013, apart from promising to look into my inquiries. See also Lerner, *Eco-Pioneers*, 381, on origins of the service.

31. On Catholic blessing practices, see below. On the 1820 Roman blessing, see Lady Morgan, *Italy*, 85–86. On Italy and Spain, see Lady Morgan and also Macmurrough, "Blessing of Animals: 'Roman' rite," 83–86; Cleghorn, "Blessing the Animals," 115; William Jones, *Credulities Past and Present*, 335–41. On Assisi, see http://www.slowtrav.com/anne/stantonio.htm. A 1927 source mentions an animal blessing in Assisi on the feast of Saint Anthony of Padua in June (Anson, *Pilgrim's Guide*, 224). On Mexico: there are references in English to the Mexican custom of having animals blessed on St. Anthony's day going back to around 1900 (Coburn, "La Benediccion," 139; Norman, *Terry's Guide to Mexico*, 108). The Los Angeles event probably began in the 1930s (Hobgood-Oster, *Holy Dogs*, 110). Guerrero's sourcebook (see note 29) is notably off base here, referring to "Saint Anthony of Abad" and calling the Macmurrough article a "rare document." On medieval origins, see King-Cohen, "Asking the Clergy"; Hess, "All Creatures," 82; Krulwich, "Blessing the Animals"; "Mission San Luis."

32. Jordan, "Animal Blessing"; "Father Alfred Boeddeker 'blessing the pets,' " photograph; Bernhard, "Dogs, Cats and Gerbil"; De Chillo, "Blessed Are the Furry Ones"; Blau, "Weekender Guide"; Pran, "Blessing of the Animals" (photo caption); "Keep This Date"; Bruske, "Pets, Owners Flock to a Blessing Event." The 1961 movie was probably *Francis of Assisi*, directed by Michael Curtiz.

33. Pran, "Creatures Large and Small" (photo caption); Sack, "A Day When the Pews"; Weil, "This Washington Cathedral Blessing."

34. Hobgood-Oster, *Holy Dogs and Asses*, 120–21; Hobgood-Oster, telephone interview with author, October 29, 2013. My assessment of locations is based on reports in the *Readers' Guide to Periodicals* and LexisNexis.

35. King-Cohen, "Asking the Clergy"; Cathy Kelly, "Blessing the Beasts"; "News from the Communities," 22–23. New Skete was founded by former Eastern Rite Franciscans in the late 1960s ("A Visit to Noah's Ark").

36. "The Rabbi Who Blesses Jewish Pets"; King-Cohen, "Asking the Clergy"; Kesterton, "Social Studies," quoting James Davis in the *South Florida Sun-Sentinel*; "Mission San Luis"; Holak, "Ritual Blessings;" "Branford Shelters Celebrate Animal Awareness Day"; Hobgood-Oster, *Holy Dogs and Asses*, 124. Jon Sweeney argued in the *Huffington Post* in 2005 that the blessing really began in Jewish tradition, but I see no direct connection with the popular blessings of today (Sweeney, "Blessing Our pets: In the Spirit of St. Francis and Judaism," http://www.huffingtonpost.com/jon-m-sweeney/blessing-our-pets-st-francis-judaism_b_951906.html.

37. Grier, *Pets in America*, 185, 228–30, 319–20; Katcher and Beck, "Animal Companions," esp. 267, 269–72, 274; De Mello, "Present and Future of Animal Domestication," 81.

38. The literature is vast. For good overviews, see Carter, "Animals"; Palmeri, "Deconstructing the Human-Animal Binary"; Franklin and White, "Animals and Modernity"; Mikhail, "Unleashing the Beast," 317–18.

39. Hobgood-Oster, *The Friends We Keep*, 127; Grier, *Pets in America*, 316. Grier notes, however, that we spend more on golf than on pets. For pet industry value in 2012, see American Pet Industry Association, "Pet Industry Market Size," http://www.americanpetproducts.org/press_industrytrends.asp. On pets as family, see Katcher and Beck, "Animal Companions," 267 [3]; Thayer, *Going to the Dogs*, 15, citing Schaffer, *One Nation Under Dog*, 18–19.

40. On Linzey, see especially his *Animal Rights: A Christian Assessment*; *Animal Theology*; and "The Theological Basis of Animal Rights." Two of many significant Jewish works are Schochet, *Animal Life in the Jewish Tradition*; Linzey and Cohn-Sherbok, *After Noah*. In Hobgood-Oster, *Friends*, see especially 147, 170–71. Webb was highly critical of Hobgood-Oster's view (Webb, review of *Friends We Keep*).

41. Guerrero, *Blessing of the Animals*, 39–46; Kesterton, "Social Studies"; Cornacchia, "Paws and Pray Service"; Jeff Martin, "Church Services Put Paws in the Pews"; Stephen Huneck Gallery and Dog Chapel, "Life Is a Ball"; Dog Mountain, "Dog Chapel."

42. Among the more thoughtful offerings are Wintz, *Will I See My Dog in Heaven?*; Carol Adams, *God Listens When You're Sad*; Debra K. Farrington, *All God's Creatures*; and Bueddemeyer-Porter, *Will I See Fido in Heaven?* For discussion, see Schaffer, *One Nation Under Dog*, on death and bereavement: 231–51, on afterlife: 241–47 (note that some of his footnotes are incorrect); also Flaim, "A Religious Debate Wages"; "Animals and the Afterlife"; Gladstone, "Dogs in Heaven?" On the controversy, see Romney, "Plans for Pet Repository in San Francisco Spur Theological Flap"; "Saint Francis Rest." The controversy over the pet columbarium appears to be tied to larger controversies at the church; see, for example, "St. Francis' Shrine Should Remain Open to All." A widely circulated bit of contemporary folklore describes a "rainbow bridge" where deceased pets wait for their humans to join them (see, for example, "Rainbow Bridge"). The pets' behavior suggests that they are mostly dogs.

43. Steinberg, "Straight from the Hearts of Children," 51; *Book of Worship for Free Churches* (Congregational), 157–59; *Book of Worship for Church and Home* (Methodist, 1945), 470, 480, 501, 506 (services for dedication of a home, school, or church, or laying a cornerstone); *Book of Worship for Church and Home* (1964), 373–74 (blessing of a dwelling); *Book of Occasional Services* (Episcopal), 45–47, 95–96, 142–43 (rites for blessing homes, food, and pregnant women); *Book of Worship* (United Church of Christ), 347–51 (blessing of a civil marriage), 260–67 (dedications and thanksgivings); *Occasional Services* (Lutheran Church in America), 183–85; Morrisroe, "Blessing," 601; *Book of Blessings*, 347–54. The *Book of Blessings* also discusses the general meanings of blessing, xxi–xxxii. *Book of Family Worship*, *Oremus* (Lutheran Student Association), and *Book of Common Worship* (Presbyterian) have no blessing services. There is no entry for "blessing" in Hillerbrand's *Encyclopedia of Protestantism* (2004), nor in *Oxford History of Christian Worship* (2006).

44. Greiner, "Blessing and Curse," 125, 129, citing Claus Westermann, *Der Segen in der Bibel und im Handeln der Kirche*, 1968; Keizer, "The Day We Bless the Chainsaws"; "Blessing of the Bicycles." I witnessed a blessing of backpacks at Immanuel Lutheran Church, Amherst, Mass., in September 2013.

45. Hobgood-Oster, *Holy Dogs and Asses*, 123, 127–28.

46. Winter, "Genesis of *Earth Mass/Missa Gaia*," 3; Winter, *Missa Gaia* [sound recording]. Winter is on dangerous ground here: a view of non-western cultures as being closer to earth or nature can easily slide into condescension or covert racism.

47. See chapter 9 in this volume for further discussion. A Google search will turn up many examples on blogs, Facebook pages, and Twitter feeds.

48. The Rev. Roger Ard of the Cathedral of Saint Philip, Atlanta, quoted in Sack, "A Day When the Pews"; the Right Rev. Mark S. Sisk of New York, quoted in Wintz, "St. Francis at St. John the Divine"; Hobgood-Oster, *Holy Dogs and Asses,* 123.

49. See, for example, Bonaventure, *Life*, chapters 5 and 8; *Little Flowers*, chapter 22.

50. Debra K. Farrington, 179–200.

51. Fordyce, "October Is the Season"; Sack, "A Day When the Pews"; Miller, "Morningside Heights"; "Duke Chapel Blessing of the Animals"; Peterson, "Pets of All Shapes, Sizes"; Reeves, "Bowwow Choir"; King-Cohen, "Asking the Clergy"; Hobgood-Oster, *Holy Dogs and Asses*, 124.

52. For the St. Paul service, see Let All Creation Praise, "Blessing of the Animals (Episcopal)." Other liturgies on this website show wide variation in their attention to Francis.

Chapter Eight

1. Morgan, *Visual Piety,* 209–12; Hobgood-Oster, *Holy Dogs and Asses*, 120–21.

2. The film was *Francis of Assisi*, directed by Michael Curtiz and starring Bradford Dillman.

3. The Tau cross takes the form of the Greek letter *tau* (T) in uppercase and is associated with eschatological biblical texts. Francis sometimes used it as a signature. It later acquired other legendary meanings (Vauchez, *Francis of Assisi*, 316–17).

Chapter Nine

1. Ehrlich, "Walking with St. Francis."

2. Boff, *St. Francis*, 19, 157.

3. On the emerging church, see Harrold, "'New Monasticism,'" esp. 182, 184; and the epilogue to this book. For Cron's comments on postmodernism, see Morrell, "Ian Cron's *Chasing Francis*."

4. Ehrlich, "On the Road with God's Fool" and "Walking with St. Francis," variant versions of the same article. In the following discussion, I have referred

where possible to "On the Road" for the sake of specific page references. This version appeared in the *New York Times Magazine*. Most of the quotes in "On the Road" also appear in "Walking," the version in *Shambhala Sun*, which is longer.

5. Ehrlich, "On the Road," 92, 96.

6. Ehrlich, "On the Road," 92.

7. The references to emptiness and compassion, to suffering, and to the 1960s appear in "On the Road," 93, 92. The other quotes are from "Walking," which uses Buddhist concepts more frequently and explicitly. On Buddhism, see also "On the Road," 90, 95, 96; on church, 95.

8. Ehrlich, "On the Road," 96.

9. Linton, "San Francisco Sacred (II)," 13, 14; Sabatier, *Road to Assisi*; Francke, *On the Road with Francis of Assisi*; Valerie Martin, *Salvation*, 231. See also Le Goff, "Francis of Assisi," 9.

10. The story about trial by fire is in Bonaventure's *Life*, chapter 9, and elsewhere. Francis issues the challenge in order to prove the truth of Christianity. He then offers to walk through fire alone, but says that if he is burned, it will be on account of his sins, not God's lack of power.

11. Tolan, *St. Francis and the Sultan*, esp. 11–12, 16.

12. Idries Shah, *The Sufis* (New York: Doubleday, 1964), cited in Tolan, *St. Francis and the Sultan*, 307–9; Matthew Fox, *Original Blessing*, 309; Ladinsky, *Love Poems*, 29; Mockler, *Francis of Assisi: The Wandering Years*, 234–47; De Beer, "St. Francis and Islam"; Hoeberichts, *Francis and Islam*.

13. Moses, *The Saint and the Sultan*; Moses, "Mission Improbable," 15. Historians may query some of Moses's interpretation; see, for example, Cunningham, "Fearless Friar." On dialogue, see also Rotzetter, "Francis of Assisi: A Bridge to Islam"; Waskow, "Celebration for People of All Faiths"; Spoto, *Reluctant Saint*, 160–61; Tolan, *St. Francis and the Sultan*, 316–21.

14. For the image and a description, see https://www.trinitystores.com/store /art-image/st-francis-and-sultan.

15. The earliest published source I have found is Burns, "Igniting Volunteers" (1994), 38, but it reads as though Burns is quoting some other source. Other versions appeared in Butz, *Christmas in All Seasons* (1995), ix, and as the epigraph to John Michael Talbot, *Lessons of St. Francis* (1997). Burns's publisher is conservative Protestant, Butz's is liberal Protestant, and Talbot is a Roman Catholic. Even the eminent Franciscan historian Lawrence Cunningham has used this aphorism without documentation, again on the basis of its being consistent with Francis's character (Cunningham, *Francis of Assisi*, 135; personal correspondence with author, January 10, 2014).

16. Ladinsky, *Love Poems from God*, 48. See also xi, xiii–xiv, and back cover. The poem is credited to Francis in Roger Housden, *For Lovers of God Everywhere: Poems of the Christian Mystics* (Carlsbad, Calif.: Hay House, 2009, 74), which also calls it a Ladinsky "rendering." Other sources circulating the poem are Margaret Bullitt-Jonas, "Wring Out the Light" [blog post], Clear Story Collective, October 2012, http://clearstorycollective.org/blog/wring-out-the-light/, accessed September

11, 2014; numerous other blogs and websites; and a newsletter from a community farm in my area (e-mail newsletter, Next Barn Over Farm, Hadley, Mass., September 1, 2014).

17. Episcopal Church, *Enriching Our Worship 1*, 71, with the citation, "Source: from St. Clare." The introduction to this book cites several earlier liturgical collections. Online references to this blessing are almost entirely from Episcopal sources.

18. Galli, "*Speak* the Gospel."

19. Ehrlich, "Walking"; Moses, *The Saint and the Sultan*; De Beer, "St. Francis and Islam," 18.

Epilogue

1. Spoto's *Reluctant Saint* accompanied a sixty-minute television "documentary" with the same title. Biographies: House, *Francis of Assisi*, 2001; Galli, *Francis of Assisi and His World*, 2002; Cunningham, *Francis of Assisi*, 2004; Murray, *A Mended and Broken Heart*, 2008; Vauchez, *Francis of Assisi*, 2012; Thompson, *Francis of Assisi*, 2012; Robson, *Cambridge Companion to Francis of Assisi*, 2012. On "new monastics" see, for example, Arpin-Ricci, *The Cost of Community*; Bessenecker, *The New Friars*; Claiborne, *The Irresistible Revolution*; and Wilson-Hartgrove, *God's Economy*. I am indebted to Michael Clawson of Baylor University for calling my attention to the place of Francis in this movement.

2. Kennedy, *St. Francis of Assisi*; Elizabeth Gilbert, *Eat, Pray, Love*, 7, 53; Bierman, "A Speaker Pulled Hard in Two Directions," A13. A Wikipedia article lists a number of other references to the prayer in religion and in popular culture, most of them without clear verification.

3. Küng, "Paradox of Pope Francis," 1, 18.

4. Glassberg, *Sense of History*, 15, citing Lipsitz, *Time Passages*.

5. *Little Flowers*, chapter 10.

6. Mehl-Laituri, "Sergeant Francis?"

7. Pelikan, *Jesus through the Centuries*, 133.

8. Meltzer and Elgner, Introduction to *Saints*, xi; Zaleski, "Saints of John Paul II," 32; McCann, "Constructing St. Francis," 147.

9. For the insight about starting points, see Glassberg, *Sense of History,* 111. Of the large literature on public history, two useful introductions are Tosh, *Why History Matters*, and *Public History: an Introduction*, edited by Howe and Kemp.

Bibliography

The Life of Francis: Sources, Biographies, and Novels

Alger, Abby Langdon, ed., *The Little Flowers of Saint Francis of Assisi, Translated with a Brief Account of the Life of St. Francis*. Boston: Roberts Bros., 1887.

Almedingen, E. M. *St. Francis of Assisi: A Great Life in Brief*. New York: Alfred A. Knopf, 1967.

Armstrong, Regis J., OFM Cap., and Ignatius C. Brady, OFM, eds. and trans. *Francis and Clare: The Complete Works*. Classics of Western Spirituality. New York: Paulist Press, 1982.

Armstrong, Regis J., J. A. Wayne Hellman, and William J. Short, eds. and trans. *Francis of Assisi: Early Documents*. 4 vols. Hyde Park, N.Y.: New City Press, 1999–2001.

Bishop, Morris L. *Saint Francis of Assisi*. Library of World Biography. Boston: Little, Brown, 1974.

Boase, T. S. R. *St. Francis of Assisi*. London: Duckworth, 1936.

Bodo, Murray. *Francis: The Journey and the Dream*. Foreword by John Michael Talbot. Cincinnati, Ohio: Saint Anthony Messenger Press, 2011. First published 1972.

Boff, Leonardo. *St. Francis: A Model for Human Liberation*. Translated by John W. Diercksmeier. New York: Crossroad, 1982.

Bonaventure. *The Life of St. Francis*. Translated by Ewert Cousins. HarperCollins Spiritual Classics. San Francisco: HarperCollins, 2005.

Bonghi, Ruggiero. *Francesco d'Assisi: Studio*. Città del Castello: S. Lapi, 1884. 2nd ed., with introduction by Paul Sabatier. Città del Castello: S. Lapi, 1909.

Chatel, Arsène de, ed. *Saint François d'Assise*. Paris: Plon, Nourrit, 1885.

Chesterton, G. K. *St. Francis of Assisi*. London: Hodder and Stoughton, 1923; New York: Doubleday, 1924; Garden City, N.Y.: Image Books, 1957, 1990.

Cunningham, Lawrence. *Francis of Assisi: Performing the Gospel Life*. Grand Rapids, Mich.: Eerdmans, 2004.

———. *Saint Francis of Assisi*. Boston: Twayne, 1976.

Cuthbert, Father, OSFC. *Life of St. Francis of Assisi*. London; New York: Longmans, Green, 1912; 2nd ed., London: Longmans, Green, 1913.

———. *The Romanticism of St. Francis*. London: Longmans, Green, 1915.

Daurignac, J. M. S. *Histoire de St. François d'Assise*. Paris, 1861.

Delecluse, E. J. *St. François d'Assise*. Paris, 1844.

Douglas, Eileen. *Brother Francis; Or, Less than the Least*. London: Salvation Army International Headquarters, 1895.

Doyle, Eric, OFM. *St. Francis and the Song of Brotherhood*. New York: Seabury, 1981.

Duffy, Mary Jo, and Roy M. Gasnick, OFM. *Francis, Brother of the Universe: His Complete Life's Story*. Illustrations by John Buscema and Marie Severin. New York: Marvel Comics Group and Franciscan Communications Office, 1980.

Egan, Maurice Francis. *Everybody's St. Francis*. New York: Century, 1912.

Englebert, Omer. *Saint Francis of Assisi: A Biography*, 2nd English ed. Translated by Eve-Marie Cooper from the 2nd French ed. (1956), revised and augmented by Ignatius Brady, OFM, and Raphael Brown. Chicago: Franciscan Herald Press, 1965.

Esser, Kajetan. *Die Opuscula des Hl. Franziskus von Assisi: Neue Textkritische Edition*. Grottaferrata: Spicilegium Bonaventurianum XIII, 1976.

Fortini, Arnaldo. *Francis of Assisi*. Translated by Helen Moak. New York: Crossroad, 1981.

———. *Nuova Vita di San Francesco*. 4 vols. in 5 bks. Assisi: 1959.

Galli, Mark. *Francis of Assisi and His World*. Downers Grove, Ill.: InterVarsity, 2002.

Goudge, Elizabeth. *My God and My All*. London: Duckworth, 1959; New York: Coward-McCann, 1959.

Green, Julien. *God's Fool: The Life and Times of Francis of Assisi*. New York: Harper, 1983.

Habig, Marion A., ed. *St. Francis of Assisi: Writings and Early Biographies: English Omnibus of the Sources for the Life of St. Francis*. Chicago: Franciscan Herald Press, 1973.

Hase, Karl von. *Franz von Assisi: Ein Heiligenbild*. Leipzig: Breitkopf u. Härtel, 1856.

Holl, Adolf. *The Last Christian*. Garden City, N.Y.: Doubleday, 1980.

House, Adrian. *Francis of Assisi*. New York: Hidden Spring, 2001.

Jewett, Sophie. *God's Troubadour: The Story of St. Francis of Assisi*. New York: Crowell, 1910.

Jørgensen, Johannes. *St. Francis of Assisi: A Biography*. Translated by T. O'Conor Sloane. New York: Longmans, Green, 1912. Reprinted Garden City, N.Y.: Image, 1955.

Kazantzakis, Nikos. *Saint Francis: A Novel*. Translated by Peter Bien. New York: Simon & Schuster, 1962. Originally published as *Ho phtōchoulēs tou Theou* (Athens: Difros, 1956).

Kennedy, Robert F., Jr. *St. Francis of Assisi: A Life of Joy*. New York: Hyperion, 2005.

Le Monnier, Leon. *History of St. Francis of Assisi*. London: K. Paul, 1894.

Little, William John Knox. *St. Francis of Assisi: His Times, Life and Work*. London: Isbister, 1891.

Malamud, Bernard. *The Assistant*. New York: Farrar, Straus, 1957.

Malan, Emile Chavin de. *Histoire de Saint François d'Assise*. Paris, 1845.

Martin, Valerie. *Salvation: Scenes From the Life of St. Francis*. New York: Knopf, 2001.

Mayo, Margaret, and Peter Malone. *Brother Sun, Sister Moon: The Life and Stories of St. Francis*. London: Orion Children's Books, 1999; Boston: Little, Brown, 2000.

Mockler, Anthony. *Francis of Assisi: The Wandering Years*. Oxford: Phaidon, 1976.

Moorman, John. *Saint Francis of Assisi*. London: SCM Press, 1950.

———. *The Sources for the Life of S. Francis of Assisi*. Manchester: Manchester University Press, 1940.

Murray, Wendy. *A Mended and Broken Heart*. New York: Basic, 2008.

Oliphant, Mrs. (Margaret). *Francis of Assisi*. Sunday Library. London: Macmillan, 1870.

Paterson, Katherine. *Brother Sun, Sister Moon: St. Francis of Assisi's Canticle of the Creatures*. San Francisco: Chronicle, 2011.

Petry, Ray C. *Francis of Assisi, Apostle of Poverty*. Durham, N.C.: Duke University Press, 1941.

Renan, Ernest. "Francis d'Assisi and the Franciscans, A.D. 1182." In *Leaders of Christian and Anti-Christian Thought*, 108–27. London: Mathieson, 1891.

———. "Saint François d'Assise, étude historique d'après le Dr. Karl Hase." *Journal des Débats* Août 20–21, 1866, 323–51. In *Nouvelles études d'histoire religieuse*, 1ère ed. Paris: Calmann Levy, 1884.

Robinson, Paschal, OFM. *The Real St. Francis of Assisi*. N.p.: Reprinted from the Catholic Mind, [1903?].

———. *The Real St. Francis of Assisi*. 2nd ed. London: Catholic Truth Society, 1904.

Robson, Michael J. P. *St. Francis of Assisi: The Legend and the Life*. London: Continuum, 1987.

———, ed. *The Cambridge Companion to Francis of Assisi*. Cambridge: Cambridge University Press, 2012.

Sabatier, Paul. *Life of St. Francis of Assisi*. Translated by Louise Seymour Houghton. London: Hodder & Stoughton, 1894; New York: Scribner, 1894.

———. *The Road to Assisi: The Essential Biography of St. Francis*. Edited by Jon M. Sweeney. Orleans, Mass.: Paraclete, 2003.

———. *Vie de S. François d'Assise*. Paris: Fischbacher, 1893.

Schmidt, Gail Ramshaw. *Francis, a Saint We Share: A Discussion Guide for Lutherans and Roman Catholics*. New York: Paulist Press, 1982.

Seton, Walter, ed. *St. Francis of Assisi: 1226–1926: Essays in Commemoration*. London: University of London Press, 1926.

Smith, John Holland. *Francis of Assisi*. London: Sidgwick and Jackson, 1972.

Spoto, Donald. *Reluctant Saint: The Life of Francis of Assisi*. New York: Viking Compass, 2002.

Stephen, James. "St. Francis of Assisi." *Eclectic Magazine of Foreign Literature and Art*, September 1847, 83–105.

———. "St. Francis of Assisi." *Edinburgh Review, or Critical Journal* 86 (1847): 1–42.

———. "Saint Francis of Assisi." In *Essays in Ecclesiastical Biography*, 1: 89–153. London: Longman, Green, Brown, and Longmans, 1849.

———. "[Life of St. Francis]." *Littell's Living Age* 14 (1847): 348–64.

Thompson, Augustine. *Francis of Assisi: A New Biography*. Ithaca, N.Y.: Cornell University Press, 2012.

Vauchez, Andre. *Francis of Assisi: The Life and Afterlife of a Medieval Saint*. New Haven, Conn.: Yale University Press, 2012.

Other Sources

A., M. L. [Marjory Adams]. "Rossellini Film at Brattle." *Daily Boston Globe*, December 31, 1956, 5.

Abbey, Edward. *The Fool's Progress*. New York: Holt, 1988.

———. *One Life at a Time, Please*. New York: Holt, 1988.

Abbott, Lawrence. *Twelve Great Modernists*. New York: Doubleday, Page and Co., 1927.

Acocella, Joan. "Rich Man, Poor Man." *New Yorker*, January 14, 2013, 72–77.

[Adams, C. K.]. "St. Francis and His Time." *The New Englander*, July 1870, 371–99.

Adams, Carol. *God Listens When You're Sad: Prayers When Your Animal Friend Is Sick or Dies*. Cleveland, Ohio: Pilgrim, 2005.

Adams, Henry. *Mont-Saint-Michel and Chartres*. Garden City, N.Y.: Doubleday, 1959. Originally published 1913 by American Institute of Architects.

Adey, Lionel. *Class and Idol in the English Hymn*. Vancouver: University of British Columbia Press, 1988.

Albanese, Catherine. *Nature Religion in America*. Chicago: University of Chicago Press, 1989.

———. *Reconsidering Nature Religion*. Harrisburg, Pa.: Trinity Press International, 2002.

"All Italy Honors St. Francis of Assisi." *New York Times*, October 5, 1926, 31.

Allen, Devere. *The Fight for Peace*. New York: Macmillan, 1930.

Allitt, Patrick. *Religion in America Since 1945: A History*. New York: Columbia University Press, 2003.

American Pet Industry Association. "Pet Industry Market Size and Ownership Statistics." http://www.americanpetproducts.org/press_industrytrends.asp. Accessed May 8, 2014.

"Among the New Books." *New York Observer and Chronicle*, September 4, 1902, 298. American Periodicals Series database.

Anderson, Chester. Papers. Folder 1, item 14. Bancroft Library, University of California at Berkeley. Reproduced on diggers.org.

Anderson, Jack. "Ted Shawn's Legacy: Men Tough and Tender." *New York Times*, October 24, 1991, C15.

Andrews, Nigel. "An Excuse for the Schmaltzathons." *Financial Times*, April 1, 1999, Arts, 23.

"Animals and the Afterlife: Do Pets Go to Heaven?" *Christianity Today*, April 2012, 66–67.

Anson, Peter F. *Pilgrim's Guide to Franciscan Italy*. London: Sands and Company, 1927.

Appelbaum, Patricia. *Kingdom to Commune: Protestant Pacifist Culture from World War I to the Vietnam Era*. Chapel Hill: University of North Carolina Press, 2009.

apRoberts, Ruth. *Arnold and God*. Berkeley: University of California, 1983.

Armstrong, Edward A. *Saint Francis, Nature Mystic: The Derivation and Significance of the Nature Stories in the Franciscan Legend*. Berkeley: University of California Press, 1973.

Armstrong, Karen. Foreword to *Francis of Assisi,* by Adrian House, ix–xi. New York: Hidden Spring, 2001.

Arnold, Gary. "Kitsch with a High Gloss." *Washington Post*, April 20, 1973, B1–2.

Arnold, Matthew. *Essays in Criticism*. London: Macmillan, 1865.

———. *Essays in Criticism, First Series*. London: Macmillan, 1932.

———. "Pagan and Christian Religious Sentiment," *Cornhill,* April 1864, 422–35.

———. "Pagan and Mediæval Religious Sentiment." In *Matthew Arnold: Lectures and Essays in Criticism*, edited by R. H. Super, 212–31. Ann Arbor: University of Michigan, 1962.

Arnstein, Walter L. *Protestant Versus Catholic in Mid-Victorian England*. Columbia: University of Missouri Press, 1982.

Arpin-Ricci, Jamie. *The Cost of Community: Jesus, Francis and Life in the Kingdom*. Downers Grove, Ill.: InterVarsity, 2011.

"Art and Architecture San Francisco: Bufano." http://www.artandarchitecture -sf.com/tag/benny-bufano. Accessed March 22, 2014.

[Article 1]. *Catholic World*, January 1895, 562–71.

"Article 3." *Friends' Intelligencer*, Seventh Month 31, 1904, 487. American Periodicals Series database.

"Article IV: Psychology and Salvation." *Methodist Review*, September 1911, 712–20. American Periodicals Series database.

[Attebery, Charles]. "Prayers for Peace: Christmas MCMLVIII." Georgian Press, 1958. Watkinson Private Press Collection. Watkinson Library, Hartford, Conn.

Auden, W.H. *The Age of Anxiety: A Baroque Eclogue*. New York: Random House, 1947.

Ayers, Robert H. "Christian Realism and Environmental Ethics." In *Religion and Environmental Crisis*, edited by Eugene C. Hargrove, 154–71. Athens: University of Georgia Press, 1986.

B. "The Epworth Pilgrimage." *Zion's Herald*, August 12, 1891, 253. American Periodicals Series database.

Bacon, Barbara. *Come Along with Us: A Year of Scouting in a Big, Little Town*. Wilton, Conn.: D. R. Converse Co., 1949; New York: Hastings, 1950.

Baedeker, Karl. *Italy: A Handbook for Travelers. Second Part: Central Italy and Rome*. 14th rev. ed. Leipzig: Karl Baedeker, 1904.

Baer, Richard. "The Church and Conservation: Talk and Action." In *Christians and the Good Earth*, edited by Albert Stefferud, 81–91. New York: Friendship Press for the Faith-Man-Nature Group, 1969.

———. "Conservation: An Area for the Church's Action." *Christian Century*, January 8, 1969, 40.

Baker, Kimball. *"Go to the Worker": America's Labor Apostles*. Milwaukee, Wis.: Marquette University Press, 2010.

Baker, Paul R. *The Fortunate Pilgrims: Americans in Italy, 1800–1860*. Cambridge, Mass.: Harvard, 1964.

Barbour, Ian. "Attitudes toward Nature and Technology." In *Earth Might Be Fair*, 146–68.

———. "An Ecological Ethic." *Christian Century*, October 7, 1970.

———, ed. *Earth Might Be Fair: Reflections on Ethics, Religion, and Ecology*. Englewood Cliffs, N.J.: Prentice-Hall, 1972.

———, ed. *Western Man and Environmental Ethics: Attitudes toward Nature and Technology*. Reading, Mass.: Addison-Wesley, 1973.

Barrett, Ellen. "A Word about the Old Saints." *Catholic World*, May 1884, 263–71. American Periodicals Series database.

Barrett, Mary Brigid. "Lawson, Robert." In *The Essential Guide to Children's Books and Their Creators*, edited by Anita Silvey, 252–53. Boston: Houghton Mifflin, 2002.

Barwell, Claire. "Jameson, Anna Brownell." In *The Europa Biographical Dictionary of British Women*, edited by Anne Crawford, Tony Hayter, and Ann Hughes, 221. Detroit: Gale, 1983.

Bauckham, Richard. "Creation Mysticism in Matthew Fox and Francis of Assisi." In *Living with Other Creatures: Green Exegesis and Theology*, 185–212. Waco, Tex.: Baylor University Press, 2011.

———. "Dominion Interpreted—A Historical Account." In *Living with Other Creatures: Green Exegesis and Theology*, 14–62. Waco, Tex.: Baylor University Press, 2011.

Beattie, Karen, and Matthew Scully. "Creating Discomforts: A Conservative Christian Makes the Case for Animal Mercy." *Christianity Today*, August 2003, 57–59.

"Being a Brother." *Outlook*, April 18, 1914, 834. American Periodicals Series database.

Bendroth, Margaret. *The Spiritual Practice of Remembering*. Grand Rapids, Mich.: Eerdmans, 2013.

"Benny Bufano Statues in San Francisco." http://gosanfrancisco.about.com/od /inandaroundsanfrancisco/a/The-Benny-Bufano-Sculptures-Of-San -Francisco.htm. Accessed March 22, 2014.

"Benny's Back." *Newsweek*, March 20, 1961, 26.

Berkeley Ecology Centre. "Four 'Changes.'" In *Environmental Handbook*, edited by Garrett DeBell, 323–33. New York: Ballantine, 1970.

Bernhard, Marianne. "The Dogs, Cats, and Gerbil Troop to Park to Be Blessed." *Washington Post*, May 16, 1980, D10.

Bess, Donovan. "Sculptor Who Embarrasses San Francisco." *Harper's*, February 1963, 53–57.

Bessenecker, Scott A. *The New Friars: The Emerging Movement Serving the World's Poor*. Downers Grove, Ill.: InterVarsity, 2006.

Bien, Peter. *Kazantzakis: Politics of the Spirit*. Princeton Modern Greek Studies.
2 vols. Princeton: Princeton University Press, 1989–2007.
———. "Nikos Kazantzakis (1883–1957)." In *European Writers*, edited by
William T. H. Jackson. Vol. 9, 1067–89. New York: Scribner, 1989.
Bierman, Noah. "A Speaker Pulled Hard in Two Directions." *Boston Globe*,
October 3, 2013, A1, A12–13.
Binyon, Mrs. Laurence. "St. Francis of Assisi." In *Paths of Peace*, book 2, 7–18.
Oxford: Oxford University Press, 1930.
"Bird Finds Friend in Statue of St. Francis of Assisi." *Life*, August 24,
1953, 104.
Birmingham, George A. "The Island of Saints." *Living Age*, October 18, 1919,
164–69. American Periodicals Series database.
Bishop, Morris L. "Song of the Creatures." *Horizon*, Summer 1974, 97–99.
Blanshard, Paul. *American Freedom and Catholic Power*. Boston: Beacon, 1949; 2nd
ed., 1958.
Blashfield, Edwin Howland, and Evangeline Wilbour Blashfield. *Italian Cities*.
New York: Scribner, 1900.
Blau, Eleanor. "Weekender Guide." *New York Times*, December 19, 1980, C1.
"Blessing of the Bicycles." Dumbarton United Methodist Church,
Washington, D.C. http://www.dumbartonumc.org/community-life
/community-life/blessing-bicycles.
Blewitt, Octavian. *A Hand-book for Travellers in Central Italy*. London: Murray,
1850.
Bliss, Shepherd. "St. Francis at Bread and Puppet Circus." *Christian Century*,
November 3, 1982, 1108–10.
Bonhoeffer, Dietrich. *Letters and Papers from Prison*. First English ed., edited by
John W. DeGruchy, translated by Isabel Best. *Dietrich Bonhoeffer Works*, vol.
3. Minneapolis, Minn.: Fortress Press, 2010.
Book of Blessings, Approved for Use in the Dioceses of the United States of
America by the National Conference of Catholic Bishops. Collegeville,
Minn: Liturgical Press, 1989.
Book of Blessings. Ottawa: Canadian Conference of Catholic Bishops, 1981.
Book of Common Worship. New York: Dutton, 1932.
*The Book of Common Worship: Provisional Services and Lectionary for the Christian
Year*. Philadelphia: Westminster, 1966.
The Book of Occasional Services. New York: Church Hymnal Corporation,
1979.
Book of Worship for Church and Home. Nashville: Methodist Publishing House,
1945.
Book of Worship for Church and Home. Nashville: Methodist Publishing House,
1964.
Book of Worship for Free Churches (Congregational). New York: Oxford, 1948.
Book of Worship: United Church Of Christ. New York: United Church of Christ,
Office for Church Life and Leadership, 1986.

"Books on St. Francis." *Congregationalist*, September 30, 1926, 438.

Boyd, Malcolm, ed. *The Underground Church*. New York: Sheed and Ward, 1968.

Bradbury, Malcolm. *Dangerous Pilgrimages: Transatlantic Mythologies and the Novel*. New York: Viking, 1996.

Bradley, Alexander. *Ruskin and Italy*. Nineteenth-Century Studies. Ann Arbor: UMI Research Press, 1987.

Bradley, Ian. *The Book of Hymns*. New York: Overlook Press, 1989.

Bradley, John Lewis, and Ian Ousby, eds. *The Correspondence of John Eliot Norton and John Ruskin*. Cambridge: Cambridge University Press, 1987.

"Branford Shelters Celebrate Animal Awareness Day with a Party." *New Haven Register*, October 3, 2013, Entertainment section.

Brann, Henry A. "Francis of Assisi: The Story of the Great Saint's Life." *New York Times*, April 14, 1912, BR 221–22.

Bratton, Susan Power. "The 'New' Christian Ecology." In *After Earth Day: Continuing the Conservation Effort*, edited by Max Oelschlager, 204–14. Denton: University of North Texas Press, 1992.

"The Bravest Are the Tenderest." *The Friend*, Eleventh Month 3, 1900, 126. American Periodicals Series database.

Brendon, Piers. *Thomas Cook: 150 Years of Popular Tourism*. London: Secker & Warburg, 1991.

Brewster, Mrs. Frederick F. (Margaret). "Factual History of Morelands." Typescript, 1953, in Dublin, New Hampshire Historical Society Archives, group 4, series A, folder NR-DLD 131.

"The Brewster Family History." In "Edgerton," supplement to *Hamden Chronicle*, September 3, 1964, 2.

Brink, Emily R., and Bert Polman, eds. *Psalter Hymnal Handbook*. Grand Rapids, Mich.: CRC Publications, 1998.

Brinton, Margaret Cooper, Mary Esther McWhirter, and Janet E. Schroeder, eds. *Candles in the Dark: An Anthology of Stories to Be Used in Education for Peace*. Philadelphia: Religious Education Committee, Philadelphia Yearly Meeting, 1964.

Bro, Margueritte Harmon. *When Children Ask*. Rev. ed. New York: Harper, 1956.

"The Brotherhood of the Kingdom." *New York Evangelist*, August 22, 1901, 28–31. American Periodicals Series database. (Note that this is listed in the database as "Abstract of paper," which is a subsection heading.)

Brown, Alice. "Little Windows into the World." *Harper's Bazaar*, March 1910, 156–57. American Periodicals Series database.

Brown, Jane. *Art and Architecture of English Gardens*. New York: Rizzoli, 1981.

Brown, John Pairman. *The Liberated Zone: A Guide to Christian Resistance*. Richmond, Va.: John Knox Press, 1969.

Brown, John Pairman, and Richard L. York, comps. *The Covenant of Peace: A Liberation Prayer Book*. New York: Morehouse-Barlow, 1971.

Brown, Raphael. *True Joy from Assisi*. Chicago: Franciscan Herald Press, 1978.

Brueggemann, Walter. "King in the Kingdom of Things." *Christian Century*, September 10, 1969.

Bruske, Ed. "Pets, Owners Flock to a Blessing Event." *Washington Post*, September 30, 1985, D1.

Buckley, Annie L. "Two Newspaper Women Abroad." *Congregationalist and Christian World*, June 3, 1905, 758–60. American Periodicals Series database.

Buddemeyer-Porter, Mary. *Will I See Fido in Heaven?* Manchester, Mo.: Eden, 1995.

"Bufano vs. Pegler." *Newsweek*, August 29, 1938, 22–23.

Burger, Nash K. "In the Field of Religion." *New York Times*, July 19, 1959, BR18.

Burns, Jim. "Igniting Volunteers to Become World Christians." In *The Short-term Missions Boom*, edited by Michael J. Anthony, 31–40. Grand Rapids, Mich.: Baker, 1994.

Bush, W. Stephen. "Simple Homages Paid to St. Francis." *New York Times*, August 29, 1926, SM 14.

Butler, Edward Cuthbert. "Francis of Assisi, St." In *Encyclopædia Britannica*, 11th ed., 10: 937–39. New York: Encyclopædia Britannica, 1910.

Butz, Geneva M. *Christmas in All Seasons*. Cleveland, Ohio: United Church Press, 1995.

Buzard, James. *The Beaten Track: European Tourism, Literature, and the Ways to Culture, 1800–1918*. Oxford: Clarendon, 1993.

C., D. [Untitled review.] Customer reviews, "Brother Sun, Sister Moon." Amazon.com. http://www.amazon.com/Brother-Sister-Moon-Graham -Faulkner/dp/B00170K9FI/ref=cm_cr_pr_pb_i>. Accessed February 2, 2015.

Caldwell, Samuel L. "The Mendicant Orders [St. Francis of Assisi and the Franciscans]," *Baptist Quarterly*, April 1877, 233–56.

Calvert, G. H. *Scenes and Thoughts in Europe*. 2 vols. Boston: Little, Brown, 1863.

Campbell, Brian J. "Religion and Ecology on the Ground: 'Practice' and 'Place' as Key Concepts." In *Inherited Land: The Changing Grounds of Religion and Ecology*, edited by Whitney A. Bauman, Richard R. Bohannon II, and Kevin J. O'Brien, 188–210. Eugene, Ore.: Pickwick Publications, 2011.

Campolo, Tony. "The Coming Spiritual Revival." *Tikkun*, Jan.–Feb. 2000, 26.

Canby, Vincent. "Which Flick Rates No. 14,684?" *New York Times*, April 29, 1973, 125.

———. "Zeffirelli's Film Study of St. Francis." *New York Times*, April 9, 1973, 48.

Cantate Domino. Geneva: World's Student Christian Federation, 1942.

Carr, Jay. "Captivating Rossellini Film Reemerges." *Boston Globe*, March 9, 1990, 27.

"Carroll Holliday of New Canaan Exhibiting at an Art Show," *Norwalk Hour*, November 18, 1930, 9.

Carter, Alan. "Animals." In *Routledge Companion to Ethics*, edited by John Skorupski, 742–53. New York: Routledge, 2010.

Cassady, Richard F. *The Emperor and the Saint*. DeKalb: Northern Illinois University Press, 2011.

Chafe, William H. *The Unfinished Journey: America Since World War II*. 7th ed. New York: Oxford University Press, 2011.

"Chapel of St. Francis and the Wolf of Gubbio, Marlborough, NH." *Frederick Warren Allen, American Sculptor, Boston School*. http://fwallen.com. Accessed July 6, 2012.

Chesterton, G. K. *Twelve Types*. London: Humphreys, 1902.

Cheuse, Alan, and Nicholas Delbanco, eds. *Talking Horse: Bernard Malamud on Life and Work*. New York: Columbia University Press, 1996.

Claiborne, Shane. *The Irresistible Revolution: Living As an Ordinary Radical*. Grand Rapids, Mich.: Zondervan, 2006.

Clark, Alden H. Foreword to *Letters by a Modern Mystic*, by Frank Laubach. New York: Student Volunteer Movement, 1937.

Clark, Sir Kenneth. *Civilisation: A Personal View*. London: BBC, 1969; New York: Harper, 1970.

"Claws of God." *Time*, June 1, 1962, 95.

Cleghorn, Sarah. "Blessing the Animals." *Fellowship*, July 1947.

"Closet and Altar." *Congregationalist and Christian World*, November 17, 1900, 697. American Periodicals Series database.

"Closet and Altar." *Congregationalist and Christian World*, October 18, 1902, 548. American Periodicals Series database.

Clowney, David, and Patricia Mosto, eds. *Earthcare: An Anthology in Environmental Ethics*. Lanham, Md.: Rowman & Littlefield, 2009.

Cobb, John B., Jr., *Is It Too Late? The Theology of Ecology*. Beverly Hills, Calif.: Bruce, 1972.

Coburn, Ida C. "La Benediccion [sic] de los Animales." *Overland Monthly*, August 1914, 139–41.

Coe, George A. "Studies in the Psychology of Religion." *Zion's Herald*, February 22, 1899, 236–37. American Periodicals Series database.

Cohen, Allen. "The San Francisco Oracle, a Brief History." In *San Francisco Oracle*, facsimile ed., xxv–lvi. Berkeley, Calif.: Regent Press, 1991.

Coleman, Simon, and John Elsner. "Pilgrimage to Walsingham and the Re-Invention of the Middle Ages." In *Pilgrimage Explored*, edited by J. Stopford, 189–214. York: York Medieval Press, 1999.

Collier, Laurie, and Joyce Nakamura. *Major Authors and Illustrators for Children and Young Adults*. Detroit: Gale Research, 1993.

Collins, Gail. *When Everything Changed*. New York: Little, Brown, 2009.

Communication Company. Untitled poster. Com/Co Bibliography CC-021, Communication Company Archives, Digger Archives, diggers.org.

Communication Company. "A Poem of Heroes." January 28, 1967, [5].

"Connecticut Letter." *Watchman*, April 25, 1901, 28. American Periodicals Series database.

Cook, John Wesley. "A Christian Vision of Unity: An Architectural History of the Riverside Church." In *The History of the Riverside Church in the City of New*

York, edited by Peter J. Paris, 137–77. New York: New York University Press, 2004.

"[Cora Babcock, dressed as the Goddess of Peace, posing next to a statue of St. Francis]." Photograph. San Francisco History Center, San Francisco Public Library, folder S. F. Monuments—St. Francis of Assisi.

Corcoran, Theresa, S.C. *Vida Dutton Scudder.* Twayne's United States Authors Series, 421. Boston: Twayne, 1982.

Cornacchia, Cheryl. "Paws and Pray Service Welcomes Dogs to Church." *Gazette* (Montréal), April 3, 2013, C18.

Council for a Summer of Love. "To sons, to daughters, to mankind . . ." (press release). May 13, 1967. Reprinted in *Oracle,* number 8, [June 1967].

"A Country House with a Private Chapel." *Town & Country,* September 30, 1905, 14–16.

"Country Life." *The Spectator,* September 10, 1932, 432.

Cox, Harvey. *The Secular City.* Rev. ed. New York: Macmillan, 1966.

———. *The Silencing of Leonardo Boff: The Vatican and the Future of World Christianity.* Oak Park, Ill.: Meyer Stone Books, 1988.

Coyote, Peter. *Sleeping Where I Fall: A Chronicle.* Washington, D.C.: Counterpoint, 1998.

Cron, Ian Morgan. *Chasing Francis: A Pilgrim's Tale.* Grand Rapids, Mich.: Zondervan, 2013.

Crothers, Samuel McChord. *The Pardoner's Wallet.* Boston: Houghton Mifflin, 1905.

Crowe, Joseph Archer, and Giovanni Battista Cavalcaselle. *A History of Painting in Italy from the 2nd to the 14th Century.* London: Murray, 1864.

Cunningham, Lawrence, ed. *Brother Francis: An Anthology of Writings By and About St. Francis of Assisi.* New York: Harper and Row, 1972.

———. "Fearless Friar." *America,* November 2, 2009, 31–32.

Curtiss, Thomas Quinn. "Next for Zeffirelli: Film on Jesus." *New York Times,* September 3, 1971.

———. "Zeffirelli to Depict Life of St. Francis in $2-million Movie." *New York Times,* January 20, 1971, 24.

D., A. E. "Pilgrimage Letters." *The Congregationalist,* June 25, 1896, 1000–1001. American Periodicals Series database.

Darlow, T. H. "M. Sabatier's Life of St. Francis," *Expositor,* March 1894, 222–31.

Davis, John. "Catholic Envy: The Visual Culture of Protestant Desire." In *The Visual Culture of American Religions,* ed. David Morgan and Sally M. Promey, 105–28. Berkeley: University of California Press, 2001.

Davis, Ozora S. "Assisi, the Home of the Little Poor Man." *Congregationalist and Christian World,* February 6, 1904, 192–93.

Davis, Philip. *Bernard Malamud: A Writer's Life.* New York: Oxford University Press, 2007.

Day, Dorothy. *The Duty of Delight: The Diaries of Dorothy Day,* edited by Robert Ellsberg. Milwaukee, Wis.: Marquette University Press, 2008.

———. "On Pilgrimage." *Catholic Worker,* June 1959, 1.

"The Day of the Birds." *New York Evangelist*, August 30, 1894, 18. American Periodicals Series database.

Deacon, J. Byron. "Assisi." *Friends' Intelligencer*, First Month 18, 1908, 37–38. American Periodicals Series database.

Dean, Ruth. "Fitly Furnishing the Everyday Garden." *Garden Magazine*, June 1924, 271–74.

Dearmer, Percy. *Songs of Praise Discussed: A Handbook to the Best-Known Hymns and to Others Recently Introduced*. Oxford: Oxford University Press, 1933.

Dearmer, Percy, Martin Shaw, and Ralph Vaughan Williams, eds. *Songs of Praise*. London: Oxford University Press, 1925.

De Beer, Francis. "St. Francis and Islam." In *Francis of Assisi Today*, edited by Christian Duquoc and Casiano Floristán, translated by Robert Nowell, 11–20. Concilium 149. New York: Seabury, 1981.

DeBell, Garrett, ed. *Environmental Handbook: Prepared for the First National Environmental Teach-in*. New York: Ballantine, 1970.

DeBenedetti, Charles, and Charles Chatfield. *An American Ordeal: The Antiwar Movement of the Vietnam Era*. Syracuse Studies in Peace and Conflict Resolution. Syracuse, N.Y.: Syracuse University Press, 1990.

De Chillo, Suzanne. "Blessed Are the Furry Ones." *New York Times*, May 9, 1982. Section 11 (Westchester), page 1.

Dellinger, David. *From Yale to Jail*. New York: Pantheon, 1993.

De Mello, Margo. "The Present and Future of Animal Domestication." In *A Cultural History of Animals in the Modern Age*, edited by Randy Malamud, 67–94. Oxford: Berg, 2007.

Derr, Thomas Sieger. "Religion's Responsibility for the Ecological Crisis: An Argument Run Amok." *Worldview*, January 18, 1975.

Didion, Joan. "Slouching Towards Bethlehem." In *Slouching Towards Bethlehem: Essays*, 84–128. New York: Farrar Straus Giroux, 1968.

Doane, William C. "Anarchism and Atheism." *Outlook*, September 28, 1901, 218–21. American Periodicals Series database.

Dog Mountain. "Dog Chapel." http://www.dogmt.com/Dog-Chapel.html. Accessed January 26, 2015.

Dombrowski, Daniel A. *Kazantzakis and God*. Albany: State University of New York Press, 1997.

Doty, Mark. *Tell Me Who I Am: James Agee's Search for Selfhood*. Baton Rouge: Louisiana State University Press, 1981.

Downes, Olin J. "The Vienna Opera Season." *New York Times*, June 29, 1924, X5.

Doyle, A. P. "St. Francis in Salvation Army Uniform." *Catholic World*, September 1897, 760–65.

Doyle, Eric, OFM. "Select Bibliography on the Life and Message of St. Francis." In *Francis of Assisi Today*, edited by Christian Duquoc and Casiano Floristán, translated by Robert Nowell, 73–77. Concilium 149. New York: Seabury, 1981.

DuBois, W. E. B. *The Souls of Black Folk*. Chicago: A. C. McClurg, 1903.

Dubos, René J. "Franciscan Conservation Versus Benedictine Stewardship." In Dubos, *A God Within*, 153–74 (New York: Scribner, 1972), and in David Spring and Eileen Spring, *Ecology and Religion in History*, 114–36 (New York: Harper and Row, 1974).

——. *A God Within*. New York: Scribner, 1972.

——. *So Human an Animal*. New York: Scribner, 1968.

——. "A Theology of the Earth." In Dubos, *A God Within*, 29–45. New York: Scribner, 1972.

Duin, Julia. "Freeing St. Francis." *Christianity Today*, December 17, 1982, 52–53.

"Duke Chapel Blessing of the Animals Service Oct. 6." Press release from Duke University, distributed by States News Service, September 30, 2013. LexisNexis.

Dumenil, Lynn. *The Modern Temper: American Culture and Society in the 1920s*. New York: Hill and Wang, 1995.

——. "Reinterpreting the 1920s." *OAH Magazine of History*, July 2007, 5–6.

Dunne, Susan. "Tribute to Christian Piety." *Hartford Courant*, September 21, 2006, 13.

Duquette, Tony. "Fantasies by the Bay: Tony Duquette's San Francisco Residence and Sculpture Pavilion." *Architectural Digest*, May 1989, 262–68, 338.

E., R. "Non-Catholic Work in Franciscan Studies." *Catholic World*, September 1906, 721–32. American Periodicals Series database.

Eddy, Sherwood. *I Have Seen God Do It*. New York: Harper, 1940.

——. *A Pilgrimage of Ideas*. New York: Farrar and Rinehart, 1934.

Eddy, Sherwood, and Kirby Page. *Makers of Freedom: Biographical Sketches in Social Progress*. New York: George Doran, 1926.

Eddy, William D. *Stone Pond: A Personal History*. Tarrytown, N.Y.: Rectory Basement Press, 1982.

"Editorial Notes." *New York Evangelist*, July 26, 1900, 7–8. American Periodicals Series database.

Ehrlich, Gretel. "On the Road with God's Fool." *New York Times Magazine*, June 6, 1999, 90–96.

——. "Walking with St. Francis." *Shambhala Sun*, May 1, 2000. http://www.shambhalasun.com/index.php?option=com_content&task=view&id=1800. Accessed September 28, 2014.

Ellis, Marc H. "Peter Maurin: To Bring the Social Order to Christ." In *A Revolution of the Heart: Essays on the Catholic Worker,* edited by Patrick G. Coy, 15–46. Philadelphia: Temple University Press, 1988.

Ellsberg, Robert. *The Saints' Guide to Happiness*. New York: North Point Press, 2003.

Encyclopedia of the Lutheran Church. Minneapolis: Augsburg, 1965.

Episcopal Church, Standing Liturgical Commission. *Enriching Our Worship 1: Supplemental Liturgical Materials*. New York: Church Publishing, 1998.

Erkins Studios. *Garden Ornaments* [catalog]. 1950.

Erkins Studios advertisement. *House and Garden*, June 1955, 41.

bibliography

Eskridge, Larry. *God's Forever Family: The Jesus People Movement in America.* New York: Oxford University Press, 2013.

"Ethel Barrymore in Premiere Here" [theater notes]. *New York Times,* November 28, 1939, 31.

Evangelical Lutheran Worship. Minneapolis: Augsburg Fortress, 2006.

Evans, Christopher H. *The Kingdom Is Always But Coming: A Life of Walter Rauschenbusch.* Grand Rapids, Mich.: Eerdmans, 2004.

Fackre, Gabriel. "Ecology and Theology." In *Western Man and Environmental Ethics,* edited by Ian Barbour, 116–31. Reading, Mass.: Addison-Wesley, 1973.

Farrington, C. "St. Francis of Assisi." *Old and New,* August 1870, 159–64.

Farrington, Debra K. *All God's Creatures: The Blessing of Animal Companions.* Brewster, Mass.: Paraclete, 2006.

[Father Alfred Boeddeker "blessing the pets" at children's playgrounds, Golden Gate Park]. July 7, 1961. Photographic print and notes. San Francisco Public Library. http://webbie1.sfpl.org/multimedia/sfphotos/AAA-5532.jpg. Accessed March 5, 2013.

Fauns and Fountains: American Garden Statuary 1890–1930. Southampton, N.Y.: Parrish Art Museum, 1985.

Ferrando, Guido, "St. Francis and Sri Ramakrishna." In *Vedanta for the Western World,* edited by Christopher Isherwood, 253–60. New York: Viking, 1945.

Finding aid. Graduate Theological Union Archives. Berkeley Free Church Collection, GTU 89-5-016. Berkeley, California, n.d.

Flaim, Denise. "A Religious Debate Wages [*sic*] on Whether There's an Afterlife for Animals." *Newsday,* January 2, 2007, B4.

"Flowers and Gardens in Art." *Carnegie Magazine,* March 1934, 291–301.

"Flowers of St. Francis." *New Yorker,* October 18, 1952, 152.

"Flowers of St. Francis." *Time,* October 6, 1952, 102–3.

Foertsch, Jacqueline. *American Culture in the 1940s.* Edinburgh: Edinburgh University Press, 2008.

Foley, Daniel J. *The Complete Book of Garden Ornaments, Complements, and Accessories.* New York: Crown, 1972.

Fordyce, Jeanette. "October Is the Season for Blessing the Animals in Honor of St. Francis of Assisi." *Twin Cities Daily Planet,* October 6, 2012. LexisNexis.

Fox, Matthew. *The Coming of the Cosmic Christ: The Healing of Mother Earth and the Birth of a Global Renaissance.* San Francisco: Harper, 1988.

———. *Confessions: The Making of a Post-Denominational Priest.* San Francisco: Harper, 1996.

———. *Original Blessing.* Santa Fe, N.M.: Bear, 1983.

Fox, Richard Wightman. *Jesus in America: Personal Savior, Cultural Hero, National Obsession.* San Francisco: Harper, 2005.

Franchot, Jenny. *Roads to Rome: The Antebellum Protestant Encounter with Catholicism.* Berkeley: University of California, 1994.

"Franciscan Drama." *Times Literary Supplement,* May 25, 1922, 334. Reprinted in *Twentieth Century Literary Criticism,* edited by Sharon K. Hall. Vol. 7. Detroit:

Gale, 1982. Accessed through Literature Resource Center, Amherst College, February 24, 2011.

Franciscan Institute Records, 1933. Society of the Companions of the Holy Cross Archives. Vida Scudder Collection. Byfield, Mass. Adelynrood.

Francis of Assisi. Film directed by Michael Curtiz. Perseus Productions, 20th Century Fox Film Corporation, 1961.

"Francis of Assisi." *New York Times*, January 8, 1888, 11.

"Francis of Assisi and the Renaissance." *Church Quarterly Review* 26 (July 1888), 340–61.

"Francis of Assisi, St." In *The Oxford Dictionary of the Christian Church*, 3rd ed., rev., edited by F. L. Cross and E. A. Livingstone, 635–36. Oxford: Oxford University Press, 2005.

Francke, Linda Bird. *On the Road with Francis of Assisi: The Timeless Journey through Umbria and Tuscany, and Beyond.* New York: Random House, 2005.

Franklin, Adrian. *Nature and Social Theory.* London: Sage, 2002.

Franklin, Adrian, and Robert White. "Animals and Modernity: Changing Relations, 1948–98." *Journal of Sociology* 37 (September 2001): 219–38.

"Free City: And the City Was Pure Gold." News sheet (poster). San Francisco: Free City Collective, fall 1967.

Friedlander, Albert H., ed. *"Never Trust a God over Thirty": New Styles in Campus Ministry.* New York: McGraw-Hill, 1967.

"Furnishings That Bring Friendliness to Gardens." *Garden Magazine*, June 1924, 299.

G., W. "Francis of Assisi, Supersaint." *Publishers Weekly*, September 26, 1980, 65.

[Gage, M.G.]. "Saint Francis of Assisi." *Christian Examiner*, January 1865, 47–64.

Galli, Mark. *"Speak* the Gospel." *SoulWork* [blog], *Christianity Today*, May 21, 2009. http://www.christianitytoday.com/ct/2009/mayweb-only/120-42.0.html?start=1.

García-Marquez, Vicente. *Massine: A Biography.* New York: Knopf, 1995.

Gasnick, Roy M., OFM., ed. *The Francis Book: 800 Years with the Saint from Assisi.* New York: Macmillan, 1980.

Gieryn, Thomas F. "A Space for Place in Sociology." *Annual Review of Sociology* 26 (2000): 463–96.

Gilbert, Creighton E. "Giotto (di Bondone)." In *The Dictionary of Art*, edited by Jane Turner, 12:681–96. New York: Macmillan, 1996.

Gilbert, Elizabeth. *Eat, Pray, Love: One Woman's Search for Everything Across Italy, India and Indonesia.* New York: Viking, 2006.

Gill, Jill K. *Embattled Ecumenism: The National Council of Churches, the Vietnam War, and the Trials of the Protestant Left.* DeKalb: Northern Illinois University Press, 2011.

Gladstone, Rick. "Dogs in Heaven? Pope Leaves Pearly Gate Open." *New York Times*, December 12, 2014, A1, A3.

Glassberg, David. *Sense of History: The Place of the Past in American Life*. Amherst: University of Massachusetts Press, 2001.

Gneuhs, Geoffrey. "Peter Maurin's Personalist Democracy." In *A Revolution of the Heart: Essays on the Catholic Worker,* edited by Patrick G. Coy, 47–67. Philadelphia: Temple University Press, 1988.

Goldsmith, Margaret Olthof. *Designs for Outdoor Living*. New York: George W. Stuart, 1941.

Goldstein, Warren. *William Sloane Coffin, Jr.: A Holy Impatience*. New Haven, Conn.: Yale University Press, 2004.

Goodman, Wendy, and Hutton Wilkinson. *Tony Duquette*. New York: Abrams, 2007.

Gordon, Lina Duff. *The Story of Assisi*. London: Dent, 1900.

Gordon, Lyndall. "Woolf [née Stephen], (Adeline) Virginia." In *Oxford Dictionary of National Biography*, 60:257–66. Oxford: Oxford University Press, 2004.

Gothein, Marie Luise. *A History of Garden Art*. Vol. 2. Edited by Walter P. Wright, translated by Mrs. Archer-Hind. New York: J. M. Dent, 1928.

Grampp, Christopher. *From Yard to Garden: The Domestication of America's Home Grounds*. Chicago: University of Chicago Press, 2008.

The Green Bible. San Francisco: HarperOne, 2008.

Gregg, Richard B. *The Power of Non-Violence*. Philadelphia: Lippincott, 1934.

———. *Training for Peace: A Program for Peace Workers*. Philadelphia: Lippincott, 1937.

Greiner, Dorothea. "Blessing and Curse." In *Religion Past and Present*, edited by Hans Dieter Betz et al., 2:124–30. Leiden: Brill, 2007.

"Grey Friars Get Back Sacred Monastery." *Daily Boston Globe*, January 22, 1928, 60.

Grier, Katherine C. *Pets in America: A History*. Chapel Hill: University of North Carolina Press, 2006.

Griggs, Edward Howard. *Great Leaders in Human Progress*. Indianapolis: Bobbs-Merrill, 1939.

———. *Moral Leaders*. New York: Abingdon, 1940.

Grissom, Carol A. *Zinc Sculpture in America, 1850–1950*. Newark: University of Delaware Press, 2009.

Griswold, Frank T. "Sermon at Service of Investiture of the XXV Presiding Bishop." January 10, 1998. http://archive.EpiscopalChurch.org/pb25_1295_ENG_HTM.htm. Accessed July 6, 2012.

Griswold, Mac, and Eleanor Weller. *The Golden Age of American Gardens: Proud Owners, Private Estates 1890–1940*. New York: Harry N. Abrams, 1991.

Grogan, Emmett. *Ringolevio: A Life Played for Keeps*. Boston: Little, Brown, 1972.

Grundy, Priscilla. "Alien Holiness." *Christian Century*, September 19, 1962, 1135–36.

Guerrero, Diana L. *Blessing of the Animals: A Guide to Prayers and Ceremonies Celebrating Pets and Other Creatures*. New York: Sterling, 2007.

Guide to Italy and Sicily. 5th ed. London: Macmillan, 1905.

Guide to Washington Cathedral. [Rev. ed.] Washington, D.C.: Cathedral Church of St. Peter and St. Paul, 1969.

Hale, Susan. "Chautauqua Special Courses," *Chautauquan*, August 1906, 568–75. American Periodicals Series database.

Halliwell, Martin. *American Culture in the 1950s.* Edinburgh: Edinburgh University Press, 2007.

Hammond, Phillip E. *The Campus Clergyman.* New York: Basic Books, 1966.

Handbook for Peacemakers. Philadelphia: Peace Section, American Friends Service Committee, [1942].

Haraszti, Zoltán. "A Library About St. Francis." *More Books*, September 1931, 273–86.

Hargrove, Eugene C., ed. *Religion and Environmental Crisis.* Athens: University of Georgia Press, 1986.

Haroutunian, Joseph. *Wisdom and Folly in Religion: A Study in Chastened Protestantism.* New York: Scribner, 1940.

Harris, Lis. "Brother Sun, Sister Moon." *The New Yorker*, April 27, 1987, 80–101.

Harrold, Philip. "The 'New Monasticism' As Ancient-Future Belonging." *Theology Today* 67 (July 2010): 182–93.

Hase, Karl von. *A History of the Christian Church.* Translated from the 7th German edition by Charles E. Blumenthal and Conway P. Wing. New York: Appleton, 1855.

Hauser, Ernest O. "Francis: A Saint for Today." *Reader's Digest*, August 1975, 157–64.

Hawthorne, Nathaniel. *Passages from Hawthorne's Note-Books in France and Italy.* Vol. 1 of *Nathaniel Hawthorne's Works.* Boston: James R. Osgood, 1872.

Hearn, Marcus. Untitled introductory essay. In "Viewing Notes," booklet accompanying Sir Kenneth Clark, *Civilisation: A Personal View: The Complete Series* (DVD), 4–17. New York: BBC America, 2006.

Heath, Richard. "The Crown of Thorns that Budded." *Contemporary Review* 46 (1884): 838–55.

Hedstrom, Matthew S. *The Rise of Liberal Religion: Book Culture and American Spirituality in the Twentieth Century.* New York: Oxford, 2012.

———. "Rufus Jones and Mysticism for the Masses." *Cross Currents* 54 (Summer 2004): 31–44.

Heimann, Mary. "St. Francis and Modern English Sentiment." In *Christianity and Community in the West: Essays for John Bossy*, edited by Simon Ditchfield, 278–93. St. Andrews Studies in Reformation History. Aldershot, UK: Ashgate, 2001.

Heineman, Kenneth J. *A Catholic New Deal: Religion and Reform in Depression Pittsburgh.* University Park: Pennsylvania State University Press, 1999.

Helbig, Alethea K., and Agnes Regan Perkins. *Dictionary of American Children's Fiction, 1859–1959: Books of Recognized Merit.* Westport, Conn.: Greenwood, 1985.

Helms, Chet. "About This Event . . . ." summeroflove.org/event.html.

Henriksen, Margot A. *Dr. Strangelove's America: Society and Culture in the Atomic Age*. Berkeley: University of California Press, 1997.

Herberg, Will. *Protestant, Catholic, Jew: An Essay in American Religious Sociology*. Garden City, N.Y.: Doubleday, 1955.

Herron, George D. *Between Caesar and Jesus*. New York: Crowell, 1899.

——. "The Recovery of Jesus from Christianity." *Arena*, September 1901, 3–21. American Periodicals Series database.

Hess, Elizabeth. "All Creatures Great and Small." *Interview*, May 2000, 82–84.

Hillerbrand, Hans, ed. *Encyclopedia of Protestantism*. New York: Routledge, 2004.

Hilton, Tim. *John Ruskin*. 2 vols. New Haven, Conn.: Yale University Press, 1985–2000.

Hinson, E. Glenn. "St. Francis of Assisi: Divine Fool." *Sojourners*, December 1981, 18.

Ho, Cynthia, Beth A. Mulvaney, and John K. Downey, eds. *Finding St. Francis in Literature and Art*. New York: Palgrave MacMillan, 2009.

Hobgood-Oster, Laura. *The Friends We Keep: Unleashing Christianity's Compassion for Animals*. Waco, Tex.: Baylor University Press, 2010.

——. *Holy Dogs and Asses: Animals in the Christian Tradition*. Urbana: University of Illinois Press, 2008.

Hoeberichts, Jan. *Francis and Islam*. Quincy, Ill.: Franciscan Press, 1997.

Holak, Susan L. "Ritual Blessings with Companion Animals." *Journal of Business Research* 61 (May 2008): 534–41.

Hollinger, David A. "After Cloven Tongues of Fire: Ecumenical Protestantism and the Modern American Encounter with Diversity." In *After Cloven Tongues of Fire: Protestant Liberalism in Modern American History*, 18–55. Princeton: Princeton University Press, 2013.

Holmes, John Haynes. *New Wars for Old*. New York: Dodd, Mead, 1916.

Hopkins, C. Howard. *The Rise of the Social Gospel in American Protestantism, 1865–1915*. Yale Studies in Religious Education, no. 14. New Haven, Conn.: Yale University Press, 1940.

——. "Walter Rauschenbusch and the Brotherhood of the Kingdom." *Church History* 7:2 (June 1938): 138–56.

Housman, Laurence. *Followers of St. Francis*. London: Sidgwick and Jackson, 1923.

——. *Little Plays Handbook*. London: Sidgwick and Jackson, 1927.

——. *Little Plays of St. Francis*. Complete edition in three volumes. London: Sidgwick and Jackson, 1935.

——. *Little Plays of St. Francis*. Great Neck, N.Y.: Core Collection Books, 1979.

——. *Little Plays of St. Francis: A Dramatic Cycle from the Life and Legend of St. Francis of Assisi*. London: Sidgwick and Jackson, 1922.

——. *The Unexpected Years*. London: Sidgwick and Jackson; Indianapolis: Bobbs-Merrill, 1937.

Howe, Barbara J., and Emory L. Kemp, eds. *Public History: An Introduction*. Malabar, Florida: Krieger, 1986.

Hoyland, John S. *The Way of St. Francis and To-day*. London: Student Christian Movement Press, 1935.

Hoyland, John S. Administrative/Biographical History, Correspondence of John S. Hoyland (1887–1957), Manuscript Collection, University of Nottingham, Hallward Library, Department of Manuscripts and Special Collections. archiveshub.ac.uk. Accessed January 12, 2012.

Hudnut-Beumler, James. *Looking for God in the Suburbs: The Religion of the American Dream and Its Critics, 1945–65*. New Brunswick, N.J.: Rutgers University Press, 1994.

Hudson, Winthrop S. Introduction to *Walter Rauschenbusch: Selected Writings*, 3–42. New York: Paulist Press, 1984.

Hurlbut, Jesse L. "The Inner Life of Madame Guyon." *Chautauquan*, December 1900, 302–6. American Periodicals Series database.

Hutchison, William R. *The Modernist Impulse in American Protestantism*. Durham, N.C.: Duke University Press, 1992.

———. "Protestantism as Establishment." In *Between the Times: The Travail of the Protestant Establishment in America, 1900–1960*, 3–18. Cambridge: Cambridge University Press, 1989.

Hutchison, William R., ed. *Between the Times: The Travail of the Protestant Establishment in America*. Cambridge: Cambridge University Press, 1989.

Hutton, Edward. *Cities of Umbria*. New York: Dutton, 1905.

Hyman, Paula E., and Deborah Dash Moore. *Jewish Women in America: An Historical Encyclopedia*. Vol. 1. New York: Routledge, 1997.

Hyman, Tom. *Village on a Hill: A History of Dublin, New Hampshire, 1752–2000*. Portsmouth, N.H.: Peter E. Randall, 2002.

The Hymnal (Presbyterian). Philadelphia: Westminster, 1933.

"Impressions of a Careless Traveler: The Yosemite." *Outlook*, October 15, 1904, 410–14. American Periodicals Series database.

The Intentional Communities. Yellow Springs, Ohio: Fellowship of Intentional Communities. Mimeograph, Author's Collection.

Isherwood, Christopher. Introduction to *Vedanta for the Western World*, 1–28. New York: Viking, 1945.

Israel, Barbara. *Antique Garden Ornament: Two Centuries of American Taste, 1740–1940*. New York: Harry N. Abrams, 1999.

Ivakhiv, Adrian, *Claiming Sacred Ground: Pilgrims and Politics at Glastonbury and Sedona*. Bloomington: Indiana University Press, 2002.

Jackson, Carl T. *Vedanta for the West: The Ramakrishna Movement in the United States*. Bloomington: Indiana University Press, 1994.

James, Henry. *Transatlantic Sketches*. Boston: James R. Osgood, 1875. Originally published as "A Chain of Italian Cities," *Atlantic Monthly*, February 1874.

James, William. *The Principles of Psychology*. 2 vols. New York: Henry Holt, 1893.

———. *The Varieties of Religious Experience: A Study in Human Nature*. New York: Longmans, Green, 1902.

Jameson, Mrs. (Anna Brownell Murphy). *Legends of the Monastic Orders, as Represented in the Fine Arts. Sacred and Legendary Art*, second series. London: Longman, Brown, Green, and Longmans, 1850.

———. *Legends of the Monastic Orders*, 2nd ed. London: Longman, Brown, Green, and Longmans, 1852; Boston: Houghton, Mifflin, n.d.

Jay, Elizabeth. *Mrs Oliphant, 'A Fiction to Herself': A Literary Life*. Oxford: Clarendon, 1995.

Jefferson, Charles Edward. *Things Fundamental: A Course of Thirteen Discourses in Modern Apologetics*. New York: Crowell, 1903.

Jekyll, Gertrude, and Christopher Husey. *Garden Ornament*. 2nd ed. London: Country Life; New York: Scribner, 1927.

Johnson, William. "Brother Sun, Sister Moon." *Film Quarterly* 26, no. 4 (summer 197): 60.

"John Wesley Bicentennial in Boston." *Christian Advocate*, July 9, 1903, 1111–12. American Periodicals Series database.

Jones, Darryl, Elizabeth McCarthy, and Bernice M. Murphy, eds. *It Came from the 1950s: Popular Culture, Popular Anxieties*. New York: Palgrave Macmillan, 2011.

Jones, Langford. *A Peace Portfolio*. Foreword by Laurence Housman. London: Friends Peace Committee, 1935.

Jones, Rufus M. "Experiments in Heroic Love." In *The New Quest*, 87–105. New York: Macmillan, 1928.

———. *The Flowering of Mysticism: The Friends of God in the Fourteenth Century*. New York: Macmillan, 1939.

———. *George Fox: Seeker and Friend*. New York: Macmillan, 1930.

———. *The Luminous Trail*. New York: Macmillan, 1947.

———. *The New Quest*. New York: Macmillan, 1928.

———. *New Studies in Mystical Religion*. New York: Macmillan, 1927.

———. *Studies in Mystical Religion*. London: Macmillan, 1909.

———. *Trail of Life in the Middle Years*. New York: Macmillan, 1934.

Jones, William. *Credulities Past and Present*. London: Chatto and Windus, 1880.

Jordan, Ida K. "Animal Blessing Has Survived the Criticism." *Virginian-Pilot*, September 22, 2013, CU 3.

"July in the Shops." *Country Life*, July 1940, 32.

Katcher, Aaron Honori, and Alan M. Beck. "Animal Companions: More Companion than Animal." In *Man and Beast Revisited*, edited by Michael H. Robinson and Lionel Tiger, 265–78. Washington, D.C.: Smithsonian Institution Press, 1991.

Kazantzakis, Helen, ed., *Nikos Kazantzakis: A Biography Based on His Letters*, translated by Amy Mims. New York: Simon & Schuster, 1968.

Keeps, David A. "The Holidays' Magic Maker." *Los Angeles Times*, December 20, 2007. http://articles.latimes.com/keyword/tony-duquette. Accessed October 1, 2013.

"Keep This Date." *Globe and Mail*, October 4, 1979, GAM.

Keizer, Garret. "The Day We Bless the Chainsaws." *Christian Century*, March 8, 2000, 263–64.

Kelly, Cathy. "Blessing the Beasts: Santa Cruz's Elias the Prophet Greek Orthodox Church Plans to Make Celebration an Annual Event." *Santa Cruz Sentinel*, December 9, 2012. LexisNexis.

Kelly, Kevin. "Zeffirelli Film Outrageous; Full of Fads and Pop Religion." *Boston Globe*, April 19, 1973, 74.

Kenneth Lynch and Company. *Garden Ornaments*. Architectural Handbook Series. Canterbury, Conn.: Canterbury Publishing Co., [1974].

Kesterton, Michael. "Social Studies." *Globe and Mail*, October 10, 2012, L10.

King-Cohen, Sylvia E. "Asking the Clergy: What Is the Meaning of Blessing the Animals." *Newsday*, October 5, 2013, B14.

Kinsolving, Lester. "A Rector, a Church and the Hippies." *Christian Century* 84:20, May 17, 1967, 667–68.

Kosek, Joseph Kip. *Acts of Conscience: Christian Nonviolence and Modern American Democracy*. New York: Columbia University Press, 2009.

Kroeker, P. Travis. "Sexuality and the Sacramental Imagination." In *Wendell Berry: Life and Work*, edited by Jason Peters. Lexington: University Press of Kentucky, 2007.

Krulwich, Sara. "Blessing the Animals" (photo caption). *New York Times*, October 7, 1985, B10.

Kuhn, Harold B. "Environmental Stewardship." *Christianity Today*, May 8, 1970.

Küng, Hans. "The Paradox of Pope Francis." *National Catholic Reporter*, May 24–June 6, 2013, 1, 18–19.

Kunitz, Stanley J., ed., *Twentieth Century Authors. A Biographical Dictionary of Modern Literature*. First Supplement. New York: H. W. Wilson, 1967.

Ladinsky, Daniel James. *Love Poems from God: Twelve Sacred Voices from the East and West*. New York: Penguin Compass, 2002.

Larsen, Timothy. "Thomas Cook, Holy Land Pilgrims, and the Dawn of the Modern Tourist Industry." In *The Holy Land, Holy Lands, and Christian History*, edited by R. N. Swanson, 329–42. Studies in Church History, 36. Woodbridge, Suffolk: Ecclesiastical History Society, 2000.

Lawson, Robert. *Rabbit Hill*. New York: Viking, 1944.

Le Goff, Jacques. "Francis of Assisi between the Renewals and Restraints of Feudal Society." In *Francis of Assisi Today*, edited by Christian Duquoc and Casiano Floristán, translated by Robert Nowell, 3–9. Concilium 149. New York: Seabury, 1981.

Lears, T. J. Jackson. *No Place of Grace: Anti-Modernism and the Transformation of American Culture, 1880–1920*. New York: Pantheon, 1981.

Leonard, Mary. "Homeless Chief Faces Tough Task." *Boston Globe*, December 2, 2002, A1.

Lerner, Steve. *Eco-Pioneers: Practical Visionaries Solving Today's Environmental Problems*. Cambridge, Mass.: MIT Press, 1997.

Let All Creation Praise. "Blessing of the Animals (Episcopal)." http://www.letallcreationpraise.org/blessing-of-the-animals-episcopal. Accessed May 8, 2014.

Lewin, Virginia. *One of Benny's Faces: A Study of Beniamino Bufano (1886–1970), the Man behind the Artist*. Hicksville, N.Y.: Exposition Press, 1980.

"Library Table." *Catholic World*, June 1, 1901, 73. American Periodicals Series database.

Lightman, Ann. "The Reverend William Henry Draper M. A. 1855–1933." Electronic document, formerly posted on AdelSt.John.org. Author's collection.

Linton, Michael. "San Francisco Sacred (II)." *First Things*, March 2003, 13–15.

Linzey, Andrew. *Animal Rights: A Christian Assessment of Man's Treatment of Animals*. London: SCM Press, 1976.

———. *Animal Rites: Liturgies of Animal Care*. London: SCM Press, 1999.

———. "Animals." In *Encyclopedia of Christianity*, edited by John Bowden, 1:50–52. New York: Oxford University Press, 2005.

———. *Animal Theology*. Urbana: University of Illinois Press, 1995.

———. "The Theological Basis of Animal Rights." *Christian Century*, October 9, 1991, 906–9.

Linzey, Andrew, and Dan Cohn-Sherbok, *After Noah: Animals and the Liberation of Theology*. London: Mowbray, 1997.

Lipsitz, George. *Time Passages: Collective Memory and American Popular Culture*. Minneapolis: University of Minnesota Press, 1990.

"Literature." *Christian Advocate*, August 13, 1894, 552. American Periodicals Series database.

Little, William John Knox. "The Last Days of St. Francis of Assisi." *Sunday Magazine* 26, November 1897, 754–62.

Loeffler, Jack. *Adventures with Ed: A Portrait of Abbey*. Albuquerque: University of New Mexico Press, 2002.

Lofting, Hugh. *Doctor Dolittle's Zoo*. Philadelphia: Lippincott, 1925.

Longfellow, Henry Wadsworth. "The Sermon of St. Francis." In *Through Italy with the Poets*, edited by Robert Haven Schauffler. New York: Moffat, Yard, 1908.

———, ed. *Poems of Places: Italy*. Vol. 1. Boston: Osgood, 1877.

Longfellow, Samuel, ed. *Final Memorials of Henry Wadsworth Longfellow*. Boston: Ticknor, 1887.

Lorbiecki, Marybeth. *Aldo Leopold: A Fierce Green Fire*. New York: Oxford University Press, 1999.

"Lord, Make Me an Instrument of Your Peace." *Life*, December 26, 1955, 168.

"Lord, Make Me an Instrument of Your Peace." *House Beautiful*, December 1962, 140–41.

Luhrmann, Tanya M. *When God Talks Back: Understanding the American Evangelical Relationship with God*. New York: Alfred A. Knopf, 2012.

Luke, Brother. "A Visit to Noah's Ark." *New Skete Monasteries Newsletter*, Fall 2014, [3].

MacDonell, Anne. *Sons of Francis*. New York: Putnam, 1902.

Macmurrough, Carola. "Blessing of Animals: 'Roman' Rite," in *Orate Fratres*, 14:2, 1939.

MacQuarrie, John. "Creation and Environment." In *Ecology and Religion in History*, edited by David Spring and Eileen Spring, 32–47. New York: Harper and Row, 1974.

Macquoid, Katharine S. *Pictures in Umbria*. New York: Scribner, 1905.

Manning, Kathleen. "Francis of Assisi." *U. S. Catholic*, December 2012, 43.

"Man of the Year: The Inheritor." *Time*, January 6, 1967, 18–23.

Marini, Stephen A. *Sacred Song in America: Religion, Music, and Public Culture*. Public Expressions of Religion in America. Urbana: University of Illinois Press, 2003.

Marlatt, Earl. *Protestant Saints*. New York: Henry Holt, 1928.

Marlborough, New Hampshire. Private photo collection, Ferranti family. Images of Meerwood, early to mid-twentieth century.

Maroff, Melissa. "How to Attend and Hold a Pet Blessing." EHow. http://www .ehow.com/how_2055563_attend-hold-pet-blessing.html. Accessed August 1, 2013.

Marshall, Ernest. "Italians Profess Threefold Faith." *New York Times*, October 10, 1926, E1.

Martin, Jeff. "Church Services Put Paws in the Pews." *USA Today*, March 31, 2009, 10D.

Martinengo Cesaresco, E. "The Friend of the Creature." *Living Age*, August 25, 1900, 483–91. American Periodicals Series database.

"Massachusetts Association Dinner." *Forest and Stream*, February 25, 1905, 157. American Periodicals Series database. (Note that this is listed in the database as "Letter 3.")

Masterman, C. F. G. "Chicago and Francis." In *In Peril of Change: Essays Written in Time of Tranquility*, 180–89. London: Unwin, 1905.

Maugham, H. Neville. *The Book of Italian Travel*. New York: E. P. Dutton, 1903.

McCann, Janet. "Constructing St. Francis for the Twenty-First Century." In *Finding St. Francis in Literature and Art*, edited by Cynthia Ho, Beth A. Mulvaney, and John K. Downey, 139–48. New York: Palgrave MacMillan, 2009.

McCauley, Elfrieda, and Leon McCauley, eds. *A Book of Family Worship*. New York: Charles Scribner's Sons, 1959.

McClintock, James I. *Nature's Kindred Spirits*. Madison: University of Wisconsin Press, 1994.

McClintock, John, and James Strong, eds. *Cyclopædia of Biblical, Theological, and Ecclesiastical Literature*. New York: Harper, 1870.

McClinton, Katharine. *Flower Arrangement in the Church*. New York: Morehouse-Gorham, 1954.

McCormick, Anne O'Hare. "Fascism Takes Francis as Patron Saint." *New York Times*, September 12, 1926, SM 13, 21.

McDannell, Colleen. *Picturing Faith: Photography and the Great Depression*. New Haven, Conn.: Yale University Press, 2004.

McHarg, Ian L. "The Place of Nature in the City of Man." In *Western Man and Environmental Ethics*, edited by Ian Barbour, 171–86. Reading, Mass.: Addison-Wesley, 1973.

McKibben, Bill, ed. Introduction to *American Earth*. New York: Library of
America, 2008.

McKinney, Claudia. [Untitled review.] Customer reviews, "Brother Sun, Sister
Moon." Amazon.com. http://www.amazon.com/Brother-Sister-Moon
-Graham-Faulkner. Accessed February 2, 2015.

McLachlan, Sarah. *Surfacing: Bonus Disc*. [Sound recording, CD.]
Vancouver, B.C.: Nettwerk, 1997.

"The Meaning and Service of Silence in Worship." *The Friend*, Third Month 30,
1900, 289. American Periodicals Series database.

Means, Richard L. "Man and Nature: The Theological Vacuum." *Christian
Century*, May 1, 1968, 579.

Meeker, Joseph W. "The Assisi Connection." *Wilderness*, April 15, 1988, 61–63.

Mehl-Laituri, Logan. "Sergeant Francis?" *The Blog, Huffington Post*, October 8,
2013. http://www.huffingtonpost.com/logan-mehllaituri/sergeant-francis_b
_4057341.html. Accessed October 9, 2013.

Meine, Curt. *Aldo Leopold: His Life and Work*. Madison: University of Wisconsin
Press, 1988.

Meltzer, Françoise, and Jaś Elgner, eds. *Saints: Faith Without Borders*. Chicago:
University of Chicago Press, 2011.

Mikhail, Alan. "Unleashing the Beast: Animals, Energy, and the Economy of
Labor in Ottoman Egypt." *American Historical Review* 118 (April 2013): 317–48.

Miles, Barry. *Hippie*. New York: Sterling, 2004.

Miller, Monica. "Morningside Heights Church Holds Annual 'Blessing of the
Animals' Service." News video, CBS New York. http://newyork.cbslocal
.com/2012/10/07/morningside-heights-church-holds-annual-blessing-of-the
-animals-service/. Accessed September 30, 2014.

Milligan, Harold Vincent, ed., *The Best Loved Hymns and Prayers of the American
People*. Garden City, N.Y.: Halcyon House, 1942.

Milman, Henry Hart. *History of Latin Christianity, Including that of the Popes to the
Pontificate of Nicolas V*. 8 vols. New York: Sheldon, 1860–62; rev. ed., 8 v. in 4.
New York: Armstrong, 1903.

Milner-White, Eric, and G. W. Briggs. *Daily Prayer*. London: Oxford University
Press, 1941.

"Ministers' Corner" [newsletter clipping], 1958. Subject file "Peace Monuments,"
Swarthmore College Peace Collection.

"Miss E. Muntz's Sculpture . . . at the Warren Gallery." *Apollo*, [December] 1928,
381–82.

"Mission San Luis Announces 9th Annual Blessing of the Animals." Press release
from Florida Department of State, distributed by States News Service,
September 30, 2013. LexisNexis.

"Money in Shakespeare, Says Mr. Evans; Star of 'King Richard II' Would Also
Like to Portray St. Francis of Assisi." *Daily Boston Globe*, March 24, 1940, C 7.

Montalembert, Charles Forbes de. *Les moines d'Occident depuis saint Benoît jusqu'à
saint Bernard*. Paris: Lecoffre, 1860–77.

———. *The Monks of the West, from St. Benedict to St. Bernard*. Edinburgh: W. Blackwood, 1861–77.

———. *The Monks of the West, from St. Benedict to St. Bernard*. Vol. 1. Boston: Marlier, 1860.

Moorman, John. *A History of the Franciscan Order From Its Origins to the Year 1517*. Oxford: Clarendon Press, 1968.

Morgan, David. *Protestants and Pictures: Religion, Visual Culture, in the Age of American Mass Production*. New York: Oxford, 1999.

———. *Visual Piety: A History and Theory of Popular Religious Images*. Berkeley: University of California Press, 1998.

Morgan, Lady (Sydney). *Italy*. London: Colburn, 1821.

Morgan, William. *Monadnock Summer: The Architectural Legacy of Dublin, New Hampshire*. Boston: David R. Godine, 2011.

Morrell, Mike. "Ian Cron's *Chasing Francis*: Why Won't This Book Go Away?" *Zoecarnate* [blog], July 30, 2010. http://zoecarnate.wordpress.com/2010/07/30 /ian-crons-chasing-francis-why-wont-this-book-go-away/. Accessed September 30, 2014.

Morrisroe, Patrick. "Blessing." *Catholic Encyclopedia*, 2:599–602. New York: Appleton, 1907.

Moses, Paul. "How Christians, Muslims Can Find Peace." CNN.com, January 2, 2011. http://www.cnn.com/2011/OPINION/01/02/moses.saint.sultan.unity /index.html. Accessed November 8, 2013.

———. "Mission Improbable: St. Francis and the Sultan." *Commonweal*, September 25, 2009, 11–16.

———. *The Saint and the Sultan: The Crusades, Islam, and Francis of Assisi's Mission of Peace*. New York: Doubleday, 2009.

Munsterberg, Margaret. "Assisi in Boston." *The Breeze: The News Magazine of Society*, July 8, 1932, 9, 33.

Murray, John. *A Handbook for Travellers in Central Italy. Part I: Southern Tuscany and Papal States*. London: John Murray, 1857.

Muste, A. J. *Non-Violence in an Aggressive World*. New York: Harper, 1940.

"My God and My All." *Booklist*, June 15, 1959, 567.

Napoleone, Caterina. "A Passion for Art and for Life." In *Franco Zeffirelli: Complete Works: Theatre, Opera, Film*, by Napoleone and Franco Zeffirelli, 18–79. New York: Abrams, 2010.

Napoleone, Caterina, and Franco Zeffirelli, *Franco Zeffirelli: Complete Works: Theatre, Opera, Film*. New York: Abrams, 2010.

Nash, Roderick. *The Rights of Nature: A History of Environmental Ethics*. History of American Thought and Culture. Madison: University of Wisconsin Press, 1989.

Nathan, Walter L. "Religion in Art." *The Living Church*, October 3, 1948, 11.

New Century Hymnal. Cleveland, Ohio: Pilgrim, 1995.

New Dictionary of Liturgy and Worship, edited by J. G. Davies. London: SCM Press, 1986.

"The New Jersey Pilgrimage." *New York Evangelist*, June 13, 1895, 8. American Periodicals Series database.

"The New Movies." *New York Times*, April 15, 1973, AL 141.

"New Oratorio by Edgar Tinel Produced for the First Time in America." *New York Times*, March 19, 1893, 13.

"News from the Communities." *From the Monastic Communities of New Skete [newsletter]*, Winter 2012, 22–23.

"A New Voice in the House." *Youth's Companion*, March 25, 1897, 138–39. American Periodicals Series database.

Nisly, L. Lamar. *Impossible to Say: Representing Religious Mystery in Fiction by Malamud, Percy, Ozick, and O'Connor*. Westport, Conn.: Greenwood Press, 2002.

Norman, James. *Terry's Guide to Mexico*. Garden City, N.Y.: Doubleday, 1962.

"Obituary: Mrs. Anna Heaton Fitch." *New Haven Evening Register*, December 31, 1896, 2.

Occasional Services: A Companion to Lutheran Book of Worship. Minneapolis: Augsburg; Philadelphia: Board of Publication, Lutheran Church in America, 1982.

"Oddity." *Youth's Companion*, February 27, 1896, 110–11. American Periodicals Series database.

Oppler, Alfred. "The Duchess of Stone Pond." Appendix to *Stone Pond*, by William D. Eddy, 38–53. Tarrytown, N.Y.: Rectory Basement Press, 1982.

Oremus: The Book of Worship for Corporate and Private Prayer. Chicago: Lutheran Student Association of America, 1962.

"The Oscar Wilde Revival." *Current Literature*, November 1906, 518–21. American Periodicals Series database.

Ozanam, Antoine Frédéric. *Les poètes franciscains en Italie au treizième siècle*. Paris: Lecoffre, 1852.

Page, Kirby. *Living Abundantly*. New York: Farrar and Rinehart, 1944.

Palmeri, Frank. "Deconstructing the Animal-Human Binary: Recent Work in Animal Studies. *Clio* 35 (2006): 407–20.

Parrish, Michael E. *The Anxious Decades: America in Prosperity and Depression, 1921–1941*. New York: Norton, 1992.

Paton, Alan. *Instrument of Thy Peace*. New York: Seabury, 1968.

"Peace Syllabus." Mount Vernon Student Association, [1939], mimeograph. Swarthmore College Peace Collection.

Peattie, Donald Culross. "Everybody's Saint—Francis of Assisi." *Reader's Digest*, December 1945, 63–68.

Pelc, Gene. "Saint Francis of Assisi . . . Superhero." *Tokyo Weekender*, November 9, 1979. Reprinted in Roy M. Gasnick, OFM., ed., *The Francis Book: 800 Years with the Saint from Assisi*, 163–66. New York: Macmillan, 1980.

Pelikan, Jaroslav. *Jesus through the Centuries: His Place in the History of Culture*. New Haven, Conn.: Yale University Press, 1985.

Penn, Nate. "Giving It All Away." *GQ*, June 2005, 176.

Penzel, Klaus, ed. *Philip Schaff: Historian and Ambassador of the Universal Church: Selected Writings*. Macon, Ga.: Mercer University Press, 1991.

Peppeard, Bertha A. "Passion Sunday Sermons in Many Churches." *Daily Boston Globe*, March 25, 1950, 9.

Perry, Charles. *The Haight-Ashbury: A History*. New York: Random House, 1984.

Peterson, Ingrid. "The Third Order of Francis." In *The Cambridge Companion to Francis of Assisi*, edited by Michael J. P. Robson, 193–207. Cambridge: Cambridge University Press, 2012.

Peterson, Judy. "Pets of All Shapes, Sizes Welcome at 'Blessing of the Animals.'" *Los Gatos Weekly-Times*, October 1, 2012. LexisNexis.

Petry, Ray C. "The Ideal of Poverty in St. Francis of Assisi." Ph.D. diss., University of Chicago, 1932.

———. *St. Francis of Assisi, Apostle of Poverty*. Chicago: University of Chicago, 1937.

Piehl, Mel. *Breaking Bread: The Catholic Worker and the Origins of Catholic Radicalism in America*. Philadelphia: Temple University Press, 1982.

Pilgrim Hymnal. Boston: Pilgrim Press, 1935.

Pittenger, W. Norman. *The Christian Situation Today*. London: Epworth Press, 1969.

Potter, Frank Hunter. "An Economic Asset." *Outlook*, July 13, 1912, 588–93. American Periodicals Series database.

Poulenc, Jérôme. "The Modern Inspiration for the Prayer." Translated by Edward Hagman, OFM. Cap. *Greyfriars Review* 10 (1996): 265–68.

Pran, Dith. "Blessing of the Animals" (photo caption). *New York Times*, May 4, 1981, B10.

———. "Creatures Large and Small, Furry and Slimy Are Blessed at Cathedral" (photo caption). *New York Times*, October 2, 1989, B8.

"Prayer: Make Me an Instrument of Thy Peace." *The Nation*, December 16, 1950, 635.

"Prayer for the New Year." *Reader's Digest*, January 1949, 80.

"Prayer of St. Francis." *Wikipedia*. https://en.wikipedia.org/wiki/Prayer_of _Saint_Francis. Accessed February 2, 2015.

"A Prayer of St. Francis of Assissi [sic]." *Friends' Intelligencer*, First Month 22, 1927, 66.

Prayers for the Church Service League. 4th ed. [Boston]: Episcopal Diocese of Massachusetts, 1930; 5th ed. [Boston]: Episcopal Diocese of Massachusetts, 1937.

Pullella, Philip. "Rockers in the Sacristy." Reuters, February 18, 2014. http:// www.reuters.com/article/2014/02/18/us-italy-book-assisi -idUSBREA1H0NH20140218. Accessed February 19, 2014.

Queen, Edward L., II, Stephen R. Prothero, and Gardiner H. Shattuck Jr. *The Encyclopedia of American Religious History*. 2 vols. New York: Facts on File, 1996.

"The Quest for Life." *Youth's Companion*, May 27, 1915, 272. American Periodicals Series database.

"The Rabbi Who Blesses Jewish Pets." *Tablet*, October 10, 2013. http://tabletmag
.com. LexisNexis.

"Rainbow Bridge." http://petloss.com/rainbowbridge.htm. Accessed May 9,
2014.

Rauschenbusch, Walter. *Christianity and the Social Crisis*. New York: Macmillan,
1907.

———. *Christianizing the Social Order*. New York: Macmillan, 1912.

———. *Social Principles of Jesus*. New York: Association Press, 1916.

———. *A Theology for the Social Gospel*. New York: Macmillan, 1917.

Rawnsley, H. D. "With Paul Sabatier at Assisi." *Contemporary Review* 74 (1898):
505–18.

Reckdahl, Katie. "The Abolitionist." *Gambit Weekly* (New Orleans), December
9, 2003, 9.

Reddy, John. "Stormy Benny." *Saturday Evening Post*, January 27, 1945, 22–23,
94–95.

Reeves, Terri Bryce. "The Bowwow Choir." *Tampa Bay Times*, October 10, 2012, 1.

Renan, Ernest. *The Life of Jesus*. Introduction by John Haynes Holmes. New
York: Modern Library, 1927. Reprinted 1955.

Richards, A. L. "A Sunbeam from the 13th Century." *Dial,* September 16, 1894,
150–52.

Ricks, Christopher. "Forgers." *New Statesman*, September 14, 1962, 330–31.

Riegle, Rosalie G. *Dorothy Day: Portraits by Those Who Knew Her*.
Maryknoll, N.Y.: Orbis, 2003.

Ritter, Richard H. *The Arts of the Church*. Boston: Pilgrim Press, 1947.

Ritvo, Harriet. *The Animal Estate*. Cambridge, Mass.: Harvard University Press,
1987.

Roddy, Joseph. "Francis of Assisi: The Hippie Saint," *Look*, April 20, 1971, 32–37.
Reprinted in Cunningham, *Brother Francis*, 3–9.

Rohr, Richard. "A Life Pure and Simple." *Sojourners*, December 1981, 13–16.

Romney, Lee. "Plans for Pet Repository in San Francisco Spur Theological
Flap." *Los Angeles Times*, August 8, 2013. http://articles.latimes.com/2013/aug
/08/local/la-me-sf-pets-20130809. Accessed August 10, 2013.

Roraback, Dick. "Looking Back: Duquette's Angels Find a Home Away from
Home." *Los Angeles Times*, December 31, 1987. http://articles.latimes.com
/keyword/tony-duquette. Accessed October 1, 2013.

———. "A Pilgrimage to the Duqal Palace." *Los Angeles Times*, April 22, 1987.
http://articles.latimes.com/keyword/tony-duquette. Accessed October 1,
2013.

Rosen, Michael J. *The Blessing of the Animals*. New York: Farrar Straus Giroux,
2000.

Ross, Ellen. "St. Francis in Soho: Emmeline Pethick, Mary Neal, the West
London Wesleyan Mission, and the Allure of 'Simple Living' in the 1890s."
Church History 83 (December 2014), 843–83.

Rossinow, Doug. *The Politics of Authenticity: Liberalism, Christianity, and the New
Left in America*. New York: Columbia University Press, 1998.

Roth, Matthew. "Coming Together: The Communal Option." In *Ten Years That Shook the City*, edited by Chris Carlsson, 192–208. San Francisco: City Lights Books, 2011.

Rothman, Hal K. *The Greening of a Nation? Environmentalism in the United States Since 1945*. Belmont, Calif.: Wadsworth/Thomson Learning, 1998.

Rotzetter, Anton. "Francis of Assisi: A Bridge to Islam." Translated by John Bowden. In *Frontier Violations*, edited by Felix Wilfred and Jose Oscar Beozzo, 107–15. Concilium. Maryknoll, N.Y.: Orbis, 1999.

Rowlands, Penelope. "Tony Duquette: Champion of Magic and Theater in Residential Design." *Architectural Digest*, January 2000, 160–63, 242.

S., L. [Leslie Stephen]. "Stephen, Sir James." *Dictionary of National Biography*. London: Smith, Elder, 1898, 54:163–64.

Sabatier, Paul. "St. Francis and the Twentieth Century." *Living Age*, February 7, 1903, 321–33.

Sack, Kevin. "A Day When the Pews Are a Jumble of Paws." *New York Times*, October 6, 1997, A12.

"St. Francis and the Birds" (advertisement from Florentine Craftsmen). *House and Garden*, July 1951, 12.

"St. Francis and the Franciscans." *American Journal of Education*, National Series, 8:30, June 15, 1873, 393–400.

"St. Francis Birdbath/Garden Statue, Marlborough, NH." *Frederick Warren Allen, American Sculptor, Boston School*. http://fwallen.com. Accessed July 6, 2012.

"St. Francis in Your Garden: Christmas for Your Birds" (advertisement from Erkins Studios). *House and Garden*, November 1946, 87; December 1946, 41.

"Saint Francis of Assisi." *Lend a Hand* 1:1886, 277–83.

"St. Francis of Assisi." *Littell's Living Age*, May 28, 1887, 515–25.

"[St. Francis of Assisi]." *Quarterly Review* 189 (1899): 1–31.

"St. Francis of Assisi 1." *Overland Monthly and Out West Magazine*, January 1895, 97–101. American Periodicals Series database.

"'St. Francis of Assisi' to be Presented by Oratorio Society." *New York Times*, March 12, 1893, 13.

"Saint Francis of the Bronx." *New Yorker*, October 15, 1949, 25–26.

"Saint Francis Rest." http://www.shrinesf.org/Columbarium/SF-Columbarium .html. Accessed August 10, 2013.

"St. Francis' Shrine Should Remain Open to All." http://www.shrinesf.org /index.html. Accessed August 10, 2013.

Salinger, J. D. *Franny and Zooey*. Boston: Little, Brown, 1961.

Samuels, Ernest. *Henry Adams*. Cambridge, Mass.: Harvard University Press, 1989.

Sanborn, Helen J. *Persephone and Other Poems*. [Wellesley, Mass.:] 1905.

"A Sanctuary Garden." *Missionary Herald*, October 1942, 26–27.

San Francisco Oracle. Facsimile Edition. Berkeley: Regent Press, 1991.

"San Francisco's Saint." *Time*, August 29, 1938, 28–29.

Santmire, H. Paul. *Brother Earth: Nature, God, and Ecology in Time of Crisis*. New York: Thomas Nelson, 1970.

———. "Struggle for an Ecological Theology." *Christian Century*, March 4, 1970, 275–77.

Schaff, Philip, ed. *A Religious Encyclopedia, or Dictionary of Biblical, Historical, Doctrinal, and Practical Theology*. 3 vols. New York: Funk and Wagnalls, 1882.

Schaffer, Michael. *One Nation Under Dog: Adventures in the New World of Prozac-Popping Puppies, Dog-Park Politics, and Organic Food*. New York: Henry Holt, 2009.

Schlueter, Paul. "Elizabeth de Beauchamp Goudge." In *An Encyclopedia of British Women Writers*, edited by Paul Schlueter and June Schlueter, 202–4. New York: Garland, 1988.

Schmidt, Gary D. *Robert Lawson*. Twayne's United States Authors Series TUSAS 686. New York: Twayne, 1997.

Schmidt, Leigh Eric. *Restless Souls: The Making of American Spirituality from Emerson to Oprah*. San Francisco: Harper, 2005.

Schochet, Elijah Judah. *Animal Life in Jewish Tradition: Attitudes and Relationships*. New York: Ktav, 1984.

Schubeck, Thomas L., S.J. "Liberation Theology." In *Encyclopedia of Christianity* 3:258–65. Grand Rapids, Mich.: Eerdmans, 2003.

Schulz, Frieder. "The So-Called Prayer of St. Francis." Translated by Peter J. Colosi. *Greyfriars Review* 10 (1996): 237–56.

Schwarzschild, Bertram M. "Earthwatch: No Birds Sing on St. Francis' Mountain." *Audubon*, March 1983, 132–35.

———. "Saving the Birds of St. Francis." *Audubon*, November 1984, 141–42.

Scudder, Vida D. *Brother John: A Tale of the First Franciscans*. Boston: Little Brown, 1927.

———. *The Church and the Hour: Reflections of a Socialist Church Woman*. New York: Dutton, 1917.

———. "Footprints of St. Francis." *Outlook*, June 6, 1903, 322–28.

———. *The Franciscan Adventure: A Study in the First Hundred Years of the Order of St. Francis of Assisi*. New York: Dutton, 1931.

———. "A Franciscan Institute." *The Commonweal*, September 1, 1933, 427–28.

———. "Joachim of Flora and the Friars." In *The Privilege of Age, Essays Secular and Spiritual*, 193–210. New York: Dutton, 1939. Originally published in *Christendom*, 1938.

———. "The Larks of St. Francis." In *The Privilege of Age: Essays Secular and Spiritual*, 187–93. New York: Dutton, 1939. Originally published in *The World Tomorrow*, 1928.

———. *The Life of the Spirit in the Modern English Poets*. Boston: Houghton Mifflin, 1895.

———. *A Listener in Babel*. Boston: Houghton Mifflin, 1903.

———. *On Journey*. New York: Dutton, 1937.

———. "The Sabatier Collection of Franciscan Literature." *More Books*, May, 1937, 218–19.

———. *Socialism and Character*. Boston: Houghton Mifflin, 1912.

———, ed. *The Journal with Other Writings of John Woolman*. London: Dent; New York: Dutton, 1922.

"Sculpture by Elizabeth Muntz" (photos). *Creative Art*, February 1929, 137.

Seelye, John. *Memory's Nation: The Place of Plymouth Rock*. Chapel Hill: University of North Carolina Press, 1998.

Selincourt, Beryl de (Beryl de Zoete). *Homes of the First Franciscans*. London: J. M. Dent, 1905.

Senn, Frank. "Happy Birthday, Francesco." *Dialog* 21, no. 1 (Winter 1982): 6–7.

Seton, Walter. "The Rediscovery of St. Francis of Assisi." In *St. Francis of Assisi: 1226–1926: Essays in Commemoration*, edited by Walter Seton, 245–263. London: University of London Press, 1926.

Shaw, George Bernard. "Poor Old Philharmonic." In *Shaw's Music: The Complete Musical Criticism in Three Volumes*, edited by Dan H. Laurence, 2:14–19. London: Bodley Head, 1981.

Sheehy, Colleen J. *The Flamingo in the Garden: American Yard Art and the Vernacular Landscape*. New York: Garland, 1998.

Sheel, Shaemas O. "On with the Dance." *Forum*, February 1911, 189–99. American Periodicals Series database.

Sheldon, Charles M. "The Law of Christian Discipleship." *Zion's Herald*, March 2, 1898, 265–66.

Sheldrake, Philip F. *Explorations in Spirituality: History, Theology, and Social Practice*. New York: Paulist Press, 2010.

———. "Human Identity and the Particularity of Place." *Spiritus* 1 (Spring 2001): 43–64.

Sherrard, Brooke. "'Palestine Sits in Sackcloth and Ashes': Reading Mark Twain's *The Innocents Abroad* as a Protestant Holy Land Narrative." *Religion and the Arts* 15 (January 2011): 82–110.

Shinn, Roger L. "Population and the Dignity of Man." *Christian Century*, April 15, 1970.

———. "Science and Ethical Decision: Some New Issues." In *Earth Might Be Fair*, edited by Ian Barbour, 141–42. Englewood Cliffs, N.J.: Prentice-Hall, 1972.

Shires, Preston. *Hippies of the Religious Right*. Waco, Tex.: Baylor University Press, 2007.

"Shopping Around." *House and Garden*, July 1938, 5.

"Shopping Around." *House and Garden*, March 1969, 140–83.

Short, Ernest. *The House of God: A History of Religious Architecture*. London: Eyre & Spottiswood, 1955.

Shuman, Joel James. "Introduction: Placing God in the Work of Wendell Berry." In *Wendell Berry and Religion*, edited by Joel James Shuman and L. Roger Owens, 1–12. Lexington: University Press of Kentucky, 2009.

Sicius, Francis. "The Chicago Catholic Worker." In *A Revolution of the Heart: Essays on the Catholic Worker*, edited by Patrick G. Coy, 337–59. Philadelphia: Temple University Press, 1988.

Sideris, Lisa H. "The Secular and Religious Sources of Rachel Carson's Sense of Wonder." In *Rachel Carson: Legacy and Challenge, edited by* Lisa H. Sideris and

Kathleen Dean Moore, 232–50. Albany: State University of New York Press, 2008.

Silvey, Anita. "Rabbit Hill, by Robert Lawson." *Anita Silvey's Children's Book-a-Day Almanac*. http://childrensbookalmanac.com/2011/07/rabbit-hill/. Accessed December 5, 2012.

Singer, Peter. *Animal Liberation: A New Ethics for Our Treatment of Animals*. New York: New York Review, distributed by Random House, 1975.

Slawenski, Kenneth. *J. D. Salinger: A Life Raised High*. Hebden Bridge, UK: Pomona, 2010.

Smith, H. Augustine. *The American Student Hymnal*. New York: Appleton-Century, 1928.

Smith, Janna Malamud. *My Father Is a Book: A Memoir of Bernard Malamud*. Boston: Houghton Mifflin, 2006

Smith, Michael G. "Troubadour of the Kingdom." *Christianity Today*. February 1985, 88.

Smith, Ryan K. *Gothic Arches, Latin Crosses: Anti-Catholicism and American Church Designs in the Nineteenth Century*. Chapel Hill: University of North Carolina Press, 2006.

Smucker, Donovan E. *Origins of Walter Rauschenbusch's Social Ethics*. Montréal: McGill-Queen's University Press, 1994.

Smyth, Newman. "Recent Revivalism and the Franciscan Rule." *Congregationalist*, March 5, 1896, 372.

Sorrell, Roger D. *St. Francis of Assisi and Nature: Tradition and Innovation in Western Christian Attitudes Toward the Environment*. New York: Oxford, 1988.

Sperry, Willard L. "The Little Flowers of St. Francis." In *Strangers and Pilgrims: Studies in the Classics of Christian Devotion*, 32–58. Boston: Little, Brown, 1939.

Spring, David, and Eileen Spring, eds. *Ecology and Religion in History*. New York: Harper and Row, 1974.

Stausberg, Michael. *Religion and Tourism: Crossroads, Destinations, and Encounters*. New York: Routledge, 2011.

Steele, Robert. "Sabatier's Life of St. Francis." *Academy* 46, no. 1162 (August 11, 1894): 96–97.

Steere, Douglas. *Time to Spare*. New York: Harper, 1949.

Stefferud, Alfred. Introduction to *Christians and the Good Earth*, edited by Alfred Stefferud, 9–11. New York: Friendship Press for the Faith-Man-Nature Group, 1969.

Steinberg, Susan. "Straight from the Hearts of Children: Animal Blessings." *Family Ministry* 19 (Winter 2005): 49–51.

Stelmach, Harlan. "The Cult of Liberation: The Berkeley Free Church and the Radical Church Movement, 1967–1972." Ph.D. diss., Graduate Theological Union, 1977.

Stephen Huneck Gallery and Dog Chapel. "Life Is a Ball" (brochure). Ca. 2011, author's collection.

Stickley, Gustav. *Craftsman Houses: The 1913 Catalog*. New York: Craftsman Publishing Company, 1913; reprint, Mineola, N.Y.: Dover, 2009.

Stoll, Steven. *U.S. Environmentalism Since 1945*. New York: Palgrave Macmillan, 2007.

Stone, James S. "Joseph Barber Lightfoot." *Church Review* 63 (October 1891), 173–208. American Periodicals Series database.

Storr-Best, Lloyd. "The Common Sense of Hypnotism." *Eclectic Magazine of Foreign Literature*, June 1893, 734–40. American Periodicals Series database.

Stowe, William W. *Going Abroad: European Travel in Nineteenth-Century American Culture*. Princeton: Princeton University Press, 1994.

Stulken, Marilyn Kay, and Catherine Salika. *Hymnal Companion to Worship*. 3rd ed. Chicago: GIA publications, 1998.

Swatos, William H., Jr. "New Canterbury Trails: Pilgrimage and Tourism in Anglican London." In *From Medieval Pilgrimage to Religious Tourism*, edited by William H. Swatos Jr., and Luigi Tomasi, 91–114. Religion in the Age of Transformation. Westport, Conn.: Praeger, 2002.

Sweeney, Jon M. "E. Stanley Jones, C. F. Andrews, Gandhi, and St. Francis." *Almost Catholic* [blog], February 28, 2010. https://jonmsweeney.wordpress.com/2010/02/. Accessed February 2, 2012.

"Table Gossip." *Daily Boston Globe*, August 18, 1935, C6.

Tagliabue, John. "A Little Dutch Angel's Cellphone Number Is in Demand." *New York Times*, March 6, 2012, A8.

Taine, H. *Italy: Florence and Venice*, translated by J. Durand. New York: Leopoldt & Holt, 1869.

Talbot, David. *Season of the Witch: Enchantment, Terror, and Deliverance in the City of Love*. New York: Free Press, 2012.

Talbot, John Michael, with Steve Rabey. *The Lessons of St. Francis: How to Bring Simplicity and Spirituality into Your Daily Life*. New York: Dutton, 1997.

"Talk about New Books." *Catholic World*, August 1894, 59, 353. American Periodicals Series database.

Tartt, Donna. Foreword to *The Life of St. Francis*, by Bonaventure, translated by Ewert Cousins, v–ix. Harper Collins Spiritual Classics. San Francisco: Harper, 2005.

Terry, Walter. "O, Brother Sun and Sister Moon." *Saturday Review*, July 29, 1967, 39–40.

Thayer, Gwyneth Anne. *Going to the Dogs: Greyhound Racing, Animal Activism, and American Popular Culture*. CultureAmerica. Lawrence: University Press of Kansas, 2013.

Thode, Henry. *Franz von Assisi und die Anfänge der Kunst der Renaissance in Italien*. Berlin: Grote, 1885.

Tinel, Edgar. *Francis: Oratorio for Soli, Chorus, Organ, and Orchestra, Opus 36*. Libretto by Lodewijk de Koninck; translated by John Fenton. New York: Breitkopf & Härtel, 1893.

———. *Franciscus: Oratorium voor Soli, Koor, Orgel en Orkest, Op. 36*. Libretto by Lodewijk de Koninck. Leipzig: Breitkopf & Härtel, 1890.

Tolan, John. *St. Francis and the Sultan: The Curious History of a Christian-Muslim Encounter*. New York: Oxford University Press, 2009.

Tomasi, Luigi. "*Homo Viator*: From Pilgrimage to Religious Tourism via the Journey." In *From Medieval Pilgrimage to Religious Tourism*, edited by William H. Swatos Jr., and Luigi Tomasi, 91–114. Religion in the Age of Transformation. Westport, Conn.: Praeger, 2002.

Tosh, John. *Why History Matters*. New York: Palgrave Macmillan, 2008.

"Toward a Hidden God." *Time*, April 8, 1966, 82–87.

Trenholme, Norman M. "The Saint of Assisi." *Dial*, December 16, 1912, 490–92. American Periodicals Series database.

Trexler, Richard C. *Naked Before the Father: The Renunciation of St. Francis of Assisi*. Humana Civilitas: Studies and Sources Relating to the Middle Ages and the Renaissance. Vol. 9. New York: Peter Lang, 1989.

Tulloch, John. "Amateur Theology." *Blackwood's Magazine* 113, June 1873, 678–92.

———. "St. Francis, Part I." *Good Words* 1877, 419–23.

———. "St. Francis, Part II." *Good Words* 1877, 449–52.

Turner, Victor, and Edith Turner. *Image and Pilgrimage in Christian Culture*. New York: Columbia University Press, 1978.

Twelve Steps and Twelve Traditions. New York: The A.A. Grapevine and Alcoholics Anonymous Publishing, [1952], 1981.

Umbria: A Complete Guide to the Landscape and Hill Towns. Milan: Touring Club of Italy. [New York]: distributed by Abbeville Press, 1999.

Vahanian, Gianni. *The Death of God: The Culture of Our Post-Christian Era*. New York: George Braziller, 1961.

Van Dijk, Willibrord-Christiaan, OFM Cap. "A Prayer in Search of an Author." Translated by Edward Hagman, OFM Cap. *Greyfriars Review* 10 (1996): 257–64.

Vidich, Arthur, and Stanford M. Lyman. *American Sociology: Worldly Rejections of Religion and Their Directions*. New Haven, Conn.: Yale University Press, 1985.

Vidor, Constance. "Lawson, Robert." In *Cambridge Guide to Children's Books in English*, edited by Victor Watson, 417. Cambridge: Cambridge University Press, 2001.

Vining, Elizabeth Gray. *Friend of Life: The Biography of Rufus M. Jones*. Philadelphia: Lippincott, 1958.

"The Virility of Goodness." *Congregationalist and Christian World*, June 25, 1904, 880. American Periodicals Series database.

Wagner-Martin, Linda. *The Mid-Century American Novel, 1935–65*. New York: Twayne, 1997.

Wainwright, Geoffrey, and Karen B. W. Tucker, eds. *Oxford History of Christian Worship*. New York: Oxford University Press, 2006.

Waller, Gary F. "From the Holy Family to the Sidney and Lee-Warner Families: The Protestantization of Walsingham." In *Walsingham in Literature and Culture from the Middle Ages to Modernity*, edited by Dominic Janes and Gary Waller, 67–81. Farnham, Surrey: Ashgate, 2010.

Wallis, Jim. "A Holy Jealousy." *Sojourners*, December 1981, 3–5.

Warfield, Benjamin B. "M. Paul Sabatier's Life of St. Francis of Assisi." *Presbyterian and Reformed Review* 6 (1895): 158–61.

Washburn, Henry Bradford. "Francis of Assisi." In *Men of Conviction*, 134–74. New York: Scribner, 1931.

———. *Religious Motive in Philanthropy*. Philadelphia: University of Pennsylvania Press, 1931.

Washington, D.C. Cathedral of Saints Peter and Paul. Archives.

Waskow, Arthur. "A Celebration for People of All Faiths." *Philadelphia Inquirer*, September 23, 2005, A23.

Watson, J. R. *An Annotated Anthology of Hymns*. Oxford: Oxford University Press, 2002.

Watson, Victor, ed. *Cambridge Guide to Children's Books in English*. Cambridge: Cambridge University Press, 2001.

Watters, Sam, ed. *American Gardens, 1890–1930*. New York: Acanthus Press, 2006.

Webb, Stephen. *On God and Dogs: A Christian Theology of Compassion for Animals*. New York: Oxford, 2002.

———. Review of *The Friends We Keep*, by Laura Hobgood-Oster. *First Things*, January 2011, 62–63.

Weil, Martin. "This Washington Cathedral Blessing Ends with an 'Arf.'" *Washington Post*, October 5, 1991, C4.

Wheeler, Michael. *Ruskin's God*. Cambridge Studies in Nineteenth-Century Literature and Culture. Vol. 24. Cambridge: Cambridge University Press, 1999.

White, Lynn, Jr. "The Historical Roots of Our Ecologic Crisis." *Science*, March 10, 1967, 1203–7.

———. "Man and Nature." *New York Times*, January 4, 1967, 40.

———"Saint Francis and the Ecologic Backlash." *Horizon*, Summer 1967, 42–47.

Wieman, Henry, and Rufus M. Jones, "What Saints and Sages See." *Christian Century,* February 12, 1930, 206–11.

Willcox, Louise Collier. "Tolstoi's Religion." *North American Review*, February 1911, 242–55. American Periodicals Series database.

Williams, Cecil. *I'm Alive!: An Autobiography*. San Francisco: Harper and Row, 1980.

Williams, Cecil, and Janice Mirikitani, *Beyond the Possible: 50 Years of Creating Radical Change in a Community Called Glide*. New York: HarperOne, 2013.

Williams, Merryn. *Margaret Oliphant: A Critical Biography*. New York: St. Martin's, 1986.

Williams, Peter. "A Mirror for Unitarians: Catholicism and Culture in Nineteenth Century New England Literature." Ph.D. diss., Yale University, 1970.

Williams, Rhys H. "Creating an American Islam: Thoughts on Religion, Identity, and Place." *Sociology of Religion* (June 1, 2011): 127–53.

Wilmington, Michael. " 'St. Francis' Breathes Life into the Thirteenth Century Icon." *Chicago Tribune*, June 16, 2006, 7A.

Wilson, Howard A. "The Lore of Francis." *The Living Church*, September 19, 1948, 25–26.

Wilson-Hartgrove, Jonathan. *New Monasticism: What It Has To Say to Today's Church*. Grand Rapids, Mich.: Brazos, 2008.

Win with Love! A Comprehensive Directory of the Liberated Church. Berkeley, Calif.: Free Church Publications, 1971.

Winter, Paul. "The Genesis of *Earth Mass/Missa Gaia*." Introduction to *Missa Gaia–Earth Mass: A Mass in Celebration of Mother Earth* [music score], by Paul Winter, Jim Scott et al., 2–6. Milwaukee, Wis.: Hal Leonard, 2006.

Winter, Paul, Jim Scott et al. *Missa Gaia–Earth Mass*. [Sound recording, CD.] Litchfield, Conn.: Talking Music, 1982.

———. *Missa Gaia–Earth Mass: A Mass in Celebration of Mother Earth*. [Music score] Milwaukee, Wis.: Hal Leonard, 2006.

Wintz, Jack, OFM. "St. Francis at St. John the Divine." *Saint Anthony Messenger*, October 2003. www.AmericanCatholic.org/messenger. Accessed October 9, 2013.

———. *Will I See My Dog in Heaven?: God's Saving Love for the Whole Family of Creation*. Brewster, Mass.: Paraclete, 2009.

With Children Leading. Philadelphia: Friends' Peace Committee of Philadelphia Yearly Meeting and Religious Education Committee of Arch Street Yearly Meeting, 1941.

"With the Corresponding Editor." *Harper's Bazaar*. April 1908, 413. American Periodicals Series database.

Wittner, Lawrence. *Rebels Against War: The American Peace Movement, 1941–1960*. New York: Columbia University Press, 1969.

Wolfe, Tom. "The 'Me' Decade and the Third Great Awakening." *New York*, August 23, 1976.

Wolff, Kenneth Baxter. *The Poverty of Riches*. New York: Oxford, 2003.

Wood, Henry. "Auto-Suggestion and Concentration." *Arena*, March 1895, 136–144. American Periodicals Series database.

"Woodbrooke Summer Settlement for Religious Study." *Friends' Intelligencer*, Tenth Month 10, 1903, 648–50. American Periodicals Series database.

Woodruff, Clinton Rogers. "Religious Intelligence: The Brotherhood of the Kingdom." *The Independent*, September 1, 1898, 652.

Woods, Ralph L., ed. *A Treasury of the Familiar*. New York: Macmillan, 1942.

———, ed. *A Second Treasury of the Familiar*. New York: Macmillan, 1950.

"A Word about the Old Saints." *Catholic World*, May 1894, 263–71. American Periodicals Series database.

"World's Tallest Statue: WPA plan for San Francisco Stirs Furious Row." *Newsweek*, August 15, 1938.

Wranovics, John. "Chaplin in the Art and Life of James Agee." In *Agee Agonistes: Essays on the Life, Legend, and Works of James Agee*, edited by Michael A. Lofaro, 157–66. Knoxville: University of Tennessee Press, 2007.

Wright, Richard. "Responsibility for the Ecological Crisis." *Christian Scholar's Review* (Fall 1970): 35–40.

Wright, Richardson L. "Instruments of Peace." *House and Garden*, December 1943, 40–41.

———. *The Story of Gardening, from the Hanging Gardens of Babylon to the Hanging Gardens of New York*. New York: Dodd, Mead, 1934.

Wuthnow, Robert. *The Restructuring of American Religion: Society and Faith since World War II*. Princeton: Princeton University Press, 1988.

"Young People and a New World." Pamphlet. New York: Fellowship of Reconciliation, [1930?] Swarthmore College Peace Collection.

Zaleski, Philip. "The Saints of John Paul II." *First Things*, March 2006, 28–32.

Zwick, Mark, and Louise Zwick. *The Catholic Worker Movement: Intellectual and Spiritual Origins*. New York: Paulist Press, 2005.

Index of Names

Talbot, John Michael, 138, 139
Tartt, Donna, 3, 100
Teilhard de Chardin, Pierre, 132, 135
Temple, Sebastian, 140
Thode, Henry, 19
Thomas à Kempis, 23, 25, 28
Thomas of Celano, 7
Thompson, Augustine, 27
Thoreau, Henry David, 87
Tolan, John, 172
Tolstoy, Leo, 27, 99, 108
Tulloch, John, 193 (n. 36)
Twain, Mark, 45

Vaughan Williams, Ralph, 75

Wadding, Luke, 7
Wallis, Jim, 127, 138
Webb, Stephen, 152
White, Gilbert, 82, 87
White, Lynn, 130, 131–32, 134, 152, 164
Whitehead, Alfred North, 132
Wilde, Oscar, 34
Winter, Paul, 136, 155
Woods, Ralph, 92
Woolman, John, 41
Wright, Richardson L., 72, 82, 201 (n. 4)

York, Richard L., 122, 125

Zeffirelli, Franco, 126–29

Index of Subjects

Adel, Yorkshire. *See* Church of St. John the Baptist

African Americans, 74, 90, 93, 95, 150

Alcoholics Anonymous, 3, 103

"All Creatures of Our God and King," 72–78, 88, 96, 139, 161–62, 163; text, 72–73. *See also* Music: church music and hymns

American Association for the Advancement of Science, 130

Anglicans and Episcopalians, 29, 40, 45, 71, 102, 123, 164, 167, 174; and "All Creatures of Our God and King," 74, 76; and blessing of the animals, 136, 149, 155; high-church influence, 13, 44, 80; and statuary, 76–77, 79–80, 82, 85

Animals, 158, 159, 163, 164, 165; and Francis, 2, 18, 34, 87, 92, 94–97, 99, 103, 131, 156, 212 (n. 66); human relationships with, 130, 150–54; in *Rabbit Hill*, 93–96; in religious practice, 152–54, 157; in religious thought, 151, 157; rights, 151, 213 (n. 6). *See also* Birds; "Blessing of the animals" ceremonies; Death: animals

Animal turn, 150–52. *See also* Liberation, as ideal

Antimodernism, 13–14, 31, 32, 170, 182

Aphorisms. *See* Attributions

Arts and Crafts movement, 26

Assisi, 11, 41, 57, 144, 160, 161, 169; early travel to, 17; and environment, 144; Fascist restoration, 60; pilgrimage to, 43–47, 144; sense of place in, 43–47, 60, 144; visits and sojourns, 39, 40–41, 45–47, 49, 108, 160–61, 165, 167, 170. *See also* Place

Attributions, 70, 155, 174–75

Authenticity, as ideal, 13–14, 19, 28, 111, 113, 115, 117

Baptists, 33, 37–38, 75, 138

Beatles, 126

Berkeley Ecology Centre, 135

Bethany Church (Foxboro, Mass.), 83

Bible, 14, 63, 66, 132; Genesis, 130, 212 (n. 70); Gospels, 7, 24, 47, 129, 139, 140, 145, 147, 151, 209 (n. 27); historical criticism, 14, 36; Job, 155; prophets, 212 (n. 70); Revelation, 129; Sermon on the Mount, 23, 24, 63, 129, 170

Birdbaths. *See* Garden statues

Birds, 99, 133, 144; imagery, 18, 93, 97, 106–7, 118, 120; imagery criticized, 101, 103; in spiritual practice, 65, 67, 163. *See also* Animals; Francis of Assisi, Saint: stories about; Garden statues; Visual art

Blessing, as practice, 151–54

"Blessing of the animals" ceremonies, 2, 136, 146–50, 152–57, 160; meanings, 147, 153–57; origins and history, 148–50, 152–54. *See also* Animals; Earth, as ideal; Pets

Body and embodiment, 16, 53, 128, 132, 184. *See also* Practice; Stigmata

Boston Public Library, 41, 79

Bread and Puppet Theater, 138, 145

British Broadcasting Corporation, 71

Brookwood Community School, 56

Brotherhood of the Kingdom, 37

Brotherhood of the New Life, 193 (n. 35)

Brother Sun, Sister Moon (movie), 126–29, 139, 160, 165

"Brother Sun, Sister Moon" (phrase), 127, 139, 146, 155, 210–11 (n. 49)

Buddhism, 24, 117, 125, 130, 136, 138, 165, 170–71; and ecology, 130, 214 (n. 19)

Campus ministry, 121–22

Canticle of the Sun, 8, 115, 162, 167; text and versions, 2, 21–22, 72–73, 192 (n. 25); uses and interpretations, 35, 92, 123, 124, 133, 136, 142, 143, 144, 145, 155, 160

Capitalism, 115; alternatives to, 27, 61, 62, 63, 66, 103; opposition to, 24, 102, 141–42

Cathedral of St. John the Divine (New York City), 96, 136, 147, 151, 155

Cathedral of Saints Peter and Paul (Washington, D.C.), 93, 97

Catholic-Protestant encounters. *See* Protestant-Catholic encounters

Catholics. *See* Roman Catholics and Roman Catholic Church

Catholic Worker movement, 53, 59, 66–68, 103–4

Chicago Theological Seminary, 43

Children, 35, 75, 83, 89, 104, 131, 160; children's books, 94–96, 103, 127, 160, 176. *See also* Youth

Christian Church (Disciples of Christ), 75, 149

Christmas, 70, 72, 92

Church, criticism of: early twentieth century, 28, 33, 38, 39, 45–46, 50, 56; later twentieth century, 100, 111, 115, 122, 123, 129, 138; and meaning of Francis, 181, 182, 183; nineteenth century, 13, 14, 23, 24; twenty-first century, 159, 171. *See also* Institutions, criticism of

Church Divinity School of the Pacific, 122

Church of St. John the Baptist (Adel, Yorkshire), 74, 102

Clare of Assisi, St., 8, 99, 103, 116, 123, 174, 194 (n. 41)

Comic books, 141

Common people, 6, 21, 24, 28, 38, 39, 100, 123, 176

Community Church of New York, 97

Congregationalists and United Church of Christ, 33, 40, 52, 54, 76, 104, 153; and garden statuary, 83, 85; place and pilgrimage, 42–43, 44

Conscience, 50, 120, 168

Consensus culture, 89–91, 95–96, 101, 105; religion in, 89–91, 92–93, 96–97

Conservation movement, 34–35, 131. *See also* Ecology; Environmentalist movement

Consumerism, 154, 159

Cooperatives, 25, 40, 64, 66

Dance, 34, 53, 162

Death, 58, 76, 212 (n. 63); animals, 152

Democracy, 17, 28, 38

Diggers, 116

Dog Chapel (St. Johnsbury, Vt.), 152

Domesticity and domestication, 72, 90, 92, 157, 178

Drugs and drug use, 111, 116, 117, 121

Duke University, 156

Earth: as ideal, 123, 132, 154–56; Francis as patron of, 154–57. *See also* Ecology; Environmentalist movement

Earth Day, 130, 134, 143, 144

Eastern Orthodoxy, 98, 100–101, 150, 173

Ecology, 88, 116, 130–35, 145, 180; and conservation, 131, 132, 212 (n. 70); Francis as patron of, 130, 139, 155; theology of, 131–33. *See also* Conservation movement; Environmentalist movement

Economics. *See* Capitalism; Consumerism; Cooperatives; Socialism and socialists

Emerging church, 170, 176
Environmentalist movement, 130, 131, 134, 143, 144–45, 159, 163, 164–65; Christian, 131–33, 155. *See also* Earth, as ideal; Ecology
Erkins Studios, 82
Evangelicals. *See* Protestants—evangelical
Existentialism, 111, 113. *See also* Theology: 1960s movements

Faith-Man-Nature Group, 131–32
Fascism. *See* Italy: under fascism
Federal Council of Churches, 32
Fellowship of Reconciliation, 63
Film, 160. *See also names of directors and titles of films*
Foolishness, 52, 53, 57–58, 172. *See also* Irony
Franciscan communities, 62, 66–67, 127, 139
Franciscan orders, 7, 41, 42, 165; defined, 9; Protestant perception of, 14–15; Third Order, 25, 59, 65, 159, 167, 200 (n. 31)
Francis of Assisi, Saint: anniversaries, 12, 27, 52, 60, 127, 136, 138, 144; and Catholicism, 1, 4, 48, 140, 189 (n. 2), 198 (n. 51); humanness and historicity of, 180–81; life of, 8–9; "lovable," 93, 101, 102, 134; personal qualities attributed to, 55–56, 131, 146, 159, 163, 165, 207 (n. 43); persons grouped with, 35–36, 41, 96–97, 124–25; as poet, 21, 22, 28, 105, 116; "real," 47–48, 139–40, 213 (n. 7); sexuality, 99, 103, 115, 116, 208 (n. 13); as spiritual ideal, 28, 38, 40, 41, 164–65, 167
—stories about: Brother Giles and King Louis IX, 39–40; Francis and the robbers, 39, 57, 65, 196 (n. 21); preaching to the birds, 2, 3, 8, 16, 18, 26, 29, 49, 115, 145, 156; "true and perfect joy," 8–9, 104, 138, 196

(n. 22), 207 (n. 43); wife of snow, 107; wolf of Gubbio, 2, 8, 65, 80, 99, 118, 156, 157, 164. *See also* Animals; Birds; Nature and natural world; Stigmata; Sultan of Egypt
—texts about: early biographies, 7; *Little Flowers*, 7, 39, 42, 47, 58, 67, 100, 115
—texts by, 189 (n. 1); Earlier Rule, 65; Testament, 7, 49–50. *See also* Canticle of the sun
Free Church of Berkeley, 122–25
Freedom, as ideal, 24, 29, 40, 41, 117, 118, 123–24, 128, 170. *See also* Liberation, as ideal
Friends, Society of. *See* Quakers
Fundamentalism. *See* Protestants—evangelical

Garden Club of America, 80
Gardens: history, 78–79; meanings, 86–88; notable, 80–81; in spiritual practice, 163, 167. *See also* Garden statues; Nature and natural world
Garden statues, 1, 3, 4, 70, 78–89, 92, 139, 147, 157, 160, 163; in church gardens, 83–87; criticism of, 98, 114–15; criticism of birdbaths, 127, 143, 157, 165; meanings, 85–88; origins, 79–80, 82–83, 204 (n. 29); in spiritual practice, 164–65. *See also* Birds; Gardens: history; Visual art: iconography
Gays, 56, 153
Gender: feminine, 47, 58, 143; and language, 76, 140, 161; masculine, 36, 53, 141, 195–96 (n. 13)
Gilded Age, 32
Golden Gate International Exposition, 205 (n. 18)
Graphic novels, 141
Great Depression, 52–54, 59–62, 66–68, 78
Guild of St. George, 25

Harvard University, 130

Hinduism and Hindus, 104–6, 117, 209 (n. 27), 214 (n. 19)

Hippies, 110, 116–21, 125–26, 128, 130; defined, 112, 116; "hippie church," 122–23; recalled after 1970s, 138, 141, 160, 171

History, 4, 6, 23, 24–25, 27, 180–81; meanings and uses of, 159, 175, 183–85; public, 183–84; and religious life, 5, 87, 88, 175, 183–85. *See also* Memory

Holy Land, 45

Hymns and hymnody. *See* "All Creatures of Our God and King"; Music: church music and hymns; Peace prayer

Iconography. *See* Visual art: iconography

Ideals and compromise, 41–42, 61, 88, 167, 181–82

Images. *See* Material culture; Visual art

Imitation of Christ: and Francis, 23, 28, 35, 124, 133, 139, 142, 159, 181; as practice, 43, 46, 104, 138, 181–82

Institutes, 60

Institutions, criticism of: early twentieth century, 37, 44, 62; later periods, 111, 116, 117, 125, 128, 138, 142, 143, 170; nineteenth century, 19, 24, 27. *See also* Church, criticism of; Postmodernity

Interbeing, 165

International Society of Franciscan Studies, 48

Interpretation, history of, 6

Interreligious dialogue, 172, 173

Interreligious relationships, 108, 144. *See also* Universalism; *and names of particular religions*

Irony, 52, 56, 58, 101, 146. *See also* Foolishness

Islam and Muslims, 169, 172–73, 175; Francis as Sufi, 143, 173. *See also* Interreligious relationships; Sultan of Egypt

Italy, 169; animal blessings, 148–49; nineteenth-century significance, 12, 18, 22–23, 28; outsiders' views of, 12, 28, 41, 100; under fascism, 60, 101, 102

Jehovah's Witnesses, 116

Jesus, 14, 36, 47, 64, 87, 147, 159; historical, 7, 14, 23, 181; in images, 87; in literature, 98, 101, 108; and place, 45. *See also* Imitation of Christ; "True Christianity," as ideal

Joy, 26, 55, 77, 78, 100, 128

Judaism and Jews, 33, 90, 103, 106–9, 160, 216 (n. 40); and animal blessings, 146–47, 149, 150, 151, 215 (n. 36); Francis as, 108–9

Kingdom of God, 37, 132–33

Land and landscape, 43, 45, 87, 128; American, 78, 96. *See also* Nature and natural world; Place

Latter-day Saints, 76

Legends. *See* Francis of Assisi, Saint—stories about

Liberal religion, 14, 23, 38, 191 (n. 12), 192–93 (n. 28). *See also* Protestants—mainline; Quakers; "Seekers"; Unitarians

Liberation, as ideal, 122, 123, 141–42, 151. *See also* Freedom, as ideal

Life of St. Francis (Sabatier), 27–29, 31, 35, 36, 38, 39, 172, 176; Catholic criticism, 48–50

Love, as ideal, 39, 92, 102, 162; and hippies, 112, 116, 125–26, 128; in nineteenth century, 14, 16, 18, 28; in pacifism, 59, 64, 65

Lutherans, 76, 149, 153, 162

Lynch, Kenneth, and Sons, 82, 91

Mainline Protestants. *See* Protestants—mainline

Material culture, 36, 43–45, 116, 145–46. *See also* Garden statues

Materialism, 113, 116, 117, 128, 146, 159. *See also* Consumerism; Money; Simplicity; Wealth

Material religion. *See* Material culture

Medievalism, 13–14, 21, 22, 25

Meditation, 83, 86, 87–88, 161, 163, 164–65, 168. *See also* Prayer; Quiet

Memory, 44, 46, 59, 88, 184; defined, 43, 184. *See also* History

Mennonites, 74, 76

Methodists, 33, 38, 44, 63, 75, 117, 149, 153

Military service, 8, 76, 111–12, 120, 128, 181

Mission and missionaries, 16, 36, 39, 65, 140, 172, 173

Modernism: artistic, 53, 54, 68–69, 78; Catholic, 33; Protestant, 32, 41. *See also* Visual art: modern

Modernity, 13–14, 32–33, 53, 54–56, 170, 175, 182; and Francis, 198–99 (n. 1)

Monastery of New Skete, 150

Money, 55; criticism of, 57–58, 62, 64, 66, 67, 117, 128, 170. *See also* Poverty; Wealth

Mormons, 76

Music, 6; church music and hymns, 74–75, 76, 77, 96, 140–41, 161; classical, 140, 160; nineteenth century, 29; popular, 139, 140–41, 176. *See also names of composers and compositions*

Mysticism, 34, 52, 54, 77, 100, 174; and Francis, 28, 36, 38–40, 99, 143, 164–65; nature mysticism, 133–34, 145. *See also* Meditation; Spirituality

National Council of Churches, 144, 211 (n. 58)

National Shrine of St. Francis of Assisi (San Francisco), 152

Nature and natural world, 8, 13, 14, 25, 32, 79; and Americans, 34–35, 77,

86–89, 133, 163–67, 180; and Christianity, 130–31, 154, 155; and Francis, 24, 26, 28–29, 49, 55, 99, 124, 128, 133–34, 144–45, 146; Francis as lover of, 91, 93, 97, 171. *See also* Animals; Birds; Conservation movement; Environmentalist movement; Gardens

New Age, 138, 143

New monasticism, 176. *See also* Emerging church

Order of Ecumenical Franciscans, 127

Peace and peacemaking, 53, 58–59, 72, 138, 162, 205 (n. 18); construction of Francis, 63–65; continuity, 59, 60, 120; and Francis, 39, 40, 113, 139, 165, 170, 176; with Islam, 172, 173; mid-century movements, 63–64, 67–68; and postwar America, 89, 90, 96; Vietnam era, 97, 99, 103, 104, 111, 112, 116, 118, 124

Peace prayer, 2–3, 88, 118, 121, 134–35, 136, 139, 171; in consensus culture, 89, 92–93, 96, 114, 164; description and history, 70–72, 102; in devotion and spiritual practice, 111–12, 160, 161–62; musical settings, 140–41; in pacifism, 68, 103, 120; in social activism, 62, 103, 124, 167

Pentecostals, 137, 150, 153

Pets, 92, 136, 147, 151, 152; Francis as patron, 154, 156–57. *See also* Animals; "Blessing of the animals" ceremonies

Pigeons, 67, 107

Pilgrimage and pilgrims, 5, 44–45, 47, 49, 52, 117, 144. *See also* Place

Pistakee Bay, Ill., 79. *See also* Garden statues

Place, 5, 42–47, 52, 88, 102, 115, 128, 144, 181; defined, 43. *See also* Assisi; Land and landscape; Pilgrimage and pilgrims; Sacred space

Pluralism, 33, 104–6, 143, 172, 173
Poetry. *See* Francis of Assisi, Saint: as poet
Possessions, 65. *See also* Money; Poverty; Simplicity
Postmodernity, 175, 182–83; defined, 169–70; and Francis, 169–72. *See also* Road, imagery of
Poverty: in Depression era, 53, 59, 61–63, 66–67; and ecology, 133; and Francis, 8, 24, 25, 52, 55, 91, 102, 105, 107, 115, 124, 128, 159; poor people, 112, 116, 123, 127, 142, 158, 167, 170, 176; in Progressive era, 32; voluntary, 40–42, 104, 133; in works of art, 21, 29, 57, 103, 127–28. *See also* Simplicity
Practice, 39, 60, 66, 103, 122, 128, 158, 170, 174–75; defined, 52, 59; as identification, 59, 77–78. *See also* Body and embodiment; Prayer; Spiritual practices
Prayer, as practice, 59, 77, 99, 102, 158, 162, 163, 164, 168, 176. *See also* Peace prayer; Practice
"Prayer of St. Francis." *See* Peace prayer
Preaching, 8, 16, 39, 98, 174
Presbyterians, 33, 44, 76, 122, 153
Private and public realms, 79, 87–88, 156–57
Progressive Era, 32, 37, 53, 141
Property. *See* Possessions
Protestant-Catholic encounters, 3, 24–25, 54–55, 168, 181–82; nineteenth century, 12–13, 16; Progressive Era, 33, 36; and social activism, 66, 68, 137; and Vatican II, 137, 153
Protestants, 3, 6, 32–33, 89, 92, 159; critical of Francis, 14–15, 16–17; Francis as proto-Protestant, 15–17, 19, 26, 92, 115, 140; and history, 10, 11, 15–17; material religion and place, 44. *See also* History; *and names of churches and denominations*

—evangelical, 87, 91, 100, 116, 139, 150, 158, 170, 174; fundamentalist, 33, 36, 76, 139; hymns, 74, 75, 76; nineteenth century, 14, 16, 25, 32, 38; since 1960s, 117, 127, 137, 138–40
—mainline, 1, 63, 117, 121, 153, 158, 162, 167, 174; in consensus culture, 90, 92, 96; history of, 32, 137, 170. *See also* Liberal religion; *and names of churches and denominations*
Psychology, 34, 164, 200 (n. 29)

Quakers, 33, 38–40, 56, 62, 63, 71, 75, 103, 135
Quiet, as countercultural, 83, 87–88, 163–64, 168. *See also* Meditation

Reversal, imagery of, 55, 56, 58
Riverside Church (New York City), 93, 206 (n. 23)
Road, imagery of, 171–72, 174
Roman Catholics and Roman Catholic Church, 1–2, 90; and animal blessings, 148–49, 152–53; First Vatican Council, 12; and hymns, 76; official teachings, 33, 66; and pilgrimage, 44; and Protestant interpretations of Francis, 26, 47–51, 56, 189 (n. 26); Second Vatican Council, 76, 112, 165. *See also* Catholic Worker movement; Francis of Assisi, Saint: and Catholicism; Protestant-Catholic encounters; Sainthood; Spirituality: creation and earth; Theology: liberation; Visual art: iconography; *and names of individuals*
Romanticism, 14

Sacred space, 87–88. *See also* Place
St. Francis Chapel (Marlborough, N.H.), 79–81
Sainthood, 5, 48; meaning, 168; and non-Christians, 180–83; and

Protestants, 3, 5, 163, 180–83; and Roman Catholics, 3, 180, 181–82

Saints, 18, 159, 168, 175, 182–83; and Protestants, 13, 52. *See also* Sainthood

Salvation Army, 29, 36, 38, 76, 97

Scholarly works and scholarship, 6, 48, 52, 168, 169, 173, 176; surveys and summaries, 12, 15, 16, 27, 43, 101–3. *See also individual authors*

Sears, Roebuck, 92

"Seekers," 14, 23, 33, 143, 190 (n. 5). *See also* Liberal religion; Spirituality

Sentimentality, 154, 157

Shrines: artistic, 17; in gardens, 79, 82; pilgrimage sites as, 44

Simplicity, 13, 27, 100, 103, 116, 128, 159, 163; voluntary, as practice, 160, 167, 170, 176

Social activism, 48, 162, 167. *See also* Economics; Peace and peacemaking; Social Gospel

Social construction, 5–6, 170

Social Gospel, 31, 33, 37–42, 60–61, 63, 111, 141, 167; defined, 37; plutocratic, 59, 80, 86. *See also* Social activism; Socialism and socialists

Socialism and socialists, 27, 40, 41, 48, 53, 62–64, 141. *See also* Cooperatives; Social Gospel

Society of St. Vincent de Paul, 23

Society of the Companions of the Holy Cross, 40, 61, 62, 82

Sojourners, 127

Spirituality, 4–5, 52, 132, 137, 146, 158, 167, 184; creation and earth, 143, 155; feminist, 140, 143, 153; inwardness, 72, 77, 87–88; in 1960s, 117–18; and place, 43–47, 88. *See also* Francis of Assisi, Saint: as spiritual ideal; Mysticism; Spiritual practices

Spiritual practices, 158–60, 161–62; classical Christian, 59, 99, 168, 184; Protestant, 168; with visual images,

161, 163, 164–65. *See also* Practice; Prayer

Stigmata, 34, 99, 118, 128, 141, 171; in life of Francis, 9; and Protestants, 16; in psychology, 34, 200 (n. 29). *See also* Body and embodiment

Sultan of Egypt, 9, 58, 65, 169, 172, 173. *See also* Islam and Muslims; Peace and peacemaking: with Islam

Summer of Love, 116–18, 121

Theater, 53, 56–59

Theology, 77, 182; feminist, 143; incarnational, 167; liberal, 14, 23–24, 63; liberation, 141–42, 170; modernist, 32–33, 41, 53; neo-orthodox, 54; nineteenth century, 13, 14, 23, 25, 28; 1960s movements, 112–13, 123, 132; popular, 14, 82, 90–91

Tourism and tourists, 17–18, 44, 45; anti-tourism, 191 (n. 15). *See also* Travel

Translation problems, 49, 145, 198 (n. 55), 203 (n. 14)

Travel, 11, 12, 27, 31, 47. *See also* Pilgrimage and pilgrims; Tourism and tourists

"True Christianity," as ideal, 24, 26, 28, 35–36, 38, 117, 122, 123, 129; exemplars of, 35–36, 41, 124–25

Underground church, 121–23, 125

Unitarians, 35, 47, 63, 75, 97

Unity Church, 161

Universalism, 117–18, 143; Francis as universal figure, 34, 43, 97, 100, 105–6, 143, 154, 170, 175

University of California at Berkeley, 121

University of Hartford, 120

Vatican Councils. *See* Roman Catholics and Roman Catholic Church

Vietnam War era, 110–13, 116, 120. *See also* Hippies; Peace and peacemaking

Visual art, 4, 6, 9, 24, 29, 95–96, 160; in church decoration, 36, 83, 96–97, 103; crosses, 161, 163, 165, 217 (n. 3); iconography, 82–83, 95, 97, 108, 173, 176, 177, 204 (n. 29); installation, 145–46; as introduction to Francis, 11, 17–19; modern, 53, 54, 68–69, 78; in spiritual practice, 161, 164–65, 167, 173. *See also* Birds; Garden statues; Material culture; *and names of artists*

War. *See* Military service; Peace and peacemaking; *and names of particular conflicts*
Wealth, 57–58, 78, 79, 116, 125–26, 133. *See also* Money; Poverty

Wellesley College, 40, 61
Western civilization, 115, 130–31
World religions. *See* Interreligious relationships; Universalism; *and names of particular religions*
World War I, 31, 53, 57, 63
World War II, 70, 71, 78, 79, 80, 89, 90, 100

Yale University, 120
YMCA and YWCA, 75, 111
Yoga, 198 (n. 48)
Youth, 75, 76, 102, 103, 104; in 1960s–70s, 111–12, 121–22, 125–26, 128; in 1980s, 139, 140–41. *See also* Children; Emerging church; Hippies